# A MEASURED APPROACH TO ENDING POVERTY AND BOOSTING SHARED PROSPERITY

Policy Research Report

# A MEASURED APPROACH TO ENDING POVERTY AND BOOSTING SHARED PROSPERITY

## CONCEPTS, DATA, AND THE TWIN GOALS

WORLD BANK GROUP

# Contents

## Figures

# Foreword

It was roughly a year ago that the World Bank Group adopted two over-arching goals to guide its work. These goals seek to end extreme poverty by 2030 and to boost shared prosperity in every society. The goals are intended to give direction and galvanize action in the organization. It is the first time the World Bank will work toward a specific poverty target, and also the first time that it has given a call for all societies to strive for shared prosperity, which combines growth with equality.

Following the formal announcement of the goals in April 2013, the World Bank has begun to assess what the new goals will mean for its work in different regions, and how the organization itself will need to change in response to the goals. This Policy Research Report contributes to this ongoing assessment, by focusing specifically on the data and measurement issues surrounding the goals. It lays out the conceptual underpinnings of the goals, assesses what reaching the goals will take, and reviews the data requirements for monitoring the goals.

A clear understanding of the empirical basis of the goals is critical to ensuring success in achieving them. One of the key contributions of the report is to provide a detailed and comprehensive account of the data and processes needed to measure global poverty and shared prosperity. It demonstrates how many different data sources are needed—beyond household surveys—and highlights how sensitive measures of poverty and shared prosperity can be to changes in the underlying data. A major takeaway from the analysis is that much more support is needed to help build the capacity of data system architectures at the country level.

While much work to date has focused either on poverty or on issues of inclusive growth, the report makes a strong case for viewing the two goals in unison. An emphasis on ending global poverty alone might lead the development community to focus almost exclusively on a few large countries where poverty is high; the shared prosperity goal ensures attention is given to the least well off in all societies. The report helps highlight cases where the goals are intimately related, such that similar policies can be used to target both goals, as well as cases where reaching the goals may require different policies aimed at different groups of people.

The report draws attention to the considerable challenge ahead of us if the twin goals are to be attained. While strong and sustained growth will be critical to meeting the goals, under reasonable growth rate assumptions extreme poverty is projected to remain well above the 3 percent target by 2030. The report shows how boosting shared prosperity, apart from being a desirable end in itself, can add considerable impetus to further poverty reduction toward the poverty target. Nevertheless, the projections suggest that reaching the global poverty target remains challenging and will require a departure from historical experience—of both growth and distributional effects and policies. This implies that achieving the goals will require concerted action and transformational policies that go well beyond "business as usual" practices.

Adoption of the new goals will not only shape the agenda of the World Bank's operational work in coming years, but will also give renewed impetus to research on these important issues. This report makes an important contribution to our understanding of global poverty and shared prosperity, but it is only a first step in this direction. I hope it will launch even more innovative research on the topic and inspire policy makers in different countries to develop and implement more effective policies toward these goals, for a better world.

*Kaushik Basu*
Senior Vice President and Chief Economist
World Bank Group

# Acknowledgments

This Policy Research Report was prepared by the Development Economics Research Group of the World Bank by a team led by Dean Jolliffe and Peter Lanjouw. The other authors of the report were Shaohua Chen, Aart Kraay, Christian Meyer, Mario Negre, Espen Prydz, Renos Vakis, and Kyla Wethli. Valuable contributions were made by Tatjana Kleineberg, Christoph Lakner, Prem Sangraula, Ilana Seff, and Liang Yu.

Overall guidance of the report was provided by Kaushik Basu, Senior Vice President and Chief Economist, and Asli Demirgüç-Kunt, Director of Research, Development Economics. The team benefited from continued engagement with the Global Poverty Working Group, including in particular Andrew Dabalen, Nobuo Yoshida, and Umar Serajuddin; and also with the poverty global practice, including in particular Ambar Narayan and Carolina Sanchez. The team also benefited from extended conversations with and feedback from Stefan Dercon, Patrick Gerland, John Gibson, and Martin Ravallion.

For valuable feedback, the team thanks Pedro Alba, Inger Andersen, Antonella Bassani, Raka Banerjee, Kathleen Beegle, Jorge Calderon, Gero Carletto, Laurence Chandy, James Close, Hai-Anh Dang, Gabriel Demombynes, Makhtar Diop, Quy-Toan Do, Marianne Fay, Caroline Heider, Vivian Y. N. Hon, Olga Jonas, Talip Kilic, Philippe Le Houérou, Jeff Lecksell, Arianna Legovini, Jeff Lewis, Norman Loayza, Misha Lokshin, Aaditya Mattoo, Nicolas Mombrial, Cyrill Muller, Rose Mungai, Kyle Peters, Sanjay Pradhan, Martin Rama, Vijayendra Rao, Ana L. Revenga, David Robalino, Luis Serven, Klaus Tilmes, Anthony G. Toft, Laura Tuck, Roy Van der Weide, Joachim von Amsberg, Axel von Trotsenburg, Jan Walliser, and Ruslan Yemtsov. The team benefited from comments received at a seminar organized by Andrew Norton and

Kevin Watkins at the Overseas Development Institute in May 2014. The team also thanks the many others inside and outside the World Bank who provided comments.

The World Bank's Publishing and Knowledge Division coordinated the design, typesetting, printing, and dissemination of the report. Special thanks to Janice Tuten, Patricia Katayama, Susan Graham, and Andrés Meneses. The report was edited by Sandy Gain. The team also thanks Merrell Tuck-Primdahl and Ryan Hahn for their guidance on communications strategy.

# Abbreviations

| | |
|---|---|
| AIDS | acquired immune deficiency syndrome |
| CAPI | computer-assisted personal interviewing |
| CPI | consumer price index |
| ELL | Elbers, Lanjouw, and Lanjouw |
| FGT | Foster-Greer-Thorbecke |
| GDP | gross domestic product |
| GPS | Global Positioning System |
| HFCE | household final consumption expenditures |
| HIES | Household Income and Expenditure Survey |
| IAM | integrated assessment model |
| ICP | International Comparison Program |
| IMF | International Monetary Fund |
| IPCC | Intergovernmental Panel on Climate Change |
| MPI | Multidimensional Poverty Index |
| NSO | national statistical office |
| NSS | National Sample Survey |
| PPP | purchasing power parity |
| WDI | World Development Indicators |
| WPP | World Population Prospects |

# Overview

The entrance to the World Bank's headquarters in Washington, DC, is inscribed with the words "Our dream is a world free of poverty." In pursuit of this dream, in April 2013, World Bank President Jim Yong Kim announced to the international community two new goals to guide the World Bank's work. First, it would seek to end global poverty, reducing the share of people living in extreme poverty to 3 percent of the global population by 2030. Second, it would seek to boost shared prosperity, understood as increasing the average incomes of the bottom 40 percent of the population in each country. The accompanying narrative emphasized that both goals should be attained in a sustainable and inclusive manner, ensuring that today's development is not reversed tomorrow and does not compromise the planet's future, or that of subsequent generations.

The adoption of these two goals marks a significant shift for the World Bank. Although poverty reduction has been a mainstay of its work for decades, the World Bank has now, for the first time, committed to a specific poverty reduction target to guide its work. Similarly, the goal to boost shared prosperity gives more explicit attention to inclusive growth than has been the case in the past and paves the way for a focus on inequality, not only of opportunity but also of final outcomes. Prosperity also needs to be shared across individuals over time, requiring forms of sustainable development that fully account for environmental degradation and natural resource depletion as well as, crucially, their close interrelation with poverty.

Articulation of and commitment to global development goals can help build momentum toward their achievement. The goals seek to provide the global development community with a unified sense of purpose and to galvanize action around clear and easily communicable objectives. Beyond this motivational function, however, the goals also have a tangible link to the manner in which the World Bank and other development agencies conduct their operations. Although the World Bank alone does not have the capacity to realize these global goals, it has pledged to place them front and center in the institution's work going forward. The indicators associated with the goals will also be used by other development agencies to target programs and allocate funding.

The two new goals provide a new context for policy assessment. They provide a framework in which to evaluate policies and their potential contribution to poverty reduction and inclusive growth. Assessing progress toward the goals (or lack thereof) provides a means to identify gaps and prioritize actions. In this way, the goals not only help regional and international donors to target available resources, but also inform national governments in their efforts to reduce poverty. However, while assessment of progress toward the goals will provide a benchmark for the World Bank's dialogue with countries about poverty reduction, the precise way in which those priorities are set and achieved should be determined at the country level, according to countries' own policies and circumstances.

How progress is measured will matter. The World Bank's choice of indicators reflects particular institutional priorities, prompted by criteria that balance precision and conceptual coherence with ease of communication and global comparability. Alternative measures may provide different insights. By offering a fuller exploration and exposition of the global poverty and shared prosperity goals, this report seeks to provide a richer basis from which individual countries can choose measures that are most relevant to their circumstances.

This report goes beyond motivating the importance of the new goals, to focusing squarely on issues of measurement and data. The objective of the report is to articulate what measuring the poverty and shared prosperity goals entails and to identify areas where improvements in data are needed to assess and monitor them. This discussion is fundamental to achievement of the goals. Action to reduce poverty and boost shared prosperity would be greatly impaired without the ability to credibly and consistently measure progress. The chapters that follow lay out the conceptual underpinnings of the World Bank's two goals and assess what reaching them will require; they discuss the relative strengths and weaknesses of the goals by contrasting them with alternative indicators; and they propose empirical approaches to tracking their progress (box O.1).

## Box 0.1 Structure of the report

This Policy Research Report is structured in three parts, mirroring the three broad aims of the report.

The first part provides a general overview of the conceptual underpinnings of the two goals and their assessment. Chapter 1 describes the World Bank's approach to poverty measurement and assesses what achievement of the poverty goal will require. Chapter 2 turns to the shared prosperity goal, demonstrating how the goal can be evaluated and highlighting some of the challenges of interpretation.

The second part of the report places the World Bank's two goals in a wider context. Chapter 3 places the global poverty and shared prosperity goals in a broader framework of poverty and welfare analysis. It shows how the World Bank's choices of measures are two options from an array of possible indicators, each with different features that provide different insights. Chapter 4 discusses poverty projections in the context of uncertainty about economic growth and large or unusual shocks, which could pose downside risk to achieving the goals and are often not adequately captured by standard economic models. Current debates around climate change and sustainability receive explicit attention in this framework. The chapter demonstrates how

confidence in achieving the goals and indeed their very attainment are sensitive to assumptions about the patterns of economic growth and the occurrence of extraordinary shocks.

Finally, while data and measurement issues are discussed throughout, the third part of the report specifically addresses issues related to the empirical monitoring of the goals in greater technical detail. Chapter 5 discusses the use of household survey data in measuring global poverty and shared prosperity, highlighting some of the challenges faced in raising the frequency and timeliness of global poverty estimates. Although household surveys are necessary inputs to the measurement of global poverty and shared prosperity, they are not sufficient. Chapter 6 thus turns to some of the key complementary data—population data, purchasing power parity (PPP) indexes that control for the differences in the cost of living across countries, and growth and inflation data—that are needed to support the World Bank's poverty and prosperity estimates. The discussion on accounting for differences in prices across countries with PPP indexes is particularly extensive, primarily because these data have significant implications for global poverty estimates.

## Evidence as the foundation for policy design

Concerns around data and measurement are often overshadowed in debates about the fundamental determinants of development and the role of policy. This report argues for a different perspective—one that acknowledges the role evidence plays in understanding structural change and the design of policy and appreciates the importance of evidence in evaluating and improving policies over time. Economists rely on the availability of consistent and reliable data not only to motivate and assess economic theory, but also to monitor and evaluate economic policies in practice—and this is as important for poverty reduction as for other areas of economics. As the eminent Indian statistician Prasanta Chandra Mahalanobis once declared, ". . . statistics is an applied science and . . . its chief object is to help in solving practical problems. Poverty is the most basic problem of the country, and statistics must help in solving this problem" (Mahalanobis 1963).

Far from being an issue of secondary importance, data and measurement are pivotal to the assessment of the World Bank's new goals and, thereby, their achievement. To assess progress toward the goals, it is necessary to have a clear understanding of how progress is defined and measured. Without a clear understanding of the goals' meaning and knowing how to measure progress, what would be the basis for selectivity and prioritization? And how would lessons be learned from past experience?

This report will argue that improved data infrastructure—consisting of many elements, including more attention to measurement methods and the collection of more and better survey data as well as complementary population and price data—is critical to ensure that progress toward the goals can be measured and policies to help achieve them can be identified and prioritized. Although the availability of poverty data has increased substantially in the past few decades, infrequent or unreliable data continue to pose a challenge to global poverty assessment (box O.2).

---

### Box O.2  Global poverty assessment since 1990

While poverty reduction has been a mainstay of the World Bank's mission for decades, the measurement of global poverty has at times lagged behind ambitions to reduce it. The 1990 *World Development Report* was an important milestone in global poverty assessment, providing one of the first comprehensive cross-country databases on poverty and a concerted effort to articulate what was needed to improve the measurement of poverty. That effort was based on single household surveys from 22 countries. The World Bank now has access to more than 1,000 surveys from 1981 to 2011 (figure BO2.1), covering nearly all developing countries—making national poverty assessments possible in most countries.

Perhaps more important is the impact this increased ability to measure poverty has had on poverty reduction efforts. Poverty assessments, drawing on country-level poverty data, inform countries' understandings of the plight of their citizens and help countries to shape policies accordingly. Such analyses have become increasingly common and detailed alongside the expansion of data. At the global level, improved data have supported international efforts to reduce poverty, including by providing the basis for the Millennium Development Goal aimed at halving global poverty between 1990 and 2015.

However, although encouraging progress has been made in improving the quantity of household

*(continued)*

## Box 0.2    continued

surveys needed to measure poverty, this report details the remaining challenges with the frequency and quality of data. Although most countries now have national poverty assessments, the global development community does not yet have the consistent and frequent data needed to understand fully the nature of poverty in countries, the evolution of poverty over time (and whether poverty is largely a chronic or transitory condition), or the determinants of poverty. Improved poverty analysis requires more than just an increase in the number of surveys available. Concerted efforts are required to improve the capacity for data collection at the country level to produce not just more, but also better-quality poverty data.

**Figure BO.2.1    Number of surveys in PovcalNet over time**

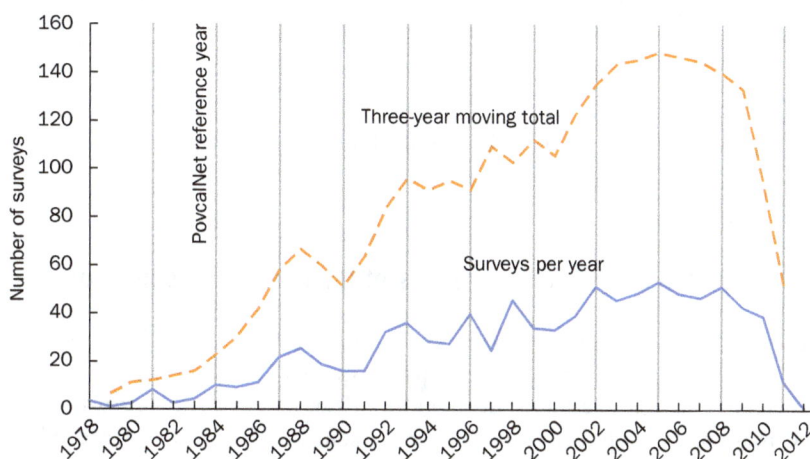

*Source:* Based on data from the World Bank PovcalNet database (accessed August 2014).
*Note:* It is quite common for there to be a delay of some months between when a survey is collected, when it is published, and when it becomes available in PovcalNet. The decline between 2010 and 2011 illustrated in the figure therefore reflects the fact that many surveys collected in 2011 are not yet available in PovcalNet, rather than a substantial decline in the number of surveys collected in 2011.

At the same time, discussion of improvements in data that are needed to measure poverty and shared prosperity consistently across countries should not ignore the progress in data measurement, access, and quality that has been achieved in recent decades. The purpose of this report is to identify areas where further improvements can build on progress that has already been made and highlight particular areas where further progress is needed.

## Ending global poverty

In the past few decades, substantial progress has been made in reducing global poverty. The World Bank assesses poverty by the number of people whose income or consumption falls below a given threshold (box O.3). Between 1990 and 2011, the number of people living in extreme poverty has halved, to around one billion people, or 14.5 percent of the world's population (17.0 percent of the developing world's population). While this progress is encouraging, the fact that so many people remain poor is sobering. To estimate the number of people living in extreme poverty, the World Bank currently uses an international poverty line of $1.25 a day, in 2005 prices—a poverty line that corresponds to an average of the national poverty lines of the 15 poorest developing countries.[1] That more than a billion people in 2011 eked out a living on such a low threshold living standard makes the need to increase efforts to reduce global poverty self-evident.

Why set the global target for poverty reduction to 3 percent of the world's population by 2030? The 3 percent target derives from conceptual and

---

### Box 0.3    Why measure poverty in terms of income or consumption?

The measurement of poverty using income or consumption has a long tradition, although consumption is usually the preferred indicator in developing countries. Consumption is typically assumed to be less volatile than income and is thus often seen as a better measure of current living standards. From a practical perspective, consumption is usually more easily and accurately measured than income in countries with relatively low levels of participation in formal labor markets. However, in countries where income is the only available indicator of economic welfare, particularly in Latin America, measuring poverty on the basis of income data is the norm.

The choice to measure poverty in terms of income or consumption should also be distinguished from multidimensional poverty measures. Although there is widespread consensus that poverty is a multidimensional phenomenon, there is much less consensus on whether it is useful to aggregate across different dimensions to construct a multidimensional measure of welfare and, if so, how to do so in a way that is conceptually sound and readily interpretable. Stopping short of attempting to construct an explicitly multidimensional measure of poverty does not, however, mean that comparisons of deprivation along various dimensions are not possible. World Bank poverty assessments, carried out at the country level, routinely look not only at consumption poverty, but also at deprivation along other dimensions. Similarly, global consumption poverty can and should be examined alongside deprivations in all other relevant dimensions. Importantly, households may experience multiple forms of hardship simultaneously and, where this happens, policy responses must recognize and address these joint deprivations. This discussion is taken up in greater detail in chapters 1, 2, and 3.

empirical considerations. Conceptually, it may be desirable to set a target to eliminate global poverty altogether. However, a global goal of zero poverty would require eliminating poverty in each and every country. Poverty in some countries remains deep and widespread, and it is simply not realistic to expect to be able to eliminate poverty in these countries by 2030. It is also the case that at any moment in time there is likely to be some churning taking place in which some people, possibly for reasons beyond their control, fall into poverty, even if only temporarily. It is thus practical to set a global target close to zero, but which allows for some heterogeneity at the country level.

Empirically, simple back-of-the-envelope simulations can be conducted to assess the plausibility of the goal to end poverty by 2030. When such simulations are based on highly stylized and rather optimistic assumptions—such as stable and continuous annual growth rates in consumption per capita of at least 4 percent in all developing countries and an unchanging distribution of income—then a global poverty rate of 3 percent is achievable.[2] Such analysis suggests that the World Bank's dream of ending global poverty by 2030 is a highly aspirational objective, but is not entirely beyond reach with concerted efforts and commitment from individual countries as well as the international development community.

To say that the global poverty goal could be reached with concerted effort, however, is not to say that doing so would be easy. Although per capita growth of 4 percent in each country is roughly equivalent to the average for developing countries as a whole from 2000 to 2010, assuming that all countries could consistently grow at this rate is highly implausible. In the past three decades, such growth rates have been far from common (figure O.1, panel a). If developing countries were instead to grow at their respective annualized growth rates of the past 20 years, global poverty would remain at around 6.8 percent of the world population by 2030, a considerable distance from the 3 percent target (figure O.1, panel b). Chapter 1 sets out a series of alternative growth simulations and assesses the likely impact of each on global poverty. Together, these combine to emphasize that the World Bank's goal to reduce poverty to 3 percent of the population by 2030, while not impossible, is certainly ambitious.

Not only would achievement of the global poverty goal require strong economic growth, there is some evidence that the poverty target may become more difficult to reach as it becomes closer. Although there has been a striking linearity in the decline of the global poverty headcount since the early 1980s, the future path toward the 3 percent target may entail a significant tapering off of progress. One reason is that, although it

**Figure 0.1    Global poverty projections are sensitive to underlying growth assumptions**

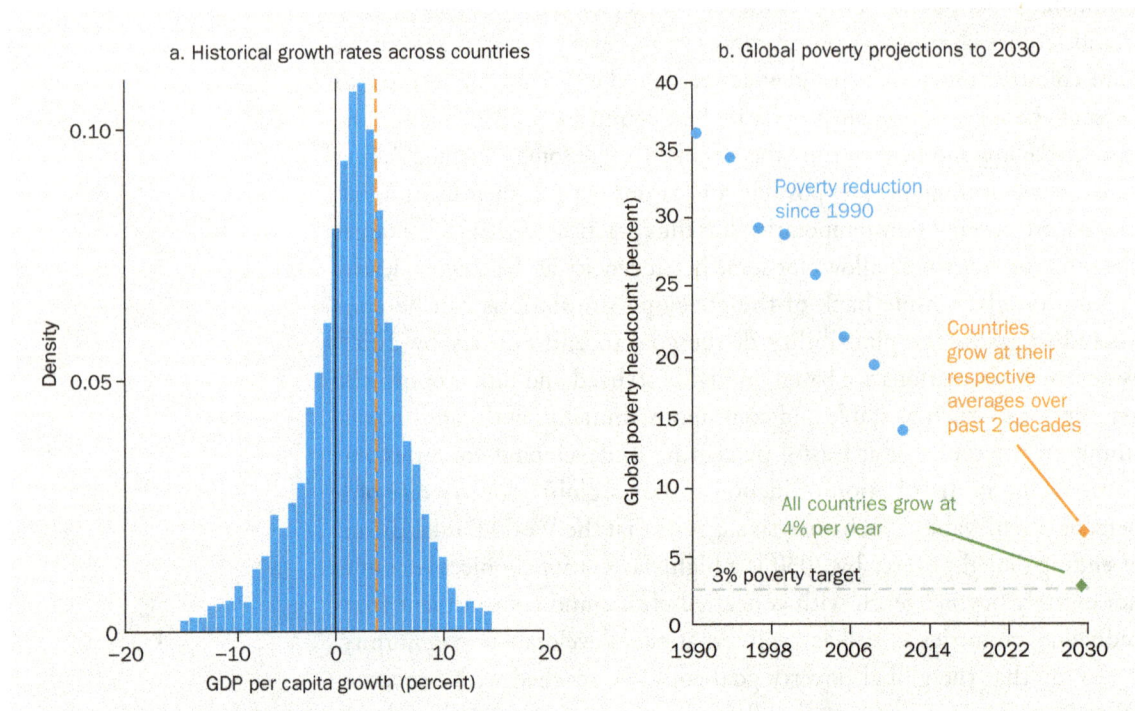

*Source:* Based on data from the World Bank World Development Indicators database, panel a, and the World Bank PovcalNet database, panel b.
*Note:* Panel a shows the frequency of different annual per capita gross domestic product (GDP) growth rates for 129 countries between 1980 and 2010. The dashed orange line denotes per capita growth of 4 percent.

may initially be possible to reach many poor people through broad-based economic growth that generates more and better-paid jobs, as poverty declines it may be relatively more difficult to reduce poverty in hard-to-reach geographic pockets or among population groups that are somehow excluded from participation in the broader economic currents. In countries experiencing conflict, it may be particularly difficult to reach populations in affected areas. In some cases, the poor may be veritably trapped in poverty because of failures in credit, land, or other key markets, or because low levels of education, skills, or health prevent them from availing themselves of new opportunities proffered by a general expansion of economic activity. Such factors, which contribute to unevenness in the rate of poverty reduction in countries, can result in a declining responsiveness of poverty reduction to a given rate of aggregate growth over time. On the other hand, experience from currently high-income countries indicate that the trajectory of poverty decline does not inevitably taper off as it approaches zero. Concerted efforts by policy makers can help to maintain progress. These efforts are likely to involve a focus not only on average income growth but particularly on raising the incomes of the poor.

## Boosting shared prosperity

The World Bank's second goal, of boosting shared prosperity, places increased focus on the least well-off in society. Discussion of inclusive growth is not new. However, although there is an extensive literature emphasizing the importance of thinking about inclusion of the poorest in society in defining goals for development, until now there has not been agreement on a single summary indicator. The World Bank's new shared prosperity goal—to boost the incomes of the bottom 40 percent of the population—provides a measure of inclusive growth (box O.4).

---

**Box O.4     Frequently asked questions about the World Bank's shared prosperity goal**

In April 2013, World Bank President Jim Yong Kim announced a global goal of promoting shared prosperity. This new goal often confronts some common questions:

*How will shared prosperity be measured?* Boosting shared prosperity is understood by the World Bank to mean fostering the well-being of the bottom 40 percent of the population in every country. This will be assessed by measuring the income or consumption growth of the bottom 40 percent of the population in each country over time.

*What does the "shared" in shared prosperity mean?* Shared refers to the extent to which the bottom 40 percent of the population takes part in and benefits from the process of economic development.

*What is "good" shared prosperity performance?* The goal does not make a normative statement about what defines good shared prosperity: the higher the growth rate of the average incomes (or consumption) of the bottom 40 percent of the population, the better.

*How is shared prosperity different from average income as a measure of development progress?* The shared prosperity measure places explicit emphasis on the least well-off in society, focusing on the bottom 40 percent. In addition, unlike growth in gross domestic product per capita, assessed from national accounts data, the shared prosperity indicator is assessed from household survey data. The two measures are thus not directly comparable.

*Is this an inequality measure?* Tracking the income growth of the bottom 40 percent of the population is not sufficient to gain insight into changes in inequality. However, by comparing the shared prosperity measure with a survey-based measure of average income or consumption, or of income growth of the top 60 percent of the population, it is easy to use the shared prosperity measure to learn about the evolution of inequality in countries over time. The details of this are explored in chapter 2.

---

One way to think about the World Bank's new shared prosperity goal is as an alternative to average income as the benchmark of development progress. Instead of assessing and measuring economic development in terms of the overall average growth in a country, the shared prosperity goal places emphasis on the bottom 40 percent of the population. In other words, good progress is judged to occur not merely when an economy is growing, but, more specifically, when that growth is reaching the least well-off in society. Thus, the shared prosperity goal seeks to increase sensitivity to distributional issues, shifting the common understanding of development progress away from average per capita income and emphasizing that good growth should benefit the least well-off in society. This discussion is relevant in developed as well as developing countries, since, notwithstanding the substantial progress that has been made in reducing absolute poverty in recent decades, in many middle- and high-income countries there is a concern that the relatively poor are being left behind. When poverty is viewed as an inability to participate and prosper in society, it remains a pervasive problem, even in developed countries.

Unlike the World Bank's global poverty goal, the shared prosperity goal is a country-specific goal, which does not have an explicit endpoint. It is unbounded, in that boosting shared prosperity requires a positive growth rate for the average incomes of the bottom 40 percent of the population, but there is no target (or limit) for what that growth rate should be. The shared prosperity indicator is thus similar to measures of average income, such as growth in gross domestic product (GDP) per capita, in its expression (as a simple growth rate over time) and in how it is evaluated (more growth is better, without a specific target rate of growth in each country).

However, the shared prosperity indicator has substantially different measurement requirements. Unlike GDP per capita, which is measured from national accounts data, the shared prosperity indicator needs to be measured from household survey data (which are also used for poverty assessment). This is because national accounts data only provide aggregated information on economic performance, not the disaggregated information on people living on different levels of income or consumption, which is needed to measure the income of the poorest 40 percent of society. Unlike national accounts data, which are produced on an annual basis in a relatively standard way, the frequency and quality of household survey data are heterogeneous, raising substantial challenges for cross-country comparisons. Although it does not seek to provide all the answers, this report offers a detailed discussion of these challenges and points to some possible improvements.

**Figure 0.2** The bottom 40 percent can encompass various income groups across countries

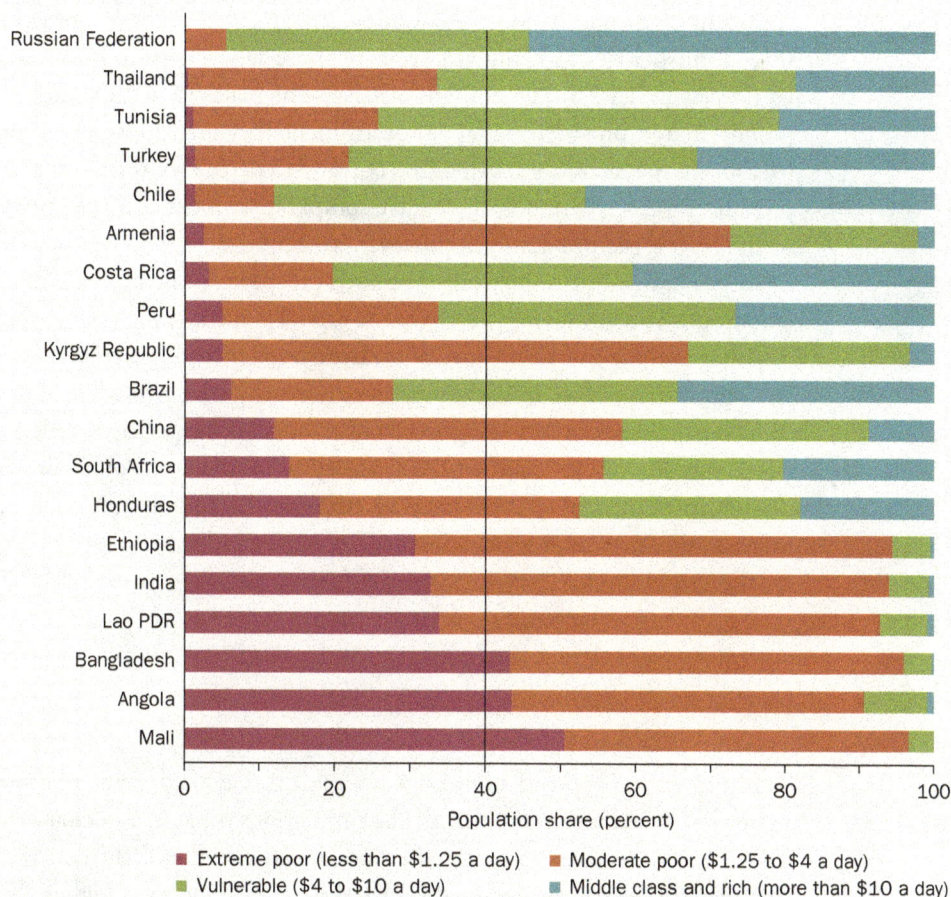

*Source:* Based on data for latest year available from the World Bank PovcalNet database (accessed August 2014).
*Note:* The vertical line in the figure illustrates the bottom 40 percent of each country's population—that is, the group that would be the focus of efforts to boost shared prosperity. The groups in the figure are the extreme poor, as defined by the World Bank's international poverty line; the moderate poor, who live on between $1.25 and $4 a day; the vulnerable, who live on between $4 and $10 a day; and the middle class and rich, who live on more than $10 a day—all measured at 2005 constant purchasing power parity (PPP). The concept of people living on between $4 and $10 a day being considered vulnerable is based on evidence that a considerable share of households above a given poverty line is usually vulnerable to falling below that line over time. See Ferreira and others (2012), López-Calva and Ortiz-Juarez (2014), and Birdsall, Lustig, and Meyer (2014).

Chapter 2 illustrates how the composition of the bottom 40 percent is very different across countries. In low- and lower-middle-income countries, there will likely be significant overlap between those living in extreme poverty and the bottom 40 percent of the population (figure O.2). Tracking shared prosperity can thus reinforce poverty reduction efforts in these countries. By contrast, a substantial proportion of the bottom 40 percent of the population in upper-middle-income countries is likely to be nonpoor according to the global $1.25 a day standard. In these countries, tracking shared prosperity can bring attention to those who may not be covered by poverty policies but who might otherwise be relatively disadvantaged.

The shared prosperity goal is not an inequality goal in and of itself. Measuring the income growth of the bottom 40 percent of the population provides no information on how that compares with the income growth of the rest of the population. However, an impression of inequality can easily be obtained by comparing the shared prosperity indicator with mean income growth (or income growth of the top 60 percent of the population). In this sense, the shared prosperity measure implicitly places emphasis on changes in inequality in society. It is noteworthy that while the World Bank has a fairly long-standing record of discussing the policies needed to create equality of opportunity, the shared prosperity entry point into the discussion of inequality is through an emphasis on equality of outcomes (in this case, in people's relative incomes). This is a rather novel perspective for the World Bank.

## Need for transformational policies

The analysis in chapter 1 highlights the critical role of continued growth in helping to reduce poverty. In all the simulations presented in chapter 1, growth contributes to poverty reduction, and the extent of the contribution increases when the assumed underlying growth rates are higher. The important role of growth is also evident in backward-looking assessments. For example, growth in average incomes has historically been strongly correlated with growth in the incomes of the bottom 40 percent of the population (figure O.3). Put differently, and as shown in chapter 2, analysis of the relative contributions from boosting overall growth (increasing the size of the pie) and reducing inequality (increasing the poor's slice of the pie) suggests that increased growth has played a more prominent role in boosting shared prosperity in the past. Achieving the World Bank's goals will therefore require strong and sustained growth in developing countries.

The analysis in chapter 1 also suggests, however, that continued growth in line with what has been experienced in recent decades will not be sufficient to end poverty. Under a variety of plausible growth rate assumptions, extreme poverty is projected to remain well above the 3 percent target by

**Figure 0.3**   Shared prosperity has been correlated with average income growth

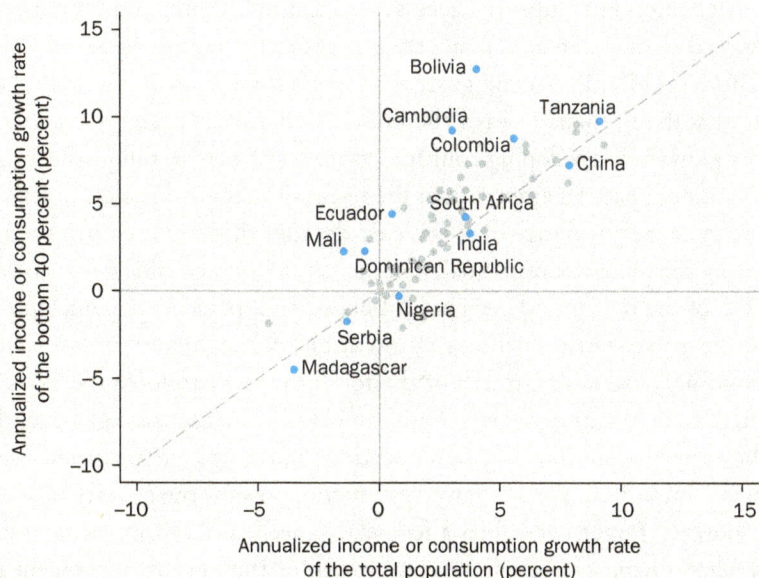

*Source:* Based on data from the World Bank PovcalNet database (accessed August 2014).
*Note:* Growth rates in shared prosperity are calculated as annualized growth rates in per capita income or consumption expenditure over the period of circa 2006–11 (all survey based). See note to figure 2.8 for further explanations.

2030; achieving the 3 percent poverty goal on the basis of growth alone would require national growth rates well above historical precedents. This suggests that achieving the poverty goal will require concerted action and transformational policies that go well beyond "business as usual" practices.

Ending global poverty and boosting shared prosperity will require not just a focus on overall levels of growth, but particular attention to the nature and patterns of growth. Although the incomes of the poorest have tended to be correlated with average income growth in the past, there are also notable exceptions, where overall growth has not translated to effective poverty reduction or has taken place alongside *increased* inequality. This suggests that it is not just growth, but also the type of growth (growth that benefits the poor) that will be important to achieving the World Bank's goals. Although this report does not set out detailed policy prescriptions for poverty reduction, given its primary focus on data and measurement issues, it is worth recognizing past analyses that emphasized the importance of different types of growth and the relative impact they have on poverty.[3] In particular, growth that is widely shared and increases the returns to assets held by the poor (especially the returns to their labor, but also to other assets, such as land holdings) is the most likely to translate into effective poverty reduction.[4] Improved access to education, health, and capital can be critical elements in enhancing the returns to the poor's assets.

The World Bank's second goal, of boosting shared prosperity, may also help in shifting focus toward the poor. Simulations in chapter 2 show that if growth in developing countries up to 2030 were to follow the same distributional pattern as growth of the respective regional leaders in terms of pro-poor performance over the past decade, this could contribute to reaching the global poverty goal. Another simulation considers increasing growth of the bottom 40 percent by 1 and then 2 percentage points more than the 10-year historical mean growth rate for each country (and correspondingly reducing growth of the top 60 percent to leave the overall mean growth rate unchanged). With some differences across regions, both of these simulations illustrate how boosting shared prosperity can add considerable impetus to further poverty reduction toward the poverty target.[5] The poverty target is reached a few years ahead of 2030 in the simulation where income or consumption growth of the bottom 40 percent is increased by 2 percentage points more than the mean. These findings point to an important complementarity between the two goals, and it is in this sense that the global poverty and shared prosperity goals can be considered "twin" goals: achieving progress in both goals will require efforts on both fronts. However, the projections suggest that reaching the global poverty target remains challenging, suggesting that a departure from the historical experience—of both growth and distributional effects and policies—will be needed if the World Bank's goals are to be met.

As discussed above, in announcing its new goals, the World Bank stressed that the path toward them must be environmentally, socially, and economically sustainable over time. Thus, while boosting growth will be crucial to meeting both the global poverty and shared prosperity goals, the extent to which development trajectories compromise future growth and sustainable development will be important. There is a substantial literature demonstrating the importance of natural resources for sustainable economic development, not only because the poor often rely disproportionately on access to natural resources to meet their immediate needs, but also because degradation of natural resources can have profound impacts on the health and livelihoods of the poor as well as future growth prospects.[6] This underscores the importance of developing policies that achieve growth in a sustainable way that does not undermine future progress.

## Alternative notions of poverty and shared prosperity

Although the World Bank has selected two indicators to measure progress toward its goals—the number of people living in extreme poverty, as a share of the world's population, and growth in the incomes of the bottom 40 percent of the population in each country—these are not the only possible indicators to measure progress in these important domains. The measures adopted by the World Bank and its development partners reflect particular institutional priorities, but individual countries may have different priorities and may choose to emphasize other specific distributional features.

The World Bank's articulation of the goals and the choice of measures to monitor and assess these goals derive from its global vantage point. Thus, the incidence of poverty in the world as a whole has been set as the poverty target, rather than a country-specific target tailored to each individual country's circumstances. Similarly, there is a clear intention not just to track shared prosperity in each country, but also to compare progress across countries. Individual countries may engage with the ideas behind these goals with a perspective that is more country specific. To that end, it is important to recognize that the specific goals defined by the World Bank can be seen as two particular applications of a whole class of approaches. An important element in clarifying and understanding the World Bank's two new goals therefore comes from appreciating where the goals fit relative to a spectrum of alternatives, with each alternative providing different insight into social welfare. Ideally, a rich understanding of poverty and distributional issues would be based on assessment of many or all of these measures.

The scope for differences in priorities is clear in the context of poverty measurement. In contrast to the World Bank's global poverty threshold, based on a single global poverty line, national governments attach priority to poverty thresholds that are more relevant to their particular countries, as evidenced by large differences across countries in national poverty lines. Countries may also prefer to go beyond the headcount measure of poverty to consider poverty measures that capture the depth and severity of poverty alongside the incidence of poverty. Similarly, the potential for different priorities can be seen in the context of the shared prosperity measure: the consumption or income share of the bottom 40 percent is just one of many measures of how equitably or inequitably income is distributed across individuals in a country, and different inequality measures imply different priorities over individuals at different points in the income distribution.

Chapter 3 uses welfare functions as a tool of analysis to set the twin goals in this broader context. Economists have long used social welfare functions to capture societal preferences over how income is distributed across individuals in a society. The chapter first discusses social welfare functions that in some way distinguish the poor from the nonpoor, as the World Bank's global poverty goal does. The choice within this group of functions is essentially about where and how to set the line distinguishing the poor from the nonpoor and whether to assess not just whether an individual is poor, but also how poor the individual is. A second group of welfare functions does not distinguish between the poor and the nonpoor. Instead, it considers the well-being of everyone in the income distribution, but places different weights on different groups of people, as is the case with the World Bank's shared prosperity goal. The main choice in this group of functions is about what weight to place on individuals at different parts of the income distribution.

## Challenges posed by uncertainty and downside risk

Chapter 4 discusses the World Bank's goals in the context of uncertainty and downside risk. The scenarios for global poverty and shared prosperity presented in chapters 1 and 2 show how projections for the World Bank's goals are sensitive to underlying assumptions, in particular about future growth. There is considerable uncertainty about the future trajectory and distributional nature of growth in developing countries, in turn implying uncertainty about trajectories for global extreme poverty and shared prosperity. Although economic models can to some extent capture uncertainty in future projections through analysis of past experience, they are inherently limited in cases where the future may systematically diverge from the past. For example, recent debates around climate change have emphasized the difficulty in anticipating and predicting the economic consequences of continued rapid rises in global temperatures.

Chapter 4 incorporates uncertainty into projections of global poverty and discusses the potential impacts of a selection of sources of downside risk. When projections are based on average growth rates from the past, the projections can be highly sensitive to the period on which the average is based (figure O.4, panel a; chapter 1). Furthermore, incorporating uncertainty and downside risk into projections of global poverty demonstrates not only that confidence in reaching the goals is diminished in the presence

**Figure O.4**   The goals appear more difficult to attain in the context of uncertainty and downside risk

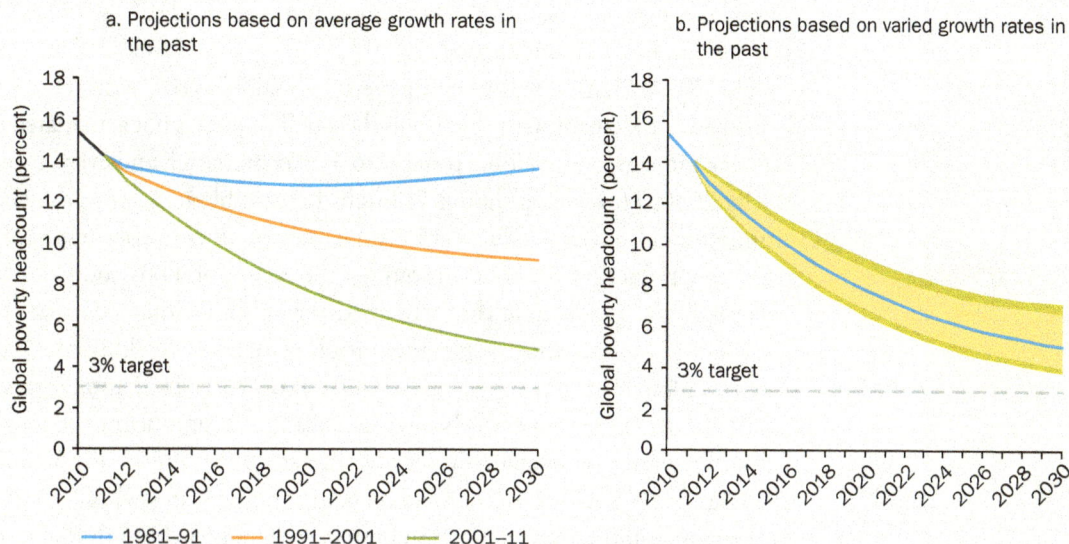

a. Projections based on average growth rates in the past

b. Projections based on varied growth rates in the past

*Source:* Based on data from the World Bank PovcalNet database.
*Note:* Panel b shows probabilistic scenarios based on random draws from past variation in growth rates between 2000 and 2010. While the median projection from this exercise is for the poverty headcount to decline to 5.1 percent by 2030, panel b shows it could also be as high as 7.1 percent.

of uncertainty, but that the goals can appear even more difficult to attain. If the growth assumptions underlying poverty projections for individual countries are allowed to fluctuate in line with patterns observed in the past (rather than assuming countries consistently grow at some average historical growth rate), the 3 percent poverty goal remains difficult to reach, even under relatively optimistic assumptions (figure O.4, panel b). Similarly, the trajectory of future poverty is much more uncertain when the incidence (distribution) of growth is allowed to vary. Although difficult to model, factors that could influence the sustainability of growth are also likely to make the World Bank goals difficult to reach. This reinforces the message from chapter 1 that the 3 percent poverty target is not easily reached.

What factors are likely to contribute to significant variation in the pace and incidence of growth in the future? There are many factors that will affect future growth, many of which are accounted for in projections of global poverty and shared prosperity by rooting the projections in the patterns of growth observed in the past. The discussion in chapter 4 thus focuses on exceptional economic and financial crises; fragility, political instability, and conflict; climate change; and global pandemics because these are factors that could have profound implications for poverty and shared prosperity. However, the likelihood and magnitude of their possible impacts are not well understood.

The World Bank's goal to end poverty is a global goal, with its target expressed as a share of the world's population. The goal is not articulated as one that aims to reduce global poverty to 3 percent in each and every country by 2030. However, although it might be possible to achieve the goal through rapid poverty reduction in some but not all countries (especially if poverty reduction occurred in some of the most populous countries), it is clear that a poverty rate that remained very high in some countries by 2030 would in some sense negate the spirit in which the World Bank's goal was articulated. In this respect the discussion of Africa in chapter 4 raises particular cause for concern. Notwithstanding the significant reduction in the incidence of armed conflict globally since the 1990s, almost half the countries in Africa are defined as being fragile states whose growth performance and poverty reduction have been lagging behind that of non-fragile states in the region. Sub-Saharan Africa is projected to be the region with the highest remaining prevalence of extreme poverty in 2030 in all the projections presented in chapter 1. Furthermore, several studies have found that the impacts on growth and poverty from temperature increases associated with climate change are likely to be particularly pronounced in Sub-Saharan Africa. Targeted support for the region will be needed to ensure that global poverty reduction leaves no country behind.

In terms of the emphasis on the World Bank's goals being achieved in a sustainable manner, the threats posed by climate change may be the most prominent source of uncertainty about future sustainability. Overall, climate change will likely have a limited aggregate impact on extreme poverty and shared prosperity by 2030. However, it is expected to affect the long-term sustainability of development progress beyond 2030, particularly in the latter part of the century when more catastrophic climate change would likely occur under current emissions scenarios.

## Monitoring poverty and shared prosperity

Having stressed the importance of data and measurement issues in assessing progress toward the twin goals, what, then, are the most important measurement and data requirements? Monitoring the goals requires many inputs, but comparable household survey data are the critical element.

Household surveys provide information on people's consumption or income—key variables in the World Bank's approach to assessing poverty. Chapter 5 discusses the measurement of poverty and shared prosperity from household survey data in detail. Although the number of household surveys has increased in countries around the world and the quantity and quality of survey data in some developing countries are excellent, overall the frequency and quality of household survey data are highly variable and there are issues of consistency and comparability across and within countries.

Heterogeneity across countries in the measure of consumption or income used to assess poverty and shared prosperity is not necessarily an indication of poor quality. In many cases, heterogeneity in surveys across countries may reflect differences that are important to take into account to assess poverty accurately at the country level, such as customization of surveys to take account of differences in living conditions in low- versus middle-income countries or differences in the types of food that are locally available. When tailoring questionnaires to local conditions produces data that are more useful to the country, then this sort of difference in the questionnaire design is desirable because it helps to produce policies that can be more effective in reducing poverty.

Heterogeneity in household surveys from the same country over time, however, may be more problematic and is often the result of happenstance rather than intentional design. For example, changes to questionnaires often reflect changes in funding sources (with surveys altered to reflect donors' interests) or simply changes in the personnel of data management teams. Changes to survey questionnaires can have substantial impacts on poverty estimates and make it difficult to answer simple questions, such as whether poverty has declined over time. For example, Beegle and others (2012) implemented an experiment where different consumption questionnaires were randomly assigned to different subsamples in Tanzania. They found large variation in measured consumption and poverty estimates that were induced simply by the differences in how questions were asked. As one example, their results show that changing the recall period from one week to two weeks (leaving everything else the same) had the effect of increasing the estimated poverty headcount from 55 percent to 63 percent. Changes to questionnaires are often based on the notion that they will improve the informational content of the data, but typically little weight is placed on the cost imposed by creating noncomparable data.

Effective policies to reduce poverty need to be informed not only by the overall level of poverty, but also by the geographic profile of poverty. Even when consumption data are consistently collected, it is impossible to accurately estimate the subnational profile of poverty if spatial differences in the cost of living within the country are not taken into account. For example, Jolliffe, Datt, and Sharma (2004) estimate region-specific poverty lines in Egypt and show that accounting for spatial differences in the cost of living had the effect of increasing the poverty rate in capital cities by more than 150 percent. Without adjusting for cost-of-living differences, policy makers would have assumed that poverty rates in metropolitan areas were about a third of what they were in the rest of the country. Thus, to inform policy empirically and design policy effectively, it is critical for surveys to be not just temporally comparable, but spatially comparable as well.

In the past, poverty has only been periodically assessed, and progress in reducing poverty was based only on these relatively infrequent measures. However, monitoring progress toward the World Bank's goals in a credible and consistent way will require more data and new methods. Although efforts should focus on improving countries' capacity to collect and assess data, innovations in statistical methods and data collection technologies offer some potential solutions. Examples include multiple-imputation and small area estimation methods, technological innovations that enhance data collection, and statistical procedures for filling in data gaps. Multiple imputation can help ensure maximum survey sizes for poverty analysis by "filling in" missing data values with (a small number of) simulated alternatives. Small area estimation techniques combine household survey and population census data to estimate poverty at more disaggregated levels and thereby pave the way for more precisely targeted policies. Chapter 5 provides details on these methods and emphasizes the importance of properly testing and validating such techniques.

## Complementary data for tracking poverty and shared prosperity across countries and over time

Although household survey data are necessary for measurement of changes in poverty and shared prosperity, they are not sufficient. At a minimum, population data are also needed to convert survey-based estimates into national poverty counts and to make inferences about poverty for the population as a whole. Poverty assessments at the country level are usually denominated in local currency and based on a poverty line that is nationally determined. Cross-country comparisons therefore require additional data to count the poor across countries with a common currency and global poverty line. Purchasing power parity (PPP) indexes, produced by the International Comparison Program, perform this role. When survey data are not available on an annual basis, two additional sources of data are needed for comparisons of poverty across countries in a common (reference) year: inflation data (to account for changes in prices between the survey year and the reference year) and real GDP growth data (to account for changes in real economic activity between the survey year and the reference year). Data on prices are also needed to account for differences in the cost of living across different areas within countries.

PPP indexes are a particularly important data input for cross-country comparisons of global poverty and shared prosperity. New rounds of PPPs can usefully update estimates of the cost of living across countries and provide price data for countries not previously covered. However, the introduction of new PPPs, which typically require reestimation of the international poverty line, can have substantial implications for the understanding of global poverty and can lead to significant reranking of countries and even regions. Table O.1 illustrates the sensitivity of the number of people who are estimated to be poor and the regional profile of poverty to changes in the PPP index and corresponding changes to the international poverty line. The 1993 count of the poor, based on the $1.08 poverty line and 1993 PPP numbers, estimated that 1.3 billion people were poor. Backcasting the 2005 PPP index to 1993, based on

**Table O.1**  Estimates of the percentage poor in 1993, based on three PPP indexes

| Indicator or region | 1985 ICP PPP index | 1993 ICP PPP index | 2005 ICP PPP index |
|---|---|---|---|
| Poverty line | $1.01 | $1.08 | $1.25 |
| East Asia and the Pacific | 26.0 | 25.2 | 50.8 |
| Europe and Central Asia | 3.5 | 3.5 | 4.3 |
| Latin America and the Caribbean | 23.5 | 15.3 | 10.1 |
| Middle East and North Africa | 4.1 | 9.0 | 4.1 |
| South Asia | 43.1 | 42.4 | 46.9 |
| Sub-Saharan Africa | 39.1 | 49.7 | 56.9 |
| Poverty headcount | 29.4 | 28.2 | 39.2 |
| *Poverty population (millions)* | *1,350* | *1,304* | *1,799* |

*Source:* Based on data from Deaton (2010).

*Note:* ICP = International Comparison Program; PPP = purchasing power parity.

the new $1.25 poverty line, resulted in an estimated count of 1.8 billion people who were poor. Adopting the new index and revising the poverty line essentially resulted in increasing the estimated number of people who were poor in 1993 by 500 million.

As discussed in chapter 6, careful review of new rounds of PPP indexes has been needed in the past. In some cases, new PPP indexes have not been adopted for global poverty measurement, while in other cases they have been adopted only after careful review and, at times, adjustments to correct for biases in the underlying data.[7] In the case of the PPP rounds from 1993 and 2005, Chen and Ravallion (2001) and Ravallion, Chen, and Sangraula (2009) provide the evidence used to justify adopting these revisions to the PPP indexes. Given the substantial revisions in the development community's understanding of poverty across countries that can occur with a new round of PPP indexes, there is a need for caution and prudence in interpreting new PPPs indexes before they are applied to global poverty data. This kind of careful review of the recently released 2011 PPP indexes is currently under way and will need to be completed before a decision is made on whether and how to adopt them for global poverty estimation.

Chapter 6 highlights the sensitivity of poverty estimates to the quality of complementary data. For example, an estimated absolute error rate of 5 percent in population projections from census data could result in the poverty status of approximately 50 million people being misclassified—leading not only to an error in the overall global poverty count, but potentially also to a distortion in the geographic profile of poverty across countries.[8] Similarly, chapter 6 illustrates how the quality of inflation data can have profound consequences for the measurement of poverty in various countries. This insight not only reinforces the discussion above on the importance of high-quality input data for measuring poverty and shared prosperity, but also speaks to the importance of the entire data architecture at the country level. Given the importance of complementary data for producing poverty estimates, focusing on improved household surveys alone will not be enough. What are needed are well-developed national statistical systems that can collect robust, complementary data as well.

## Concerted effort is needed to improve measurement methods and data

A well-functioning system of data sources and tools is needed to measure poverty and shared prosperity in a way that helps to monitor and improve policy. This report describes the detailed analysis needed to assess poverty and shared prosperity in a robust and consistent way. The report argues that although the World Bank's twin goals are a useful and important umbrella around which essential distributional issues can be considered and discussed, the global perspective inherent in these goals may not necessarily coincide directly with the priorities of individual countries. This dual purpose of distributional analysis has been borne in mind in the discussion of this report.

A key message of the report is that strengthening data measurement and collection capacity at the country level is of utmost importance. Although the World Bank's goals are global, they will be achieved through policies at the national level, and the path to reaching the global poverty and shared prosperity goals will be heterogeneous across countries. The primary purpose of collecting data on extreme poverty and shared prosperity should therefore be to inform policy at the national level. The ability to make cross-country comparisons, while important, is secondary to having a solid evidence base to guide countries' policies. This in turn implies that the data needs of national statistical agencies should not take a back seat to the data demands of international organizations, quality of data should not be compromised in favor of cross-country comparability, donors should accordingly be cautious in the emphasis they give to cross-country comparisons, and technologies and statistical approaches to bridge gaps in data measurement may offer some partial solutions.

A useful comparison of different approaches to data collection can be made between the World Bank's Living Standards Measurement Study (LSMS) and the United States Agency for International Development's (USAID's) Demographic and Health Surveys (DHS). The LSMS seeks to strengthen household data collected by national statistical agencies through intensive collaboration with those agencies, and focuses on improving data collection methods and developing an instrument that is tailored to the country context. One outcome of the focus on collection methods and capacity building has been that some countries have continued to manage and fund the survey even when external support has tapered off. A trade-off, however, of tailoring the instrument to the country context is that many of the indicators and data collected are frequently difficult to compare across countries. In contrast, the DHS data collection activities tend to be much more focused on defining and measuring indicators in a manner that maintains comparability across countries. Similarly, DHS training is relatively more focused on international standards for measuring an extensive set of key health and nutrition indicators. As a result of this, the DHS effort has enjoyed great success in increasing the coverage and standardization of health data, which has promoted an explosion of detailed analysis of health issues in countries and has helped donors to make cross-country comparisons and thereby target funding for health aid more effectively.

To some extent, whether to emphasize cross-country comparability or the need to be sensitive to the country context is determined by the overarching purpose of the survey. In the case of DHS, the focus is on measures of health and well-being for which the items to be measured are similar across countries and units are the same (or conversion factors are well known). In contrast, a primary objective of the LSMS is to measure consumption poverty, which consists of items that vary significantly across countries (for example, rice in India, teff in Ethiopia) and units are not standardized internationally (for example, sacks and piles). The twin goals of shared prosperity and poverty reduction rest heavily on the measure of consumption, which does not lend itself as readily to standardization. Since the primary aim of measurement and collection of poverty and prosperity data is to support policy making at the national level, strengthening the statistical systems of countries is a key priority. The LSMS approach of working closely with national statistical agencies has been important in this respect. Greater support to enhance the capacity of statistical agencies and more funding for improved data systems are needed.

The timeliness and frequency of data collection need to increase. Even where data have been collected, processing lags can be lengthy and in some cases governments are reluctant to provide access. Even more emphasis needs to be placed on the importance of open access to data: it is regrettable that even in cases where data are produced some governments remain reluctant to make them available in an open and timely way. Beyond producing more frequent surveys, however, more attention to the careful design and collection of data is needed. There is ample scope to improve the standardization of data. Indeed, there needs to be more standardization of guidelines for estimating poverty and more emphasis on maintaining comparable measures of consumption and income. However, in many cases countries may have good reasons to follow a particular approach, which is different from that followed in other countries. Although this heterogeneity comes at the cost of comparability across countries, the benefits of data that can provide locally useful information may at times outweigh this cost. In all cases, the quality of national data, rather than its comparability, should be the primary concern. The implication is that donors and development practitioners need to be realistic about how much can be inferred from cross-country comparisons, not only because poverty and shared prosperity estimates may be imprecise, for many reasons discussed in the chapters that follow, but also because of heterogeneity in data across countries. This underscores the importance of informing funding decisions on the basis of a wide spectrum of evidence, rather than only a few indicators.

New technologies and statistical approaches can help to bridge some of the gaps in data measurement and assessment. For example, technological innovations, such as computer-assisted personal interviews or mobile phone–based data collection, can help improve the frequency of surveys, especially in geographically dispersed countries. Similarly, when the desired or standard sources of complementary data are not available, it may still be possible to measure poverty with alternative data sources and modeling techniques. The use of technologies that can improve data collection and the use of well-designed survey-to-survey imputations should be scaled up. However, the first-best solution is to strengthen countries' capacity to collect data in a manner that produces high-quality, time-sensitive, and well-documented inputs for policy making. The development community urgently needs to mobilize efforts to spur the availability of data for the purpose of poverty analysis (box O.5).

---

### Box 0.5    Summary of the report's key recommendations

- As countries begin to consider what policy changes will be needed to end poverty and boost shared prosperity, **attention should be given to the nature of growth in countries**. While strong and sustained growth will be critical to meeting the goals, attention to the type of growth (sustainable growth that benefits the poor) is also needed.

- Rather than gauging progress toward the World Bank's goals separately, **progress toward the two goals should be assessed in unison**, as "twin" goals. Achieving progress in both goals will require efforts on both fronts.

- Measuring progress toward ending poverty and boosting shared prosperity requires increased capacity at the national level, where improved

data are most relevant for policy. **Strengthening the capacity of national statistical agencies to collect these data should not be neglected in favor of data collection by international organizations**. Data system architectures at the country level are needed not only to support credible measurement of the twin goals, but also for effective national development policy.

- **Quality of data should be the primary aim of efforts to improve data measurement and collection at the country level**. Although increased frequency of data is desirable, it should not come at the cost of improved quality. Similarly, for the purpose of well-designed poverty mitigation policies, producing high-quality data that suit national contexts is more important than having data that is comparable across countries.

## Notes

1. Chapter 1 sets out the World Bank's approach to measuring global poverty in more detail. See Chen and Ravallion (2010) for a fuller description of how the $1.25 a day international poverty line was derived.
2. The scenarios explored in Ravallion (2013) reach qualitatively similar conclusions but are based on less restrictive assumptions.
3. See World Bank (1990) for a rich discussion of this issue.
4. The Green Revolution in India is a prominent example of an episode of extensive poverty reduction supported by growth that substantially improved the returns to agriculture. By contrast, high growth driven by commodity booms has not always translated to effective poverty reduction when the returns from extractive industries have remained concentrated in the hands of relatively few people.
5. The regional leader simulations in chapter 2 highlight some interesting differences across regions. In particular, they suggest that changing the incidence of growth could have a substantial impact on poverty in Latin America and the Caribbean and South Asia, while the effect may be relatively smaller in Sub-Saharan Africa. This partly reflects that nature of the exercise: the distribution of income (consumption) of the regional leader in Sub-Saharan Africa (Rwanda) is significantly less progressive than that of the regional leader in Latin America and the Caribbean (Brazil), thus the simulated impact of the exercise for countries in Sub-Saharan Africa is smaller. These regional effects are muted in the second simulation where the income or consumption growth of the bottom 40 percent is raised by 1 and then 2 percentage points more than their country's respective mean growth rates. See chapter 2 for a full discussion.
6. See World Bank (2012) for a comprehensive discussion of the importance of sustainable development for poverty reduction and future growth.
7. The first comprehensive attempt at producing global poverty estimates was completed in 1979, on the basis of the 1975 International Comparison Program (ICP) PPP data. Since then the 1985, 1993, and 2005 ICP PPP revisions have been incorporated into the World Bank's global poverty estimates—although often with a delay of five or more years—but the 1980 revisions were not incorporated. See chapter 6 for a full discussion.
8. In an extensive review of population counts, the National Research Council (2000) assessed the overall quality of population projections across the globe. Across several sets of United Nations and World Bank forecasts, the absolute value of the errors in projected country populations averaged 4.8 percent in five-year projections and 17 percent in 30-year projections.

## References

Beegle, Kathleen, Joachim De Weerdt, Jed Friedman, and John Gibson. 2012. "Methods of Household Consumption Measurement through Surveys: Experimental Results from Tanzania." *Journal of Development Economics* 98 (1): 3–18.

Birdsall, Nancy, Nora Lustig, and Christian J. Meyer. 2014. "The Strugglers: The New Poor in Latin America?" *World Development* 60 (August): 132–46. doi:10.1016/j.worlddev.2014.03.019.

Chen, Shaohua, and Martin Ravallion. 2001. "How Did the World's Poorest Fare in the 1990s?" *Review of Income and Wealth* 47 (3): 283–300.

———. 2010. "The Developing World Is Poorer Than We Thought, but No Less Successful in the Fight Against Poverty." *Quarterly Journal of Economics* 125 (4): 1577–1625.

Deaton, Angus. 2010. "Price Indexes, Inequality, and the Measurement of World Poverty." *American Economic Review* 100 (1): 5–34. doi:10.1257/aer.100.5.

Ferreira, Francisco H. G., Julian Messina, Jamele Rigolini, Luis-Felipe López-Calva, Maria Ana Lugo, and Renos Vakis. 2012. *Economic Mobility and the Rise of the Latin American Middle Class.* Washington, DC: World Bank.

Jolliffe, Dean, Gaurav Datt, and Manohar Sharma. 2004. "Robust Poverty and Inequality Measurement in Egypt: Correcting for Spatial-Price Variation and Sample Design Effects." *Review of Development Economics* 8 (4): 557–72. doi:10.1111/j.1467-9361.2004.00252.x.

López-Calva, Luis F., and Eduardo Ortiz-Juarez. 2014. "A Vulnerability Approach to the Definition of the Middle Class." *Journal of Economic Inequality* 12 (1): 23–47.

Mahalanobis, Prasanta C. 1963. *The Approach of Operational Research to Planning in India.* Indian Statistical Series 18. New York: Asia Publishing House.

National Research Council (United States). 2000. *Beyond Six Billion: Forecasting the World's Population.* Edited by John Bongaarts and Rodolfo A. Bulatao. Washington, DC: National Academy Press.

Ravallion, Martin. 2013. "How Long Will It Take to Lift One Billion People Out of Poverty?" *The World Bank Research Observer* 28 (2): 139–58.

Ravallion, Martin, Shaohua Chen, and Prem Sangraula. 2009. "Dollar a Day Revisited." *The World Bank Economic Review* 23 (2): 163–84. doi:10.1093/wber/lhp007.

World Bank. 1990. *World Development Report 1990: Poverty.* New York: Oxford University Press.

———. 2012. *Inclusive Green Growth: The Pathway to Sustainable Development.* Washington, DC: World Bank.

# CHAPTER ONE

# Defining and Assessing the Goal of Ending Poverty by 2030

Monitoring poverty at the global level has been an important pillar of the World Bank's analytical work on poverty since an early attempt in the late 1970s to estimate the fraction of the developing world's population in poverty (Aluwahlia, Carter, and Chenery 1979) and a subsequent effort for the 1990 *World Development Report* (Ravallion, Datt, and van de Walle 1991). What has changed now is that the World Bank has set an explicit goal and timetable. In the spring of 2013, World Bank President Jim Yong Kim presented to the international development community the World Bank's new goal of ending global poverty by 2030. Ending poverty was defined as occurring when global poverty has fallen to no more than 3 percent of the world's population. Thus, the World Bank is focusing on reducing global poverty from an estimated 14.5 percent in 2011 to 3 percent or lower in a period of two decades.[1]

This chapter starts with a brief review of the World Bank's approach to measuring global poverty. The World Bank's methodology has been widely described and discussed and so the review here will be selective, focusing in particular on the data-intensive nature of the effort and the accompanying sensitivity of poverty estimates to changes in data and empirical methods.

The chapter then turns to an assessment of what reaching the poverty goal will require, demonstrating that the goal of ending poverty by 2030 is highly aspirational. The chapter examines a range of scenarios and shows that "business as usual" at the country level is unlikely to bring the world all the way to the 3 percent target. This implies, therefore, that success will depend on transformational policies that succeed either in markedly raising growth rates in countries or in improving the responsiveness of poverty reduction to growth through greater inclusion of the poor in the growth process.

What do evidence and analysis tell us about the likely pathway that global poverty reduction will trace during the coming decades? Poverty has fallen at a fairly steady rate of about 1 percentage point per year between 1980 and 2011, with China having a central role in shaping this global picture. But maintaining such a pace of poverty reduction through growth alone will become increasingly difficult. The reason for this can be understood in a simple stylized framework that analyzes the impact of growth on poverty when changes in the distribution of income are ruled out. Of course, given that policy makers can intervene and income distribution can and does change, it is necessary to look beyond stylized examples to actual country experience.

The chapter documents that, on the one hand, in many developing countries the poverty of certain subgroups of the population is relatively insensitive to overall rising income levels. These pockets of poverty can emerge for a variety of reasons. They can be linked, for example, to geographic remoteness, patterns of social stratification and discrimination, as well as market failures that generate poverty traps. As overall poverty levels fall and these pockets come to represent the majority of those who remain poor, progress in further reducing poverty may slow. On the other hand, evidence of poverty decline among those countries that, today, have already ended poverty suggests that in some cases policy makers were able to adopt the policies needed to maintain a steady rate of progress in eliminating extreme poverty. It is clear that for the global target of 3 percent by 2030 to be achieved, countries will need to look beyond accelerating growth toward ensuring that the poor in particular benefit from growth. This message motivates the examination in chapter 2 of the World Bank's second goal, which is to boost shared prosperity.

## A brief overview of global poverty measurement

### Measurement of poverty with household surveys

The World Bank's approach to measuring poverty has been widely documented.[2] Household surveys play a pivotal role in this effort; they are critical not only for global poverty estimation, but also for country-level poverty estimation. The surveys are organized at the country level and are commonly administered by government statistical agencies. The key indicator of interest from such surveys is a measure of household consumption or income. In what follows, the discussion provides a brief overview of the procedure to put together a consumption measure. Additional remarks are provided on the distinction between income and consumption.

In a typical survey, a nationally representative sample of households is interviewed and asked to specify purchases against a list of market products over a given period of time. Information is also collected about consumption of nontransacted (home produced) goods and services, access to publically provided goods and services, as well as ownership of assets such as housing and consumer durables. By combining the responses to such questions, it is possible to arrive at an estimate of the level of consumption in each surveyed household.[3] Sampling weights that accompany the household survey data can be used to extrapolate from the sample data to the underlying population. The resultant data on the distribution of consumption across the population can be combined with a poverty line to identify the poor. Specific methodologies can be applied to aggregate up from the household-specific poverty indicators to a national-level poverty measure.

Consumption per capita is the preferred welfare indicator for the World Bank's analysis of global poverty. This position needs to be explained with respect to two important but distinct alternatives. First, it is well understood and widely acknowledged that poverty is a complex phenomenon that involves multiple dimensions of deprivation. So shouldn't global poverty be measured in an explicitly multidimensional framework? A focus on consumption poverty could otherwise be construed to imply that the World Bank regards other, nonconsumption dimensions of deprivation as of secondary importance. Such an interpretation would be unfortunate. Recognition that there are multiple dimensions of deprivation does not mean that they are best assessed simultaneously, within a single indicator. There is a good deal of consensus that a comprehensive consumption aggregate captures many important economic dimensions of well-being. Other critical dimensions of well-being—such as health, education, social inclusion, empowerment, and so on—are difficult to incorporate into a consumption measure. This is because it is difficult to construct a multidimensional measure that respects households' own perspectives on how the various dimensions interact with each other and the trade-offs between the dimensions.

Stopping short of attempting to construct an explicitly multidimensional measure of poverty does not, however, mean that comparisons of deprivation along various dimensions are not possible. World Bank poverty assessments, carried out at the country level, routinely look not only at consumption poverty, but also at deprivation along other dimensions.

These studies draw important insights not only from quantitative household survey data, but also from qualitative surveys and from techniques that "mix" qualitative and quantitative analysis. Only when all relevant indicators are closely scrutinized and considered can an overall assessment of poverty be regarded as complete. The key point is that the dimensions can be examined alongside one another and do not necessarily need to be combined in a single indicator—with the additional proviso that one must not lose sight of the possibility that individuals and households may suffer multiple deprivations simultaneously. At the global level, the challenges of estimating multidimensional poverty measures are further aggravated. However, the central point remains that global consumption poverty can and should be examined alongside deprivations in all other relevant dimensions. Thus, the Millennium Development Goals were articulated with respect to a wide range of indicators, in addition to global consumption poverty. Similarly, there are large literatures exploring the cross-country correlations of health and education outcomes with poverty outcomes, as well as a growing literature investigating the association between economic well-being and subjective assessments of welfare. Chapter 3 offers additional discussion of some of the issues around multidimensional poverty measurement.

The second alternative to a consumption-based analysis of poverty is to measure poverty on the basis of income. Income is a widely available alternative measure of economic well-being and can be calculated from many household surveys in a manner similar to the procedure followed for constructing a consumption measure. In some countries, notably in Latin America, income is the only available indicator of economic welfare. In these countries, the most common nationally representative household surveys are employment surveys, designed to collect information on employment patterns and labor incomes. The surveys readily yield a measure of household income, but they provide no information on household consumption. In those instances where household income is the only possible indicator of economic well-being, the World Bank's global poverty monitoring effort uses income as the welfare indicator to measure a country's poverty rate. However, income is not, in general, the preferred indicator.

It can be argued that, in measuring poverty, policy makers are interested in capturing the living standards *achieved* by individuals. These are directly reflected in a well-constructed, comprehensive consumption measure. Incomes, in contrast, reflect an *opportunity* to reach a given welfare but may provide only an imperfect proxy of what welfare level was finally achieved. In the face of a particularly poor agricultural harvest, for example, a farmer might generate a very low or even negative income. But by drawing down on stocks and by borrowing from friends and relatives, it may be possible for the farmer's family to maintain its consumption levels, at least for some time.[4] Consumption may thus provide a smoother, less volatile measure of living standards than income, reflecting not only the financial inflows that are available to a household (as captured by a current income measure), but also the ability of a given household to (dis) save or borrow.

More generally, the preference for consumption derives from the fact that these data are typically more easily and accurately collected in the developing country context. This is particularly the case when attention is focused on the poor. The poor are likely to consume a rather modest range of goods and services, primarily staple food items and a small set of essential nonfood goods and services. Compiling information on the consumption levels of the poor may thus be reasonably straightforward. By contrast, collecting information on the income levels of the poor can be much more complex. The poor are likely to be employed in the informal sector and may derive income from multiple sources—each of which contributes in a small way to total income. If income is measured over a long period, like a year, it could be easy to overlook some of these income sources. Furthermore, many of the developing world's poor are subsistence farmers with incomes that may be particularly difficult to calculate given long lags and uncertain attribution across seasons, between when costs of cultivation are incurred and when associated farming revenues accrue.[5]

## Comparison of poverty across countries

In the 1990 *World Development Report* on poverty, the World Bank applied a concerted effort to estimate the world's population in poverty (World Bank 1990). As described in Ravallion, Datt, and van de Walle (1991), this effort was based on what was, at the time, a rather thin empirical foundation, consisting of a single household survey available in only 22 countries. The empirical base underpinning the World Bank's global poverty estimates has since increased substantially. Chen and Ravallion (2010) estimated global poverty in 2005 based on 675 household surveys for 115 countries covering the period 1979 to 2006. Ravallion (2013), drawing on Chen and Ravallion (2013), estimated global poverty at three points in time between 1990 and 2008, drawing on 900 surveys for 125 countries.

The most recent World Bank estimates, covering the period 1981 to 2011, expand that database further, to well over 1,000 surveys covering nearly all developing countries.[6]

Assembly of the survey data that support the World Bank's global poverty monitoring task is carried out by a designated team in the World Bank's research department. The resultant internationally comparable poverty estimates are published in a database called Povcal. An accompanying website and online computational tool called PovcalNet provide access to these data to users within and outside the World Bank.[7] A key feature of PovcalNet is that users can access and manipulate the Povcal data remotely, either to replicate the World Bank's calculations or to tailor the analysis to their own specific needs.

The process governing the collection of household survey data in each country varies on a case-by-case basis. In some countries, household survey data collection is an integral part of the mandate of the national statistical office (NSO). Surveys are programmed into the NSO's work plan, and survey-based consumption data are regularly published and disseminated. In many countries, however, there is no such systematic effort to collect and distribute survey data. Household surveys are collected on an ad hoc basis—as a result of specific requests from a particular government department or ministry and depending on the availability of funding. Often donors provide the impetus and funding for data collection. Even in those countries where survey data have been collected and compiled, there is great heterogeneity across countries as to when and to what degree the data are made available to analysts outside the NSOs. Delays between the fielding of household surveys and the release of the data for analysis can be lengthy. In quite a few countries, access to survey data remains altogether restricted. Occasionally, as in the case of China, even though access to microdata is restricted, aggregated data on the distribution of consumption is published in official NSO reports. In such cases, indirect estimates of poverty might still be feasible, although not without the imposition of additional assumptions.

These considerations account for the lack of a consistent and predictable flow of new data into PovcalNet from all countries. Even in those cases where new data do become available, the fact that they stem from choices, decisions, and implementation at the country level implies that there are numerous ways in which comparability across countries of the underlying consumption data can be compromised. Before any calculation of global poverty can proceed, therefore, it is necessary to undertake an exhaustive assessment and evaluation of each country's respective data. In some cases, adjustments can be introduced so as to strengthen comparability; often, harmonization will be far from complete and a degree of noncomparability will remain. Some imprecision in the resulting global poverty estimates will be unavoidable.

Scrutiny of the household surveys that enter the World Bank's Povcal database occurs at multiple levels. First, household surveys are identified and acquired (and occasionally procured directly) by World Bank teams working in specific countries and regions. These data are checked and analyzed by the World Bank country teams for the purpose of national-level poverty work in the respective country and region. The survey data are then sent to the Povcal team and are subjected to a further round of scrutiny, this time from the point of view of their comparability with data from all other countries.

Second, the Povcal team is in some cases able to identify and acquire household surveys that have been collected outside the purview of the World Bank's country teams. Such data include surveys collected in developed countries where there is no presence of a World Bank operational unit or data that have been collected by NSOs that do not have a dialogue with the World Bank's operational units (for example, Iran). The way in which these additional data sources are accessed can range from a routine downloading of the data from officially approved websites (as is the case for many developed country data sets) to the acquisition of data via personal networks and ad hoc requests. As these data have not undergone any World Bank scrutiny, they must be assessed by the Povcal team from first principles. The challenges with such data can be particularly onerous, as the quality of survey documentation received on an ad hoc basis may be quite variable.

Third, several household surveys are collected by NSOs with substantial technical assistance from the World Bank research department's Living Standards Measurement Study (LSMS). This program focuses on methods of data collection with an eye toward providing guidance on the most appropriate methods for collecting data on living standards. The current LSMS-Integrated Surveys for Africa program involves the LSMS team in informing the collection of household survey panels in seven African countries. More generally, some 80 surveys included in the research department's global poverty monitoring effort have come directly from such data collection efforts involving the LSMS team. Although, again, there is no assurance that these data are strictly comparable across countries, the data have generally received close scrutiny by World Bank researchers and are usually well documented.

Irrespective of how the data are sourced, they are all vetted and assessed for their suitability for cross-country comparability in the global poverty monitoring effort. Although considerable efforts are made, it is clear that comparability remains partial and will hopefully strengthen further over time, as additional methodological refinements are developed and introduced. Chapter 5 provides a further discussion of the challenges in assembling a global database of comparable country-level surveys. It describes some of the innovations under consideration aimed at increasing the frequency of country-level poverty estimates and the timeliness of global poverty estimates.

### National and global poverty lines

Poverty analysis at the World Bank is most commonly carried out at the country level. It is important that this work is done in a way that is relevant to the respective country, producing empirical results that can be readily interpreted and endorsed by stakeholders, and providing reliable information to support decision making. Country-level analysis commonly builds on a solid measure of per capita consumption and combines this with a poverty line that has been derived in the respective country, representing a well-understood and widely accepted minimum threshold of consumption. The intention of such a poverty line is to delineate the threshold standard of living in a given society below which an individual is judged to be poor by the standards of that particular society. The standards are likely to vary across societies. Indeed, empirical evidence indicates that across countries, national poverty lines tend to rise with average income levels. Box 1.1 provides a detailed overview of the various approaches that have been taken in the specification of national poverty lines.

Global poverty estimates represent the sum of country-level estimates but are based on a common poverty line across all countries. The World Bank currently uses an international poverty line of $1.25 a day, in 2005 prices. As described in Chen and Ravallion (2010), this line corresponds to an average of the national poverty lines of the 15 poorest developing countries and must therefore be understood to represent a very low threshold standard of living.[8] In setting the global poverty line at $1.25 per person per day in real terms, the World Bank has elected to monitor global poverty by the standards that apply in the very poorest countries of the world. It is sobering that, even at that standard, there were about one billion poor people in the world in 2011.

## Box 1.1 Setting national poverty lines around the world

Poverty lines are commonly used as cutoff points that delineate who in a country or region is considered poor at any given point in time, based on some predefined standard of living. The choice of poverty line—what type and how it should be set—depends on the local context and intended use. In high-income countries, where absolute deprivation is less common, poverty lines are often relative—that is, they are defined in relation to the overall distribution of income. For example, a poverty line could be set as a percentage of the overall population mean or median income. In developing countries, where large parts of the population cannot meet their basic needs, it often makes sense to define some absolute standard and thus set an absolute poverty line.

The challenge of defining an absolute poverty line at the country level can be summarized by two related questions. First, what is the adequate *minimum level of well-being* at which an individual is not considered poor in the specific local context (often called the referencing problem)? Second, how can the *minimum amount of money* that corresponds to that level of well-being be identified (the identification problem)? Commonly, these two problems are approached in what is called the *cost of basic needs method*. This approach first stipulates a consumption bundle that is deemed adequate for basic consumption needs in the local context and then estimates the cost of this specific bundle.

What is an adequate consumption bundle? One potential starting point is the average nutritional requirement for an individual to be in good health, often approximated to be 2,100 calories per person per day. Based on this food energy requirement, a local consumption basket is compiled for a diet that reflects the consumption habits of local households near the poverty line. The cost of this basket is estimated based on the prices of the various foodstuffs that are included. This is not a trivial task, since the

calorie requirement can be met with various food baskets and, depending on the cost composition of the basket and local price levels, the resulting poverty line can vary widely (Pradhan and others 2000; Haughton and Khandker 2009).

In addition to the food component (which gives the so-called food poverty line), the overall poverty line often also includes a nonfood component that is added to reflect costs for housing, clothing, electricity, and so on. There are various ways to estimate the nonfood component—and no consensus on best practice. One way is to stipulate a second consumption bundle that reflects an adequate level of nonfood items. Parallel to the approach for the food component, that bundle could then be priced accordingly. In the absence of an objective caloric requirement, however, it is difficult to define "adequate" nonfood consumption needs. An alternative approach to estimate the nonfood component is to divide the food component by the average share of food in total household expenditure (Orshansky 1963), although this approach raises the question of whether the food share of the average household, a poor household, or a nonpoor household should be used.

An alternative to the cost of basic needs approach is the *food energy intake method*, which does not require information on the prices of the goods that are included in the estimated consumption basket. Instead, this approach plots total household (food and nonfood) consumption expenditure or income against food consumption as measured in calories per person per day to find the level at which a household can meet its basic energy requirements. However, this requires analysts to assume a relationship between household expenditure and food energy, and this approach does not lend itself to comparisons across time or regions. Yet another potential approach to set absolute lines is based on asking people what minimum consumption or

*(continued)*

## Box 1.1    Continued

income level they need just to make ends meet. These *subjective poverty lines* remain relatively rare in practice, but they can be useful supplements to more objective measures.

Conceptually, the cost of basic needs approach provides the most reliable framework to set national absolute poverty lines and is widely used in practice. In a data set of national poverty lines compiled by the World Bank's Global Practice for Poverty, 38 of 45 national poverty lines set in low- and middle-income countries between 2001 and 2011 were based on the cost of basic needs method. The Russian Federation is one of the few countries that use the food energy method, while the remaining countries in Eastern Europe and Central Asia predominantly rely on relative poverty lines.

The common practice in high-income countries is to use relative lines. In the European Union, the main poverty measure identifies as "at risk of poverty" all households that have net incomes of less than 60 percent of the national median. Similarly, the Organisation for Economic Co-operation and Development uses national median household income as a yardstick and applies thresholds of 50 percent and 60 percent. A noteworthy exception is the United States, where the federal poverty measures are based on absolute thresholds. In 1963, U.S. government statistician Mollie Orshansky calculated the cost of a minimum food diet and multiplied it by three to account for nonfood expenditure. Since then, her results have been adjusted for inflation and today form the basis for a detailed matrix of poverty lines, varying by family size, number of children, and so on.

Empirically across countries, national absolute poverty lines tend to drift upward with average income, although for the very poorest countries the relationship is initially flat (Ravallion, Chen, and Sangraula 2009). The median poverty line across countries of Sub-Saharan Africa (using data from around 2000) was roughly equal to the World Bank's international poverty line of $1.25 a day (at 2005 purchasing power parity [PPP]). Across countries in Latin America and the Caribbean around 2010, the median national poverty line was a little over $4 per capita per day (at 2005 PPP). In contrast, in the United States in 2013, a household with two adults and two children under 18 years old was considered poor if its daily income was less than about $16 (at current 2013 prices, around $13.50 at 2005 prices).

Ultimately, the choice of a specific absolute or relative poverty line is a social and policy decision that depends on the local context. No matter how precisely a specific poverty line is estimated, it is important to keep in mind that living standards of those just above the poverty line are not very different from those just below. In other words, nothing happens to individuals in terms of their consumption, income, health, or any other indicator when their income crosses an absolute poverty line (Deaton 1997; Pritchett 2006). The key issue, then, in setting an absolute poverty line is not its precise location, but to ensure comparability and consistency across areas and over time.

*Source:* Based on Deaton (1997); Haughton and Khandker (2009); Ravallion (1988); and Ravallion, Chen, and Sangraula (2009).

### Global poverty counts

The World Bank employs a specific measure of poverty in its calculations. It reports the extent of global poverty by calculating the percentage of the world's population with a consumption or income level below the international poverty line. Producing global poverty counts in this way is intuitive and easily communicated. Yet it has disadvantages as well. Notably, this manner of measuring poverty is insensitive to the fact that there may be great variation in living standards among the poor across countries. Two countries could record the same headcount rate of poverty, although in one country the poor have consumption levels far below the poverty line, while in the other the poor's consumption levels are only just below the poverty line. Other poverty measures, more sensitive to differences in consumption levels among the poor, can be readily calculated and reported but are less easy to communicate. Chapter 3 provides further discussion of some of the alternative methods for measuring poverty.

The three key steps involved in measuring global poverty can be summarized as follows: construct a survey-based measure of household consumption, define a global poverty line, and aggregate across households to calculate an overall measure of poverty. While these steps capture the overall process, there remain a few measurement details to consider further. First, although household surveys typically collect information on consumption at the household level, poverty headcounts seek to assess the poverty of *individuals* and the percentage of the population that is poor. Conventional practice is to divide household consumption by household size and attribute to each individual in the household a per capita consumption level accordingly. Those individuals whose per capita consumption level is below the poverty line (also expressed in per capita terms) are designated as poor. It is important to note that proceeding in this manner involves several important assumptions: that household resources are shared equally across family members; that family members have identical needs, such that two individuals with the same per capita consumption level enjoy the same living standard; and that there are no differential costs of reaching a given welfare level per person for households of different sizes. All three of these assumptions are unlikely to hold in practice. Yet it would be difficult to relax the assumptions in a way that is transparent and widely accepted. An imperfect but tractable solution is to maintain the assumptions but to subject all conclusions to sensitivity analysis in which the assumptions are in turn allowed to be relaxed. Country-level work along these lines indicates that conclusions as to, for example, the relative poverty of the elderly versus children, or of the particular vulnerability of widows, can be quite sensitive to these assumptions.[9]

Second, important adjustments must be made to the survey results to account for differences across places and time. Differences in the cost of living between countries must be accommodated by converting consumption levels in each country into comparable international prices, or purchasing power parity (PPP) terms. In addition, consumption levels from a given survey may need adjustment if there are important differences in the cost of living across regions of a given country, or if the year of the survey does not coincide with the year for which global poverty is being estimated. In the interval between the two time periods, economic growth may have occurred, as well as changes in the cost of living. To line up the data for all countries to a given reference year, adjustments are introduced on the basis of national accounts data on consumption growth and consumer price indexes that capture the rate of inflation over time. Chapter 6 provides further details on the various price and growth adjustments.

Third, to be certain that poverty estimates are based on accurate population figures, population census data are used to translate the poverty rates in a country into numbers of poor people based on population estimates. In many cases, the household survey data are accompanied by accurate population weights that allow for a direct conversion of survey-based counts to the underlying population. But often these weights are outdated or incomplete and must be adjusted with census data. Further discussion of these issues is provided in chapter 6.

## Assessment of the global poverty target

Given the broad approach taken by the World Bank to measure global poverty, this section attempts to provide a perspective on the target to end poverty by 2030. As was noted above, the World Bank's target is to end poverty by reducing global poverty to 3 percent or less. Why should a global poverty rate of 3 percent be interpreted to imply an ending of poverty? As discussed below, poverty in many countries remains extremely widespread. Reducing poverty to zero in such countries over any reasonable time frame would be extremely unrealistic. However, a global goal of zero poverty would require the elimination of poverty in each and every country. It is also important to acknowledge that at any moment in time, some churning is likely to be taking place in which some people, possibly for reasons beyond their control, fall into poverty, even if only temporarily. It is difficult to imagine a world in which nobody at all is poor. For these reasons, it seems reasonable to view global poverty as having effectively ended even if some frictional poverty remains at a very low level. Hence, the global target is 3 percent or lower.

What is the current picture of poverty around the world? In 2011, it is estimated that about one billion people in the world had a consumption level below the $1.25 a day global poverty line (table 1.1).[10] This represents about 17 percent of the population of the developing world and 14.5 percent of the entire global population.[11] In 2011, poverty was most prevalent in Sub-Saharan Africa and South Asia. These two regions accounted for about 80 percent of the global poor.

Taking the 2011 poverty estimates as a point of departure, figure 1.1 illustrates in a stylized way the changing patterns of global poverty in selected developing regions. In each of the three panels, the vertical gray line indicates today's $1.25 global poverty line, and the vertical axis can be read as the poverty headcount at each consumption or income level. In 1981 (panel a), the estimated number of people below the $1.25 line was about 1.9 billion, representing about 52 percent of the developing world's population. Poverty was most prevalent in East Asia and the Pacific, where about 77 percent of the population had a consumption or income level below the $1.25 line, and South Asia, where about 61 percent of the population was considered poor. As the graph illustrates, the headcount in these regions was mostly driven by China and India; the total number of poor people in each of these two countries accounted for about three-quarters of the headcount in East Asia and the Pacific and South Asia, respectively. In Sub-Saharan Africa, slightly more than half the regional population was considered poor.

**Table 1.1**  **Poverty in 2011 at $1.25 a day 2005 PPP**

| Region | Headcount (%) | Number of poor (millions) |
| --- | --- | --- |
| East Asia and the Pacific | 7.9 | 160.8 |
| Europe and Central Asia | 0.5 | 2.3 |
| Latin America and the Caribbean | 4.6 | 27.6 |
| Middle East and North Africa[a] | 1.7 | 5.6 |
| South Asia | 24.5 | 399.0 |
| Sub-Saharan Africa | 46.8 | 415.4 |
| Total developing world | 17.0 | 1,010.7 |
| World | 14.5 | 1,010.7 |

*Source:* Based on data from the World Bank PovcalNet database (accessed August 2014).
*Note:* Benchmark year estimates generated following methodology described in Chen and Ravallion (2010). For countries without survey data, such as Eritrea or Somalia, the poverty headcount is assumed to be equal to the respective regional average headcount.

a. This is a provisional estimate, in part because it is based on survey data covering only about one third of the population and because the 2011 estimate for Egypt is a projection from 2008 data.

**Figure 1.1    Changing patterns of global poverty, 1981–2030**

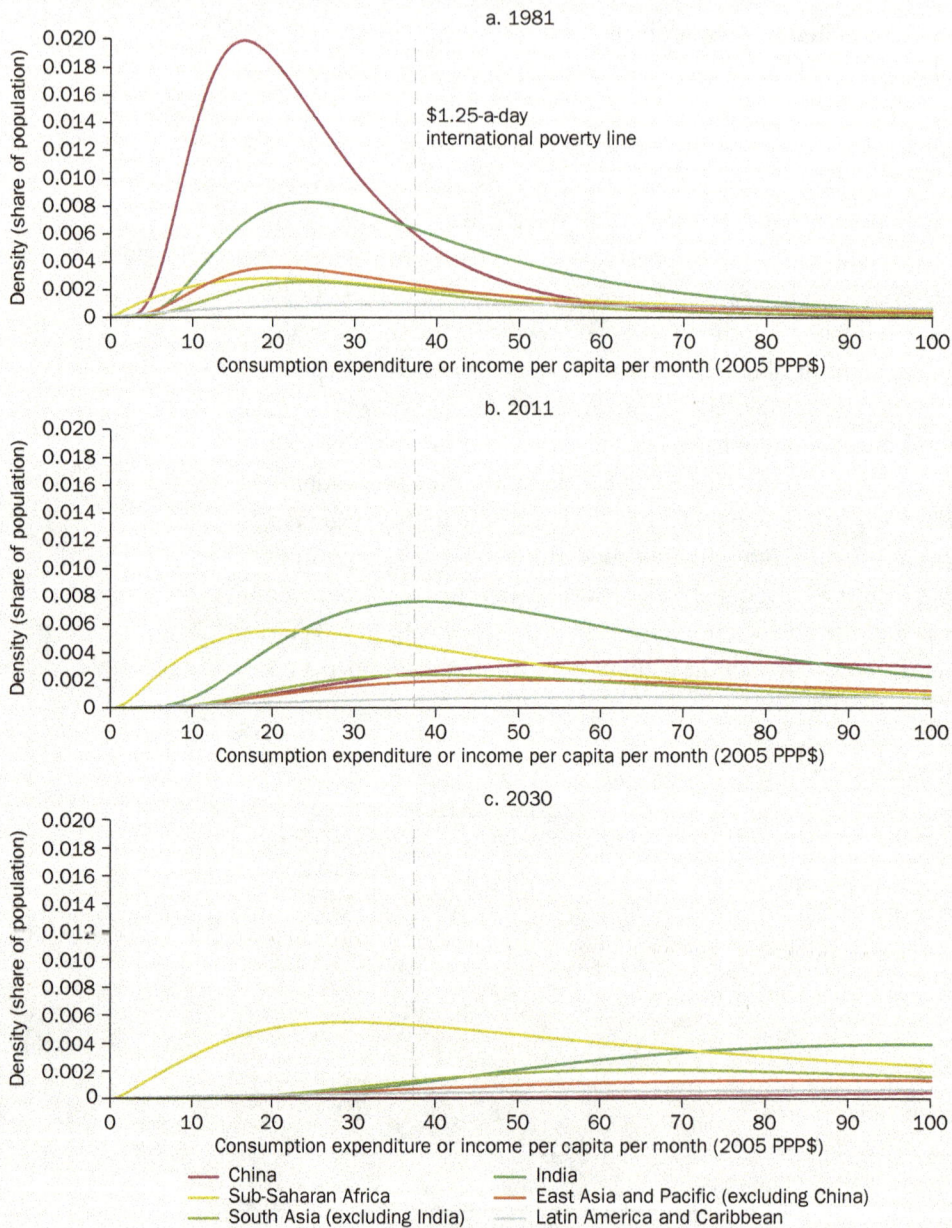

*Source:* Based on analysis of World Bank PovcalNet data.
*Note:* Calculations assume lognormal distributions, based on the mean and variance of the country-specific consumption or income distributions in each reference year. To generate annual reference years, survey means are log-linearly interpolated between survey years and extended backward to 1980 and forward to 2011, using real household consumption growth. The graph for 2030 shows a projection under the assumption that countries grow between 2011 and 2030 at their historical average growth rates over the period 2000 to 2011 and constant inequality since the last available survey year. PPP = purchasing power parity.

In comparison, panel b in figure 1.1 illustrates the central role of India and China in the global reduction of poverty as measured by the $1.25 line over the following three decades. In East Asia and the Pacific, the headcount fell from about 77 percent of the regional population in 1981 to about 8 percent in 2011. In South Asia, the headcount more than halved, from 61 percent in 1981 to about 24 percent in 2011. Still, of the one billion people in the world below the poverty line in 2011, about 40 percent were in South Asia, about 30 percent in India alone. As shown in table 1.1, poverty in 2011 was most prevalent in South Asia and in Sub-Saharan Africa.

In 2030 (figure 1.1, panel c), assuming historical, country-specific growth rates and no changes in the distribution of income, continued progress in global poverty reduction, particularly in South Asia, would likely leave Sub-Saharan Africa as the region with the highest poverty headcount. The rest of this section will now turn to a more detailed examination of scenarios tracing out the possible evolution of poverty to 2030.

In a comprehensive approach to projecting poverty declines, Ravallion (2013) poses the question of how long it would take to lift one billion people out of poverty. Projecting poverty rates forward on the basis of a variety of alternative growth scenarios, Ravallion found that achievement of this goal could take half a century or longer if a relatively pessimistic growth scenario is assumed. However, he found that this time span could be halved if the developing world could maintain the progress against extreme poverty that it was able to achieve during the first decade of the 2000s. Drawing on the line of reasoning outlined by Ravallion (2013), it is possible to construct a stylized scenario for reducing global poverty to 3 percent by 2030 by assuming, first, that each developing country grows at 4 percent per person per year (roughly equivalent to the average rate of growth of the developing world as a whole during the 2000s, as reflected in household survey data); second, that the distribution of consumption or income in each country remains unchanged throughout; and third, that between-country inequality remains unchanged. That means that population growth in each country is assumed to be equal to the global average population growth rate. Table 1.2 shows that, conditional on these assumptions, poverty in the developing world will have fallen to 3.5 percent of the developing world's population by 2030, corresponding to an overall global poverty rate of 3 percent.[12]

It is noteworthy that even with this growth scenario, poverty in Sub-Saharan Africa would remain at just over 19 percent in 2030, accounting

**Table 1.2   Ending global poverty**

| Region | Headcount (%) | Number of poor (millions) |
|---|---|---|
| East Asia and the Pacific | 0.3 | 8.0 |
| Europe and Central Asia | 0.1 | 0.4 |
| Latin America and the Caribbean | 2.1 | 15.1 |
| Middle East and North Africa | 0.2 | 0.8 |
| South Asia | 1.3 | 24.9 |
| Sub-Saharan Africa | 19.2 | 202.5 |
| Total developing world | 3.5 | 251.8 |
| World | 3.0 | 251.8 |

*Source:* Based on analysis of World Bank PovcalNet data.

*Note:* Values are for poverty in 2030 at $1.25 a day purchasing power parity (2005), assuming constant inequality and average per capita consumption growth of 4 percent per year. The projection assumes that each country's survey mean per capita household income or consumption expenditure grows at about 4 percent per year, keeping between-country and within-country inequality constant. To keep between-country inequality constant, population growth rates in each country are assumed to be equal to the global average population growth rate between 2011 and 2030. This in effect shifts the entire world income or consumption expenditure distribution from 2011 to 2030.

for nearly 80 percent of the global poor in that year. Poverty in South Asia, by contrast, would have fallen sharply, from about 24 percent in 2011 to about 1.3 percent in 2030. It is also of interest that, even with this assumed progress in poverty reduction over the coming two decades, several countries would remain with poverty rates above 30 percent. Scrutiny of country-specific poverty outcomes following the projections of this scenario shows that six countries would have poverty rates above 30 percent in 2030: Burundi (39 percent), the Democratic Republic of Congo (57 percent), Haiti (33 percent), Madagascar (52 percent), Malawi (37 percent), and Zambia (48 percent).

As emphasized in Ravallion (2013), the assumption of a global per capita growth rate of 4 percent per year cannot be taken for granted. While the developing world as a whole achieved such progress during the past 10 to 15 years, many countries certainly did not grow at this rate. To gauge the realism of achieving the 3 percent target, it is thus instructive to consider a few additional growth scenarios. The discussion refrains, for the time being, from considering alternatives to the basic assumption that within-country inequality does not change.

## Ending global poverty: An ambitious target

A first alternative simulation assumes that individual countries grow at their respective average annualized rates of the past 20 years, instead of a 4 percent growth rate in all countries. First, growth rates as captured in the national accounts are considered, before turning to discussion of growth rates that are based instead on household survey data. As is discussed in chapter 6, there is often less than perfect agreement between survey and national accounts data on aggregate consumption or income measures, as well as on growth rates, so it is useful to consider both sets of economic performance data in turn.

Not surprisingly, table 1.3 reveals that when countries grow at their respective average national accounts growth rates of the past two decades, the poverty target appears more difficult to achieve. With this assumed growth performance, the global poverty estimate falls to 6.8 percent of the world's population in 2030, much higher than the 3 percent achieved

**Table 1.3  Alternative One: Projections based on countries' experiences over the past 20 years**

| Region | Headcount (%) | Number of poor (millions) |
|---|---|---|
| East Asia and the Pacific | 0.4 | 8.5 |
| Europe and Central Asia | 0.1 | 0.7 |
| Latin America and the Caribbean | 3.1 | 22.1 |
| Middle East and North Africa | 1.6 | 7.0 |
| South Asia | 3.5 | 69.2 |
| Sub-Saharan Africa | 32.8 | 465.4 |
| Total developing world | 7.9 | 572.8 |
| World | 6.8 | 572.8 |

*Source:* Based on data from the World Bank PovcalNet database.

*Note:* Values are for poverty in 2030 at $1.25 a day purchasing power parity (2005), assuming country-specific national accounts–based growth rates over the past 20 years. This projection assumes that each country's mean per capita household income or consumption expenditure grows at past country-specific national accounts growth rates, keeping country-specific distributions constant. Past national accounts growth rates are calculated as the annualized growth rates of real gross domestic product per capita (countries in Sub-Saharan Africa) or the annualized growth rates of household final consumption expenditure per capita (all other countries) over the period 1990–2010. Endnote 14 provides a more detailed discussion. National accounts growth and population projections are based on the World Bank's World Development Indicators database.

under the benchmark scenario. Under this scenario, the number of countries with projected poverty rates above 30 percent in 2030 increases dramatically from 6 to 23.[13]

Recognizing that (national accounts) growth picked up in most of the developing world from around 1999 onward, a third scenario retains the assumption of country-specific growth rates, but applies the annualized rate achieved during the past 10 years, rather than the past 20 years (table 1.4).[14] This scenario yields a projected global poverty rate of 4.8 percent of the world's population, a rate lower than in the preceding scenario, but still well above the aspirational global target of 3 percent. Under this scenario, too, some 17 countries would remain with projected poverty rates above 30 percent in 2030.[15] Maps 1.1 and 1.2 illustrate the poverty rates in all developing countries in 2011 compared with the projected poverty rates in 2030 according to this scenario. The maps highlight the geographical concentration of poverty in Sub-Saharan Africa.

As noted above, national accounts and survey-based annual growth rates for a given country can vary significantly (chapter 6 of this report provides

**Table 1.4** Alternative Two: Projections based on countries' experiences over the past 10 years

| Region | Headcount (%) | Number of poor (millions) |
|---|---|---|
| East Asia and the Pacific | 0.3 | 5.6 |
| Europe and Central Asia | 0.0 | 0.1 |
| Latin America and the Caribbean | 3.2 | 22.6 |
| Middle East and North Africa | 1.1 | 5.0 |
| South Asia | 1.6 | 32.7 |
| Sub-Saharan Africa | 23.9 | 339.4 |
| Total developing world | 5.6 | 405.4 |
| World | 4.8 | 405.4 |

*Source:* Based on data from the World Bank PovcalNet database.

*Note:* Values are for poverty in 2030 at $1.25 a day purchasing power parity (2005), assuming country-specific national accounts–based growth rates over the past 10 years. This projection assumes that each country's mean per capita household income or consumption expenditure grows at past country-specific national accounts growth rates, keeping country-specific distributions constant. Past national accounts growth rates are calculated as the annualized growth rates of real gross domestic product per capita (countries in Sub-Saharan Africa) or the annualized growth rates of household final consumption expenditure per capita (all other countries) over the period 2000–10. Endnote 14 provides a more detailed discussion. National accounts growth and population projections are based on the World Bank's World Development Indicators database.

**Map 1.1  Poverty headcount at $1.25 a day, 2011**

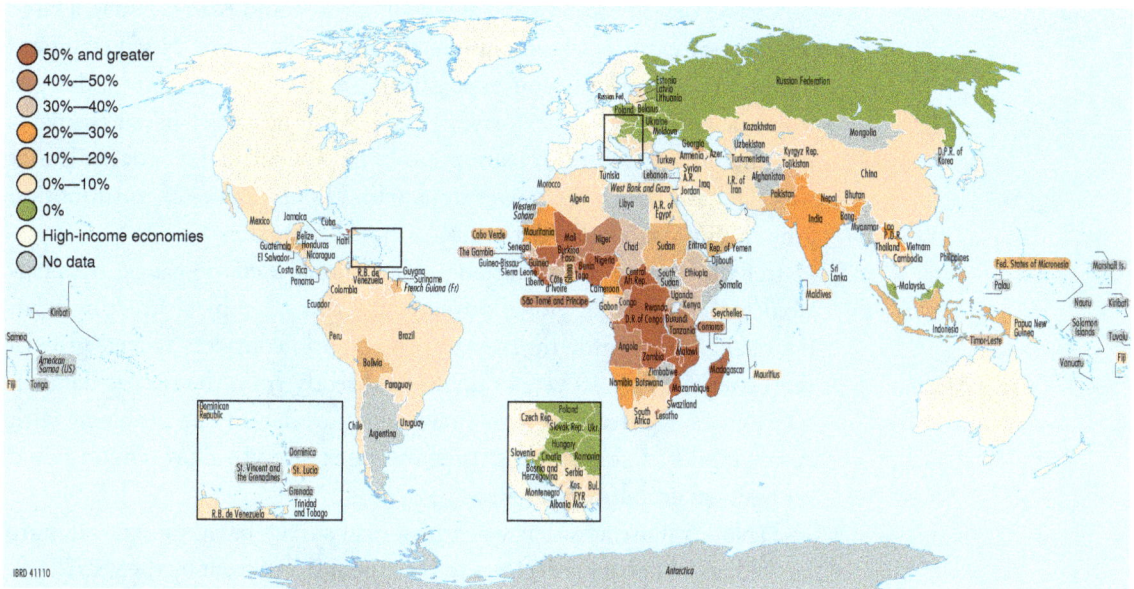

Source: Based on World Bank PovcalNet data.
Note: See notes to table 1.1 for further explanations.

**Map 1.2  Poverty headcount at $1.25 a day, 2030**

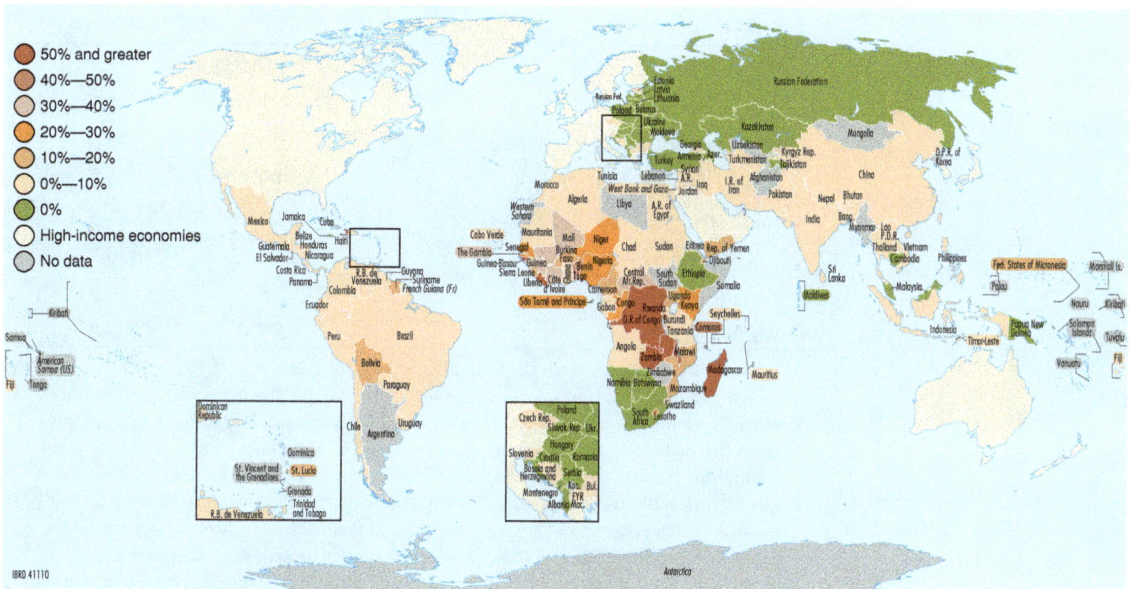

Source: Based on World Bank PovcalNet data.
Note: Projections of poverty rates are based on countries' experience over the past 10 years. See table 1.4 for further details on projection methodology.

a further discussion). India represents a striking illustration of such divergences. As described in several entries in Deaton and Kozel (2005), a large discrepancy exists between National Accounts Statistics (NAS) estimates of household consumption expenditure in India and estimates derived from the National Sample Survey (NSS), with the survey-based estimates pointing to much lower consumption levels. Of particular concern is that this gap has been growing over time, with NSS estimates of consumption growth significantly lower than NAS-based estimates.

In light of these considerations, an additional scenario gauges the plausibility of a 3 percent global poverty target in 2030 by abstracting from national accounts growth. Instead this scenario considers average growth rates over the past 10 years calculated directly from the survey data. In a few cases, there are gaps in survey data availability or problems with comparability across surveys. In those cases, growth rates remain based on national accounts estimates.

Table 1.5 illustrates that when historical survey-based growth rates are applied, global poverty declines to just under 6.7 percent by the year 2030. This is significantly higher than the 4.8 percent that would be achieved if

**Table 1.5** Alternative Three: What do household surveys say?

| Region | Headcount (%) | Number of poor (millions) |
|---|---|---|
| East Asia and the Pacific | 1.0 | 21.7 |
| Europe and Central Asia | 0.1 | 0.7 |
| Latin America and the Caribbean | 2.9 | 20.3 |
| Middle East and North Africa | 0.9 | 4.0 |
| South Asia | 2.4 | 47.5 |
| Sub-Saharan Africa | 33.2 | 470.7 |
| Total developing world | 7.8 | 564.8 |
| World | 6.7 | 564.8 |

*Source:* Based on data from the World Bank PovcalNet database.

*Note:* Values are for poverty in 2030 at $1.25 a day purchasing power parity (2005), assuming country-specific household survey–based growth rates over the past 10 years. This projection assumes that each country's mean per capita household income or consumption expenditure grows at past country-specific household survey growth rates, keeping country-specific distributions constant. Past survey growth is calculated over a period of about 2000 to 2012. When survey growth is not available, national accounts growth rates are used as described in endnote 14. In 11 countries where survey growth rates over that period are negative, a survey mean growth rate of 1 percent per year is assumed. National accounts growth and population projections are based on the World Bank's World Development Indicators database.

national accounts growth rates of the past 10 years had been applied and accords with expectations that survey-based estimates of aggregate consumption, and of consumption growth, are often (but not always) lower than national accounts estimates.

A final scenario explores a more aspirational setup, again using historical national accounts growth, but aiming to preserve a degree of plausibility. This scenario examines episodes of growth (covering periods of 8 to 10 years) during the past 20 years, in each country in turn. The scenario identifies the growth rate associated with the episode of most rapid growth during this reference period and postulates that the country will manage to match that growth rate going forward over the coming two decades. Although this is the basic principle that underpins this scenario, several filters are applied to ensure that the scenario remains broadly plausible.[16]

Table 1.6 reveals that with these ambitious, but not entirely unachievable, growth projections, the target of 3 percent poverty in the world comes tantalizingly close to being within reach. This growth scenario is predicated

**Table 1.6    Alternative Four: An aspirational scenario**

| Region | Headcount (%) | Number of poor (millions) |
|---|---|---|
| East Asia and the Pacific | 0.1 | 0.9 |
| Europe and Central Asia | 0.0 | 0.1 |
| Latin America and the Caribbean | 2.9 | 20.7 |
| Middle East and North Africa | 0.4 | 1.8 |
| South Asia | 0.6 | 12.0 |
| Sub-Saharan Africa | 21.0 | 297.4 |
| Total developing world | 4.6 | 332.9 |
| World | 4.0 | 332.9 |

*Source:* Based on data from the World Bank PovcalNet database.

*Note:* Values are for poverty in 2030 at $1.25 a day purchasing power parity (2005), assuming country-specific household survey–based growth rates associated with the highest 10-year growth episode observed during the past 20 years. This projection assumes that each country's mean per capita household income or consumption expenditure grows at the rate achieved during the best past country-specific national accounts growth spell, keeping country-specific inequality constant. Past national accounts growth spells are calculated as the annualized growth rates of real gross domestic product per capita (countries in Sub-Saharan Africa) or the annualized growth rates of household final consumption expenditure per capita (all other countries) over 8 to 10 years, observed during 1992–2012. When the best annual growth rate is less than 1 percent per year, a growth rate of 1 percent per year is assumed. Endnotes 14 and 16 provide a more detailed discussion. National accounts growth and population projections are based on the World Bank's World Development Indicators database.

on growth rates that would need to be sustained over the next two decades but that do, at least, have some historical precedence in each respective country. If all countries were to manage to grow at these rates, then this simulation exercise indicates that a global poverty rate of 3 percent is close to being achievable. If growth can be accelerated further or inequality can be brought down, then the goal becomes more readily attainable (see chapter 2). At the same time, there should be no mistaking that a requirement of sustained growth at the very high levels postulated by this scenario, over a period of two decades, is quite onerous and is one that historical experience suggests is far from certain (chapter 4 explores this point further).

### Country-specific projections

It is instructive to consider how countries will need to adjust, on a country-by-country basis, to come close to the projected 3 percent global poverty estimate in 2030. Table 1.7 and figure 1.2, panel a, report for the 10 countries currently contributing the most to global poverty in 2011 the rates

**Table 1.7**  Actual and required growth rates in the 10 countries contributing most to poverty in 2011

| Country | Current headcount (%) | Number of poor (millions) | Current growth rate (%) | Required growth rate (%) |
|---|---|---|---|---|
| India (Rural) | 25.5 | 213.9 | 3.52 | 3.52 |
| India (Urban) | 22.9 | 87.5 | 3.94 | 3.94 |
| Nigeria | 60.1 | 98.6 | 2.28 | 3.17 |
| China (Rural) | 12.3 | 81.7 | 7.73 | 7.73 |
| Bangladesh | 39.6 | 60.5 | 2.32 | 4.97 |
| Congo, Dem. Rep. | 84.0 | 53.7 | 1.51 | 1.65 |
| Indonesia | 16.2 | 39.5 | 4.29 | 6.43 |
| Ethiopia | 36.8 | 32.9 | 1.72 | 3.42 |
| Pakistan | 12.4 | 21.8 | 3.68 | 5.52 |
| Tanzania | 43.5 | 20.2 | 1.35 | 5.75 |
| Philippines | 19.3 | 18.3 | 1.43 | 7.92 |

*Source:* Based on data from the World Bank PovcalNet database.

*Note:* Values reflect those needed to achieve the aspirational scenario presented in table 1.6, which assumes country-specific household survey–based growth rates associated with the highest 10-year growth episode observed during the past 20 years.

**Figure 1.2** What does it take? Actual and required growth rates to achieve the aspirational scenario

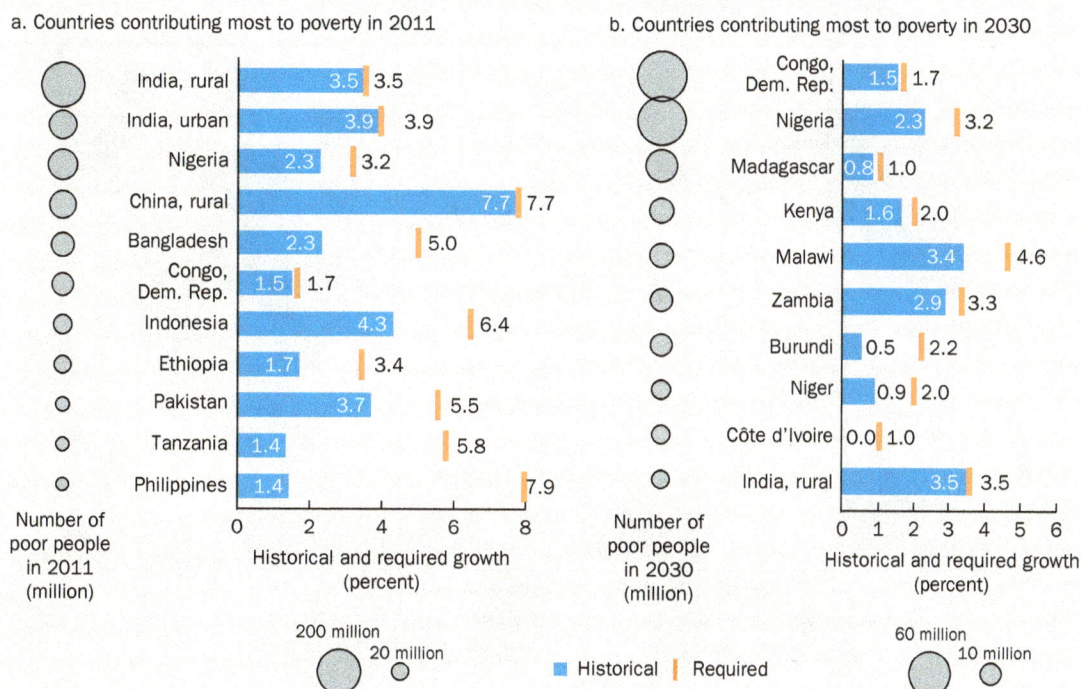

a. Countries contributing most to poverty in 2011

| | Number of poor people in 2011 (million) | Historical and required growth (percent) |

India, rural — 3.5 / 3.5
India, urban — 3.9 / 3.9
Nigeria — 2.3 / 3.2
China, rural — 7.7 / 7.7
Bangladesh — 2.3 / 5.0
Congo, Dem. Rep. — 1.5 / 1.7
Indonesia — 4.3 / 6.4
Ethiopia — 1.7 / 3.4
Pakistan — 3.7 / 5.5
Tanzania — 1.4 / 5.8
Philippines — 1.4 / 7.9

Historical and required growth (percent): 0, 2, 4, 6, 8

b. Countries contributing most to poverty in 2030

Congo, Dem. Rep. — 1.5 / 1.7
Nigeria — 2.3 / 3.2
Madagascar — 0.8 / 1.0
Kenya — 1.6 / 2.0
Malawi — 3.4 / 4.6
Zambia — 2.9 / 3.3
Burundi — 0.5 / 2.2
Niger — 0.9 / 2.0
Côte d'Ivoire — 0.0 / 1.0
India, rural — 3.5 / 3.5

Number of poor people in 2030 (million)
Historical and required growth (percent): 0, 1, 2, 3, 4, 5, 6

200 million / 20 million

60 million / 10 million

■ Historical ▮ Required

*Source:* Based on data from the World Bank PovcalNet database.

of growth that would be needed in each country respectively to comply with the "aspirational" scenario discussed above. The scenario requires that in Nigeria, currently contributing heavily to global poverty numbers, growth rates need to rise, but not to a degree that is entirely unimaginable. In Nigeria, the growth rate needs to pick up from 2.3 to 3.2 percent. More onerous challenges are confronted by countries such as Tanzania (having to raise growth from a current 1.4 percent to 5.8 percent) and the Philippines (requiring an increase from 1.4 to 7.9 percent per year).

Table 1.8 and figure 1.2, panel b, report the growth rates that are required for the 10 countries that, in the year 2030, will remain as the main contributors to global poverty. If all developing countries manage to achieve their historically highest growth rates, then in 2030 the Democratic Republic of Congo will be the single largest contributor to global poverty, accounting for 64.3 million poor people. To comply with

**Table 1.8**  Actual and required growth rates in the 10 countries that will remain as principal contributors to global poverty in 2030

| Country | 2030 headcount (%) | Number of poor (millions) | Current growth rate (%) | Required growth rate (%) |
|---|---|---|---|---|
| Congo, Dem. Rep. | 62.0 | 64.3 | 1.51 | 1.65 |
| Nigeria | 22.5 | 61.5 | 2.28 | 3.17 |
| Madagascar | 73.3 | 26.4 | 0.82 | 1.01 |
| Kenya | 23.2 | 15.4 | 1.62 | 2.02 |
| Malawi | 56.5 | 14.7 | 3.37 | 4.59 |
| Zambia | 51.9 | 13.0 | 2.88 | 3.34 |
| Burundi | 75.4 | 12.4 | 0.53 | 2.21 |
| Niger | 27.8 | 9.6 | 0.89 | 2.0 |
| Côte d'Ivoire | 29.8 | 8.7 | 0 | 1.0 |
| India | 0.6 | 8.1 | 3.52 | 3.52 |

*Source:* Based on data from the World Bank PovcalNet database.

*Note:* Values reflect those needed to achieve the aspirational scenario presented in table 1.6, which assumes country-specific household survey–based growth rates associated with the highest 10-year growth episode observed during the past 20 years.

the aspirational scenario, the Democratic Republic of Congo will need to have lifted its annual growth rate, as captured in household survey data, from 1.5 to 1.7 percent as captured in household survey data. Nigeria will contribute another 61.5 million poor people to the global total. To achieve the aspirational scenario, the country will need to have raised its annual growth rate from 2.3 to 3.2 percent.

## Does the ending poverty target become more elusive when nearing success?

One of the important features of the past three decades of global poverty reduction has been that poverty has been declining at a steady rate of approximately 1 percentage point per year. Figure 1.3 shows that there has been a striking linearity in the decline of the global headcount index since the early 1980s. In his original exploration of the prospects for

**Figure 1.3**  Poverty reduction in the developing world, global measures 1980–2010

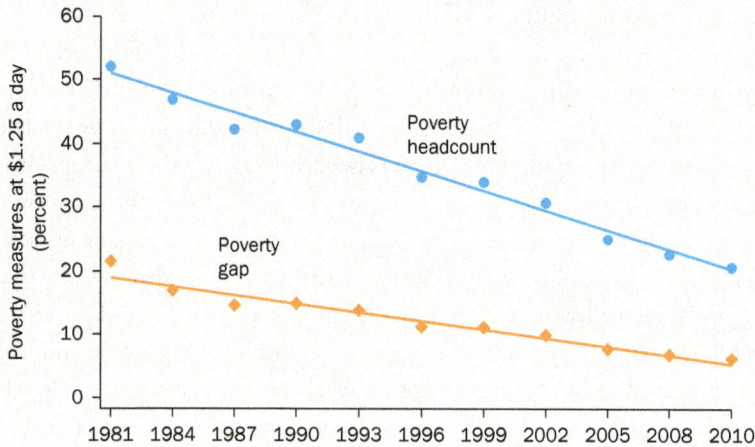

*Sources:* Based on data from the World Bank PovcalNet database and Chen and Ravallion (2013).

ending global poverty, Ravallion (2013) assumed that the developing world would achieve and sustain a growth rate in per capita consumption of just over 4 percent per year. Coupled with an additional assumption of uniform population growth in all countries, Ravallion's (2013) analysis implied that global inequality was also assumed not to change over the decades to 2030. If one were to apply the assumptions in Ravallion (2013) to, say, the world's income distribution in 1990 and then project poverty forward to 2010, a similar path of global poverty reduction would be traced as was empirically observed during these two decades. How realistic is it to assume that, going forward from 2011, poverty reduction will maintain this constant pace?

## Why might the pace of poverty reduction be lower in the future?

Suppose that the world could be thought of as just one large country and that per capita consumption in this country was growing at a steady rate, without any accompanying change in distribution. Why would one expect eventually to see a declining rate of poverty reduction in this setting? Empirically, distributions of consumption take a shape that reflects a concentration of the population around the middle of the income distribution, with a thinning of the population density around either of the two tails.

As was described earlier, one can think of a poverty line as representing a fixed standard of living indicated by a particular consumption level. Persons with consumption levels below that line are considered poor, while those whose consumption is higher are counted among the nonpoor. As the distribution of consumption shifts along the consumption scale (the result of economic growth that essentially scales up the consumption levels of all persons in the population, which is needed to satisfy the assumption of unchanged inequality), it is clear that poverty will fall as economic growth progresses. However, because the bulk of the population is concentrated around the middle of the consumption distribution, it is also the case that, progressively, the fraction of the population that are lifted out of poverty as a result of economic growth will decline. To put it simply, a large number of people tend to live on consumption levels near the average, while relatively fewer live on very high or very low consumption levels. After poverty reduction has reached the mass of people concentrated in the middle of the consumption distribution, poverty reduction will increasingly reach fewer people, even if the pace of growth remains unchanged.

Figure 1.4 plots this empirical result for two stylized distributions of per capita consumption. For illustrative purposes, consumption is transformed to a normal distribution by taking the logarithm of consumption.[17] The two panels show how many people hold what level of consumption: panel a plots the share of individuals at each point of the distribution while panel b plots the cumulative population share. At the point where the curve in panel b intersects the poverty line, the vertical axis provides the total poverty headcount. The earlier period is represented by the red curve $t_0$ while the later period is represented by the orange curve $t_1$. Between the two periods, all consumption levels increase by the same proportion, so that inequality remains constant. In other words, each person gets richer by the same rate (but richer individuals gain more in absolute terms than poorer individuals). As a result, the curve of log consumption shifts to the right but the shape remains the same. Consider the earlier period $t_0$. In figure 1.4, panel a, a large share of the population is lifted out of poverty as the peak of the red curve moves beyond the poverty line. In panel b, the same shift of the red curve means that the poverty line is crossed at the point where the curve is very steep. Now consider the later period $t_1$, where growth remains the same but the majority of the population has already escaped poverty. In panel b, the curve crosses the poverty line at a relatively less steep point, which means that the same growth in consumption will translate into a less marked decline in the poverty headcount. The slope at

**Figure 1.4**  **The effect of growth on poverty under the assumption of unchanged inequality**

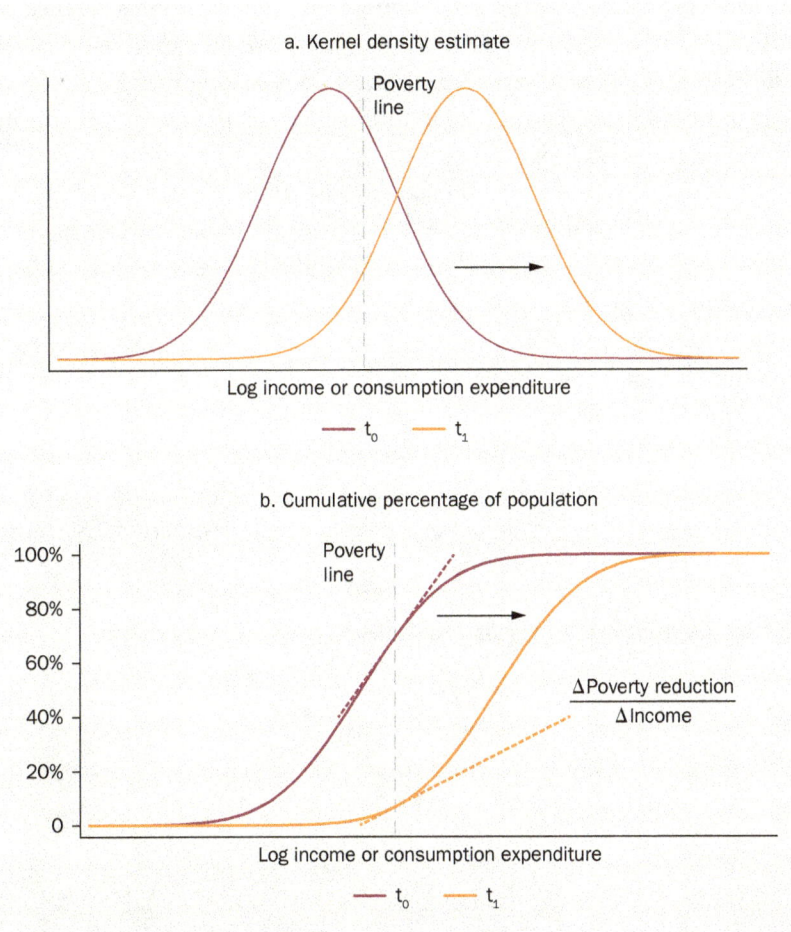

a. Kernel density estimate

Poverty
line

Log income or consumption expenditure

— $t_0$  — $t_1$

b. Cumulative percentage of population

Poverty
line

100%

80%

60%

$\Delta$Poverty reduction

40%

$\Delta$Income

20%

0

Log income or consumption expenditure

— $t_0$  — $t_1$

*Note:* Panel a illustrates a stylized density of income, that is, the share of individuals at each point of the distribution, plotted on a logarithmic scale. Panel b illustrates the cumulative population share of the same distribution on the same logarithmic scale. The two angled lines in panel b represent the slope of the tangent at the point where the poverty line intersects with the cumulative distribution function, which is the point that marks the total poverty headcount for each distribution.

each of the two intersections (dashed lines) can be thought of as the growth elasticity of poverty reduction.[18]

Thus, under the assumed conditions of unchanging inequality and constant growth, there exists virtually a mechanical relationship between growth and the sensitivity of poverty reduction to that growth. In the face of such conditions, the only way that a constant rate of poverty decline can be delivered all the way to zero is if growth, in fact, accelerates over time. Yoshida, Uematsu, and Sobrado (2014) offer the striking finding that, if one were to assume that the world consumption distribution as existed in 2010 could be regarded as that of just one global country, then to maintain a steady rate of global poverty reduction all the way to zero by 2030, global growth would have to accelerate to rates as high as 48 percent per year by the end of the period (figure 1.5).

The discussion in this section so far has assumed that, somehow, all countries would grow at the same rate. Yet it was emphasized in the preceding section that a plausible assessment of the global poverty targets must allow for growth rates across countries to vary. Given that, historically, growth rates have differed across countries, it was argued above that imposing a single, uniform growth rate across all countries is an important departure from realism.

What do heterogeneous growth rates imply for the trajectory of poverty reduction over time? In the previous section it was shown that, if growth rates are allowed to vary across countries, only the aspirational scenario

**Figure 1.5** Declining sensitivity of poverty reduction would require ever-increasing growth

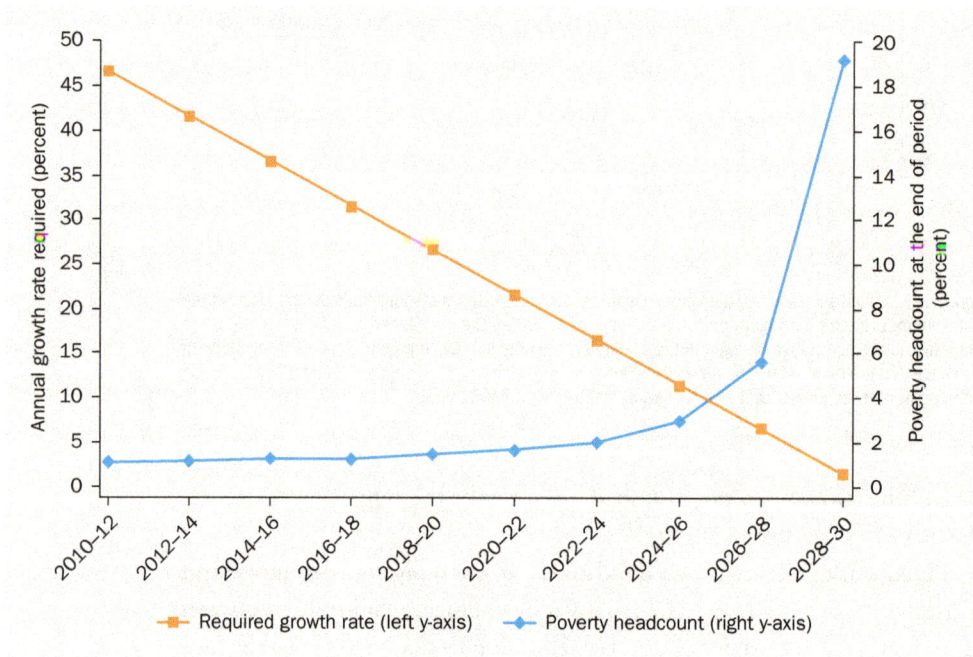

Source: Based on data from the World Bank PovcalNet database.

would yield a global poverty rate by 2030 in the vicinity of the 3 percent target. This scenario assumed constant growth rates at the country level that were sufficiently high to ensure that the reduction in poverty achieved each year and in each country was on aggregate sufficient to bring global poverty down to very nearly 3 percent by 2030. The precise trajectory of poverty reduction that this scenario implies is displayed in figure 1.6. In the figure, progress toward the 3 percent target in 2030 occurs not as a linear reduction of poverty over time, but rather through a trajectory of a gradually declining pace of poverty reduction as overall global poverty falls.

The reason for the diminishing pace of global poverty reduction observed in figure 1.6 can be understood in terms of the differential pace of growth, and hence poverty reduction, across countries. Some countries, such as China, with initially high levels of poverty, but also very rapid growth rates, would initially see rapid rates of poverty reduction over time. Initially, because China contributed substantially to the global poverty count, global poverty would fall commensurately with China's falling poverty. Over time, however, continued growth and poverty reduction in China would translate into a progressively smaller impact on global

**Figure 1.6**  **The trajectory of future poverty reduction may not be obviously linear**

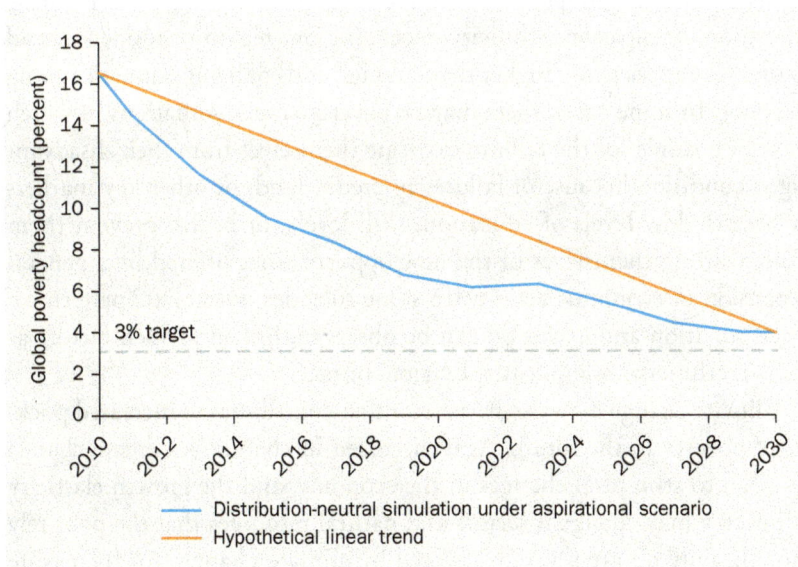

*Source:* Based on data from the World Bank PovcalNet database.

poverty, because China's poverty would account for an ever smaller contribution to global poverty. At some point prior to 2030, China can be expected to have essentially eliminated poverty at the global poverty line, so further growth in China would have no further impact on global poverty. Thus, as the faster-growing countries, such as China, essentially grow themselves out of any further contribution to global poverty reduction, it is clear that the pool of countries accounting for the remaining global poverty will, on average, be growing less rapidly and will be reducing poverty at a slower pace.

### Pockets of poverty and the dynamics of poverty reduction at the country level

Just as it is difficult to imagine that global poverty would decline at a constant rate all the way through to 2030, one would not expect poverty decline at the country level to display a straight-line trajectory. Within countries, too, there are reasons why poverty decline might be expected to slow with continued economic growth. Poverty reduction is an uneven process. In many countries, pockets of poverty exist whereby certain parts of the population appear not to be participating to the same extent as others in the broader development process. Country-level poverty assessments, in which household survey data are broken down to assess the poverty status of various groups, routinely identify specific groups—defined by education, occupation, ethnicity, race, religion, region of residence, and so on—as experiencing higher than average odds of being counted among the poor. In some cases, there may be poverty traps—situations in which it is not possible for the poor to extricate themselves from their disadvantaged condition because of failures in credit, land, or other key markets or because low levels of education, skill levels, or health prevent them from availing themselves of the new opportunities offered by a general expansion of economic activity. In some societies, systematic patterns of discrimination and exclusion can be observed, linked to such factors as gender, ethnicity, origin, caste, religion, or race.

Climate change may also be a factor that contributes to increased pockets of poverty in the future. As is discussed in chapter 4, climate change can lead to structural changes in the economy, and the growth elasticity of poverty may change if sectors and natural resources that the poor rely more heavily on are severely affected by climate change. An increasing number of studies suggest that climate change will disproportionately affect the poorest because of their dependence on natural resources and ecosystem-based services—as a means to support consumption and accumulate assets, and as a form of safety nets that strengthen resilience in the face of shocks—because the poorest live in regions where the impact of climate change is expected to be most severe, or because they have less capacity (financial, institutional, and technical) to adapt to climate change.[19] More broadly, changing climatic patterns may affect agriculture, biodiversity, and access to water, among other things, in a very localized manner, thus disproportionately affecting some areas or groups of people. Green growth strategies that aim to decouple economic growth from the emission of greenhouse gases can play an important role in limiting the disproportional effect of climate change on the poor.[20]

Empirical evidence of the existence of poverty traps, formally understood as self-reinforcing mechanisms that prevent the poor from escaping poverty, is difficult to assemble and remains scarce. Kraay and McKenzie (2014) survey the literature on the existence of poverty traps at the level of countries as well as among population groups within countries. They find relatively little evidence for the truly stagnant incomes that would be predicted by canonical models of poverty traps. At the same time, they acknowledge that this should not be taken to imply that poverty cannot be persistent among certain population groups. In fact, Kraay and McKenzie (2014) point to plentiful evidence of pockets of poverty related to geographic location, arising from people being trapped in low-productivity locations, such as remote rural regions or low-productivity countries. The mechanisms underpinning such geographic poverty traps can vary across settings, but are usually related to physical and geographic characteristics that prevent households' consumption levels from rising over time. Jalan and Ravallion (2002) discuss, for example, how in China the productivity of farmers' investments is lower in poor areas, constraining their ability to lift themselves out of poverty.

The poverty of people in such poverty pockets, whether they arise from proper poverty traps (representing a low-level equilibrium) or simply result from low resource endowments or patterns of discrimination, does not necessarily decline hand-in-hand with economic growth. As a result, as overall economic development generates employment and lifts the bulk of the population out of poverty, a core subset of the population may remain poor and constrained in its ability to benefit from growth. When poverty is spatially concentrated, one might expect overall growth to benefit some locations more than others and for the spatial concentration of poverty to become increasingly accentuated over time. This will then reduce the responsiveness of aggregate poverty to further growth and will translate into a declining rate of poverty reduction with respect to growth.

This process can be readily illustrated with the evidence recently assembled for Vietnam by Lanjouw, Marra, and Nguyen (2013). Two poverty maps were constructed for Vietnam, providing a snapshot of poverty at the district level in 1999 and 2009. During this time period, aggregate poverty in Vietnam fell sharply, from around 47 percent to 15 percent. Although poverty declined overall, some districts grew much more slowly than other districts and saw a much lower rate of poverty reduction than elsewhere. In other words, the spatial concentration of poverty increased noticeably (map 1.3). For example, districts in the Red River Delta region, surrounding the city of Hanoi, and in the south of the country saw significant reductions in poverty, while the mountainous regions in the northwest and along the central coast and highlands of Vietnam saw slower progress.

The growing spatial concentration revealed by the two poverty maps for Vietnam suggests that lagging districts will experience relatively less economic progress over time and will fall progressively behind the leading

**Map 1.3** Increased spatial concentration of poverty in Vietnam, 1999 and 2009

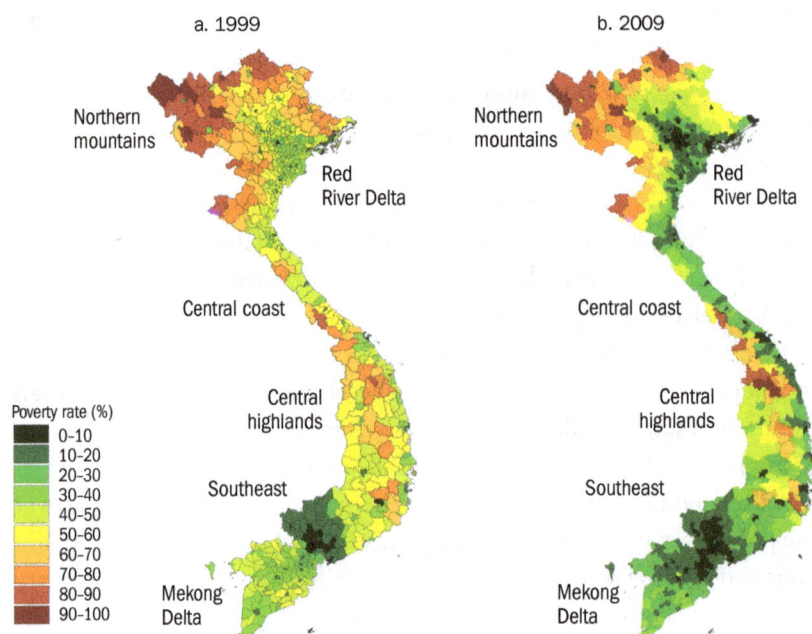

*Source:* Lanjouw, Marra, and Nguyen (2013).

regions. Heterogeneity in growth rates in turn implies that aggregate poverty will fall more slowly for a given overall national growth rate than would be the case if all districts grew at the same rate. Figure 1.7 illustrates this point by postulating alternative spatial patterns of growth for Vietnam over the decade from 2009 to 2019. In the first simulation, per capita expenditures are projected to grow at the same national rate of growth as was observed over the interval between 1999 and 2009. Poverty falls from just below 20 percent in 2009 to essentially zero by 2019. In subsequent simulations, household expenditure levels within a given region, province, or district are assumed to grow at the respective regional, provincial, or district-level growth rate that was observed between 1999 and 2009. Aggregate poverty reduction slows increasingly as the level of spatial heterogeneity is allowed to increase.

In sum, just as at the global level countries vary in their growth rates and their pace of poverty reduction, the existence of factors that result in unevenness in the rate of poverty reduction across population groups within a country, whether they are defined in terms of location of residence or some other criterion, can result in a declining responsiveness of poverty reduction to a given rate of aggregate growth. The presence of such factors at the country level will thereby also translate into a declining

**Figure 1.7** Heterogeneous subnational growth in Vietnam leads to slower national poverty reduction

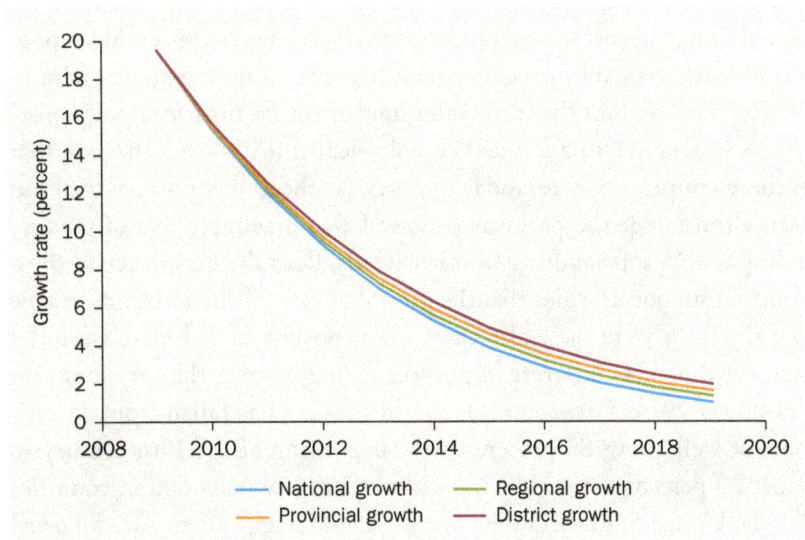

*Source:* Based on data from Lanjouw, Marra, and Nguyen (2013).

responsiveness of global poverty reduction to growth and will serve to delay achievement of the global poverty target.

It is important to note that so far the discussion has ignored the possibility of changes in the distribution of income. However, there is, of course, no cast-iron law stating that the distribution of income will remain unchanged in the future. Indeed, as will be shown in chapter 2, there have been important changes in the distribution of income in many countries—with inequality increasing in some and decreasing in others. Once one allows for changes in growth rates and inequality, the trajectory of poverty decline may be different from the scenarios described above. Changing underlying economic forces and policy choices may also substantially influence the future trajectory of poverty reduction. Some economic forces will play out on the global stage, but the relationship between growth and poverty decline will also often be driven by factors occurring at the country level or even at the subnational level.

### What does past country experience suggest about the likely pace of poverty reduction in the future?

Although the discussion so far suggests that there are multiple reasons to expect poverty decline to slow with continued growth, the extent to which this may occur can vary. In principle, arguments in favor of an *accelerating* rate of poverty decline can also be made. As countries grow richer, they may move away from (imperfect) targeting of social policies and transfers toward universal entitlement programs that reach previously excluded populations. Alternatively, over time countries may acquire stronger administrative data systems that can better implement means-tested programs.

It is instructive to ask whether, empirically, it has been the case that in those countries where, today, poverty (at the global poverty line) has been eliminated, the pathway followed was inevitably one of poverty ending with a soft landing. In other words, does the experience of these countries support the idea that the pace of poverty reduction tends to slow over time? Or were there also cases where poverty ended more abruptly? Figure 1.8 depicts progress in poverty reduction over the very long run (Ravallion 2014, forthcoming). World poverty has fallen from an estimate of well above 80 percent in the beginning of the 19th century to under 20 percent today. The trajectory of poverty reduction in countries like the United States and the United Kingdom appears to have followed a fairly steady rate of decline until rates in the vicinity of 5 percent were

**Figure 1.8** Poverty reduction in countries that have already achieved zero extreme poverty, 1820–2000

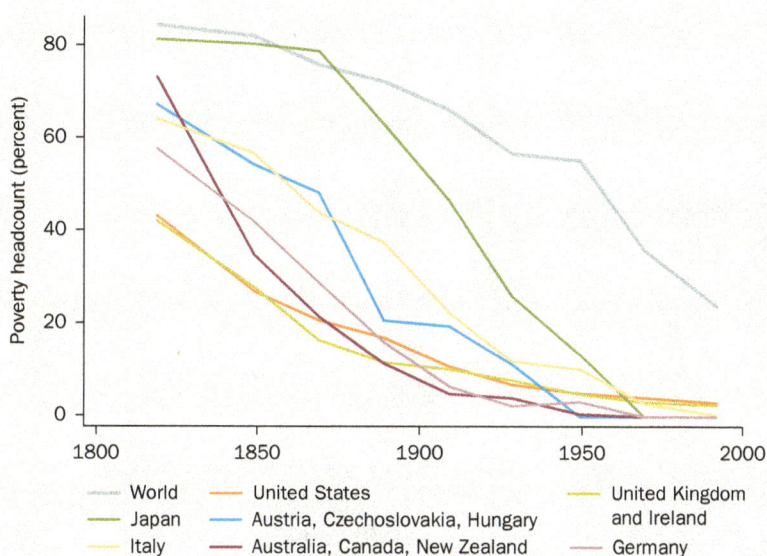

Source: Based on data from Ravallion (2014) and Ravallion (forthcoming).
Note: Based on estimates using parameterized Lorenz curves calibrated to the data set developed by Bourguignon and Morrisson (2002). See Ravallion 2014 for a more detailed explanation

achieved. Subsequent poverty declines appear to have occurred more slowly. However, the path of poverty decline achieved in Japan—and in Austria, Czechoslovakia, and Hungary—appears to have followed a steady decline to zero. Although poverty ended later in these countries than in the United States and the United Kingdom, the percentage point decline in poverty was maintained to the end, and there is less clear evidence of a tapering off of poverty reduction in these countries.

A more current picture of progress from the developing world can be observed in the case of Thailand. Figure 1.9 shows that in Thailand poverty estimated at the $1.25 global poverty line fell to 3 percent around 1995. Poverty reduction in Thailand prior to 1995 occurred at a constant rate and, indeed, there is some sign of acceleration relative to progress prior to 1990. As in the cases of Japan and Austria-Czechoslovakia-Hungary, there is little sign of a declining rate of progress in approaching the 3 percent poverty rate. Interestingly, after 1995, further progress in reducing poverty in Thailand displays the familiar tapering-off tendency, with evidence of a small increase in poverty around 2000, at the time of the

**Figure 1.9**   **Poverty reduction in Thailand, 1981–2010**

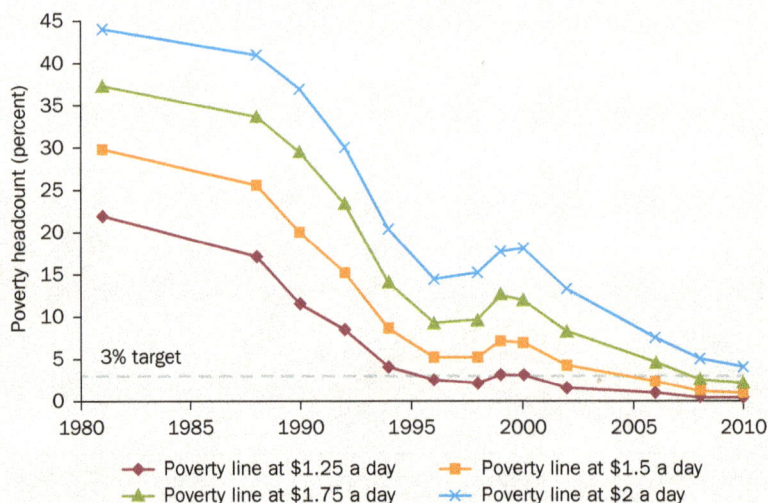

Source: Based on data from the World Bank PovcalNet database.

East Asian crisis. Note further that if an alternative poverty line of $1.50 or $1.75 is taken, poverty in Thailand can be seen to end (reach 3 percent) only in the second half of the 2000s. The trajectory of the poverty line in these cases is less steep than was observed in the early 1990s. However, again, there is no evidence that the pace of poverty reduction diminished in the years immediately prior to the dates when poverty reached the 3 percent target.

A detailed diagnosis of how the Thais were able to ensure that progress in poverty reduction was maintained all the way to the effective elimination of poverty is beyond the scope of the present discussion. The point to emphasize, however, is that the actual experience of poverty reduction achieved by countries can be affected by policies and policy choices that bear not only on growth, but also on the distribution of growth. In other words, the rate at which poverty falls can be influenced by countries themselves. This chapter argues that, most likely, achievement of the 2030 goal of ending global poverty will depend on countries pursuing a combination of growth and distribution policies that aim to supplement the attenuating impetus that can be expected from continued growth alone. Efforts to boost the incomes of the lower deciles in particular are needed. This discussion is taken up further in chapter 2.

## Poverty and shared prosperity

Reducing world poverty has long been an overarching objective of the World Bank. In recent years, the institution has taken the additional step of setting an explicit goal for itself and for the development community. A target has been articulated: to reduce global poverty to no more than 3 percent of the world's population by 2030. This chapter has examined this target with a view toward gauging just what it means and what it implies. In particular, the chapter has attempted to assess whether business as usual, a continuation of recent global trends in poverty reduction, can be expected to be sufficient to reach the global poverty target.

In thinking about the progress necessary for ending global poverty, it is important to have a clear understanding of the yardstick against which progress will be measured. This chapter has revisited the basic steps and procedures involved in the measurement of global poverty. A key concern has been to emphasize that not only are there many conceptual issues and choices involved in establishing a tractable means to monitor global poverty, but the quality and reliability of the underlying information database is critical. The development community continues to face important challenges in strengthening its ability to gauge the extent of global poverty and how it is evolving over time. Several of these challenges will be examined in further detail in subsequent chapters of this report.

This chapter has indicated that the explorations of poverty trends and trajectories that fed into the initial definition of the 3 percent global target were based on stylized assumptions—not necessarily intended to represent reality. The chapter has attempted to assess whether a path to the 3 percent target can be readily discerned once somewhat more realistic assumptions are made. In particular, the analysis in this chapter has focused on the kinds of growth scenarios that might unfold over the coming decades. Notably, the chapter has argued that these scenarios must accommodate different rates of growth across countries. The analysis cautions against complacency with regards to the achievability of future growth rates that are somehow anchored to historical experience and that are also able to generate poverty trajectories leading to an end of poverty by 2030. The chapter thus argues that the 3 percent target should be viewed as ambitious and far from assured.

The chapter discusses further the point that, although past experience suggests that global poverty reduction up to around 2011 was achieved at a fairly constant pace of around 1 percentage point per year, there are many reasons to doubt that such a steady rate of poverty decline is feasible as global poverty approaches the end target of 3 percent or lower. In the absence of targeted policies to the contrary, the pace of poverty decline associated with a given rate of economic growth can be expected, at some point, to diminish markedly. If this occurs well before the global target is reached, the burden on growth as an engine of global poverty reduction will become very significant: ever-increasing growth rates would be needed to maintain the overall pace of global poverty reduction.

An important assumption maintained throughout the analysis in this chapter has been that income distribution within countries does not change. This assumption was needed to establish a benchmark against which the actual experience of countries can be gauged. Although the arguments pointing to a declining sensitivity of poverty reduction to growth follow readily when income distribution is held fixed, things are less clear once inequality is allowed to vary. Clearly, if inequality increases alongside economic growth, progress in poverty reduction may slow further. This chapter has illustrated this possibility in the context of uneven within-country spatial patterns of poverty reduction, where the persistence of pockets of poverty in a country results in a slower overall rate of poverty reduction. However, if inequality were somehow to fall alongside economic growth, particularly inequality associated with the relative position of the poor in the income distribution, then the rate of progress in poverty decline might hold steady or even accelerate as overall poverty approached zero.[21] Indeed, there does seem to be some evidence of this from the experience of present-day countries in which extreme poverty has been eliminated. How this was achieved is likely to depend on a constellation of highly context-specific circumstances and policies. What is clear, though, is that if the incomes of the bottom segments can be boosted alongside overall economic growth, the prospects for ending global poverty are much enhanced. This observation motivates the focus in the next chapter on the World Bank's second goal of boosting shared prosperity.

## Notes

1. Several additional details about the World Bank's poverty goal are worth noting. First, the reference population for the poverty estimates is that of the world as a whole. Thus, poverty is to be brought down to under 3 percent of the world's population, not that of the developing world only. Second, although 3 percent by 2030 is the ultimate objective, there is a need to galvanize energies and efforts right away. Accordingly, at the World Bank and International Monetary Fund Annual Meetings held in the autumn of

2013 in Washington, DC, the World Bank pointed to an interim target of 9 percent by 2020.

2. Ravallion, Datt, and van de Walle (1991); Chen and Ravallion (2004, 2010); Ravallion, Chen, and Sangraula (2009); and Ravallion (2013) describe the World Bank's methods in considerable detail. Broader surveys of poverty measurement can be found in Ravallion (1994), Deaton (1997), and Ravallion (forthcoming). A useful overview of the World Bank's approach can be found in Chandy (2013).

3. Deaton and Zaidi (2002) provide a useful guideline for constructing a comprehensive measure of consumption.

4. Of course, difficult-to-interpret situations can also arise with consumption. For example, Lanjouw and Stern (1991) discuss the case of a rich individual in a small Indian village who chose to live (and consume) like an ascetic for religious reasons and who would have been categorized as poor on the basis of a consumption measure.

5. Note that in assessing the relative appeal of consumption over income as an indicator of economic well-being, one should not lose sight of the fact that when the focus moves from an assessment of welfare to an analysis of drivers of change, then income data become extremely useful as they can point to the differential roles played by different income sources (wages, remittances, profits). This underscores that deliberation around strategies for data collection may well wish to look beyond the gathering of reliable data on consumption only.

6. Prominent exceptions include the Democratic People's Republic of Korea, as well as fragile and conflict-affected states such as Eritrea, Somalia, and Somaliland.

7. For details, see http://iresearch.worldbank.org/PovcalNet.

8. The 15 countries are mainly in Sub-Saharan Africa and comprise Chad, Ethiopia, The Gambia, Ghana, Guinea-Bissau, Malawi, Mali, Mozambique, Nepal, Niger, Rwanda, Sierra Leone, Tajikistan, Tanzania, and Uganda. See Chen and Ravallion (2010).

9. See Lanjouw, Lanjouw, Milanovic, and Paternostro (2004); Lanjouw and Ravallion (1995); and Drèze and Srinivasan (1997).

10. All regional and global poverty estimates in this chapter are based on an internal working version of the World Bank's PovcalNet database with data as of August 2014. While every effort was made to use the most up-to-date data available, the estimates presented in this report should be seen as approximate; the official global and regional poverty estimates will be published in the forthcoming *Global Monitoring Report.* Concurrent with the publication of the *Global Monitoring Report,* the World Bank's PovcalNet website will be updated.

11. The estimation of the global poverty headcount assumes that nobody lives below the $1.25 a day in high income countries. Although there are a number of people with household incomes below $1.25 per person in rich countries, estimated per capita consumption is above this threshold for nearly everyone. For example, Chandy and Smith (2014) find that 1 to 4 percent of the population in the United States live below $2 a day when using income

measures, but that fewer than 0.1 percent live below this threshold when using consumption data.

12. The procedure outlined in Ravallion (2013) does not insist on between-country inequality remaining constant, and therefore that all countries should grow at the same rate. We impose the additional assumption here in order to contrast it with the additional scenarios that follow.

13. These countries are Benin, Burundi, the Central African Republic, Comoros, the Democratic Republic of Congo, Republic of Congo, Côte d'Ivoire, The Gambia, Guinea, Guinea-Bissau, Haiti, Kenya, Madagascar, Malawi, Mali, Niger, Nigeria, Rwanda, Sierra Leone, Swaziland, São Tomé and Principe, Togo, and Zambia.

14. For the projections summarized in tables 1.3, 1.4, 1.5, and 1.6, annualized growth rates from national accounts are used to adjust mean per capita household income or consumption expenditure from household surveys, keeping country-specific distributions constant. Following Chen and Ravallion (2010), national accounts growth rates are based on household final consumption expenditure per capita for all countries outside Sub-Saharan Africa. In Sub-Saharan Africa, real gross domestic product per capita growth is used because of better data availability. Before applying national accounts growth rates to survey mean per capita income and consumption expenditure, an adjustment factor of 0.87 times the growth rate is used to reflect empirically observed differences between national accounts growth and survey growth. Lower factors are used for China and India (0.72 and 0.57, respectively) to account for historically larger gaps between national accounts and survey growth there. These factors are based on a simple cross-country regression for the growth rate in survey means on the growth rate from national accounts. Using an adjustment factor to account for such differences is common practice in related exercises. Birdsall, Lustig, and Meyer (2014) and Chandy, Ledlie, and Penciakova (2013) make a similar adjustment, but use different scaling factors. See Ravallion (2003) and Deaton (2005) for a more detailed discussion of the differences between national accounts growth and survey growth.

15. These are Benin, Burundi, the Central African Republic, Comoros, the Democratic Republic of Congo, Côte d'Ivoire, The Gambia, Guinea, Guinea-Bissau, Haiti, Liberia, Madagascar, Malawi, Mali, Swaziland, Togo, and Zambia.

16. The filters are as follows: (a) If the observed growth rate during the high-growth episode exceeded 10 percent per year, this was regarded as a case of noncomparable survey data and the case was dropped in favor of the second highest growth episode during the reference period. (b) In three cases, national accounts data revealed an even higher growth rate than that from the surveys; in these three cases, the high-growth rate, higher than 10 percent, was used. (c) If scrutiny of growth rates suggested that the surveys were noncomparable, they were replaced with national accounts estimates. (d) When the highest growth rate was positive but below 1 percent per year, a high growth of 1 percent was applied. (e) In the case of rural India, a high-growth rate equal to the rate achieved in the high-growth episode observed for urban India was applied. (f) If growth rates over the 10-year window

were always negative, a positive growth rate from an episode shorter than the 10-year high-growth episode was considered. If there was no positive growth observed anywhere, a high-growth rate of 1 percent was assigned.

17. Empirically, per capita income often takes a shape in which there is a concentration of the population around the middle of the distribution with a thinning around the two tails. In most cases, the mass of the distribution is concentrated on the left side (right-skewed). Such distributions can be approximated with a lognormal distribution, which means that the logarithm of income will be approximately normally distributed. Lopez and Servén (2014) show empirically that lognormal distributions provide a very close approximation of actual per capita income distributions.

18. See Bourguignon (2003) for a more formal treatment of the growth elasticity of poverty reduction.

19. For example, a recent study by Angelsen and others (2014) measures environmental incomes, showing that environmental income shares are higher for low-income households than the rest.

20. See World Bank (2012) for a comprehensive discussion of green growth strategies.

21. One potential indication of this would be if economic growth was greater for the poor relative to the country average growth rate. Chapter 2 introduces the shared prosperity indicator, which measures growth for the bottom 40 percent of each country. In those countries for which we have data, in about two thirds of the countries, this growth rate is greater than the overall average growth rate.

## References

Ahluwalia, Montek S., Nicholas G. Carter, and Hollis B. Chenery. 1979. "Growth and Poverty in Developing Countries." *Journal of Development Economics* 6 (3): 299–341. doi:10.1016/0304-3878(79)90020-8.

Angelsen, Arild, Sven Wunder, Ronnie Babigumira, Brian Belcher, Jan Börner, and Carsten Smith-Hall. 2014. "Environmental Incomes and Rural Livelihoods: A Global-Comparative Assessment." *World Development*. In press.

Birdsall, Nancy, Nora Lustig, and Christian J. Meyer. 2014. "The Strugglers: The New Poor in Latin America?" *World Development* 60 (August): 132–46. doi:10.1016/j.worlddev.2014.03.019.

Bourguignon, François. 2003. "The Growth Elasticity of Poverty Reduction: Explaining Heterogeneity across Countries and Time Periods." In *Inequality and Growth: Theory and Policy Implications*, edited by Theo S. Eicher and Stephen J. Turnovsky, 3–26. CESifo Seminar Series 1. Cambridge, MA: MIT Press.

Bourguignon, François, and Christian Morrisson. 2002. "Inequality among World Citizens: 1820–1992." *American Economic Review* 92 (4): 727–44. doi:10.1257/00028280260344443.

Chandy, Laurence. 2013. "Counting the Poor: Methods, Problems, and Solutions Behind the $1.25 a Day Global Poverty Estimates." Investments to End Poverty Working Paper 3, Development Initiatives, Bristol, U.K.

Chandy, Laurence, Natasha Ledlie, and Veronika Penciakova. 2013. "The Final Countdown: Prospects for Ending Extreme Poverty by 2030." Global Views Policy Paper 2013-04, The Brookings Institution, Washington, DC.

Chen, Shaohua, and Martin Ravallion. 2004. "How Have the World's Poorest Fared since the Early 1980s?" *The World Bank Research Observer* 19 (2): 141–69.

———. 2010. "The Developing World Is Poorer Than We Thought, but No Less Successful in the Fight Against Poverty." *The Quarterly Journal of Economics* 125 (4): 1577–1625. doi:10.1162/qjec.2010.125.4.1577.

———. 2013. "More Relatively-Poor People in a Less Absolutely-Poor World." *Review of Income and Wealth* 59 (1): 1–28.

Deaton, Angus. 1997. *The Analysis of Household Surveys: A Microeconometric Approach to Development Policy.* Baltimore, MD: The Johns Hopkins University Press.

———. 2005. "Measuring Poverty in a Growing World (or Measuring Growth in a Poor World)." *Review of Economics and Statistics* 87 (1): 1–19. doi:10.1162/0034653053327612.

Deaton, Angus, and Valerie Kozel. 2005. "Data and Dogma: The Great Indian Poverty Debate." *The World Bank Research Observer* 20 (2): 177–99. doi:10.1093/wbro/lki009.

Deaton, Angus, and Salman Zaidi. 2002. "Guidelines for Constructing Consumption Aggregates for Welfare Analysis." Living Standards Measurement Study (LSMS) Working Paper 135, World Bank, Washington, DC.

Drèze, Jean, and P. V. Srinivasan. 1997. "Widowhood and Poverty in Rural India: Some Inferences from Household Survey Data." *Journal of Development Economics* 54 (2): 217–34.

Haughton, Jonathan Henry, and Shahidur R. Khandker. 2009. *Handbook on Poverty and Inequality.* Washington, DC: World Bank.

Jalan, Jyotsna, and Martin Ravallion. 2002. "Geographic Poverty Traps? A Micro Model of Consumption Growth in Rural China." *Journal of Applied Econometrics* 17 (4): 329–46. doi:10.1002/jae.645.

Kraay, Aart, and David McKenzie. 2014. "Do Poverty Traps Exist?" Policy Research Working Paper 6835, World Bank, Washington, DC.

Lanjouw, Jean O., Peter Lanjouw, Branko Milanovic, and Stefano Paternostro. 2004. "Relative Price Shifts, Economies of Scale and Poverty During Economic Transition." *Economics of Transition* 12 (3): 509–36.

Lanjouw, Peter F., Marleen Marra, and Cuong Nguyen. 2013. "Vietnam's Evolving Poverty Map: Patterns and Implications for Policy." Policy Research Working Paper 6355, World Bank, Washington, DC.

Lanjouw, Peter, and Martin Ravallion. 1995. "Poverty and Household Size." *Economic Journal* 105 (433): 1415–34.

Lanjouw, Peter, and Nicholas Stern. 1991. "Poverty in Palanpur." *The World Bank Economic Review* 5 (1): 23–55.

Lopez, Humberto, and Luis Servén. 2014. "A Normal Relationship? Poverty, Growth, and Inequality." *Annals of Economics and Finance* 15 (2): 593–624.

Orshansky, Mollie. 1963. "Children of the Poor." *Social Security Bulletin* 26 (7): 3–13.

Pradhan, Menno, Asep Suryahadi, Sudarno Sumarto, and Lant Pritchett. 2000. "Measurements of Poverty in Indonesia—1996, 1999, and Beyond." Policy Research Working Paper 2438, World Bank, Washington, DC.

Pritchett, Lant. 2006. "Who Is Not Poor? Dreaming of a World Truly Free of Poverty." *The World Bank Research Observer* 21 (1): 1–23. doi:10.1093/wbro/lkj002.

Ravallion, Martin. 1988. "Expected Poverty Under Risk-Induced Welfare Variability." *The Economic Journal* 98 (393): 1171–82. doi:10.2307/2233725.

———. 1994. *Poverty Comparisons*. Fundamentals of Pure and Applied Economics 56. Chur, Switzerland: Harwood Academic Publishers.

———. 2003. "Measuring Aggregate Welfare in Developing Countries: How Well Do National Accounts and Surveys Agree?" *The Review of Economics and Statistics* 85 (3): 645–52.

———. 2013. "How Long Will It Take to Lift One Billion People Out of Poverty?" *The World Bank Research Observer* 28 (2): 139–58. doi:10.1093/wbro/lkt003.

———. 2014. "Poverty in the Rich World When It Was Not Nearly So Rich," Blog Post, Center for Global Development, Washington, DC. http://international.cgdev.org/blog/poverty-richworld-when-it-was-not-nearly-so-rich.

———. Forthcoming. *The Economics of Poverty: History, Measurement, Policy.* New York and Oxford: Oxford University Press.

Ravallion, Martin, Shaohua Chen, and Prem Sangraula. 2009. "Dollar a Day Revisited." *The World Bank Economic Review* 23 (2): 163–84. doi:10.1093/wber/lhp007.

Ravallion, Martin, Gaurav Datt, and Dominique van de Walle. 1991. "Quantifying Absolute Poverty in the Developing World." *Review of Income and Wealth* 37 (4): 345–61. doi:10.1111/j.1475-4991.1991.tb00378.x.

World Bank. 1990. *World Development Report 1990: Poverty.* New York: Oxford University Press.

———. 2012. *Inclusive Green Growth: The Pathway to Sustainable Development.* Washington, DC: World Bank. http://elibrary.worldbank.org/doi/book/10.1596/978-0-8213-9551-6.

Yoshida, Nobuo, Hiroki Uematsu, and Carlos E. Sobrado. 2014. "Is Extreme Poverty Going to End? An Analytical Framework to Evaluate Progress in Ending Extreme Poverty." Policy Research Working Paper 6740, World Bank, Washington, DC.

# CHAPTER TWO

# Understanding Shared Prosperity

Economic development is often equated with average growth in gross domestic product (GDP) per capita. A country with a high growth rate is deemed to be successful, while a country with a low or negative growth rate is considered to be falling behind. But this concept of development provides little insight into who may be benefiting (or not) from growth in a given country. For example, incomes in two countries could be growing at the same average rate, but in the first country all the growth is concentrated among the richest members of society, while in the second, most of the growth benefits the poorest. Although both countries are progressing at the same pace, not everyone in each country benefits to the same extent.

How should economic development be measured and assessed then? Should the emphasis be only on the overall performance of a country or should there be some additional focus to ensure that the poor are not left behind? This question, in essence, is what the World Bank's new goal of boosting shared prosperity aims to address. The idea is to retain an emphasis on growth (as measured in national surveys by income or consumption, as opposed to growth measured from national accounts), but shift attention to the growth of the average income (or consumption) of the bottom 40 percent of the people in a given country. In this way, shared prosperity remains an indicator of economic dynamism and progress and the benchmark of good progress is income growth of the bottom 40 percent of society.

By introducing this goal, the World Bank explicitly brings income inequality to the forefront of the policy dialogue. The shared prosperity goal is not an inequality measure in itself, since it focuses exclusively on income growth of the bottom 40 percent of the population. However, as this chapter discusses, shared prosperity is intimately linked to inequality. The evolution of shared prosperity can be decomposed into a part that can be attributed to overall (survey mean) income (or consumption) growth, while another part accounts for changes in the share of overall income that accrues to the bottom 40 percent. This simple relationship implies that shared prosperity reveals a lot about overall income distribution and, therefore, inequality. Although distributional issues have been part of the development debate for decades, this is the first time that an indicator with close links to inequality of outcomes (incomes) has become a benchmark of development progress for the World Bank.

This chapter discusses the conceptual and empirical underpinnings of the World Bank's shared prosperity goal. The chapter highlights some of the historical antecedents leading to the adoption of the shared prosperity goal and discusses the empirical requirements and challenges for calculating shared prosperity trends in countries around the world. The chapter also presents some of the insights and benefits from tracking the income growth rate of the bottom 40 percent and argues why this measure is relevant even in countries where poverty is low. Finally, the chapter shows how the goal of shared prosperity goes hand in hand with the goal of ending global poverty and how boosting shared prosperity may be instrumental for achieving the poverty goal. The chapter also discusses some of the data challenges in measuring and monitoring shared prosperity (which are discussed in more detail in chapters 5 and 6).

## The evolution of shared prosperity

The desire to establish a measure that captures the notion that economic growth should benefit everyone is not new by any means. The debate on why and how to define such a measure can be traced to the 1950s. The discussion within the developing community on the concept of shared prosperity reached an important milestone in the early 1970s, as part of the process of refining the broad goals of development (box 2.1). One important influence on development thinking came from John Rawls' *Theory of Justice*, with its implication that, in a society, promoting the well-being of the least fortunate member should be an important priority (Rawls 1971).

An influential book published by the World Bank, *Redistribution with Growth*, by Chenery and others (1974), set in motion an active academic and policy debate on how best to measure such a concept. The authors argue that overall economic growth (measured by growth in gross national product [GNP]) is too narrow and cannot adequately be used as a social

## Box 2.1   The World Bank's early discussions of shared prosperity

The development community's rich debate on inclusive growth in the 1970s is reflected in a speech given by then World Bank President Robert McNamara during the Annual Meetings of the Board of Governors in 1972.

In the speech, McNamara first motivates the importance of focusing on the bottom 40 percent of the population: ". . . the poorest 40 percent of the citizenry is [a population] of immense urgency since their condition is in fact far worse than national averages suggest."

He then calls for action:

> . . . Policies specifically designed to reduce the deprivation among the poorest 40 percent in developing countries are prescriptions not only of principle but of prudence. Social justice is not merely a moral imperative. It is a political imperative as well . . . it is possible to design policies with the explicit goal of improving the conditions of life of the poorest 40 percent of the populations in the developing countries and that this can

be done without unacceptable penalties to the concomitant goal of national growth. Without specific emphasis on such programs, there will not be significant progress in reducing poverty within acceptable time periods.

Finally, he introduces the idea of monitoring and benchmarking:

> . . . The first step should be to establish specific targets, within the development plans of individual countries, for income growth among the poorest 40 percent of the population. I suggest that our goal should be to increase the income of the poorest sections of society in the short run—in five years—at least as fast as the national average. In the longer run—ten years—the goal should be to increase this growth significantly faster than the national average.

*Source:* Based on McNamara (1972).

welfare indicator. By showing how growth in GNP can be decomposed into the growth of the incomes of socioeconomic groups with weights proportional to the groups' existing share in the national product, the book presents a policy dilemma: in the process of maximizing overall growth, the best strategy would be to focus on those groups whose original share of GNP was the largest (in other words, the richest). As an alternative, the authors propose looking at the income growth performance of the poor to address the concern of maximizing social well-being. In this way, the concept of the growth performance of the bottom 40 percent and the goal of inclusive growth were introduced, although not widely used, as concrete measures emerging from this work.

By the 1980s, a new strand of the literature emerged that contributed to the broadening of the goals of development and, as a consequence, the measurement of these goals. Led by the writings of Amartya Sen and consistent with Rawlsian concepts, these pieces argue that access to or ownership of material goods should not be the goal of development (Sen 1983, 1985, 1999). Instead, development and progress should be seen in terms of functioning (what a person manages to do) and capability (what a person is able to do). Sen points out that this approach goes back to the work of Adam Smith and Karl Marx, but it was lost in the increasing effort to measure the progress of nations by their incomes. A direct consequence of this work was the emergence of a broad range of nonmonetary measures of living standards, such as the United Nations Development Programme's Human Development Index or, more recently, the Oxford Poverty and Human Development Initiative's multidimensional poverty index and the World Bank's Human Opportunity Index (see chapter 3 for a full discussion on these and other alternative welfare measures). This perspective was also implicit in the "broad-based growth" discussions that pervaded the 1990 *World Development Report* (World Bank 1990) and the focus over the past few decades on measuring development progress on the basis of a broader set of indicators related to human development (not just income).

Following concerns about the unequal impacts of growth and in the context of explicit global commitments to poverty reduction in the Millennium Development Goals, a new strand of work in the 2000s recatalyzed the discussion on who should benefit from growth. An academic debate on the conceptualization and operationalization of pro-poor growth emerged, with various prevailing views. The "absolute approach," suggested by Ravallion and Chen (2003) and Kraay (2006), defines any poverty-reducing episode as being pro-poor. The "relative view," held by Kakwani and Pernia (2000), Son (2004), Klasen (2004, 2008), Essama-Nssah and Lambert (2009), and Negre (2010), requires the poor to benefit disproportionately from growth. In another strand of work, Subramanian (2011) points to the notion of "egalitarian growth," which requires that at least 40 percent of increases in GDP accrue to the bottom 40 percent. Depending on initial inequality, pro-poor growth could require the growth in incomes of the bottom 40 percent to exceed dramatically the growth in incomes of the overall population. These concepts gave rise to several indicators and measures, with no overall agreement on how to balance the trade-offs in adopting a single measure.

Basu (2001, 2006) takes a step further by providing some practical suggestions on how to go about measuring an inclusive growth concept in a systematic way at the global level. He argues that development goals that go beyond income growth to broader objectives—a better quality of life, increased education, and a more equitable distribution of goods and services—are indeed desirable. Basu notes that a meaningful summary measure that would capture these multiple objectives is urgently needed. By reasoning that a perfect measure that encompasses all the desired properties does not exist, Basu concludes that a careful balance between conceptual coherence, empirical tractability, and ease of communication needs to be considered. He proposes to focus on the per capita income of the poorest 20 percent of the population and, specifically, the growth rate of the per capita income of the poorest people. Basu further shows how the quintile income has many attractive properties, among them the fact that it correlates more strongly than average per capita income with other (nonmonetary) indicators of well-being, such as greater life expectancy and higher literacy.

Although this brief description of the evolution of the discussions around the concept of shared prosperity does not aim to be comprehensive, three main messages emerge. First, shared prosperity is a concept that has been discussed, debated, and of concern to the development community for many decades. Second, for any measure of shared prosperity to be of meaningful use, it needs to reconcile multiple challenges, both technical and practical. And finally, the adoption of the goal of achieving shared prosperity inherently implies that ensuring the well-being of the most vulnerable in a society is a key goal of development.

## Shared prosperity decoded

The shared prosperity goal adopted by the World Bank is to boost the per capita income or consumption growth of the poorest 40 percent in a given country.[1] In the debates leading to the adoption of this indicator, three aspects influenced the discussion and final choice of the indicator: its simplicity, target population, and theoretical considerations. These are described below.

### Simplicity

An attractive feature of the shared prosperity goal is its conceptual simplicity. To track shared prosperity, the only requirement is data on the income (or consumption) growth rate of those in the bottom 40 percent of the population between two periods. The development community has used and will continue to use national GDP growth rates to track the overall progress of a given country over time; given the appropriate data, the calculation of the income growth of the bottom part of the distribution is an easy extension. However, there are two important differences. First, income growth in the shared prosperity measurement refers to growth in mean income or consumption of the bottom 40 percent of the population from household surveys.[2] As chapter 6 discusses, a key difference between the shared prosperity measure and GDP growth is that living standards measured from surveys and those from national accounts are often strikingly different. In this sense, the two growth measures are not comparable.

Second, shared prosperity in this framework does not track the growth rate of the same bottom 40 percent of people over time. The shared prosperity indicator is an "anonymous" measure, expressed as the growth in mean income of the bottom 40 percent of the income distribution between two periods, irrespective of the individuals belonging to this group at either point in time. It is likely that many of the people in the bottom 40 percent of the income distribution in the first period will not be in the bottom 40 percent in the second period. This highlights an important distinction between shared prosperity measured with cross-sectional data at two points in time and the concept of mobility. The latter concept explicitly focuses on tracking the *same* individuals (nonanonymous) over time and analyzing their income growth over time (upward or downward), which requires panel data.

Unlike the goal to end extreme poverty, the shared prosperity goal is country specific. Therefore, tracking progress only requires monitoring the income growth of the bottom 40 percent over time in a given country. Since it is country specific, there is no explicit target set at the global level. Even at the country level, the shared prosperity goal is more of a moving target than an absolute target. Although the goal of minimizing extreme poverty has a specific target, the goal of boosting shared prosperity does not have a specific numerical target. Shared prosperity is "unbounded" in this way: there is no absolute standard that every country should reach. Even for a given country, the standard is unlikely to remain constant, as societies, along with people's aspirations, evolve along the development path.

### Target population

The shared prosperity goal's emphasis on the bottom 40 percent focuses the goal on an explicit objective population. The goal emphasizes that, within a country, different subpopulations will be able to take advantage of economic opportunities in different ways. The focus on growth of the bottom 40 percent ensures that, irrespective of what is happening in the country overall, economic growth should also reach the least well-off people in the population. In this way, the focus provides guidance for policy design. Policy design must directly consider the potential impact of policies on the bottom 40 percent and how those at the bottom can benefit the most from the policies. Box 2.2 discusses considerations underlying the choice of 40 percent as the cutoff for defining the shared prosperity goal.

Yet, in sharp contrast to Rawls, who emphasizes the poorest person, the shared prosperity indicator is in fact not an egalitarian measure. Although the prosperity indicator does not put any weight on people above the bottom 40 percent, it gives more weight to the richest person within the bottom 40 percent since, by construct, increased shared prosperity can be achieved more quickly by first raising the incomes of those at the top of the bottom 40 percent (chapter 3 discusses this in more detail).

---

### Box 2.2    Why 40 percent?

The decision to have a shared prosperity goal that focuses on a specific target population required a choice for what cutoff to use for the target population. The main arguments given for the use of 40 percent as the cutoff relate to practical compromises regarding trade-offs in the empirical implementation of the goal. On the one hand, placing the threshold "too high" could result in mean per capita (household survey) incomes of the target population that are very close to national mean per capita incomes (also survey based) and hence provide little information beyond GDP per capita. On the other hand, in many low-income countries, extreme poverty is concentrated in the bottom quintile, so placing the threshold at 20 percent would provide little information beyond that provided by the extreme poverty goal. Placing the threshold "too low" could also be problematic if income data on the poorest people, being at the tail of the distribution, tended to have higher measurement errors. The very poor often have no steady source of income and the income they do have comes from multiple, informal sources that are not always easy to document, which could contribute to higher measurement error for this part of the population.[a] The choice of the 40th percentile as the cutoff point to define the "least well-off" part of the population is admittedly a somewhat arbitrary threshold, although the criticism of arbitrariness would apply to any such threshold.

Interestingly, the threshold of 40 percent may have some separate empirical relevance. Palma (2011) explores recent trends in distributional income disparities within countries and finds two stylized facts. First, the disparity between the income shares of the top 10 percent of the population and the bottom 40 percent has been increasing over time. At the same time, the income share of the fifth to ninth deciles has remained roughly constant. Palma argues that half the world's population has acquired strong "property rights" over their respective share of national income, while the other half of the income is increasingly up for grabs between the very rich and the bottom 40 percent. This narrative provides some further rationale for focusing specifically on the incomes of the bottom 40 percent.

a. Note that the frequently asserted claim that measurement error is highest for the poorest has not been comprehensively substantiated empirically.

### Theoretical considerations

Beyond simplicity and focus, it is also desirable for any measure of living standards to satisfy some of the standard axioms of welfare functions. It is worthwhile to mention briefly two of the axioms.[3] First, the shared prosperity measure satisfies the criterion of anonymity: in a given society, it should not matter who is at the bottom (or the top) of the income distribution. For the shared prosperity measure, all that matters is the growth rate of the incomes of the bottom 40 percent, irrespective of who they may be.

The shared prosperity indicator also satisfies the weak Pareto principle, which states that if the income of every individual in a group rises, the group is considered better off. Since the aim of the shared prosperity goal is to track the income growth of the bottom 40 percent of the population, while the income of those outside the range is not relevant for the indicator, an increase in the incomes of the bottom 40 percent will by design improve shared prosperity and hence be interpreted as an improvement in the well-being of the group.

No welfare index is perfect, and the shared prosperity indicator is not an exception. For example, the shared prosperity indicator does not satisfy the weak transfer axiom, which requires lump-sum transfers from a richer person to a poorer one within a group to lead to improvement in the value of the indicator. Since the shared prosperity indicator focuses on the bottom 40 percent and does not differentiate within this group, such a transfer would not affect shared prosperity. The weak transfer axiom would likely be less of an issue for a cutoff point of, say, 20 percent, highlighting one of the trade-offs in the choice of the threshold, as discussed in box 2.2. An interesting implication of the shared prosperity indicator is that any change in the distribution of income within the bottom 40 percent that maintains the same total share of income accruing to the bottom 40 percent would not affect the value of the measure. This aspect of the indicator is discussed further below.

## Tracking shared prosperity in practice

### Who are in the bottom 40 percent?

As is the case with the measurement of poverty, an important entry point for reflecting on government action and policy on shared prosperity relates to the profile of the bottom 40 percent. In what way do the characteristics of the population in the bottom 40 percent of a given country differ from those of the population as a whole (or the top 60 percent or the poor)? Since shared prosperity is a relative concept, it corresponds to different income groups across countries. In other words, the bottom 40 percent differs across countries. For example, the average household in the bottom 40 percent of the income distribution in the United States would be among the richest 10 percent in Brazil (figure 2.1). Similarly, the average household in the bottom 40 percent of Brazil's income distribution would be at approximately the 90th percentile of the income distribution in India.

Not only does the average income of the bottom 40 percent differ across countries, but the composition of incomes among the bottom 40 percent is also likely to vary substantially. Figure 2.2 plots the sizes of various income-based groups across a selection of countries. The groups are the

**Figure 2.1** The bottom 40 percent in the United States, Brazil, and India, 2008

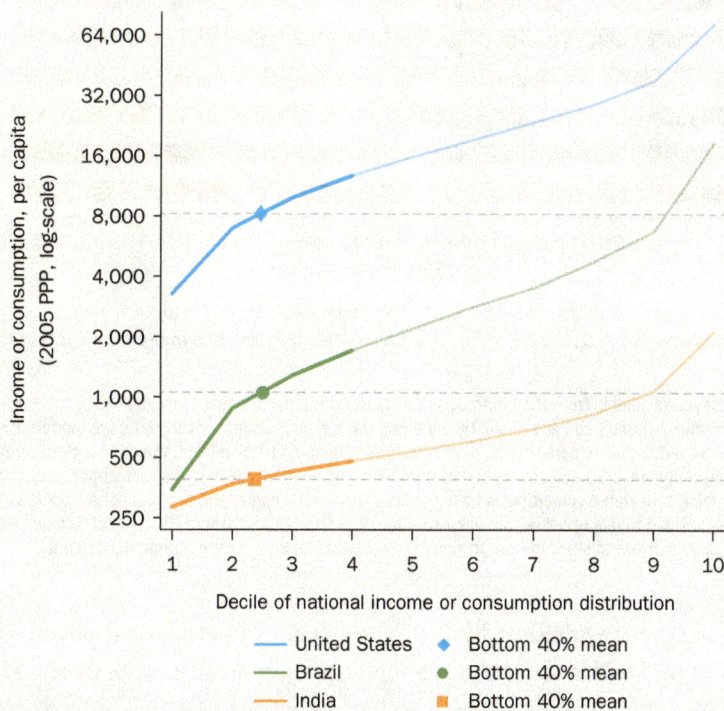

Source: Based on Lakner and Milanovic (2013).
Note: The lines connect decile means for each country, where the thicker portion of each line connects the decile means of the bottom 40 percent. PPP = purchasing power parity.

81

**Figure 2.2** The bottom 40 percent can encompass various income groups across countries, circa 2009

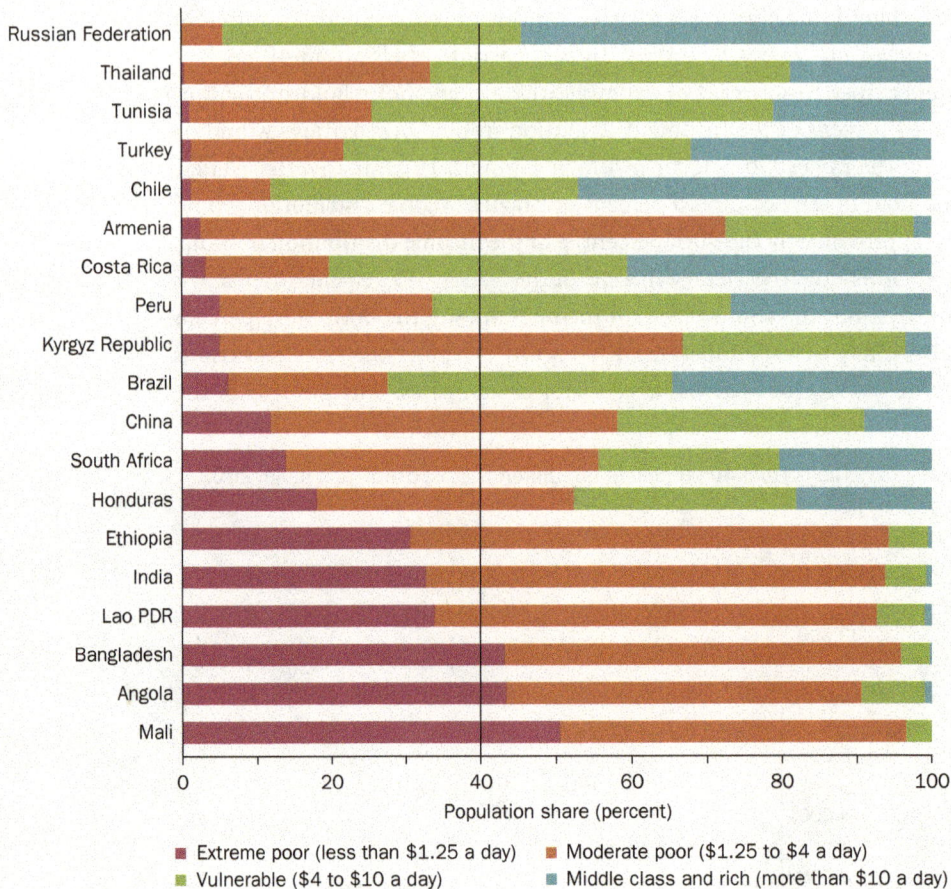

**Source:** Based on data for latest year available from the World Bank PovcalNet database (accessed August 2014).
**Note:** The groups in the figure are the extreme poor, as defined by the World Bank's international poverty line; the moderate poor, who live on between $1.25 and $4 a day; the vulnerable who live on between $4 and $10 a day; and the middle class and rich, who live on more than $10 a day—all measured at 2005 constant purchasing power parity (PPP). The concept of people living on between $4 and $10 a day being considered vulnerable is based on evidence that a considerable share of households above a given poverty line is usually vulnerable to falling below that line over time. See Ferreira and others (2012) and Birdsall, Lustig, and Meyer (2014). The vertical line is drawn to show the proportion of the population living in the bottom 40 percent.

extreme poor, as defined by the World Bank's international poverty line (less than $1.25 a day); the moderate poor, who live on between $1.25 and $4 a day; the vulnerable, who live on between $4 and $10 a day; and the middle class and rich, who live on more than $10 a day, all measured at 2005 constant purchasing power parity (PPP).[4] In countries such as Angola, Bangladesh, and Mali, the bottom 40 percent essentially captures the extreme poor (using the international poverty line). In Ethiopia and India, 80 percent of those in the bottom 40 percent are extremely poor and the rest are moderately poor. In other countries, such as China, the bottom 40 percent predominantly comes from the moderately poor (with the rest extremely poor).

A different picture emerges in countries in Latin America and the Caribbean and in Europe and Central Asia. In some of the richer, upper-middle-income countries in these regions, such as Chile and the Russian Federation, the large majority of individuals in the bottom 40 percent are in the vulnerable group. The vulnerable are nonpoor individuals with a high risk of falling back into poverty. In all, these trends highlight the great range of people that constitute the bottom 40 percent across the world. Consequently, the concept of shared prosperity and its associated policy discussion will have different meanings in each country.[5]

Since the concept of shared prosperity focuses attention on the poorest members of society within a country, it is useful to compare the bottom 40 percent with the poor as defined by each country's respective national poverty line. In figure 2.3, data on national poverty lines from the data set compiled by Ravallion, Chen, and Sangraula (2009) are matched with corresponding surveys from the PovcalNet database. In some cases, focusing on the bottom 40 percent captures a narrower group than those living below national poverty lines. For example, in Colombia, Georgia, the Republic of Congo, República Bolivariana de Venezuela, Tajikistan, and The Gambia, the bottom 40 percent implies a much narrower focus on the poor than the national poverty line. By contrast, in China, India, and Tunisia, the concept of shared prosperity encompasses a much larger part of the population than the poor as defined by the national poverty line.

Overall, the comparison of who constitutes the bottom 40 percent across countries illustrates the benefit of a "moving target" that can be interpreted differently in different countries, rather than a common goal for all countries. In some cases, especially in low- and lower-middle-income countries, the shared prosperity indicator can reinforce national poverty lines and strengthen the focus on the poor. In other cases, especially in upper-middle-income countries, the shared prosperity indicator may help broaden the policy agenda for nonpoor parts of the population that might otherwise face the risk of being left behind or falling into poverty. In the latter case, policy agendas for the bottom 40 percent may introduce trade-offs or complementarities with those for the poor. Although a discussion of this type of trade-off is beyond the scope of this report, it is worth noting

**Figure 2.3**  The bottom 40 percent compared to the poor as defined by national poverty lines

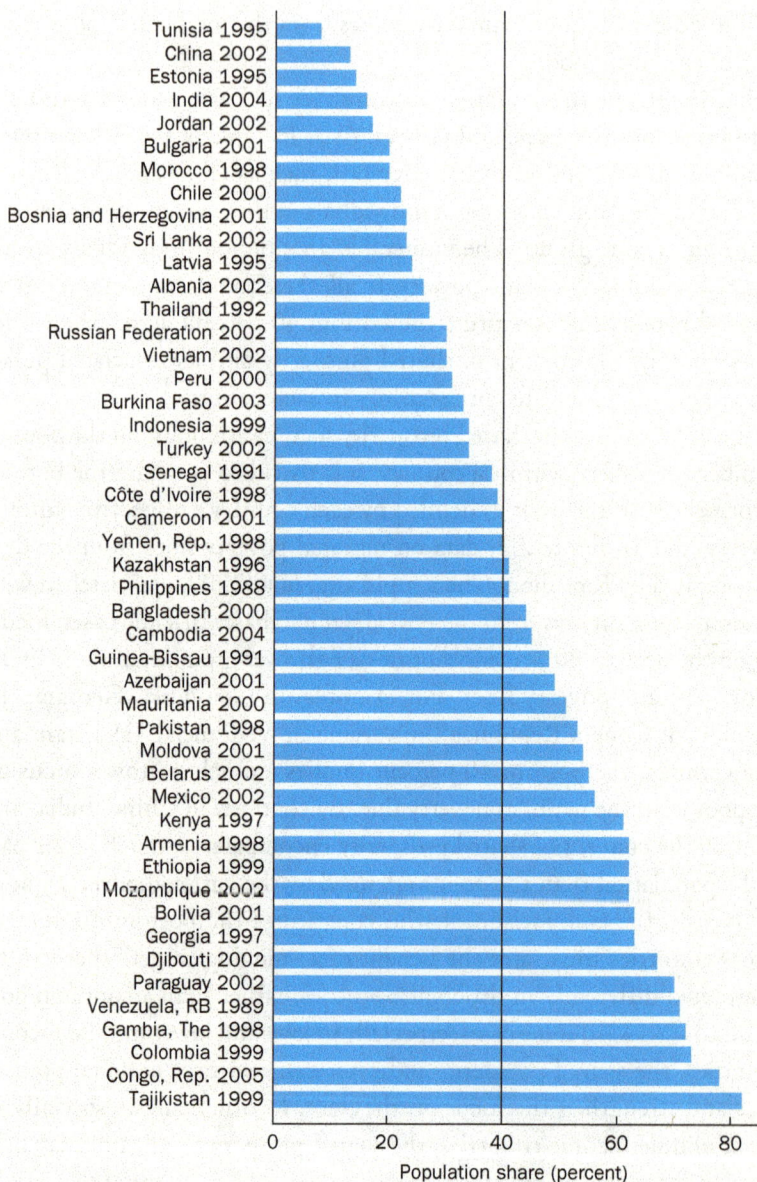

*Sources:* Based on data from the World Bank PovcalNet database (accessed August 2014) and Ravallion, Chen, and Sangraula (2009).
*Note:* The blue bars show the percentage of the population below the national poverty line. The vertical line is drawn to show the proportion of those in the bottom 40 percent who are also living below the national poverty line.

that such trade-offs are likely to be a country-specific issue and a function of the connections between growth and poverty reduction in specific contexts, which are discussed further below and in chapter 3.[6]

## Measurement of shared prosperity at the country level: What constitutes success?

Calculating shared prosperity requires measuring income or consumption in a given country and year for those in the bottom 40 percent. Then, by replicating this calculation in a comparable manner in another year, shared prosperity in a particular country can be measured as the annualized growth rate between the two periods (box 2.3 discusses the data requirements). What, then, constitutes success? A positive number would suggest that the bottom 40 percent of the population saw increases in their incomes, but, given the fact that the goal is unbounded, the number would not provide meaningful information about how good the growth rate was. This section discusses some ways to think about assessing the performance of the shared prosperity goal.

A first insight about a country's performance can be inferred by having multiple periods of data, so that the evolution of shared prosperity can be tracked over time. Figure 2.4 shows examples from four countries where multiple surveys exist from the 1980s onward. In Sri Lanka, shared prosperity increased slowly in the late 1980s and early 1990s before increasing more sharply in the 2000s. Similarly, in Brazil, shared prosperity fluctuated in the 1990s before beginning a strongly increasing trend from the early 2000s. In this sense, performance has been better in both countries in more recent years. This is also the case in South Africa and Uganda.

Another possibility is to compare the performance of the bottom 40 percent with that of other parts of the income distribution (for example, the top 60 percent of the population) or overall national average performance. Alongside trends in the average income of the bottom 40 percent, figure 2.4 also shows annualized growth rates for the population as a whole. In addition to providing a means to compare the performance of shared prosperity across countries, this comparison also allows an assessment of the evolution of income inequality (this point is discussed further below). For example, the bottom 40 percent in South Africa did better than average during the mid-1990s (suggesting not only that incomes of the bottom 40 percent grew, but also that there was some catching up). By contrast, by the 2000s, income growth for the bottom 40 percent increased compared with

## Box 2.3 Measuring and tracking shared prosperity at the country level

Measurement of the shared prosperity indicator, like any measure, implies information requirements and potentially some underlying assumptions. Chapter 1 discusses some of the issues related to the measurement of poverty, this chapter discusses shared prosperity, and chapter 5 discusses additional data challenges and promising areas that can improve measurement for both goals.

### What data to use?

The shared prosperity measure refers to growth of the per capita real household income or consumption of the bottom 40 percent of a population. Although aggregate growth statistics like GDP growth are typically derived from national income accounts, these aggregate data cannot provide disaggregated information on the growth of income fractiles, such as the bottom 40 percent. Instead, shared prosperity can be calculated from nationally representative surveys that provide income or consumption data at the household level. These surveys directly allow the identification of the bottom 40 percent of the population and their incomes.[a]

### Which measure of well-being?

To construct the shared prosperity indicator with at least two data points for a given country over time, strict comparability is required between the respective surveys used. Constructing a growth rate with consumption levels in one year and income in the other year is a meaningless option. Even when the same indicator is used, special attention is needed to ensure that the methodology used to construct the measure of well-being is consistent in the two years. Many countries periodically update their survey methodologies to account for changes in population structures, spatial prices, caloric requirements, and imputation techniques—adding new sources of consumption or income, treatment of taxes, and food consumed away from home, to name a few. Growth rates can be sensitive to such changes and thus comparability is essential.

As discussed in chapter 1, the use of income or consumption to measure poverty has a long tradition, although consumption is usually the preferred indicator, particularly in developing countries. As with the measurement of poverty, data on consumption, if available, are preferred over data on income to construct the shared prosperity indicator. Conceptually, consumption is usually less susceptible to measurement errors and temporary fluctuations and thus it is often seen as a better measure of current living standards.[b] Even poor households can usually rely on some form of saving and dissaving mechanisms to smooth income shocks. Consumption is usually also seen as more indicative of long-term living standards.[c] Empirically, the difference between a shared prosperity measure based on consumption and one based on income is not trivial (as figure 2.5 shows).

### Which time interval to consider?

In many countries, data availability will dictate the interval in which shared prosperity can be estimated. But in cases where data from multiple years are available, how should the shared prosperity measure be calculated? When there are more data, the best approach is to take advantage of all the information available (see figure 2.6 for an illustration).

a. Note that while these surveys are well designed to capture population averages, it is still the case that they may not adequately capture information from specific subpopulations where extreme poverty is concentrated.

b. There is a large literature on the use of income or consumption in the measurement of poverty. Ravallion (1994), Deaton (1997), and Deaton and Zaidi (2002) provide a comprehensive overview of the conceptual background and empirical issues. For a broader review of the literature on living standards measurement, see Slesnick (1998).

c. In economic theory, the permanent income hypothesis essentially states that individuals base their consumption decisions on their anticipated long-term income rather than shorter-term fluctuations. However, Deaton concludes that "the standard argument—that by the permanent income hypothesis, consumption is a better measure of lifetime living standards than is current income—is much weaker than the arguments based on practicality and data" (Deaton 1997, 148).

**Figure 2.4** Evolution of mean income or consumption of the bottom 40 percent and the overall population, 1980–2010

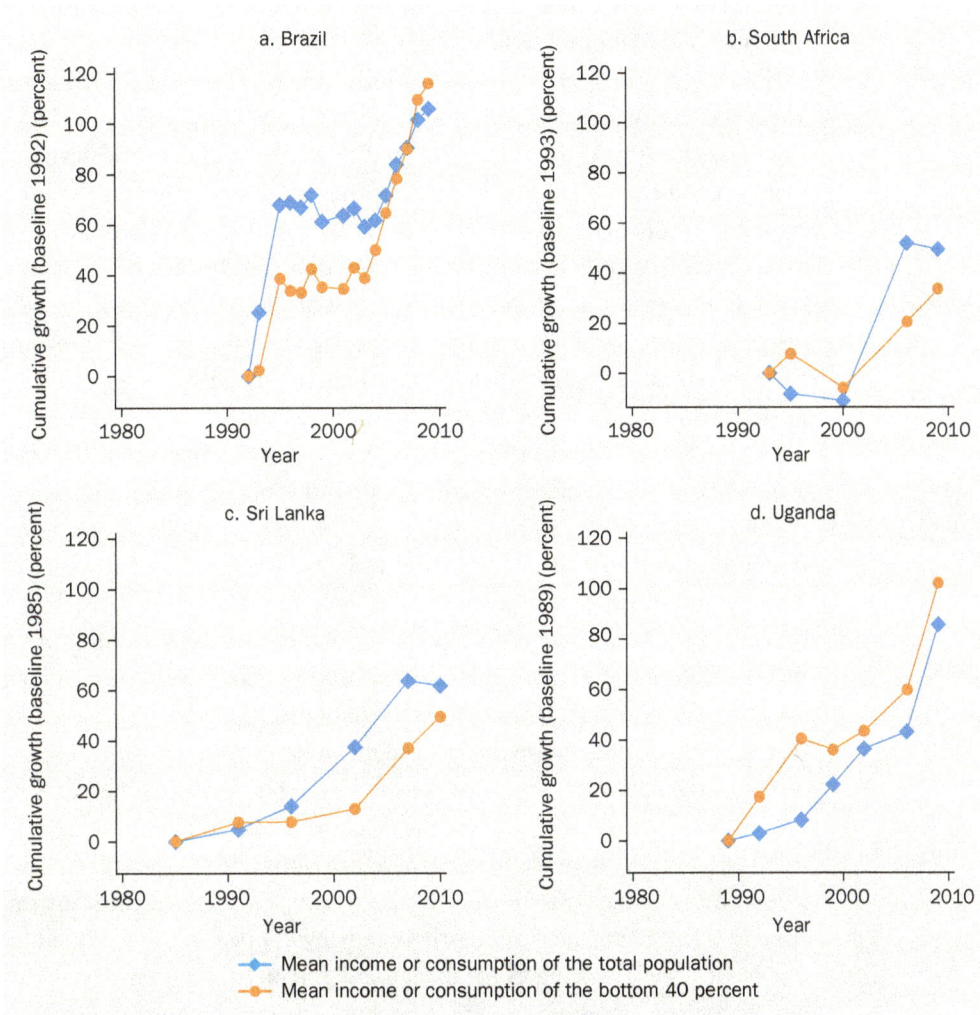

Source: Based on data from the World Bank PovcalNet database (accessed August 2014).
Note: Cumulative growth of household consumption expenditure or income per capita in constant 2005 purchasing power parity (PPP).

the mid-1990s but was significantly slower than average income growth, implying increased inequality. Although shared prosperity was boosted over this period in South Africa (average incomes of the bottom 40 percent increased), the bottom 40 percent underperformed relative to the rest of the population. The same is true in Sri Lanka in the 1990s and 2000s. In Uganda, the trends suggest not only that shared prosperity has been increasing over time, but the bottom 40 percent also did at least as well as the rest of the population (the growth rate was the same as or exceeded the overall average). The same is true for the bottom 40 percent in Brazil in the second half of the 2000s.

The aggregate shared prosperity indicator provides no information about the performance *within* the bottom 40 percent. As is the case for the measurement of poverty, or indeed any other indicator of development outcomes, subnational divergence may confound the interpretation of shared prosperity. The perceived performance of shared prosperity can vary depending on whether the income or consumption growth of the bottom 40 percent is calculated at the level of the country, state, or even district—particularly in large and heterogeneous countries. This problem can arise through a scale effect, where the level of aggregation can determine the findings for a specific area (for example, state averages can smooth out district-level heterogeneity), and a zoning effect, where the choice of groupings of households at the same scale can similarly influence results.[7]

The challenge of interpreting shared prosperity at the subnational level is illustrated by the case of rural India, where regional disparities in poverty and other development indicators have traditionally been large, between and within states. In figure 2.5, shared prosperity using growth in household monthly per capita expenditure for *rural* India is calculated for the bottom 40 percent at the national level, the state level, and the district level. At the national level, the mean household per capita expenditure of the rural bottom 40 percent fell by about 4 percent (red dashed line in both panels). Despite the weak performance during this period, these results hide the wide heterogeneous performance at the subnational level. For example, the mean household per capita expenditure of the rural bottom 40 percent in Rajasthan grew by 4.4 percent, while it fell by 6 percent in neighboring Gujarat (figure 2.5, panel a). Similar trends can be seen within states: within rural Gujarat, the state's poor performance masks the fact that the mean of the bottom 40 percent grew by 2 percent in the state's most populous district of Ahmedabad, while it fell in most other districts (panel b). Thus, the overall decrease in shared prosperity at the national level masks mixed performances within states and districts.

The source of data or time interval chosen can also affect the performance and interpretation of the shared prosperity indicator. Since Peru collects annual data on consumption and income, it is a natural candidate to examine sensitivity to the source of data and time period used. Figure 2.6 shows the growth rates for the bottom 40 percent measured with

**Figure 2.5** Shared prosperity in rural India at various levels of disaggregation, 2007/08–2009/10

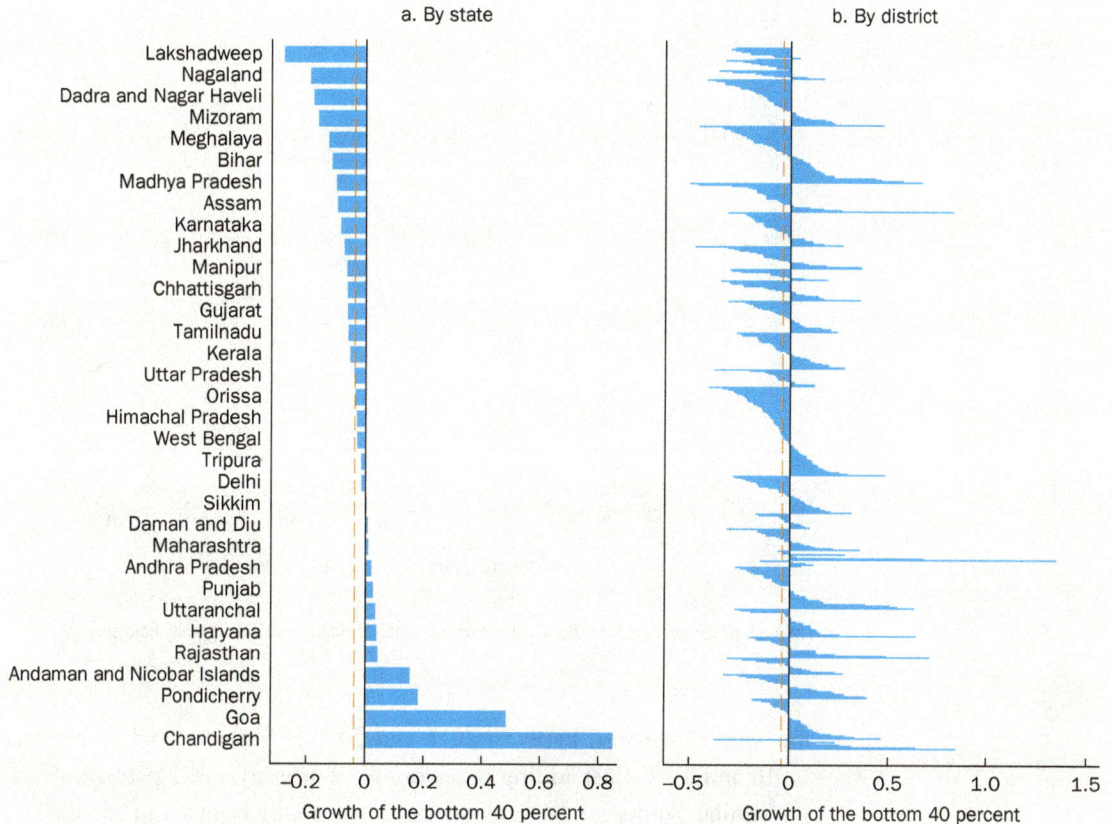

Source: Based on data from India's NSSO National Sample Survey rounds 64 (2007/08) and 66 (2009/10).
Note: Orange dashed line marks the annualized growth in consumption expenditure of the rural bottom 40 percent for the nation. Growth rates calculated using real household monthly per capita expenditure (mixed reference period), deflated using the consumer price index (CPI) for agricultural laborers with base 1986/87 = 100.

income and consumption, using different time intervals. The end year is fixed at 2012, but the initial year from which the annualized growth rate is estimated ranges from 2011 to 2004. A few results stand out. First, the shared prosperity indicator for a given interval with consumption data is different (in most cases lower) than the one with income data. The growth rates can differ by as much as 2 percentage points (about 30 percent), thus providing substantially different interpretations about the performance of Peru. Even more striking, the choice of time interval used to calculate shared prosperity makes a significant difference to Peru's performance. At the extreme, shared prosperity (growth in mean consumption of the

**Figure 2.6** Illustration of how the choice of data and time interval influence shared prosperity estimates

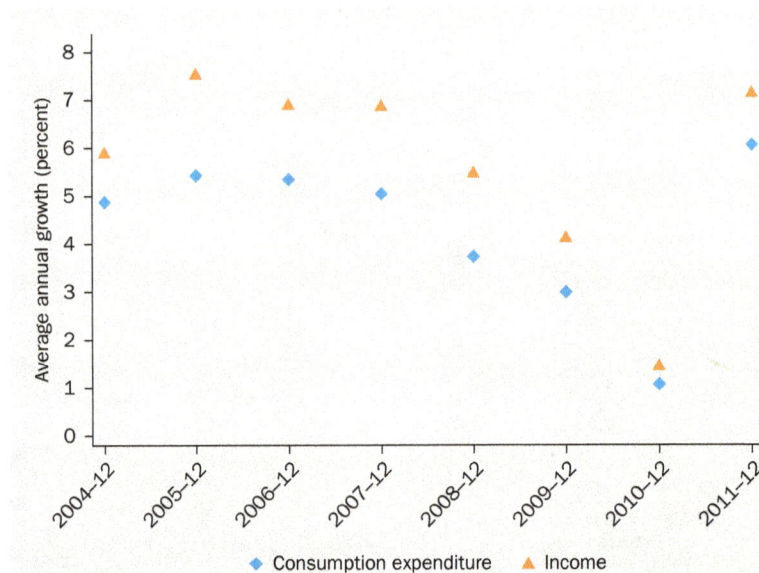

*Source:* Based on data from Peru's Encuesta Nacional de Hogares (ENAHO) household survey.

bottom 40 percent) between 2011 and 2012 is 6 percent, while between 2010 and 2012 (just adding one more year), it is around 1 percent.

Similar points can be made when deciding which start and end dates to use. Instead of holding the end year constant and varying the time interval, as in figure 2.6, the end years in figure 2.7 vary to compose estimates of equal duration over a different range of years. Once again, the results vary when consumption or income data are used to estimate the shared prosperity indicator. In addition, the choice of which five-year interval one uses affects the performance of shared prosperity. For the five-year span between 2004 and 2008, income growth of the bottom 40 percent in Peru is estimated at 6 percent (annualized) compared with 10 percent if the period used shifts by one year (2005 to 2009).

Given the sensitivity of estimates to the source of data and time intervals used, a last exercise is to consider how the performance of shared prosperity fares by estimating moving averages of income and consumption growth (as depicted in figure 2.7). The results strongly show how both two- and three-period moving averages smooth considerably the estimated shared prosperity.

**Figure 2.7** Moving averages provide more stable shared prosperity estimates

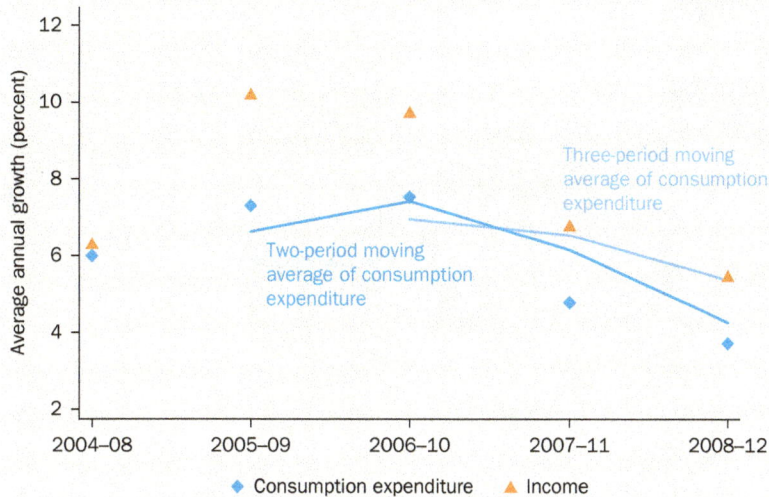

*Source:* Based on data from Peru's Encuesta Nacional de Hogares (ENAHO) household survey.

A take-away message from this section is that in the presence of more rounds of comparable data, they should be used to improve the interpretation and better assess the performance of a country in boosting shared prosperity. Moving averages provide a simple and effective way to smooth some of the inherent variations observed in the underlying data and thereby produce more stable results. In most countries, annual consumption or income data are not consistently available. The case of Peru, used to illustrate the scenarios above, is an outlier in terms of good data availability. Although the presence of good data in Peru is closer to the situation of some more developed countries, it is not the norm in the majority of developing countries (see chapter 5 for a more detailed discussion of data availability across countries). Still, Peru showcases a second take-away and an aspirational scenario that other countries will need to move to, so that frequent data can better accommodate measuring and tracking development goals like shared prosperity.

## Monitoring performance in a global context

Shared prosperity is a country-specific goal that can help a given country better understand whether growth is benefiting those at the bottom 40 percent of the population. Still, monitoring of shared prosperity could also involve country-by-country comparisons, which may reveal some

**Figure 2.8   Shared prosperity, by country**

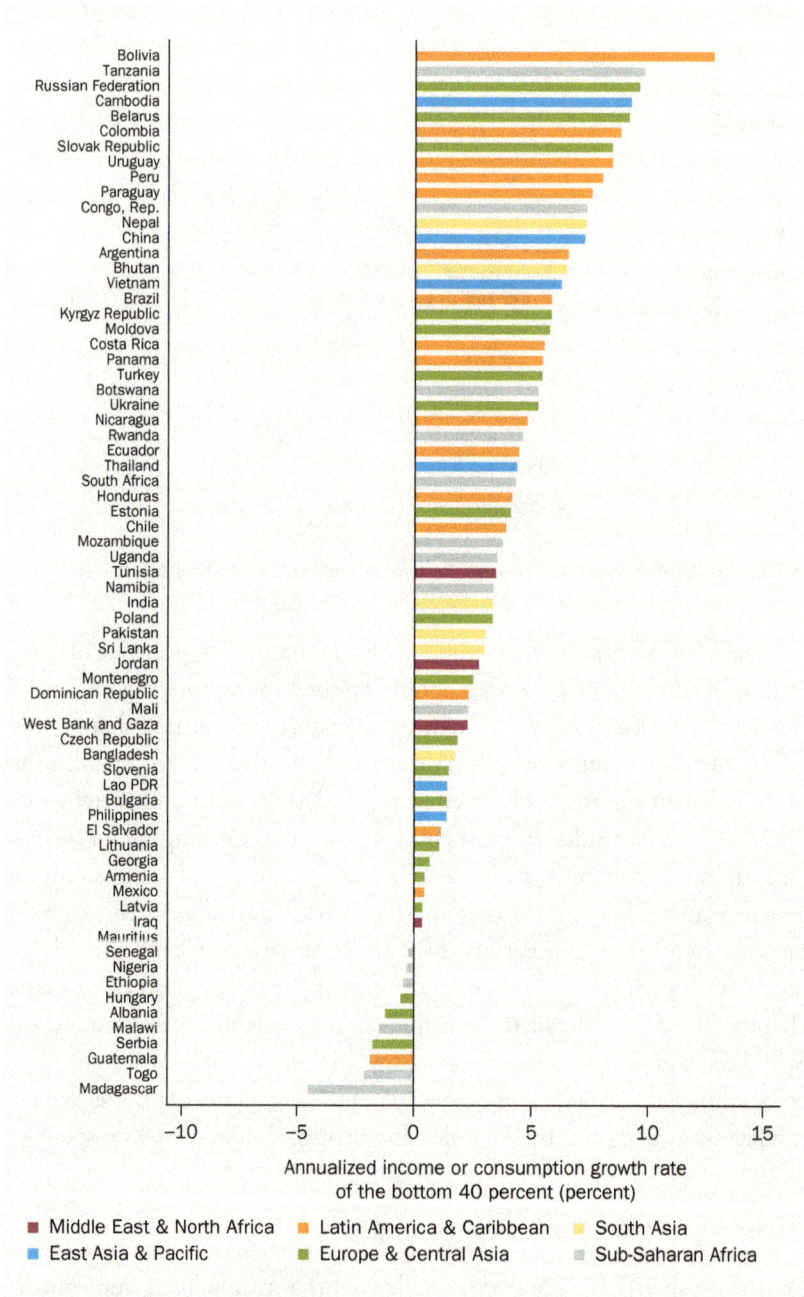

Annualized income or consumption growth rate
of the bottom 40 percent (percent)

■ Middle East & North Africa   ■ Latin America & Caribbean   ■ South Asia
■ East Asia & Pacific   ■ Europe & Central Asia   Sub-Saharan Africa

*Source:* Based on data from the World Bank PovcalNet database (accessed August 2014).
*Note:* Growth rates in shared prosperity are calculated as annualized growth rates in per capita income or consumption expenditure over the period 2006–11. Given the data available from PovcalNet for each country, surveys that use the same welfare indicator are matched as closely as possible to this period.

interesting regional or global trends in how countries are performing with respect to growth of the income of the bottom 40 percent of their populations. Figure 2.8 presents a summary of comparable shared prosperity performances for 69 countries for the period 2006 to 2011.[8] Overall, the bottom 40 percent has performed well. With the exception of 11 of the countries of this sample, the bottom 40 percent in all countries experienced increases in their incomes during this period. However, there is considerable variation across countries. Countries such as Belarus, Bolivia, Colombia, Russia, Tanzania, and Uruguay have experienced annual growth rates in income or consumption of the bottom 40 percent of more than 8 percent, while countries such as Albania, Guatemala, Madagascar, Malawi, Serbia, and Togo have experienced negative annual growth.

In addition, a more nuanced understanding of the comparison may result from considering the drivers of shared prosperity growth. The cases of Honduras and Vietnam help illustrate this point. Over approximately the same period, the growth rate of the bottom 40 percent in Honduras was 4 percent (per year), while in Vietnam it was 6 percent. Does that mean that Vietnam did better at boosting shared prosperity during this period? A strict interpretation of the shared prosperity measure would imply that this was the case. Still, overall growth in Honduras for the whole population during this period was 2 percent, while in Vietnam it was 8 percent. Therefore, in Honduras, income growth of the bottom 40 percent was almost double the national average. In Vietnam, despite the gains for the bottom 40 percent and a high overall growth rate, growth of the bottom 40 percent has lagged behind the national average. Given the discussion on how shared prosperity is a moving target, as well as its inherent connection with inequality, this kind of nuance is worth keeping in mind when comparing trends between countries. Box 2.4 offers some additional discussion and suggestions on cross-country comparisons of shared prosperity.

### The "sharing" in shared prosperity

To what extent does "sharing" prosperity imply the bottom 40 percent of the population should have a larger slice of the pie, beyond simply sharing in the proceeds of growth? The shared prosperity indicator on its own is not an inequality measure; it is a simple growth measure that tracks how the bottom 40 percent of a given country are doing, without any need to compare this progress with other parts of the population. Still, *comparing* the growth of the bottom 40 percent to the average for the total population

## Box 2.4 The challenges of measuring and tracking shared prosperity at the global level

Cross-country comparisons and tracking of shared prosperity pose several additional challenges to monitoring shared prosperity at the country level, since to create a global cross-country data set, comparability across various dimensions needs to be met. Many of these issues are similar to those when comparing poverty numbers across countries, although the dynamic aspect of the shared prosperity indicator brings some additional technical obstacles. The main message below is that, despite the best efforts and intentions, comparisons of shared prosperity across countries should be interpreted with considerable caution.

*Which measure of well-being?* As with the country level, strict comparability of the well-being indicator being used is desirable to make comparisons across countries. In practice, consumption data are not always available, and in recent years many countries (especially middle-income countries) have tended to use income to measure well-being. Following strict requirements of comparability can seriously restrict the scope of any exercise to compare shared prosperity across countries, but even when the same measure of well-being is used, there can still be important differences in the quality of data and their comparability across countries and over time. Most of these issues are a direct or indirect result of variability in how data on different categories of expenditures or income are collected and treated in household surveys across countries and over time.

*Timing—which period and how often to update?* Cross-country comparisons will involve fixing a specific common time interval in all countries over which to assess shared prosperity. Since household surveys are infrequent in most countries and misaligned in terms of their timing, perfect comparability is impossible without drastically reducing the number of countries for which the indicator can be reported. Countries do not generally coordinate the fielding of household surveys, and, as a result, at any point in time there will only be partial coverage across

countries of household survey data. Furthermore, although poverty historically has been tracked only for developing countries, shared prosperity aims to provide measures in all countries across the world (data permitting), adding to the harmonizing complexity in the scope as well as the technical differences involved. The choice of the time period over which to assess growth can also matter significantly at the global level: electoral cycles, country-specific economic upswings or downturns, and natural disasters can all affect individual country performance and thereby render comparisons difficult to make.

*Data.* The primary data source for cross-country comparisons of shared prosperity is the World Bank's PovcalNet database. It comprises income or consumption aggregates from household surveys conducted by statistical offices of individual countries and harmonized to achieve some degree of comparability across countries and years. Since PovcalNet is used for estimating poverty rates at international poverty lines, using it to estimate shared prosperity can also have the advantage of ensuring the consistency of shared prosperity numbers with country-level poverty trends. One limitation is that PovcalNet does not include information from advanced countries, implying that comparisons that aim to present estimates for all countries around the world will require a blend of data sets, rendering comparability issues more difficult.

*Imputing or using survey data?* One way to compare shared prosperity across countries with PovcalNet data is to base the comparison on a *common base year*—an extension of the approach used to measure extreme poverty across countries discussed in chapter 1. This requires that country estimates are "lined up" first to a common reference year, interpolating for countries in which survey data are not available in the reference year but are available either before or after, or both. The more survey data are available for different years, the more accurate the

*(continued)*

## Box 2.4 Continued

interpolation. This approach has the advantage of aligning shared prosperity estimates to those for poverty, so that monitoring of both goals can provide contemporaneous information and insights. By lining up the year of comparison, this approach would also potentially make it possible to construct regional shared prosperity aggregates, which could shed light on more general aggregate patterns of growth for the bottom 40 percent.

Unfortunately, to line up countries in a common year, the process of interpolation requires adjusting the mean income or consumption observed in the survey year by a growth factor to infer the unobserved level in the reference year. In practice, since survey data in most countries are not available on an annual basis, the change in private consumption per capita as measured from the national accounts is used to calculate this growth factor. There can be no guarantee that the survey-based measures of income or consumption change at exactly the same rate as private consumption in the national accounts, even if this appears to be the best currently available option for global poverty estimates. Chapter 6 discusses this further and provides examples of this problem in practice. Perhaps more troublesome, this calculation rests on the assumption of distributionally neutral growth: income or expenditure levels are adjusted for growth between periods assuming that the underlying relative distribution of income or expenditure observed in survey years remains unchanged. This assumption is problematic since changes in the underlying relative distribution of income or expenditure are exactly what the shared prosperity indicator seeks to capture.

An alternative approach is to use actual surveys *around a fixed interval*. The large benefit of this approach is that it uses actual surveys as opposed to projections for those countries and years where data do not exist for the reference year. This approach requires a decision on the interval of interest; whether consumption, income, or both can be used (for different countries); and how conservative or

not the analyst wants to be in terms of the surveys being close to the interval of interest. These are again not trivial decisions, as has been shown throughout this chapter, since all three choices will affect inferences about performance for each country in specific (and different) ways, making comparability complicated. As an example, in a recent application of this approach, Narayan, Yoshida, and Mistiaen (2013) chose the time interval to be the five-year period between 2005 and 2010. For the choice of living standards measure, the authors use annualized average growth rates in per capita real income and consumption, which has the advantage of increasing the number of countries in the pooled sample. Finally, growth rates for the bottom 40 percent are calculated only for those countries meeting the following survey criteria: (a) the latest household survey for a given country is no older than 2008; (b) the survey year for the initial period is close to $(t_1 - 5)$ within a bandwidth of ± 2 years; and (c) living standards aggregates (consumption or income) for both years within a country are comparable. Based on these rules, the final set of countries only covers 79 of a potential 150 countries in PovcalNet, comprised to a large extent of countries in Latin America and the Caribbean and Eastern Europe and Central Asia.

What is the take-away message of all this? First, use of actual surveys is more sensible for estimating shared prosperity. Second, whatever assumptions can be made from the use of existing surveys, making cross-country comparisons on the performance of shared prosperity should be done with considerable caution, since the results for a given performance can differ depending on which rules are used. In addition, although the notion of an aggregate global or regional measure of shared prosperity is indeed appealing, given the data limitations, its interpretation would be misleading. Whatever decisions are made, shared prosperity should remain a country-specific goal, and each country should decide on the specific goals and metrics by which to monitor its performance over time.

can provide a gauge as to whether people at the bottom are doing better or worse than the average (or, in practice, the top 60 percent of the population). Moreover, changes in shared prosperity can be driven as much by changes in inequality as by changes in national growth. A nice way to illustrate this is to decompose the change in shared prosperity between two years into two parts: the change in the average income of the bottom 40 percent is a combination of change in the share of the total income accruing to the poorest 40 percent and change in the average income for the population as a whole—in other words, differences in how much of the total pie the bottom 40 percent has managed to accrue and how quickly the overall pie has grown.[9]

Figure 2.9 shows an approximation of this decomposition of the shared prosperity indicator across 69 countries from around 2006 to 2011. The graph plots the annual growth in household survey mean income or consumption expenditure against the annual growth in the share of total income or consumption accruing to the bottom 40 percent in each

**Figure 2.9    Growth and changing shares of income**

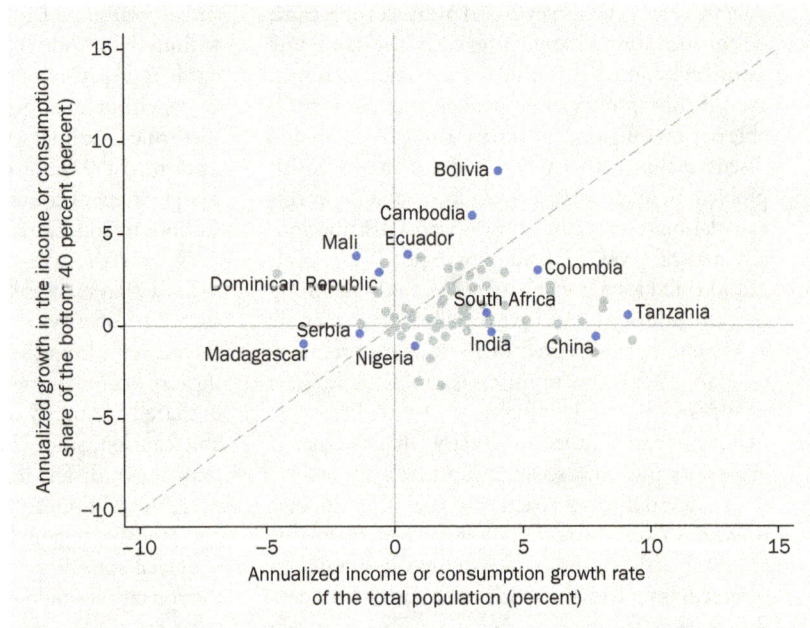

*Source:* Based on data from the World Bank PovcalNet database (accessed August 2014).
*Note:* Growth rates in shared prosperity are calculated as annualized growth rates in per capita income or consumption expenditure over the period of circa 2006–11. See note to figure 2.8 for further explanations.

country. The decomposition can illustrate the range of country experiences in terms of the source of the changes in shared prosperity. For example, in Colombia, South Africa, and Tanzania, growth in mean incomes contributed a larger part to the overall increase in shared prosperity than the increase in the share of total income accrued by the bottom 40 percent. By contrast, in countries such as Bolivia, Cambodia, and Ecuador, increases in the share of income accruing to the bottom 40 percent was the factor that contributed more to shared prosperity as opposed to the increase in overall mean growth. In countries such as China or India, boosting shared prosperity was a result of high overall growth in mean income, compensating small declines in the share accrued to the bottom 40 percent. Finally, in Madagascar and Serbia, overall shared prosperity decreased, driven by a reduction in both overall mean incomes as well as the share component.

In general, these insights showcase how cross-country comparisons should be treated with some caution, as equivalent performances could be the result of different economic processes at play. More conceptually, although policies that promote overall growth can be beneficial for the bottom 40 percent, increased participation of the bottom 40 percent is an alternative way to boost shared prosperity. The shared prosperity goal itself is agnostic on whether changes in shared prosperity should come from changes in growth or changes in inequality. However, this review of past experience shows that different combinations have played a role in boosting shared prosperity in different countries. This is an important aspect of tracking shared prosperity, as it can inform how changes in this mix influence living standards for the bottom 40 percent.

## Can boosting shared prosperity help end global poverty?

As chapter 1 shows, solely accelerating GDP per capita growth rates will not suffice to reduce global poverty to 3 percent by 2030. Is there a link between poverty reduction, shared prosperity, and overall growth? Dollar, Kleineberg, and Kraay (2013) argue that overall income growth accounts for most of the variation in income growth of the bottom 40 percent, thereby suggesting that overall prosperity and shared prosperity are closely related. Skoufias, Tiwari, and Shidiq (2014) also find a strong positive correlation between the growth rate of overall consumption and the growth rate of the consumption of the bottom 40 percent across provinces in

## Box 2.5   Does inequality affect income growth "equally"?

In their paper, van der Weide and Milanovic (2014) explore the relationship between initial inequality and subsequent growth at various parts of the income distribution. As they note, the fact that many studies do not find a systematic relationship between inequality and growth could be driven by the simple insight that most studies explore how inequality is associated with growth of the *average* income as opposed to growth at *different parts* of the distribution. This is what they set out to explore with data from the United States covering five decades between 1960 and 2010. Specifically, they assess the impact of overall inequality, as well as inequality among the poor and among the rich, on the growth rates along various percentiles of the income distribution.

Three sets of results stand out. First, among the poor, overall initial inequality is negatively correlated with subsequent growth. By contrast, the correlation is positive among the rich. Second, these associations suggest large income growth effects among the poor: a one standard deviation reduction of the overall Gini (0.04 points) would imply a doubling of the growth of the bottom 10 percent of the population (from an annualized 0.8 percent to 1.7 percent), while the effect of the inequality reduction for the richest 10 percent is muted, at only 0.3 percent (from 2.0 percent to 1.7 percent). Finally, the authors find similar trends when they separately test whether initial inequality in the bottom or top 40 percentiles affects subsequent income growth: both top and bottom inequalities are negatively associated with real income growth for the poor, while bottom inequality is positively associated with the income growth for the rich (no association is found between top inequality and income for the rich).

*Source:* Based on van der Weide and Milanovic (2014).

Thailand. They find a significant negative correlation between changes in overall inequality at the province level and the growth rate of consumption of the bottom 40 percent, suggesting that reductions in overall inequality may have an impact on the consumption growth of the poor. Similar results are found in developed settings, as in the case of the United States, in van der Weide and Milanovic (2014; box 2.5).

As figure 2.9 indicates, strong overall growth performance is indeed good for the bottom 40 percent. This is confirmed directly in figure 2.10: the same data from around 2006 to 2011 show a positive association between the income growth of the bottom 40 percent and growth in average income. A correlation coefficient of 0.82 suggests that the relationship is strong. However, this correlation also implies that overall growth does not fully explain changes in shared prosperity, which is consistent with the discussion of figure 2.9. In fact, the mean growth rate of mean income of the bottom 40 percent across this sample of 69 countries was 3.6 percent, higher than the 2.6 percent per capita income growth of the overall

**Figure 2.10  Shared prosperity and average income growth**

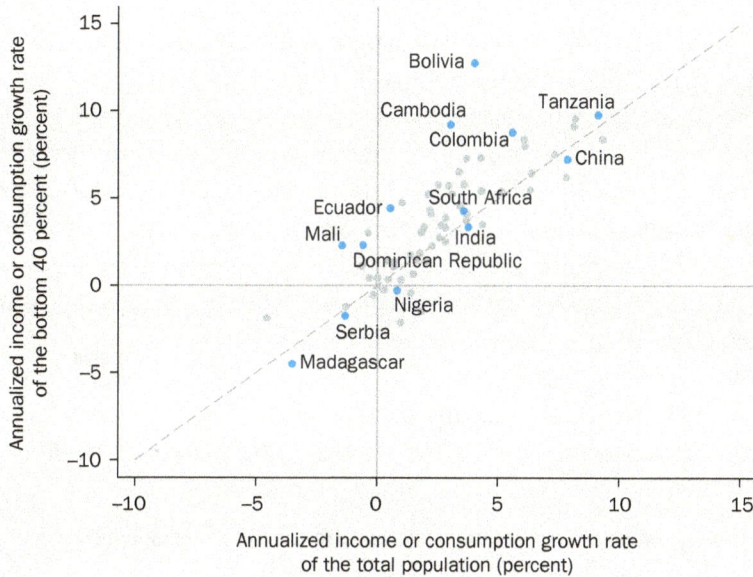

*Source:* Based on data from the World Bank PovcalNet database (accessed August 2014).
*Note:* Growth rates in shared prosperity are calculated as annualized growth rates in per capita income or consumption expenditure over the period of circa 2006–11 (all survey based). See note to figure 2.8 for further explanations.

population (in line with preliminary estimates done by Narayan, Saavedra-Chanduvi, and Tiwari [2013]). During this period, the bottom 40 percent experienced higher growth rates compared with the overall population in 48 of the 69 countries in the sample. Interestingly, these trends contrast earlier results (for example see Dollar and others 2014) that show a more distribution-neutral nature of growth for similar spells (in length) during the last few decades. It is not clear to what extent these recent trends represent a departure from the previous patterns and if they will continue. But, the likelihood of achieving the poverty goal is certainly improved if this trend continues, as chapter 1 illustrates that growth alone is unlikely to be sufficient to reach the 3-percent goal.

Given the relationship between shared prosperity and growth, how does shared prosperity relate to poverty reduction? A high correlation between shared prosperity and poverty reduction is expected, given that the bottom 40 percent of many countries overlaps strongly with those below the poverty line (as shown in figure 2.3). In addition, as chapter 1 and the discussion above suggest, both growth and inequality reduction—which are interconnected with shared prosperity—are closely interlinked with poverty reduction.

Figure 2.11 shows the annual change in the poverty headcount rate using the $1.25 international poverty line against the annual growth rate of household income or consumption for the total population (panel a) and the bottom 40 percent (panel b) for the same set of 69 countries and time interval (2006 to 2011). The figure differentiates the countries by poverty rate in the initial period, with a larger circle denoting a higher initial poverty rate. The correlation between overall income or consumption growth and poverty reduction as well as the correlation between shared prosperity and poverty reduction are strong (and negative) but imperfect.

A comparison of the panels can also help explore whether shared prosperity is particularly relevant for poverty reduction. In order to evaluate this, two regressions are done: regressing the change in the poverty

**Figure 2.11** The association of poverty reduction with overall income growth and shared prosperity

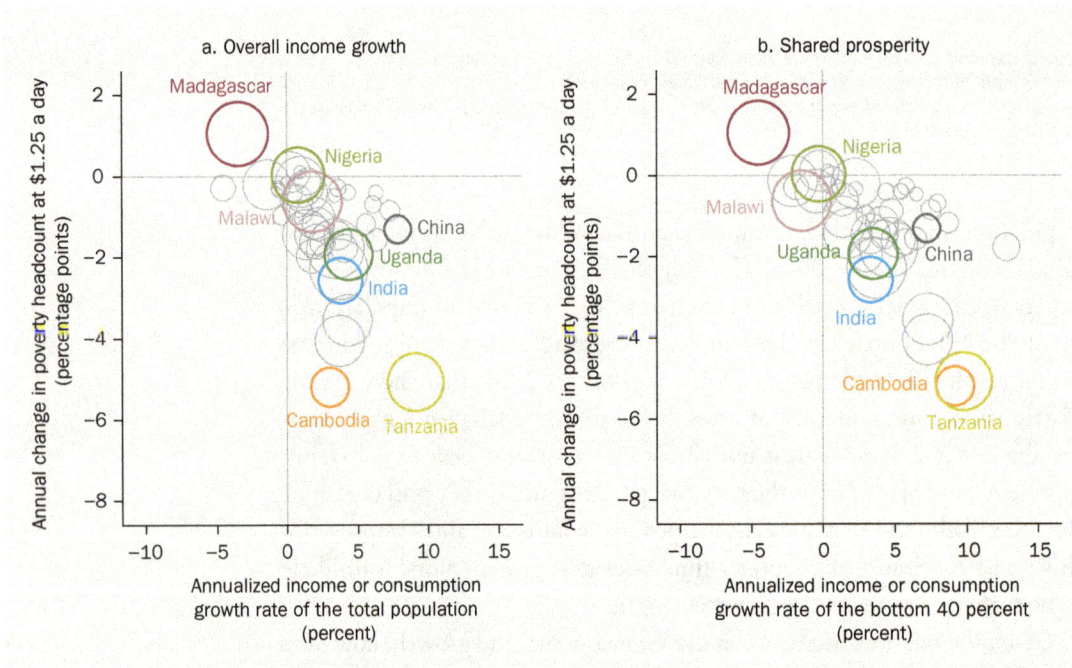

*Source:* Based on data from the World Bank PovcalNet database (accessed August 2014).
*Note:* The size of the circles in the figure denotes poverty headcount rate in the initial period. Growth rates in shared prosperity are calculated as annualized growth rates in per capita income or consumption expenditure over the period of circa 2006–11. See note to figure 2.8 for further explanations. Excluding countries with an initial poverty headcount rate below 3 percent.

headcount first on the growth of mean income or consumption for the population as a whole and then on the growth of mean income or consumption for the bottom 40 percent of the population. This reveals that the slopes of the two lines are not statistically different from each other, but the goodness of fit as measured by the R-squared is higher for growth of the bottom 40 percent than for growth of the population as a whole. This suggests that growth in shared prosperity explains more of the variation in observed changes in poverty.[10] Although this evidence is not causal, it does suggest that boosting shared prosperity could be particularly relevant for poverty reduction.

Finally, to explore the relationship between shared prosperity and poverty reduction explicitly, this section ends by posing the following question: how would global poverty in 2030 change if countries performed well by boosting shared prosperity? As chapter 1 shows, even the most aspirational growth scenario (assuming each country will grow at the rate of its best growth episode during the past 20 years) does not manage to bring poverty down to the goal of 3 percent globally. This section revisits the simulations by extending the projections to include scenarios where both growth and the distribution of growth change. Table 2.1 presents the results.

As a benchmark, the first column in table 2.1 assumes that each country grows at its annualized growth rate over the last 10 years (with no changes in the distribution of growth). In this scenario, the extreme poverty headcount among developing countries by 2030 would be 5.6 percent, while the global headcount would be 4.8 percent.

Now, consider a scenario where each country again grows at its annualized growth rate over the last 10 years, but this time the bottom percentiles grow faster than those at the top. For this simulation, in each country, the same growth incidence curve is imposed using the respective regional best performers in terms of relative pro-poorness while maintaining the country-specific annualized growth rate projection fixed. The incidence curves are chosen based on the difference between growth of the bottom 40 percent relative to the mean while trying to maximize comparability of data and periods. For this simulation, the best performers in their respective regions are Brazil (2001 to 2009), Jordan (2003 to 2011), Rwanda (2000 to 2011), Sri Lanka (2002 to 2010), and Thailand (2000 to 2010). In all these spells, the bottom 40 percent grew faster than the mean, with the difference ranging between 0.34 percentage points in Rwanda and 3.20 percentage points in Brazil.[11] The growth incidence of these countries is then imposed on the 44 countries used for the exercise up to 2030 while

**Table 2.1**   Reaching the 2030 extreme poverty goal in a world of higher shared prosperity

*(percent of population below $1.25-a-day poverty line)*

| Region | Scenario 1.<br>10-year growth rate with actual income distributions | Scenario 2.<br>10-year growth rate with income distributions of the best regional performers | Scenario 3.<br>10-year growth rate with income distributions of the best regional performers and additional 1% growth in Sub-Saharan Africa |
|---|---|---|---|
| East Asia and the Pacific | 0.3 | 0.2 | 0.2 |
| Europe and Central Asia | 0.0 | 0.0 | 0.0 |
| Latin America and the Caribbean | 3.2 | 1.5 | 1.5 |
| Middle East and North Africa | 1.1 | 1.1 | 1.1 |
| South Asia | 1.6 | 0.3 | 0.3 |
| Sub-Saharan Africa | 23.9 | 22.6 | 16.5 |
| Total developing world | 5.6 | 4.7 | 3.6 |
| World | 4.8 | 4.1 | 3.1 |

*Source:* Based on data from the World Bank PovcalNet database (accessed August 2014).

*Note:* The three scenarios present year 2030 projections of headcount poverty rates using the $1.25-a-day international poverty line. Scenario 1 assumes that each country grows at its historical 10-year national accounts growth rate. Scenarios 2 and 3 assume distributional changes in all 44 countries that are projected to have more than one million poor people in 2030 when distributions remain unchanged. Scenario 2 assumes that countries will grow at the same historical 10-year national accounts growth rate, but that the bottom of the income (or consumption) distribution benefits relatively more from growth than the top of the distribution. The incidence of growth in each country is determined by the observed past growth incidence curve of a regional leader over the past 10 years in terms of growth of the bottom 40 percent relative to mean growth. Poverty headcounts in 2030 are then projected by combining incidence curves with country-specific regional growth rates. Scenario 3 adds the assumption that national accounts growth in Sub-Saharan Africa is 1 percentage point faster than over the past 10 years. Also see endnote 11.

maintaining country-specific overall projected annualized growth rates. To simplify the exercise, rather than considering all developing countries, the estimation focuses only on changes in the 44 countries that contribute the most to the global headcount in 2030 and that have populations of more than one million poor people. The results can thus be seen as a lower bound to the distributional effect.[12]

In this scenario of higher shared prosperity, the extreme poverty headcount for developing countries is decreased by an additional percentage point to 4.7 percent, while the global headcount decreases to 4.1 percent. Although these outcomes are significantly better, distributional shifts do not close the gap to reach the 3 percent goal compared with the growth-alone scenario. A primary reason seems to be that although this scenario contributes to faster poverty reduction in middle-income countries, particularly in Latin America and the Caribbean and South Asia, it does not help to decrease poverty in low-income countries, particularly in Sub-Saharan Africa. This partly reflects that nature of the exercise: the distribution of income (consumption) of the regional leader in Sub-Saharan Africa (Rwanda) is significantly less progressive than that of the regional leader in Latin America and the Caribbean (Brazil), thus the simulated impact of the exercise for countries in Sub-Saharan Africa is smaller. In addition, countries in Sub-Saharan Africa experienced zero or even negative per capita growth rates during the period the simulation covers. For these countries, the potential impact on poverty reduction from distributing a small amount of growth more widely is clearly limited.

To demonstrate the particular sensitivity of poverty reduction in Sub-Saharan Africa to overall growth, a third scenario illustrates how much additional impact on poverty can be achieved by twinning improved growth performance with a more pro-poor incidence of growth. Table 2.1 therefore presents an additional scenario, which adds to scenario 2 an extra assumption of 1 percentage point additional growth in Sub-Saharan African countries. In this scenario, the global headcount falls to the vicinity of 3 percent of the world's population; the global extreme poverty goal is reached.

Figure 2.12 provides two additional simulations. Each country's initial mean is projected to grow between 2011 and 2030 following the historical annualized growth rate over the last 10 years (similar to simulation 1 in table 2.1). The two new simulations add the twist that the bottom 40 percent of the distribution grows faster than the top 60 percent of the distribution, while preserving the growth in the mean.

If the growth rate of the bottom 40 percent is assumed to be 1 percentage point greater than the growth rate of the mean, the global extreme poverty headcount would decrease by an additional 1.1 percentage points relative to the scenario where all incomes grow at the annualized growth rate over the last 10 years (figure 2.12, red line).[13] With even higher shared prosperity of 2 percentage points above the mean, the global 3 percent poverty target would be reached by 2028. Thus, twinning growth with improvements in shared prosperity can make the difference in closing the gap to meet the global poverty target.

Regionally, however, the picture is not that simple. While shared prosperity can have a significant effect on the global headcount, particularly in a context where growth is low, Sub-Saharan Africa stands out as an

**Figure 2.12**  Twinning growth and shared prosperity to reach the 2030 extreme poverty goal

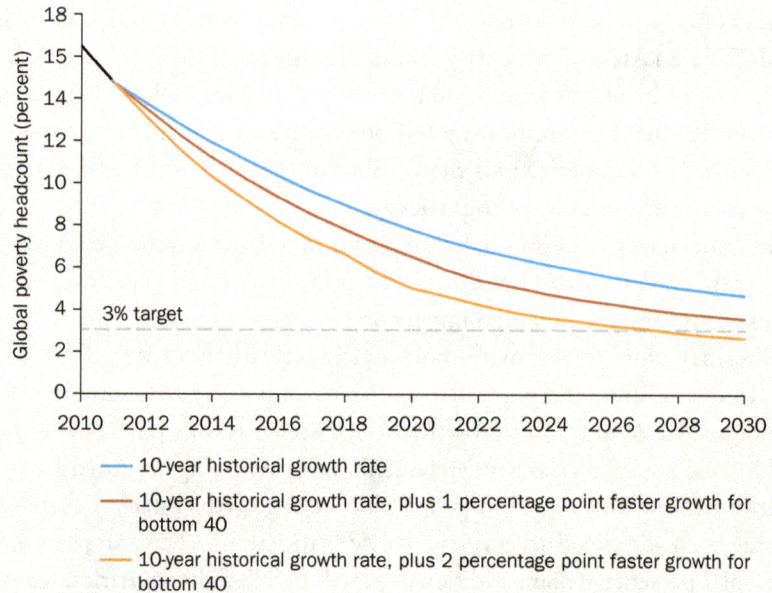

*Source:* Based on data from the World Bank PovcalNet database (accessed August 2014).
*Note:* The three scenarios present projections from 2011 to 2030 of the global poverty headcount using the $1.25-a-day international poverty line. Scenario 1 (blue line) assumes that each country grows at its historical 10-year national accounts growth rate. Past national accounts growth rates are calculated as the annualized growth rate of real GDP per capita (countries in Sub-Saharan Africa) or the annualized growth rate of household final consumption expenditure per capita (all other countries) over the period 2000–10 (see also notes to table 1.4 in chapter 1). Scenario 2 (red line) assumes that the bottom 40 percent have an annualized 19-year growth rate (between 2011 and 2030) that is 1 percentage point greater than the annualized growth in the mean over this period. Scenario 3 (orange line) repeats scenario 2 but with a growth differential of 2 percentage points.

exception. Distributional shifts in this region's countries would contribute relatively less to reducing the regional headcount. Chapter 1 shows that projecting the annualized growth from the 2000s would bring the proportion of the poor in Sub-Saharan Africa from 46.8 percent to 23.9 percent. If the bottom 40 percent grows 1 or 2 percentage points faster than the mean, this would reduce the regional headcount by an additional 4 or 8 percentage points, respectively. Although this effect is greater than the simulation based on regional best performers, it still suggests that extreme poverty rates would remain very high in Sub-Saharan Africa under all of the simulations considered.

Overall, these results point to the inherent complementarities between the World Bank's two goals whereby a combination of substantial growth and comparatively higher growth rates of the income of the bottom 40 percent could significantly improve the chances of reaching the global headcount goal of 3 percent.

## Key conclusions on shared prosperity

This chapter has explored the conceptual and empirical underpinnings of the World Bank's new shared prosperity goal. Five take-away messages stand out. First, the shared prosperity goal seeks to increase sensitivity to distributional issues, shifting the common understanding of development progress away from per capita income and emphasizing that good growth should benefit not just the wealthiest, but the least well-off in society as well. Although distributional issues have been part of the development debate for decades, this is the first time that an indicator with close links to inequality of outcomes (incomes) has become a benchmark of development progress.

Second, unlike the global poverty goal, boosting shared prosperity is a country-specific goal with no explicit target. This has an inherent simplicity in that countries can track their own performance and have different aspirational targets. Still, interpreting performance at the country level may not be straightforward in the absence of a clear standard of what constitutes "good" performance. Looking at trends in shared prosperity over time and comparing the average income growth of the bottom 40 percent with the rest of the population over time provide two simple ways of assessing performance.

Third, the goal is relevant for poor countries. In low- and lower-middle-income countries, there will likely be significant overlap between those living in absolute poverty and the bottom 40 percent of the population. Boosting shared prosperity should therefore reinforce poverty reduction efforts in these countries. In doing so, the added emphasis to improve the living standards of the poor may be instrumental for achieving the ambitious goal of ending global poverty. As the evidence in chapter 1 suggests, growth in GDP in the most optimistic scenarios will not be sufficient to reach the 3 percent global poverty target unless a structural shift happens. This chapter indicates that a scenario with higher shared prosperity can facilitate reaching the extreme poverty goal. At the same time, the chapter makes clear that transformational changes in growth and shared prosperity are needed to reach the poverty goal: repeating historical performance is not enough.

Fourth, the goal is also relevant for richer countries. A substantial proportion of the bottom 40 percent of the population in upper-middle-income countries is likely to be nonpoor by the $1.25 per day global standard. The shared prosperity focus in these settings will bring attention to those not covered by poverty policies but who might otherwise be relatively left behind and highly vulnerable to reentering poverty if shocks affect them.

Finally, many challenges in measuring and tracking shared prosperity remain. Monitoring the goal requires high-quality and frequent household survey data. Issues of comparability across surveys—relevant also for consistently tracking global poverty—become more pronounced when looking at the performance of shared prosperity. Given that estimates of shared prosperity are sensitive to the time period and intervals used, comparisons over time should be treated with caution. It is advisable to take advantage of all information (for example, calculating moving averages in shared prosperity when feasible). Cross-country comparisons should also be treated with caution. The frequency and quality of household survey data across the world are heterogeneous, with some countries having a considerable way to go in producing the consistent and reliable data needed to track shared prosperity over time. Supporting these efforts is an important policy priority.

## Notes

1. This chapter uses income and consumption interchangeably, although, as chapter 1 notes, consumption is the preferred choice.
2. The official World Bank approach endorses use of the mean of the bottom 40 percent of the population, but it is worth noting that IDA17's Results Measurement Framework has instead adopted the *median* income growth rate of the bottom 40 percent as an indicator of progress (World Bank 2014a).
3. Chapter 3 provides a more in-depth discussion of these issues. A discussion of the axiomatic requirements of welfare functions can also be found in Foster and others (2013) and Campbell and Kelly (2002).
4. The concept of people living on between $4 and $10 a day being considered vulnerable is based on evidence that a considerable share of households above a given poverty line is usually vulnerable to falling below that line over time. See López-Calva and Ortiz-Juarez (2014); Ferreira and others (2012); and Birdsall, Lustig, and Meyer (2014).
5. The World Bank regions have begun producing operational reports that provide more detailed profiles of the bottom 40 percent in each country (see World Bank 2014b, Rama and others 2014, or Bussolo and López-Calva 2014).

6.  See also Beegle and others (2014) for a discussion of the potential trade-offs.
7.  For the technically curious, this is a case where the weak transfer axiom discussed earlier in this chapter comes into play.
8.  Official estimates of shared prosperity will be published in the forthcoming *Global Monitoring Report*.
9.  Chenery and others (1974) discuss these issues in the context of overall growth. See Rosenblatt and McGavock (2013) for a more recent discussion.
10. The results hold when the regressions are weighted by the initial poverty headcount.
11. These are not based on the official shared prosperity estimates.
12. Three other caveats should be noted. First, the estimates are mostly based on consumption data, which typically present lower inequality values because savings uniformly increase with income. The consumption share of the top earners is not as high as their income share. The effects of distributional changes in income could therefore be considerably higher than shown for consumption. Second, the estimates are very sensitive to missing data on top earners, as the latter contribute significantly—and proportionally—more to average income, which directly biases upward the difference between growth in the bottom 40 percent and that of the mean. Finally, since distributive government social expenditures such as in health and education are not always captured in consumption surveys, important government inequality-reducing tools are not captured in this framework.
13. To ensure that the mean growth rate is equal to the historical 10-year average, the growth rate of the top 60 percent is adjusted downward to compensate for the faster growth of the bottom 40 percent. In some cases, the differential growth rates lead to a reranking of incomes across the 40th percentile of the distribution. To account for the reranking, the growth rate differential between the bottom 40 percent and the mean in each year is assumed to be somewhat greater than 1 percentage point, so that the measured (ex post) annual growth rate differential between 2011 and 2030 is equal to exactly 1 percentage point.

## References

Basu, Kaushik. 2001. "On the Goals of Development." In *Frontiers of Development Economics: The Future in Perspective*, edited by Gerald M. Meier and Joseph E. Stiglitz, 61–86. Washington, DC, and New York: World Bank and Oxford University Press.

———. 2006. "Globalization, Poverty, and Inequality: What Is the Relationship? What Can Be Done?" *World Development* 34 (8): 1361–73. doi:10.1016/j.worlddev.2005.10.009.

Beegle, Kathleen, Pedro Olinto, Carlos E. Sobrado, Hiroki Uematsu, and Yeon Soo Kim. 2014. "Ending Extreme Poverty and Promoting Shared Prosperity: Could There Be Trade-Offs Between These Two Goals?" *Inequality in Focus* 3 (1): 1–6.

Birdsall, Nancy, Nora Lustig, and Christian J. Meyer. 2014. "The Strugglers: The New Poor in Latin America?" *World Development* 60 (August): 132–46. doi:10.1016/j.worlddev.2014.03.019.

Bussolo, Maurizio, and López-Calva, Luis F. 2014. *Shared Prosperity: Paving the Way in Europe and Central Asia*. Washington, DC: World Bank Group.

Campbell, Donald E., and Jerry S. Kelly. 2002. "Impossibility Theorems in the Arrovian Framework." In *Handbook of Social Choice and Welfare*, 1: 35–94. Handbooks in Economics 19. Amsterdam: North-Holland.

Chenery, Hollis B., Montek S. Ahluwalia, C. L. G. Bell, John H. Duloy, and Richard Jolly. 1974. *Redistribution with Growth: Policies to Improve Income Distribution in Developing Countries in the Context of Economic Growth*. London: Oxford University Press.

Deaton, Angus. 1997. *The Analysis of Household Surveys: A Microeconometric Approach to Development Policy*. Baltimore, MD: Johns Hopkins University Press.

Deaton, Angus, and Salman Zaidi. 2002. "Guidelines for Constructing Consumption Aggregates for Welfare Analysis." Living Standards Measurement Study Working Paper 135, World Bank, Washington, DC.

Dollar, David, Tatjana Kleineberg, and Aart Kraay. 2013. "Growth Still Is Good for the Poor." Policy Research Working Paper 6568, World Bank, Washington, DC.

Essama-Nssah, B., and Peter J. Lambert. 2009. "Measuring Pro-Poorness: A Unifying Approach with New Results." *Review of Income and Wealth* 55 (3): 752–78. doi:10.1111/j.1475-4991.2009.00335.x.

Ferreira, Francisco H. G., Julian Messina, Jamele Rigolini, Luis-Felipe López-Calva, Maria Ana Lugo, and Renos Vakis. 2012. *Economic Mobility and the Rise of the Latin American Middle Class*. Washington, DC: World Bank.

Foster, James E., Suman Seth, Michael Lokshin, and Zurab Sajaia. 2013. *A Unified Approach to Measuring Poverty and Inequality: Theory and Practice; Streamlined Analysis with ADePT Software*. Washington, DC: World Bank.

Kakwani, Nanak Chand, and Ernesto M. Pernia. 2000. "What Is Pro-Poor Growth?" *Asian Development Review* 18 (1): 1–16.

Klasen, Stephan. 2004. "In Search of the Holy Grail: How to Achieve Pro-Poor Growth?" In *Proceedings from the Annual World Bank Conference on Development Economics—Europe, 2003: Toward Pro-Poor Policies: Aid, Institutions, and Globalization*, edited by Bertil Tungodden, Nicholas Stern, and Ivar Kolstad, 63–93. Washington, DC, and New York: World Bank and Oxford University Press.

———. 2008. "Economic Growth and Poverty Reduction: Measurement Issues Using Income and Non-Income Indicators." *World Development* 36 (3): 420–45. doi:10.1016/j.worlddev.2007.03.008.

Kraay, Aart. 2006. "When Is Growth Pro-Poor? Evidence from a Panel of Countries." *Journal of Development Economics* 80 (1): 198–227. doi:10.1016/j.jdeveco.2005.02.004.

Lakner, Christoph, and Branko Milanovic. 2013. "Global Income Distribution: From the Fall of the Berlin Wall to the Great Recession." Policy Research Working Paper 6719, World Bank, Washington, DC.

López-Calva, Luis F., and Eduardo Ortiz-Juarez. 2014. "A Vulnerability Approach to the Definition of the Middle Class." Journal of Economic Inequality: 12(21), 23–47.

McNamara, Robert S. 1972. *Annual Address to the 1972 Annual Meetings of the Boards of Governors*. Washington, DC: International Bank for Reconstruction and Development, International Finance Corporation, International Development Association.

Narayan, Ambar, Jaime Saavedra-Chanduvi, and Sailesh Tiwari. 2013. "Shared Prosperity. Links to Growth, Inequality and Inequality of Opportunity." Policy Research Working Paper 6649, World Bank, Washington, DC.

Narayan, Ambar, Nobuo Yoshida, and Johan A. Mistiaen. 2013. "Computing Shared Prosperity Indicator for a Global Database." Unpublished manuscript, World Bank, Washington, DC.

Negre, Mario. 2010. "Concepts and Operationalization of Pro-Poor Growth." WIDER Working Paper 2010/47, United Nations University, Helsinki.

Palma, José Gabriel. 2011. "Homogeneous Middles vs. Heterogeneous Tails, and the End of the 'Inverted-U': It's All About the Share of the Rich." *Development and Change* 42 (1): 87–153. doi:10.1111/j.1467-7660.2011.01694.x.

Rama, Martin, Tara Beteille, Yue Li, John Newman, and Pradeep Mitra. 2014. *Inequality in South Asia*. Washington, DC: World Bank Group.

Ravallion, Martin. 1994. *Poverty Comparisons*. Fundamentals of Pure and Applied Economics 56. Chur, Switzerland: Harwood Academic Publishers.

Ravallion, Martin, and Shaohua Chen. 2003. "Measuring Pro-Poor Growth." *Economics Letters* 78 (1): 93–99. doi:10.1016/S0165-1765(02)00205-7.

Ravallion, Martin, Shaohua Chen, and Prem Sangraula. 2009. "Dollar a Day Revisited." *The World Bank Economic Review* 23 (2): 163–84. doi:10.1093/wber/lhp007.

Rawls, John. 1971. *A Theory of Justice*. Cambridge, MA: Belknap Press of Harvard University Press.

Rosenblatt, David, and Tamara J. McGavock. 2013. "A Note on the Simple Algebra of the Shared Prosperity Indicator." Policy Research Working Paper 6645, World Bank, Washington, DC.

Sen, Amartya. 1983. "Development: Which Way Now?" *The Economic Journal* 93 (372): 745–62. doi:10.2307/2232744.

———. 1985. *Commodities and Capabilities*. Amsterdam: North-Holland.

———. 1999. *Development as Freedom*. Oxford: Oxford University Press.

Skoufias, Emmanuel, Sailesh Tiwari, and Akhmad Rizal Shidiq. 2014. "Sharing Prosperity: The Poverty, Growth and Equity Nexus in Thailand." Policy Research Working Paper, World Bank, Washington, DC.

Slesnick, Daniel T. 1998. "Empirical Approaches to the Measurement of Welfare." *Journal of Economic Literature* 36 (4): 2108–65.

Son, Hyun Hwa. 2004. "A Note on Pro-Poor Growth." *Economics Letters* 82 (3): 307–14. doi:10.1016/j.econlet.2003.08.003.

Subramanian, Subbu. 2011. "'Inclusive Development' and the Quintile Income Statistic." *Economic and Political Weekly* XLVI (4): 69–72.

van der Weide, Roy, and Branko Milanovic. 2014. "Inequality Is Bad for Growth of the Poor (But Not for That of the Rich)." Policy Research Working Paper 6963, World Bank, Washington, DC.

World Bank. 1990. *World Development Report 1990: Poverty*. New York: Oxford University Press.

———. 2014a. Report from the Executive Directors of the International Development Association to the Board of Governors, Additions to IDA Resources: Seventeenth Replenishment—IDA17: Maximizing Development Impact. World Bank Group, Washington, DC.

———. 2014b. *Social Gains in the Balance: A Fiscal Policy Challenge for Latin America and the Caribbean*. Washington, DC: World Bank.

# CHAPTER THREE

# The Twin Goals in a Broader Context

The previous two chapters have discussed in detail the conceptual under-pinnings and data requirements of the World Bank's twin goals of eliminating global extreme poverty and promoting shared prosperity. This chapter provides further conceptual and empirical perspective on the twin goals by setting them in a broader context. While the twin goals set by the World Bank imply a particular set of institutional preferences or priorities across individuals, this does not mean that these should be the only valid priorities for all development partners. National governments, other aid donors, or any other group might choose to emphasize other priorities that best reflect their particular objectives.

The scope for such differences in priorities is perhaps clearest in the context of poverty measurement. Although the World Bank has placed emphasis on the fraction of people living below the global poverty line as a global objective, national governments attach priority to poverty thresholds that are relevant to their particular countries—as evidenced by large differences across countries in national poverty lines. Similarly, when analyzing poverty in a particular country, best practice quickly goes beyond the headcount measure of poverty to consider other poverty measures that capture the severity as well as the incidence of poverty.

The scope for different priorities can also be seen in the context of the shared prosperity measure, which ascribes particular importance to the share of total income that goes to the poorest 40 percent of people in a country. Yet the income share of the bottom 40 percent is just one of many measures of how equitably or inequitably income is distributed across individuals in a country. Different inequality measures imply very different priorities over individuals at different points in the income distribution. For some purposes, a country might choose to prioritize those in the bottom 20 percent, or even the bottom 90 percent, rather than the bottom 40 percent. Or it might choose to evaluate the benefit of a policy intervention in terms of its effects on individuals throughout the entire income distribution, with different weights for people at different income levels.

This chapter uses social welfare functions as a tool of analysis to set the twin goals in this broader context.[1] Economists have long used social welfare functions to capture societal preferences over how income is distributed across individuals in a society (box 3.1). The twin goals set by

## Box 3.1    Social welfare functions articulate priorities across individuals

The World Bank's twin goals of eliminating extreme poverty and boosting shared prosperity are two particular cases in a large class of *social welfare functions,* which economists have long used to represent preferences over how income is distributed across individuals.

Two key ingredients are required for this analysis:

- The first ingredient is the distribution of income across a population of interest (typically, a country). A convenient way of representing this is to use a *quantile function,* which gives the income level $y(p)$ corresponding to each percentile $p \in [0,100]$ of the income distribution in that country. The quantile function is the inverse of the cumulative distribution of income, that is, $y(p) = F^{-1}(p)$, where $F(y)$ is the distribution function of income and $F^{-1}(p)$ is the inverse of this function. The orange line in figure B3.1.1 shows a quantile function, which is upward sloping since poorer percentiles have lower income levels while richer percentiles have higher income levels. The steeper the quantile function is, the greater are the income gaps between the rich (those to the right in the graph) and the poor (those to the left).

- The second ingredient consists of the *welfare weights* that a given social welfare function assigns to different percentiles of the income distribution. The blue line in figure B3.1.1 shows a possible set of such welfare weights across percentiles, based on the income of each percentile, that is, $w(y(p))$. In this case, social preferences assign higher weights to the poor and lower weights to the rich. In other words, the welfare weights are downward sloping. These weights show the importance that a society assigns to individuals at different points in the income distribution. These in turn can be used to evaluate policies. For example, the downward-sloping welfare weights shown in the figure imply that this society would be in favor of policies that redistribute income from the rich to the poor. The extent of desired redistribution depends on the relative weights assigned to the poor versus the rich—the greater the weights assigned to the poor relative to the rich, the more redistribution is desired.

Based on these two ingredients, the social welfare function is the average of the welfare weights, represented as the shaded area below the blue line in figure B3.1.1—formally, $W = \int w(y(p))dp$. The

*(continued)*

## Box 3.1    Continued

**Figure B3.1.1    Income distributions and social welfare functions**

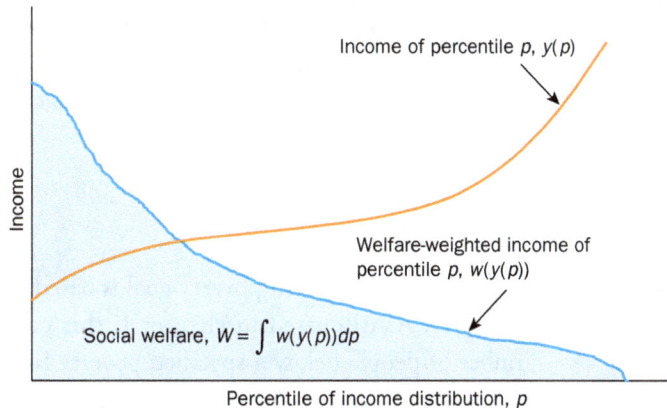

social welfare function illustrated in the figure assigns greater weights to those at lower percentiles of the income distribution. However, other social welfare functions may assign greater weight to the rich. For example, average income is itself an example of a social welfare function with increasing rather than decreasing weights. Since average income weights the incomes of everyone equally, it naturally assigns *greater* weight to those in richer percentiles of the income distribution, since richer percentiles have higher incomes. Intuitively, a 1 percent increase in the income of a rich person raises average income by more than a 1 percent increase in the income of a poor person does, since the absolute change in income of the rich person is larger.

The next section of this chapter discusses social welfare functions featuring a given poverty line, such as the headcount measure of poverty on which the World Bank's first goal is based. Such social welfare functions assign positive weights to those below the poverty line, but imply zero weight for those above the poverty line. This is because changes in the incomes of anyone above the poverty line do not affect the poverty measure. The following section then discusses social welfare functions that do not rely on a poverty line. Social welfare functions that value equality will assign higher weights to poorer percentiles. However, they may or may not assign positive weights throughout the entire distribution. For example, the World Bank's second goal is based on average incomes in the bottom 40 percent, which implies zero welfare weights for those above the 40th percentile of the income distribution. Finally, it is worth noting that these social welfare functions are chosen because of their links to standard poverty and inequality measures. In contrast, many theoretical models define welfare in terms of the present value of the lifetime utility of an agent, which will depend on all the ingredients in the particular model under consideration. The final section of this chapter discusses how such measures can be used to aggregate across different dimensions of well-being in a theory-consistent way.

the World Bank can be thought of as two particular cases of such social welfare functions and valuable insights about the twin goals can be learned by considering them in this broader context. Specifically, setting the twin goals in the context of a broader class of social welfare functions helps to clarify the precise institutional priorities implied by the goals and contrasts them with other potential priorities implied by other social welfare functions. The chapter also provides empirical perspective on the twin goals by documenting trends in the relevant measures and comparing them with the trends implied by other social welfare functions.

## Welfare functions with poverty lines

The World Bank's global poverty goal is based on the headcount measure of poverty. As discussed in chapter 1, this consists of counting up the number of people below a specified poverty line and expressing the sum as a fraction of the total population. By simply counting up the poor, this measure has the virtue of clarity, a key quality to crystalize political traction around goals. This clarity comes at a cost, however, since it provides no information on the well-being of those below the poverty line, beyond the fact that they are poor. The cases of Pakistan (in 2007) and Senegal (in 2005), shown in figure 3.1, provide a vivid illustration. In both countries, the proportion of the population living on less than $2 per day was the same, at 60 percent. However, average consumption levels below the poverty line were substantially lower in Senegal than in Pakistan. In the case of Pakistan, average consumption of the poor fell 60 cents short of the poverty line, whereas the shortfall in Senegal was considerably larger, at 82 cents.

Such differences in the distribution of income below the poverty line are not captured by the headcount measure of poverty, and so other distributionally sensitive measures are commonly used to capture how "deep" or "severe" poverty is. The Foster-Greer-Thorbecke (FGT) class of poverty measures is the most commonly used because of its straightforward interpretation.[2] The FGT class weights poor people according to their distance from the poverty line. Specifically, the weight assigned to each poor person is the gap between their income and the poverty line, expressed as a fraction of the poverty line, and raised to an exponent. When the exponent is zero, the index weights everyone below the poverty line equally, resulting in the headcount measure. When the exponent is one, the index is the

**Figure 3.1** The headcount provides an incomplete picture of well-being below the poverty line

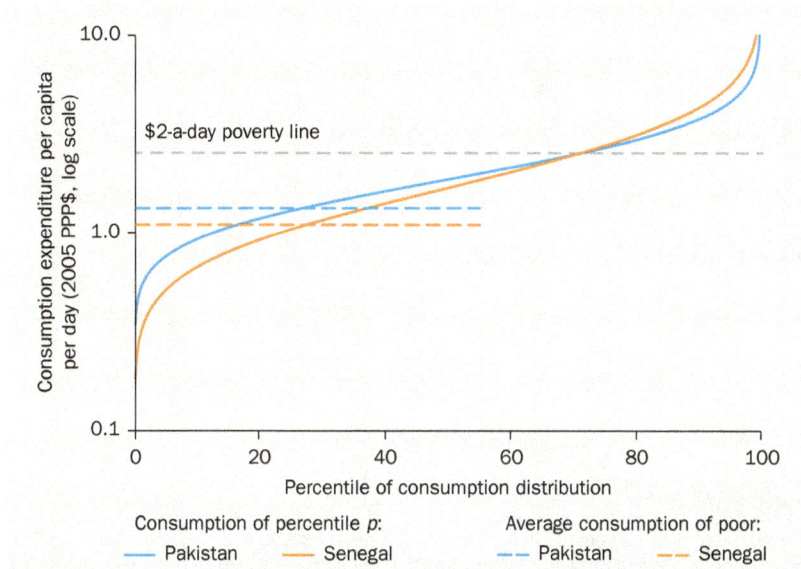

*Source:* Based on data from the World Bank PovcalNet database.
*Note:* This graph shows the distribution of consumption (on the vertical axis) for Pakistan in 2007 (the blue line) and Senegal in 2005 (the orange line). The horizontal gray line shows the $2-a-day line. The red and blue dashed lines show average income of those below the poverty line in Pakistan and Senegal, respectively. The consumption distributions are lognormal approximations to the true distributions. PPP = purchasing power parity.

average gap between the incomes of the poor and the poverty line, as a fraction of the poverty line. When the exponent is two, the measure is the squared poverty gap. By placing greater weight on those further below the poverty line, this measure also reflects inequality among the poor.

Figure 3.2 summarizes the weights that members of the FGT class of poverty measures assign to individuals in different percentiles of the income distribution. The headcount measure weights everyone below the poverty line equally. In contrast, the poverty gap and the squared poverty gap are social welfare functions that place successively higher weights on the poorest. These weights have important implications for policy choices. For a fixed amount of resources, if reducing the headcount is taken as the primary goal, the most effective use of funds would imply focusing on the poor nearest to the poverty line, so that as many of them as possible go over the poverty threshold and hence decrease the poverty headcount. This may not be ideal, however, because it biases poverty reduction efforts away

**Figure 3.2** Welfare weights implied by different poverty measures

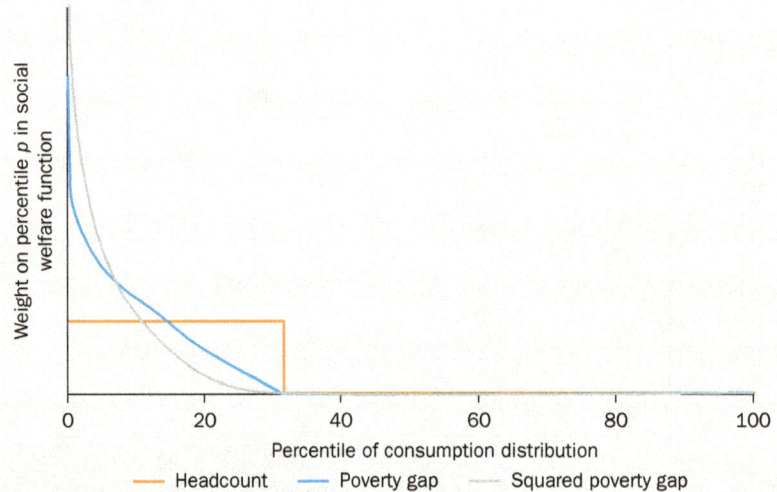

Source: Based on data from the Bangladesh Household Income and Expenditure Survey (2010).
Note: This graph plots the weights assigned by common poverty measures to individuals at different points in the income distribution. The weights are $w(y(p)) = I_{y(p)<z}\left(\dfrac{z - y(p)}{z}\right)^{\theta}$ with $\theta = 0$ for the headcount, $\theta = 1$ for the poverty gap, and $\theta = 2$ for the squared poverty gap. The weights have been normalized to sum to one, and are drawn for the observed distribution of household consumption expenditures in Bangladesh in 2010. The poverty line is set at 1,487 Bangladesh taka per month, which generates a headcount in 2010 of 31.5 percent.

from the poorest among the poor. Means-tested antipoverty programs can be thought of as a way of avoiding this problem. For example, food stamps (vouchers to be used for food purchases by the poor) are an important part of the social safety net in the United States. Food stamp benefits are means tested, in the sense that the value of the benefit declines as the incomes of the poor increase. Since this program provides a greater benefit to the poorest, it has a greater proportional impact on the poverty gap and the squared poverty gap than it does on the poverty headcount (Jolliffe and others 2005).

Figure 3.3 provides a systematic look at the practical consequences of these different approaches to weighting individuals below the poverty line, drawing on the most recent household survey available in the PovcalNet database. The figure shows recent data for 81 countries for which the $1.25 a day headcount measure of poverty constitutes at least 5 percent of the population. Panels a and b, respectively, graph the headcount and the poverty gap (on the vertical axis) against the logarithm of the household

**Figure 3.3**   **Different poverty measures fall with income, but tell different stories**

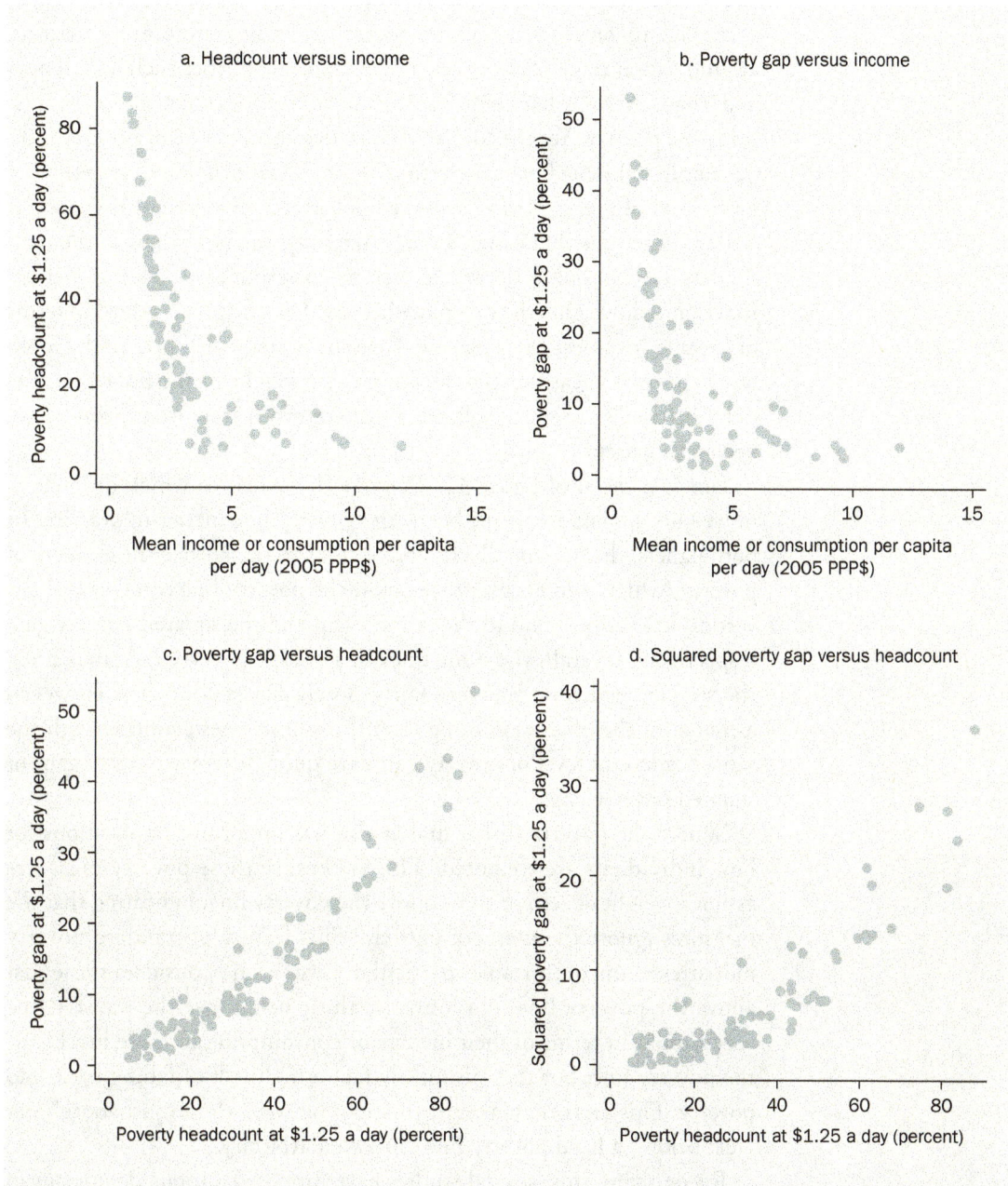

a. Headcount versus income

b. Poverty gap versus income

c. Poverty gap versus headcount

d. Squared poverty gap versus headcount

*Source:* Based on data from the World Bank PovcalNet database.
*Note:* Panels a and b graph the headcount and poverty gap against household survey mean income or consumption. Each data point corresponds to the most recently available survey in PovcalNet (as of July 2014) for a country. The sample is restricted to countries where the headcount ratio is greater than 5 percent of the population. PPP = purchasing power parity.

survey mean (on the horizontal axis). Both panels show a strong negative relationship: across countries, both measures of poverty fall sharply as average incomes increase. However, there is also substantial variation around this average relationship. For example, countries such as Ethiopia and Togo, in 2011, have similar levels of survey mean consumption, just below $2 per day. Yet the $1.25 a day headcount measure of poverty is 37 percent in Ethiopia but 52 percent in Togo. This variation in poverty at a given level of average living standards illustrates the value of using social welfare functions that assign greater weight to the poor than to the rich. As discussed in box 3.1, average income corresponds to a social welfare function that weights the rich more heavily than the poor. Judged in terms of average incomes, Ethiopia and Togo are equally well-off. Yet by looking at poverty measures that assign greater weight to the poor than the rich, differences in social welfare across countries at a given income level become apparent.

Panels c and d of figure 3.3 illustrate the extent to which differences in weights applied to people below the poverty line matter in practice. In both panels, the horizontal axis corresponds to the headcount measure of poverty (which weights everyone below the poverty line equally) and the vertical axes correspond to the poverty gap and the squared poverty gap, respectively. Overall, the more bottom-sensitive poverty measures track the simple headcount measure fairly closely across countries. However, as noted in the discussion of figure 3.1, in some cases countries with the same headcount level of poverty can have quite different poverty gaps or squared poverty gaps.

Where the poverty line is drawn also has important implications for how individuals are weighted. This is because these poverty measures assign a weight of zero to those above the poverty line, indicating that the measures ignore the nonpoor entirely. This feature of standard poverty measures is uncomfortable, particularly when one considers those just above the poverty line. Not only are those just above the poverty line very similar in terms of their income or consumption to those just below the poverty line, but they also likely face a high risk of falling back into poverty. This, in turn, makes distinctions between those "just above" and "just below" a fixed poverty line somewhat arbitrary.

Recognizing this, several studies have proposed various definitions of "vulnerability" to poverty, which seek to convey the sense that individuals currently above the poverty line face nonnegligible risks of falling back into poverty.[3] For example, López-Calva and Ortiz-Juarez (2011) define a *vulnerability zone* just above the poverty line. This zone is defined in terms of an income level above the poverty line where the risk of falling back into poverty is 10 percent or more over a five-year interval. This higher threshold income level is estimated with panel data on transitions into and out of poverty in Chile, Mexico, and Peru. For national poverty lines between $4 and $5 in terms of purchasing power parity (PPP), a vulnerability zone between the poverty line and a higher threshold of $10 PPP a day is estimated. López-Calva and Ortiz-Juarez find that this seems to correspond well with subjective self-assessments of the risk of falling into poverty. This approach has the appeal of explicitly recognizing poverty dynamics: individuals who are not poor in one period may very well become poor in the next period. At the same time, however, the approach is somewhat asymmetric, since it does not recognize that those who are poor in one period might become nonpoor in the next period.

A further drawback of a fixed poverty line is that the accompanying poverty measures may become less and less relevant over time, as countries grow richer and the fraction of the population below the poverty line falls. The same is true for a poverty line that is fixed across countries, as its relevance may be very different in countries at different income levels. For example, based on the World Bank's global poverty line, 71 percent of the population of Malawi was poor in 2011, while only 5 percent of Brazil's and 1 percent of Chile's populations were poor. Setting a fixed poverty line across countries implies different social welfare functions across countries. In the case of the headcount below the global poverty line, a fixed poverty line implies a particular concern for 71 percent of the population of Malawi but only 5 percent of the population of Brazil. Box 3.2 discusses how national poverty lines vary across countries, as well as proposals for a "weakly relative" international poverty line that varies with income levels.

## Beyond the poverty line: Social welfare functions that care about everyone

The discussion in the previous section focused on social welfare functions featuring a fixed poverty line. A key feature of these measures is that they assign zero weight to individuals above the poverty line. This section turns to social welfare functions that do not distinguish between "the poor" and "the nonpoor" but rather assign weights throughout the income distribution. The discussion here encompasses the second of the twin goals, in the

## Box 3.2  Where to draw the poverty line?

It is a common occurrence to see eyebrows rise when visitors from low per capita income countries are in a high per capita income country and read local poverty statistics in the media. The visitors find, to their surprise, that the figures are not far from the ones back at home. Based on national poverty lines, countries such as Greece, Romania, and Spain had poverty rates around 23 percent in 2012, slightly above the poverty rate in India based on national poverty lines. Since these European countries are vastly richer on average than India, these differences come from the fact that the national poverty lines used are very different.[a] Figure B3.2.1, panel a, shows that in the poorest

**Figure B3.2.1** Weakly relative poverty lines, and global poverty based on weakly relative lines

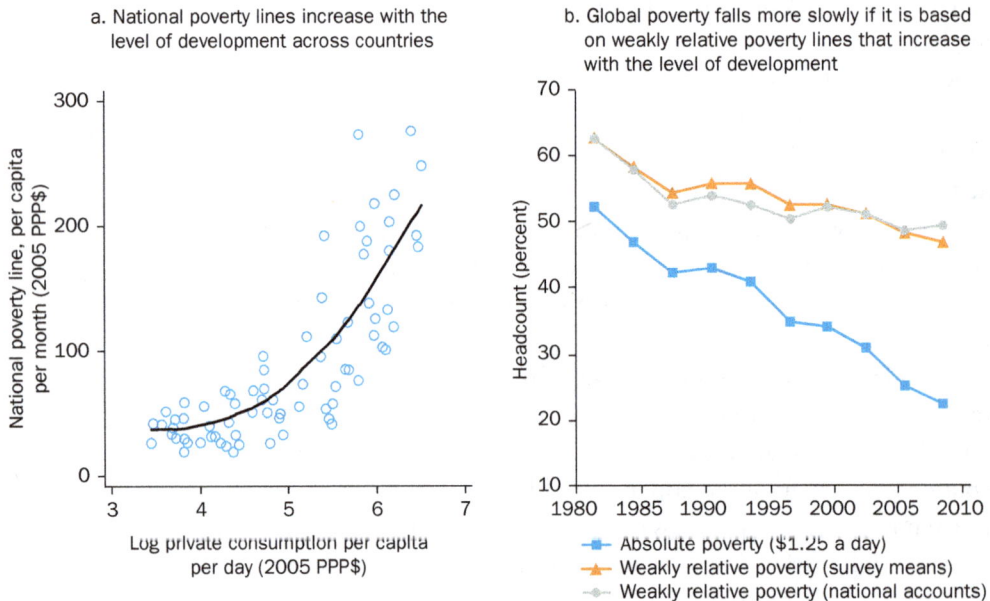

a. National poverty lines increase with the level of development across countries

b. Global poverty falls more slowly if it is based on weakly relative poverty lines that increase with the level of development

Absolute poverty ($1.25 a day)
Weakly relative poverty (survey means)
Weakly relative poverty (national accounts)

*Source:* Adapted from Ravallion, Chen, and Sangraula (2009); Ravallion and Chen (2011); Chen and Ravallion (2013).
*Note:* Solid line in panel a is a locally weighted regression smoother (lowess) with bandwidth = 0.8. PPP = purchasing power parity.

*(continued)*

sense that the average income of the bottom 40 percent of the population is not a social welfare function with a fixed poverty line. Like measures with a fixed line, the shared prosperity measure assigns zero weight to individuals in one part of the income distribution (those in the top 60 percent of the income distribution). However, this measure is just one particular

## Box 3.2    Continued

countries in the world, poverty lines are not very different and are unrelated to per capita incomes. After a certain point, however, national poverty lines tend to increase more or less in line with the level of national income. In European countries, a person is generally considered poor if his or her income falls below 60 percent of median income, so the poverty line automatically increases as median income increases.[b]

For the purpose of international comparisons, Ravallion, Chen, and Sangraula (2009) construct the World Bank's current global international poverty line of $1.25 a day at 2005 purchasing power parity by taking the mean of the poverty lines in the poorest 15 countries in terms of consumption per capita.[c] They show that this is quite robust to the choice of countries and that it is consistent with the fact that poverty lines in the poorest countries do not vary much. Chen and Ravallion (2013) and Ravallion and Chen (2011) bring together the two views by combining the global absolute poverty line of $1.25 for the poorest countries in the world with a "weakly relative poverty line" for richer countries, where the latter increases with per capita income (shown as the solid line in figure B3.2.1, panel a).[d]

Chen and Ravallion (2013) estimate the global poverty headcount based on this weakly relative

line and project it forward through 2030 (figure B3.2.1, panel b).[e] Global poverty is higher with the weakly relative line rather than the fixed global poverty line, since the weakly relative line implies higher poverty lines in richer countries. In addition, global poverty based on the weakly relative line declines more slowly over time, since poverty lines increase as countries' incomes increase over time.

*Sources:* Figures adapted from Ravallion, Chen, and Sangraula (2009); Ravallion and Chen (2011); and Chen and Ravallion (2013).

a. Government of India Planning Commission, in http://planningcommission.nic.in, visited on May 5, 2014; EUROSTAT, in http://appsso.eurostat.ec.europa.eu, visited on May 5, 2014.

b. See box 1.1 for a full discussion of how national poverty lines are set.

c. See chapter 6 for a full discussion of how the international poverty line is set.

d. In closely related work using the same data set of national poverty lines, Greb and others (2011) propose a weakly relative poverty line that increases smoothly with the level of development, rather than imposing a "kink" as Chen and Ravallion (2013) do.

e. In the notation of box 3.1, the weakly relative poverty line corresponds to a set of welfare weights given by $w(y(p)) = I_{y(p)<z(\mu)}$, where $\mu$ is average income, $z(\mu)$ is a poverty line that increases with average income, and $I_{y(p)<z(\mu)}$ is an indicator function taking on the value 1 if $y(p)<z(\mu)$, and zero otherwise.

choice; other common social welfare functions discussed in this section apply nonzero weights to individuals throughout the income distribution.

Panel a of figure 3.4 illustrates one such classic social welfare function introduced by Atkinson (1970), which assigns nonzero weights throughout the entire income distribution.[4] The Atkinson social welfare function is in essence an average of income raised to the power $1 - \alpha$. When $\alpha = 0$, the exponent on income in the Atkinson social welfare function is equal to one and so this measure simply corresponds to mean income. In this common type of social welfare function, the rich receive greater weight than the poor. By emphasizing reductions in poverty and growth among

**Figure 3.4    Welfare weights implied by different social welfare functions**

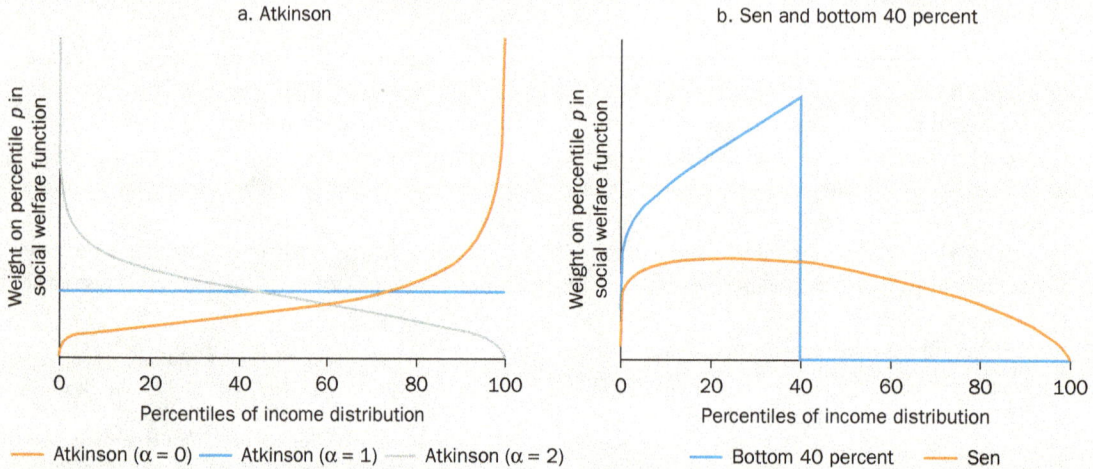

*Source:* Based on data from the Bangladesh Household Income and Expenditure Survey (2010).
*Note:* This figure graphs the welfare weights assigned by different welfare functions to percentiles of the income distribution. Panel a graphs weights implied by the Atkinson social welfare function, that is, $w(y(p)) = y(p)^{1-\alpha}$, for $\alpha = 0, 1, 2$. Panel b graphs weights implied by the Sen index, that is, $w(y(p)) = (1 - p)y(p)$, and by the average income in the bottom 40 percent of the income distribution, that is, $w(y(p)) = I_{p<0.4}y(p)$. The weights have been normalized to sum to one, and are drawn for the observed distribution of monthly consumption expenditures in Bangladesh in 2010.

the bottom 40 percent rather than simply growth in average incomes, the World Bank's twin goals represent an endorsement of much more egalitarian social welfare functions than simply average income.

Another important case occurs when $\alpha = 1$, so that the exponent in the Atkinson social welfare function is equal to zero. In this case, the social welfare function weights all individuals equally, setting a conceptually interesting "democratic" benchmark social welfare function. There is an interesting connection between this particular social welfare function and a recent proposal by Birdsall and Meyer (2014) that a good proxy for "equitable development" is the growth rate of median income. Although their justification for this measure is mostly intuitive, it turns out that if incomes are lognormally distributed, the growth rate of median income is in fact exactly the same as the growth rate of the Atkinson social welfare function with $\alpha = 1$.[5] Finally, for values of $\alpha$ that are greater than one, the Atkinson measure assigns greater weight to poorer individuals.

The parameter $\alpha$ in the Atkinson measure is important because it determines the weights the social welfare function assigns to the rich relative to the poor. As such, this parameter can be thought of as reflecting preferences for redistribution. Arthur Okun (1975) proposed a thought experiment in which income is transferred from a rich person to a poor person using a "leaky bucket" in which some of the income taken from the rich "leaks" out of the bucket and does not reach the poor recipient of the transfer. Consider transferring one dollar of income from a rich person to a poor person with half the income of the rich person. If a bucket in which half the transfer "leaks" in transit is acceptable, this implies a value of $\alpha = 1$.[6] If, instead, a bucket in which only 25 percent of the transfer reaches the poor person is tolerable, this would imply a value of $\alpha = 2$.

Yet another way to think about $\alpha$ is to consider the case where the Atkinson social welfare function is constructed over a distribution of consumption expenditures. In this case, it is simply an average of $c^{1-\alpha}$, which is a standard isoelastic utility function. In many quantitative studies of growth or business cycles, it is standard to calibrate $\alpha$ so that the intertemporal elasticity of substitution, $1/\alpha$, falls somewhere between 1 and 2. This implies values of $\alpha$ ranging from $\alpha = 0.5$ to $\alpha = 1$. This, in turn, implies that standard macroeconomic calibrations of $\alpha$ imply a social welfare function with increasing weights, that is, that weight the rich more than the poor.

Panel b of figure 3.4 reports the welfare weights assigned to individuals by two other notable social welfare functions. The first is the measure of "real national income," which Sen (1976) defined as a weighted average of individuals' incomes, with weights inversely proportional to each person's rank in the income distribution. This implies an inverted U-shaped pattern of welfare weights across individuals, reflecting the balance of two offsetting forces. On the one hand, as individuals' incomes increase, their weight in the social welfare function increases. On the other hand, the weights assigned to their incomes fall, as their ranks in the income distribution increase.

The other notable category of social welfare functions is represented in panel b of figure 3.4 by the average income of the bottom 40 percent of the income distribution. This measure is of particular interest in the context of this report because it corresponds to the notion of shared prosperity that the World Bank has proposed as an institutional goal. As discussed in the previous chapter, the threshold of 40 percent is somewhat arbitrary, and, depending on one's purpose, it could be set at other points. For example, Dollar and Kraay (2002) study growth in the average incomes of the bottom 20 percent of the income distribution, suggesting a social welfare function that values those in the bottom quintile only. At the other extreme, one can interpret the "we are the 99 percent" slogan of the Occupy Wall Street movement in the United States as an implicit endorsement of a social welfare function that values average incomes in the bottom 99 percent. Wherever the cutoff is drawn, use of the average income of the bottom X percent implies a social welfare function that places greater weight on the richer among those in the bottom X percent and less weight on the poorer, as shown in figure 3.4. As discussed in box 3.1, any average income measure weights the incomes of each member of the average equally. However, since richer members of the group have higher income than poorer members of the group, the weights assigned to richer members are higher. Beyond X percent, the social welfare function assigns zero weight.

How do these social welfare functions look in practice? Figure 3.5 shows the relationship between selected social welfare functions and per capita income. Across countries, the social welfare functions track average incomes quite closely, with higher average incomes corresponding to higher social welfare on average. At a given level of average income, however, there can be some differences in rankings of countries based on which social welfare function is of interest. Consider, for example, the cases of Ethiopia and Togo, discussed earlier. Both have roughly the same level of per capita consumption. As noted above, average consumption implies a social welfare function that weights the rich more than the poor. However, the four social welfare functions in figure 3.5 all value equality. Since inequality is lower in Ethiopia, it ranks higher than Togo in social welfare terms.

Figure 3.6 illustrates trends over time in inequality and social welfare in the United States, as measured by the Atkinson social welfare function and based on the World Top Incomes database assembled by Thomas Piketty and his coauthors (Piketty 2014). A notable feature of Piketty's data for the United States is the steep rise in the share of income going to the richest 1 percent of the income distribution (panel a of figure 3.6). Panel b of figure 3.6 illustrates the implications of this trend in inequality for social welfare. The top line in the graph is the Atkinson measure with $\alpha = 0$. As noted above, this corresponds simply to average income in the United States (based on tax return data assembled by Piketty). A striking feature of the data is that income measured in this way increases steadily in the 30 years between 1950 and 1980, but then essentially stagnates in the 30 years thereafter.

The second and third lines in panel b of figure 3.6 are the Atkinson measure with $\alpha = 0.25$ and $\alpha = 0.5$. Since inequality aversion is higher,

**Figure 3.5** **Social welfare increases with average income**

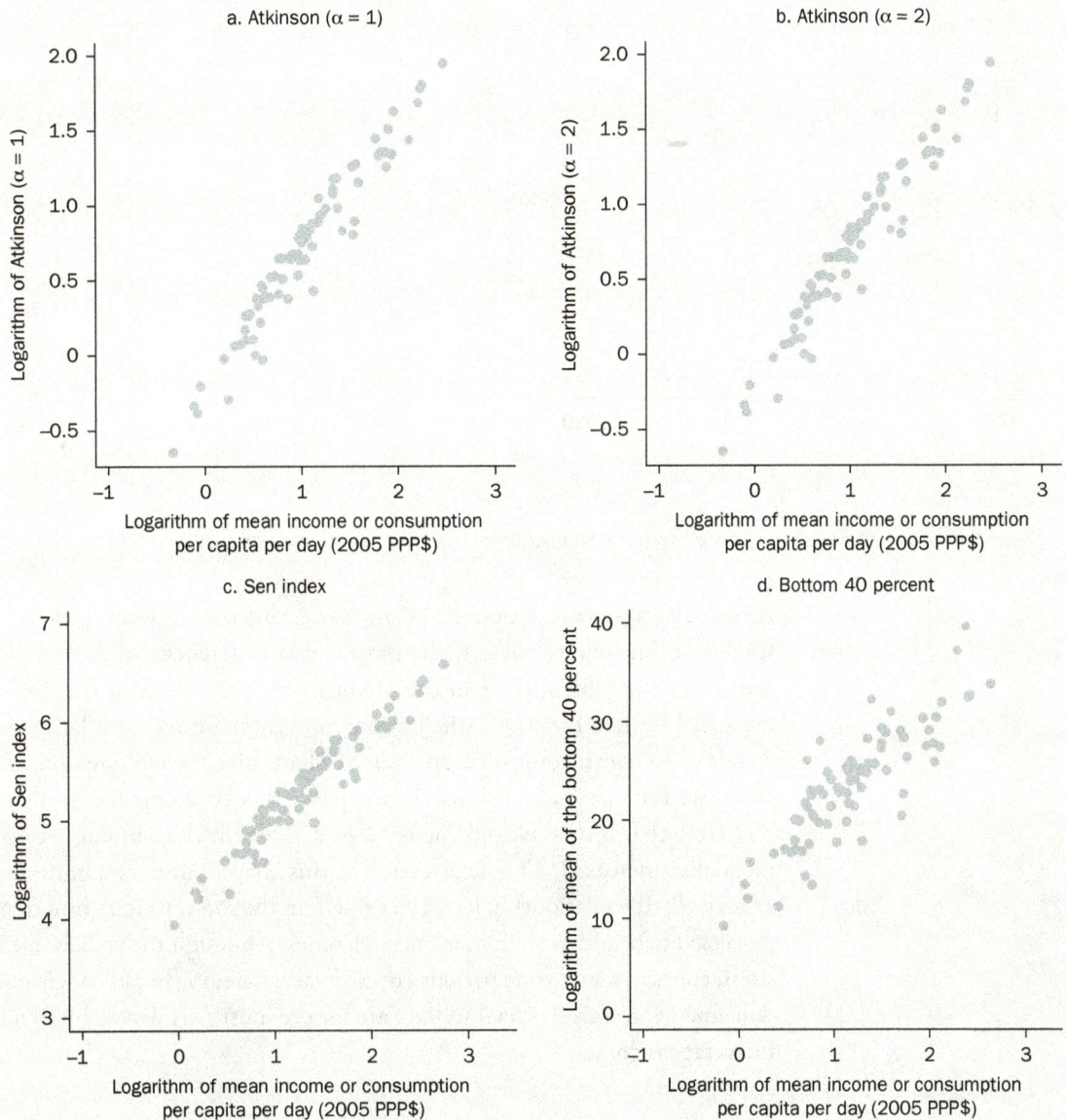

a. Atkinson (α = 1)

b. Atkinson (α = 2)

c. Sen index

d. Bottom 40 percent

*Source:* Based on data from the World Bank PovcalNet database.
*Note:* Each panel plots the logarithm of survey mean income or consumption (on the horizontal axis) against the logarithm of the indicated social welfare function (on the vertical axis). Each data point corresponds to the most recent available survey in PovcalNet (as of July 2014) for a country. The Atkinson measures are constructed based on decile-average income shares, and assuming that income or consumption are equally distributed within each decile. The Sen index is constructed as mean income or consumption times the corresponding Gini coefficient. Average income in the bottom 40 percent is constructed as the share of the bottom 40 percent, times average income or consumption, divided by 0.4.
*Note:* PPP = purchasing power parity.

**Figure 3.6    High-end inequality and social welfare in the United States, 1950–2010**

a. Income share of top 1 percent

b. Social welfare

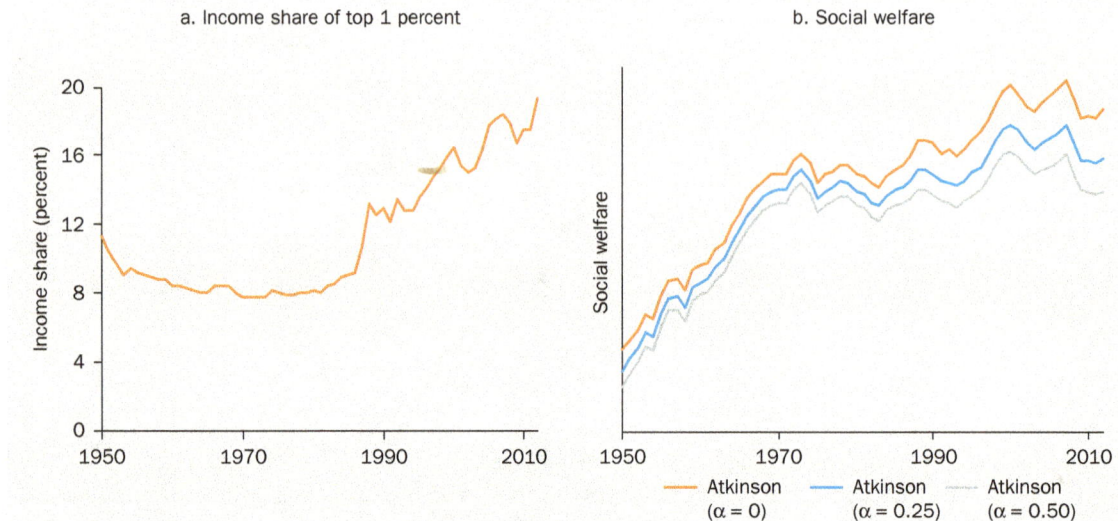

Atkinson (α = 0)    Atkinson (α = 0.25)    Atkinson (α = 0.50)

*Source:* Based on the Global Top Incomes database, available at http://topincomes.g-mond.parisschoolofeconomics.eu/.

these social welfare functions lie below average income, indicating that the level of social welfare is lower the more social preferences value equality. However, a notable feature of the graph is that the trends in the different social welfare functions (the bottom two lines) are very similar to the trends in average income (the top line). Mechanically, the main reason why social welfare grew more slowly in the past 30 years compared with the 30 before that is that average incomes grew more slowly, and not because inequality increased. The next section of this chapter discusses more systematically the relationship between growth in the social welfare functions discussed here and growth in average incomes. Although the welfare measures, countries, and time periods covered vary, the same broad conclusion will emerge: trends in social welfare are for the most part driven by trends in average incomes.

## Growth and social welfare

The previous two sections have shown that there is a strong relationship between all the measures of social welfare discussed and the level of development: social welfare is on average higher in richer countries than in poorer countries. This section documents evidence on the relationship between incomes and social welfare within countries. The discussion focuses on trends in aggregate social welfare. Data limitations prevent tracking of welfare at the individual level in a large cross-section of countries, since true panel data that allow tracking of individuals into and out of poverty, for example, are scarce.

The question of how fast social welfare increases as economies grow is of particular interest in the context of the World Bank's shared prosperity goal, which is defined in terms of the growth rate of the average income of the bottom 40 percent. As discussed in chapter 2, growth in average incomes in the bottom 40 percent can be usefully decomposed into growth in average incomes and growth in the income share of the bottom 40 percent. The latter is the change in one particular measure of inequality or, more precisely, equality: other things equal, an increase in the income share of the bottom 40 percent suggests a *reduction* in inequality and an increase in *equality*.

The same simple decomposition is also true for the Sen and Atkinson social welfare functions. The Sen index is the product of average incomes and one minus the familiar Gini measure of income inequality. Similarly, the Atkinson social welfare function is the product of average incomes and one minus the somewhat less familiar Atkinson inequality measure. This means that for both measures, growth in social welfare is the sum of growth in average incomes and growth in the relevant equality measure, either one minus the Gini coefficient or one minus the Atkinson inequality measure.

Panels a through c of figure 3.7 show the relationship between growth in these three social welfare functions and growth in average incomes. Each data point represents an episode or "spell" between two household surveys for a given country. Spells are defined so that they are nonoverlapping and at least five years long. Average annual growth in social welfare and average annual growth in the survey mean income (or consumption) are calculated for each spell and then graphed against each other. The graph suggests two key stylized facts.[7]

First, the contribution of changes in inequality to changes in social welfare is, on average, much smaller than the contribution of growth itself. Consider, for example, the contrasting cases of Nigeria between 2004 and 2010 on the one hand, and China between 2005 and 2010 on the other. Growth in the average income of the bottom 40 percent was –0.3 percent in Nigeria, while growth in the average income of the bottom 40 percent was 7.2 percent in China. These differences are largely because of

**Figure 3.7**   **Growth and social welfare**

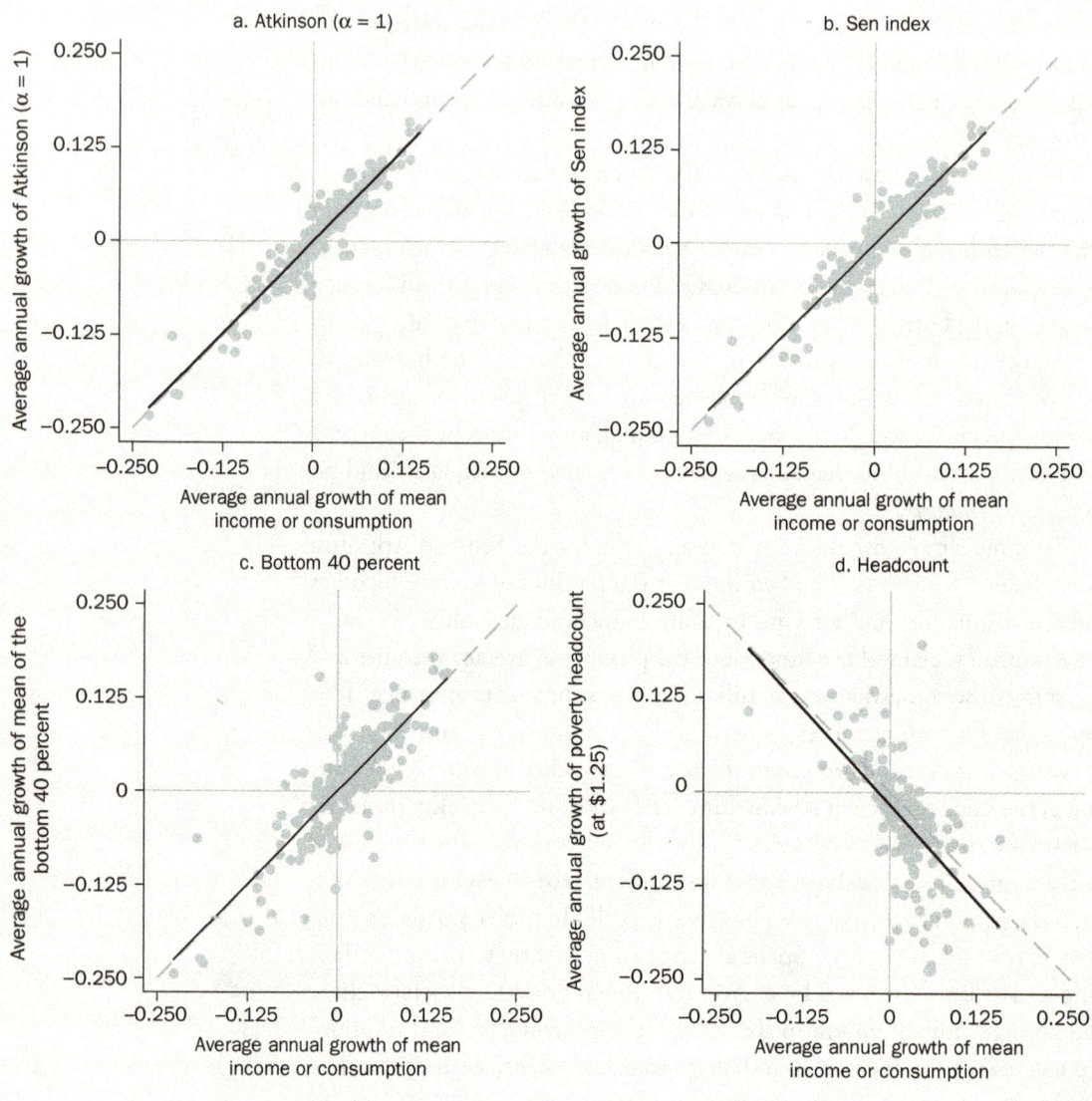

*Source:* Based on data from the World Bank PovcalNet database.
*Note:* This graph plots the average annual change in the logarithm of household survey mean income or consumption expenditure (on the horizontal axis) against the average annual change in the logarithm of the indicated social welfare function (on the vertical axis). The dashed gray line is a 45-degree line; the solid black line is a linear fit. Average annual changes are calculated over nonoverlapping "spells" in between surveys that are at least five years long. Each data point corresponds to a country. Data from PovcalNet are as of July 2014.

differences in average growth performance: growth in the survey mean was 0.8 percent in Nigeria but 7.9 percent in China. These examples highlight a more general pattern. Changes in the inequality measures relevant for social welfare growth (that is, the vertical distances between each data point in these panels and the 45-degree line) are much smaller than the dispersion in countries' average growth performance (that is, the variation along the horizontal axis in the graphs).

Second, social welfare on average increases more or less equiproportionately with average incomes. This can be seen from the fact that the slope of the estimated relationships is close to one. This reflects the fact that the contribution of changes in inequality to changes in social welfare are not correlated with the contribution to growth in average incomes: on average, episodes of fast growth are not systematically associated with particularly fast increases in inequality, nor are episodes of slow growth associated with declines in inequality. As a result, if average incomes are growing, it is likely that social welfare is growing at more or less the same rate.[8]

Panel d of figure 3.7 shows the relationship between average annual growth in the headcount measure of poverty (on the vertical axis) and average annual growth in mean income (on the horizontal axis). The graph shows a well-known and clear relationship: poverty reduction and growth are strongly correlated. Consider, for example, the contrast between Mozambique over the period 2003 to 2009 versus Senegal over the period 2006 to 2011. In Senegal, a period of very slow growth (0.3 percent) in the survey mean coincided with a slight increase in poverty of 0.3 percent per year. In Mozambique, growth in the survey mean was a healthy 3.7 percent per year, and poverty declined at the rate of 3.1 percent per year.

However, panel d of figure 3.7 also shows that, at a given rate of growth, there can be substantial differences in the rate of poverty reduction. For example, growth in the survey mean in Malawi over the period 2004 to 2010 was 1.8 percent per year, similar to that of Namibia over the same period, at 1.9 percent per year. However, while poverty fell at 4.4 percent per year in Namibia, the decline was only 0.8 percent per year in Malawi. These differences reflect the combination of two factors. First, as discussed in chapter 1, the sensitivity of poverty to distribution-neutral growth depends on the shape of initial income distribution at the poverty line. Intuitively, if there are many poor people just below the poverty line, a given amount of growth will reduce poverty faster than if there are fewer people just below the poverty line. Second, the rate of poverty reduction also depends on changes in the distribution of income: if the incomes of those below the poverty line grow faster than those above, the headcount measure of poverty will fall faster at a given rate of growth than if the opposite were true.

These considerations imply that there is no simple additive breakdown of growth in the headcount measure of poverty into growth and inequality changes, as is the case for the other social welfare functions shown in figure 3.7. However, it is possible to decompose poverty changes into a "growth component"—reflecting the reduction in poverty that would have occurred had inequality not changed over the course of the spell—and a "distribution component"—reflecting the reduction in poverty that would have occurred had average incomes not increased, but relative incomes changed the way they did in reality.[9] Kraay (2006) empirically analyzes this decomposition in a large sample of spells of changes in poverty in the 1980s and 1990s, as recorded in an earlier version of the World Bank's PovcalNet database. In a sample of 77 spells averaging eight years long, he finds that 97 percent of the variation across spells in the rate of headcount poverty reduction is attributable to variation in the growth component, while changes in inequality account for only 3 percent of the variation. This finding underscores the importance, also emphasized in chapters 1 and 2, of the role of sustained growth in supporting the achievement of the World Bank's twin goals. Moreover, the finding highlights the fact that, to the extent that attaining the twin goals will involve systematic reductions in inequality over the coming 15 years, it will represent a significant break from the past 30 years, where changes in inequality have played a much smaller role.

The growth component in this calculation is itself the combination of growth in average incomes and the sensitivity of poverty to growth in average incomes. Kraay (2006) finds that most of the variation across spells in the growth component is caused by cross-spell differences in average growth, rather than cross-spell differences in the sensitivity of poverty to growth. In addition, for a given country, the "distribution component" of changes in the poverty gap can be taken as an indicator that measures the direction and extent of pro-poorness of shifts affecting income distribution when the poor disproportionately benefit from growth. Negre (2010) shows that this perspective has useful applications for the discussion of pro-poor growth, where attempts have been made at capturing the contribution of inequality changes to poverty reduction, as discussed in chapter 2.

## Going global: From country-level to global social welfare functions

This section discusses the distinction between social welfare functions defined at the country level and social welfare functions defined at the global level. This distinction is important given the fact that the World

Bank's poverty goal is global in nature—seeking to reduce the *global* poverty headcount ratio, that is, the share of the developing world's population living on less than $1.25 a day. A useful feature of this target is that there is a direct connection between progress at the country level and progress at the global level toward meeting the target. The connection is that the global number of poor people below the global poverty line is simply the sum of the number of poor people below the same line in each country. When the number of poor people in a given country falls, the global number of poor people falls by the same amount. Similarly, the contribution of the poverty *rate* in a given country to the fraction of the world's population below the global poverty line is simply that country's poverty rate times its share in world population.

The same simple addition across countries can be done for the poverty gap and for the squared poverty gap as well. As a result, it is easy to aggregate from the country level to the global poverty gap, or the global squared poverty gap, and examine how these have evolved in the past and into the future (figure 3.8). Although there are important conceptual differences between the poverty measures and the headcount measure, at the global level all three have shown similar trends in the past. Figure 3.8 shows the

**Figure 3.8**  Trends in global poverty measures, 1980–2030

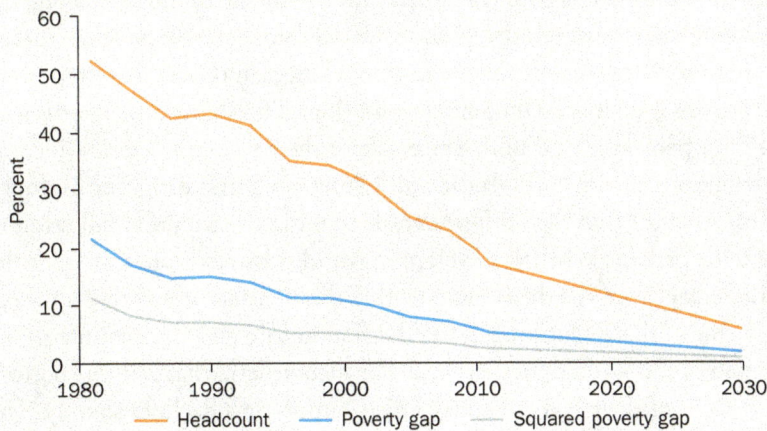

*Source:* Based on data from the World Bank PovcalNet database.
*Note:* This graph reports the global headcount, poverty gap, and squared poverty gap. Historical data through 2011 are actuals based on data in the World Bank PovcalNet database. Projection through 2030 assumes that each country's mean per capita household income or consumption expenditure grows at past country-specific national accounts growth rates over the period 2000–10, keeping country-specific distributions constant. See table 1.4 and endnote 12 in chapter 1 for details.

projected trends in all three measures through 2030, based on the scenario discussed in chapter 1, where all countries are projected to grow over the next 20 years at their historical rate during the 2000s.

Although the poverty line–based social welfare functions aggregate naturally to the global level, the same is not true for all the other social welfare functions discussed in this chapter. Consider, for example, the World Bank's second goal of promoting growth of the bottom 40 percent in all countries. This goal places particular emphasis on policy interventions that would disproportionately benefit those in the bottom 40 percent of the income distribution in each country. The conceptual challenge of aggregating to the global level comes from the fact that not everyone in the bottom 40 percent of their home country's income distribution is also in the bottom 40 percent of the world income distribution. The converse is also true—it is possible for individuals to be in the bottom 40 percent of the global income distribution but not in the bottom 40 percent of their own country's distribution.

These scenarios can be seen in figure 3.9. The horizontal axis in the figure traces out percentiles of the developing world's income distribution. The vertical axis reports the fraction of people in each percentile of the developing world's income distribution that is in the bottom 40 percent of their own country's income distribution. Naturally, virtually all the very poorest people in the world (on the left in figure 3.9) are in the bottom 40 percent of their home country's distribution. Moving to the right along the horizontal axis, however, this proportion falls, since some people who are in the bottom 40 percent of the world are no longer in the bottom 40 percent of their own country's income distribution. The sharp drops at around the 25th percentile and 60th percentile of the developing world's income distribution are driven by India and China. The first drop, for example, reflects the fact that the 40th percentile of India's distribution falls around the 25th percentile of the developing world's distribution. Crossing the 25th percentile of the developing world's distribution means that all those above the 40th percentile of India's distribution are no longer counted. The fraction of the world's population at this income level that is in the bottom 40 percent of their home country's distribution thus declines sharply. The same occurs crossing the 60th percentile of the developing world's distribution, which corresponds to crossing the threshold of the bottom 40 percent in China.

Figure 3.9 is also helpful for thinking about the relationship between the World Bank's two goals. The blue vertical line shows the global $1.25

**Figure 3.9    Bottom 40 percent at home and in the world**

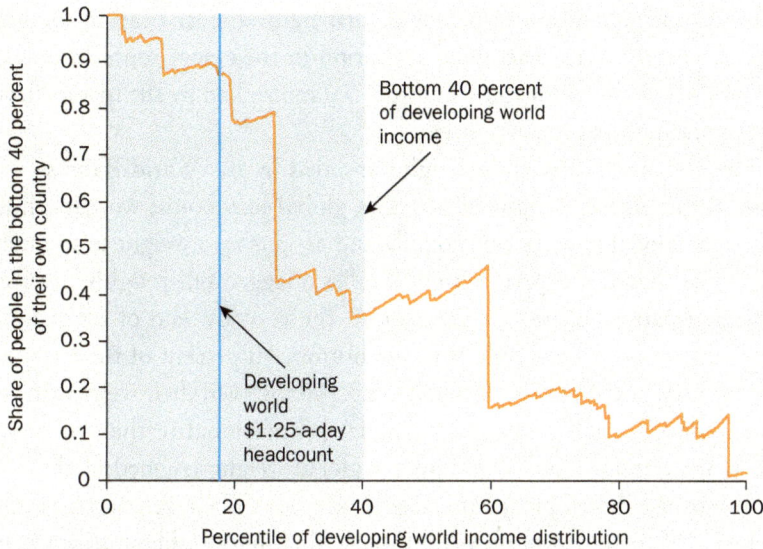

*Source:* Based on data from the World Bank's PovcalNet database.
*Note:* This figure plots the proportion of people at each percentile of the developing world's income distribution who are also in the bottom 40 percent of their home country income distribution.

a day headcount. Virtually everyone to the left of this line is poor relative to the global poverty line and in the bottom 40 percent of their respective country distribution. However, there are many people who are not poor by the standard of the global poverty line, but are in the bottom 40 percent of their own country's distribution. As discussed in chapter 2, this crucial feature of the shared prosperity goal makes it more relevant to middle- and even high-income countries than the goal of reducing global $1.25 a day poverty. This is because in these countries, the number of poor according to the austere global poverty line is very small.

It is possible to go one step further and consider the *global* social welfare functions that are implied by the World Bank's twin goals. For the goal of eliminating global headcount poverty, this is straightforward, as it implies a social welfare function that weights everyone below the poverty line equally, while those above the poverty line receive no weight. Things are slightly more involved for the goal of promoting shared prosperity. In a given country, the average income of the bottom 40 percent implies a social welfare function that weights individuals in the bottom 40 percent according to their income levels and assigns zero weight to those in the top 60 percent. Aggregating this to the global level would imply that each percentile of the global distribution is weighted by the product of its income and the fraction of people in that percentile that fall in the bottom 40 percent of the income distribution in their own country, that is, the product of the orange line in figure 3.9 multiplied by the income level corresponding to each percentile.

The global social welfare weights implied by the World Bank's twin goals are depicted in figure 3.10. The global headcount weights those below the global poverty line equally and assigns zero weight to the nonpoor. The shared prosperity target implies a jagged but roughly inverted U-shaped pattern of welfare weights. At the very low end of the income distribution, nearly everyone is in the bottom 40 percent of their respective country distributions (recall figure 3.9). However, their weights in the country-level social welfare function are proportional to their incomes, which are very low, and so the overall global weight assigned to the very poorest by the shared prosperity target is very low. The reverse is true at the high end of the developing world income distribution. Here incomes are much higher, but relatively few people with these high incomes are in the bottom 40 percent of the income distribution of their home country and

**Figure 3.10  Who in the world do the twin goals address?**

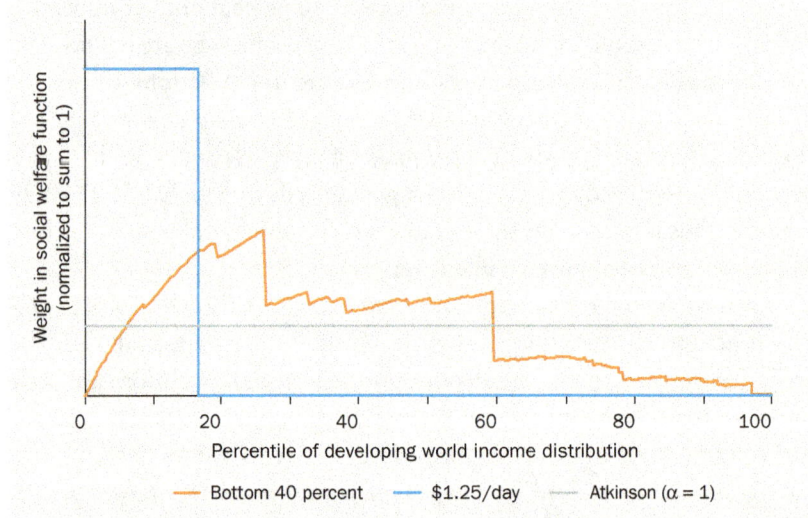

*Source:* Based on data from the World Bank PovcalNet database.
*Note:* This graph shows the welfare weights that are assigned to people in each percentile of the developing world income distribution by the indicated social welfare functions at the country level.

so these percentiles also receive a low weight. The welfare weights in the middle of the distribution reflect the balance of these two forces. Moving up the world income distribution, the fraction of people in each percentile that receives positive weight according to the shared prosperity metric falls, but, at the same time, their weight in the implied social welfare function increases as their incomes increase.

Figure 3.10 also shows an alternative, highly egalitarian, global social welfare function that may be of interest for some purposes. The Atkinson social welfare function with $\alpha = 1$ is a benchmark social welfare function that assigns equal weight to everyone throughout the income distribution. If the distribution of income is lognormal, this is equivalent to a social welfare function that tracks median income. Because the weights assigned to individuals are equal, it is easy to move from social welfare functions at the country level to a global social welfare function for the world as a whole, since this too will feature equal weights for all individuals regardless of their position in the global income distribution. Thus, an alternative metric for tracking shared prosperity might be a "democratic" growth rate that weights the growth rates of all individuals in the world income distribution equally.

## Beyond income: Multidimensional social welfare functions

All the social welfare functions that have been considered so far in the preceding sections are based only on households' income or consumption. The same is true for the specific goals that the World Bank has set for itself, to eliminate extreme poverty and to promote shared prosperity. The focus on income or consumption is limiting because welfare at the individual level can in principle depend on much more than just income, including other dimensions such as health, longevity, insecurity, access to nonmarket goods and services, and so on. In fact, there is wide recognition that poverty is a multidimensional phenomenon reflecting deprivations in multiple dimensions, in line with Sen's capabilities approach (Sen 1999). However, there is much less consensus on *whether* and *how* deprivation in different dimensions should be combined into broader measures of social welfare.[10] This section discusses two directions in the literature to move "beyond income" by constructing empirical welfare measures that reflect multiple dimensions of well-being.

A useful starting point is the observation that standard poverty or social welfare measures based on consumption are already multidimensional in that they aggregate across many items in the consumption basket of the households being surveyed. Total consumption at the household level reflects households' choices among many consumption items, which are then aggregated across "dimensions" of consumption using *prices*: total consumption is the *value*, that is, price times quantity, of consumption of food, clothing, transportation, and so on. One could consider measures of food consumption poverty, clothing consumption poverty, and transportation consumption poverty separately, or one could consider a multidimensional poverty measure that aggregates these together using the value of consumption in each category.

Measuring welfare based on aggregate expenditures rather than individual commodities is conceptually attractive because it respects the choices that households make for themselves, given the prices they face and the resources they have at their disposal. For example, with the same income level, one household might choose to consume relatively more food, while another consumes relatively more clothing and another relatively more transportation. As long as these choices reflect utility-maximizing behavior by the household, there is no obvious rationale for measuring consumption poverty for individual commodities. A multidimensional index consisting simply of total consumption expenditures is a sufficient statistic for welfare at the household level.

This tidy logic in favor of a basic poverty or welfare measure based on observed total household expenditure or income can break down for at least two reasons. First, a wide variety of market failures might imply that households' observed expenditure choices are not their preferred ones. For example, a household may spend nothing on education, not because it does not value schooling, but simply because no school is available in the location where the household lives. Alternatively, a school might be available, but if the fixed cost of annual tuition is high and the family is unable to borrow to finance the cost because of credit market imperfections, spending on schooling might also be zero although the marginal valuation of education by the household is high. Second, this approach is difficult to implement when considering dimensions of well-being for which it is difficult to assign prices and consumption values. Although it is straightforward to calculate the value in Indian rupees of rice consumption of a household in India, it is far from obvious how to value other dimensions of well-being in monetary terms. For example, how should one value differences in health outcomes across households? What is the "value" of an additional year of life expectancy? What "price" can be assigned an individual's sense of dignity, or empowerment, and what is the monetary value of being more empowered? The difficulty in assigning monetary values for such crucial dimensions of well-being is an important motivation for considering multidimensional indicators of poverty or social welfare.

In these situations, there is a strong rationale for assessing welfare in multiple dimensions and specifically in dimensions other than the monetary value of income or consumption. Figure 3.11 provides a simple illustration with two dimensions of well-being. For this figure, the unit of observation is a country, and the graph plots per capita income (on the horizontal axis, measured in 2005 dollars [PPP]) against life expectancy at birth (on the vertical axis, measured in years). Income and life expectancy are arguably important dimensions of well-being. Indeed, both are

**Figure 3.11** **E pluribus unum? Constructing multidimensional social welfare indicators**

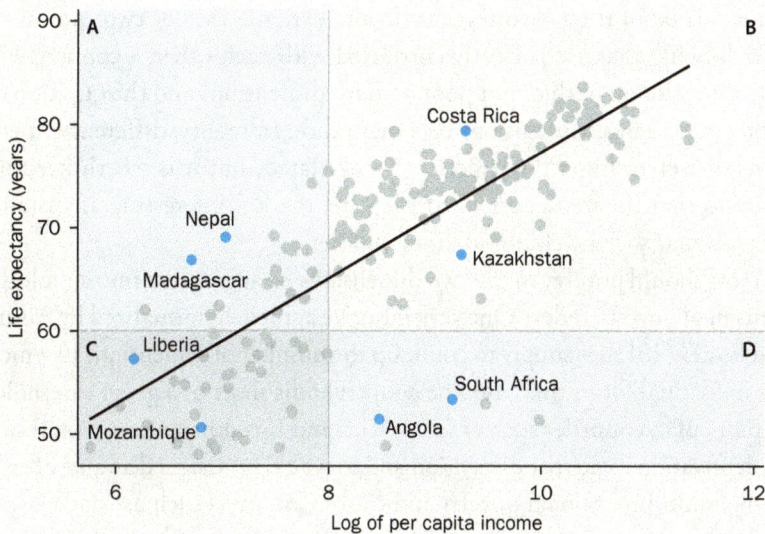

Source: Based on data from the United Nations Development Programme's Human Development Index database.
Note: This graph plots log income per capita (on the horizontal axis) against life expectancy (on the vertical axis), with data referring to 2012. The solid black line is a linear fit. Letters A and B denote regions in which countries are considered poor according to the the dimensions on the horizontal and vertical axis, respectively. Countries in region C are considered poor according to both dimensions; countries in region B are not considered poor.

included, together with a measure of educational attainment, in the United Nations' widely referenced Human Development Index.

The horizontal and vertical lines in the graph reflect possible cutoff values that might be used as poverty lines in both dimensions, which could be used to construct a social welfare function analogous to the headcount measure of poverty. Countries falling below the line in each dimension are classified as poor according to that dimension, while those above the line are not poor. The key questions are then *whether* and *how* poverty (or more generally, welfare) in these two dimensions should be combined into a multidimensional measure reflecting deprivation in the two dimensions.

Before answering either of these questions, it is important to keep in mind a basic statistical feature of the data that matters for the relevance of a multidimensional measure. In figure 3.11, income and life expectancy are strongly positively correlated across countries, but they are far from being perfectly correlated. Since they are only imperfectly correlated with each other, it is possible for a country to be poor in one dimension but not in the other, as is the case with countries such as Nepal and Angola falling in regions A and D in the graph, respectively. The more correlated the two dimensions of well-being under consideration are, the fewer observations there will be in these two regions. In the extreme case of two indicators of well-being that are perfectly correlated with each other, a country will either be poor on both or not poor on both dimensions and the question of aggregation across dimensions becomes moot. In reality, different dimensions of well-being are not perfectly correlated, but it is worth keeping in mind that the more correlated they are, the less interesting any multidimensional social welfare function will be.

How should poverty in the two dimensions be aggregated into a multidimensional poverty index? One very intuitive approach, formalized by Alkire and Foster (2011), is simply to count up the number of dimensions in which the individual (or in this case, the country) falls short of a given threshold. In particular, countries such as Costa Rica and Kazakhstan in region B suffer deprivation in neither dimension and so would be assigned a value of zero in the multidimensional poverty indicator. Countries such as Madagascar and South Africa in regions A and D, respectively, are deprived in one of two dimensions, and so both are assigned a value of one in the multidimensional indicator. Finally, countries such as Liberia and Mozambique in region C are deprived in both dimensions and would receive a value of two. This approach is transparent and simple and, moreover, Alkire and Foster (2011) show that the resulting multidimensional poverty indicator satisfies a number of very desirable axiomatic properties. This methodology of counting up dimensions of poverty is used by the Multidimensional Poverty Index (MPI) featured in the United Nations' *Human Development Report* since 2010. The MPI is based on three equally weighted poverty dimensions—health, education, and living standards—that are captured by a total of 10 indicators. Each person who is deprived in less than 33 percent of weighted attributes is not considered poor, whereas each person deprived above this mark is considered poor. Moreover, the value of the index assigned to each person reflects the number of dimensions in which he or she is poor, but ignores the depth of deprivation below the cutoff.

This approach suggests a high degree of substitutability across the dimensions of poverty. In the example in figure 3.11, a country that is only income poor but not poor in terms of life expectancy is treated in exactly the same way as another country for which the opposite is true. This high degree of substitutability across the dimensions can appear somewhat arbitrary. The identification method developed by Rippin (2010, 2012, 2014) instead differentiates between degrees of severity of poverty that depend on the number of weighted attributes in which individuals are deprived as well as on the correlation between those attributes. Each person receives an individual weight that increases with the number of attributes in which the person is deprived. The size of the increase depends on the correlation between the attributes: the more difficult it is to compensate for the loss in one attribute with the achievements in other attributes (that is, the less statistical correlation between the former and the latter), the larger the increase. In her simplest identification form, Rippin's Correlation Sensitive Poverty Index provides an index similar to the MPI with the additional benefit of accounting for inequality-changing transfers among the poor and incorporating information for all individual attribute deprivations without ignoring those below a certain cutoff.

Another approach to aggregating two dimensions of welfare—such as income and life expectancy—is to draw explicitly on economic theory that provides links between the dimensions under consideration. For example, many economic models feature agents who seek to maximize the present discounted value of utility over their lifetime. In any given period, more income leads to higher utility within the period, and greater longevity means that lifetime utility is higher because the period over which income can be enjoyed is longer.

This basic idea was implemented empirically by Becker, Philipson, and Soares (2005), who found that inequality in welfare across countries is smaller than inequality in income. The difference is because the welfare effects of differences in life expectancy across countries are more equitably distributed across countries than income is. Fleurbaey and Gaulier (2009) expand on this idea to add leisure and within-country inequality and find a substantial reranking of countries in welfare compared with that based on per capita gross domestic product. In yet another application, Jones and Klenow (2011) use data for consumption, leisure, inequality, and mortality to measure welfare across countries. They also find nontrivial rerankings of countries whereby Western European countries almost catch up with the United States thanks to higher leisure and developing countries fall further behind because of shorter life expectancy, as shown in figure 3.12. Jones and Klenow (2011) also calculate growth rates of welfare across countries and find that welfare has grown roughly 1 percent per year faster than income over the period 1980 to 2000, reflecting rising life expectancy.

Beyond the question of *how* to aggregate across different dimensions of well-being is the perhaps more important question of *whether* this should be done at all. To be sure, aggregate measures such as the MPI have great presentational appeal in that they bring together many dimensions into a single summary statistic. However, arriving at such a simple statistic may

**Figure 3.12    Welfare and per capita GDP**

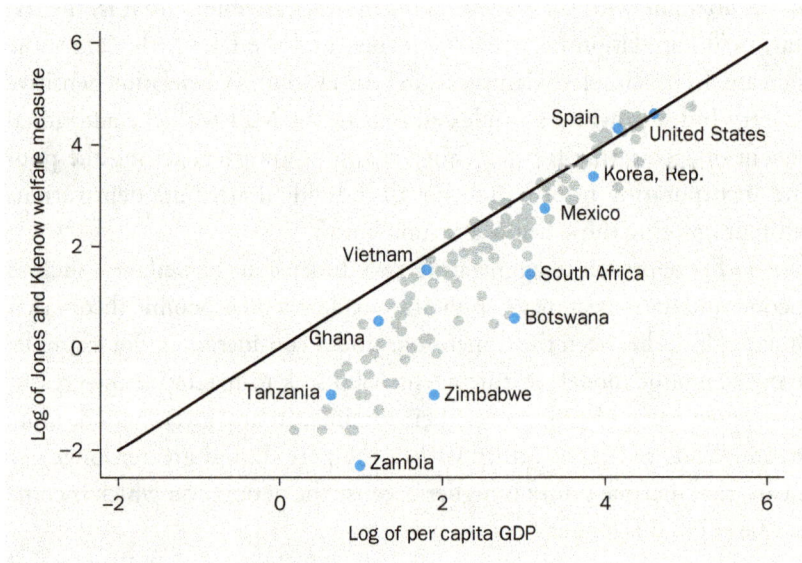

*Source:* Based on data from Jones and Klenow (2011).
*Note:* GDP = gross domestic product.

come at the cost of reduced policy relevance. Consider, for example, an international aid donor with a comparative advantage in health interventions. For such a donor, a multidimensional index that aggregates together income and life expectancy into a single measure will not be especially useful for the purpose of identifying countries or regions where the need for health interventions to improve life expectancy is particularly acute. Instead, such a donor would find it more useful to look at indicators of health separately from indicators of other dimensions of well-being.

Overall, there is widespread consensus that poverty is a multidimensional phenomenon. However, there is much less consensus on whether it is useful to aggregate across dimensions to construct a multidimensional measure of welfare and, if so, how to do so in a way that is conceptually sound.

## Notes

1. Since the twin goals are expressed in terms of income (or consumption) based on available household survey data, most of the discussion here focuses on social welfare functions defined over income (or consumption). To avoid terminological awkwardness, this chapter will generally refer to distribution of income, recognizing that available distributional data will refer to income in some countries and consumption in others. However, when referring to a specific country where consumption is the relevant measure in the household survey, the chapter will refer to consumption.

2. In the notation of box 3.1, the FGT class corresponds to welfare weights $w(y(p)) = I_{y(p)<z}\left(\dfrac{z-y(p)}{z}\right)^{\theta}$, where $I_{y(p)<z}$ is an indicator function taking on the value one if $y(p)<z$ and zero otherwise. See Foster, Greer, and Thorbecke (1984) for the original introduction of this class of poverty measures.

3. See, for example, Calvo and Dercon (2013); Christiaensen and Subbarao (2005); Dang and Lanjouw (2014); Pritchett, Suryahadi, and Sumarto (2000); and Suryahadi and Sumarto (2003).

4. For the Atkinson social welfare function, the welfare weights are $w(y(p)) = y(p)^{1-\alpha}$.

5. To see this, note that the median value of income is the same as the median value of log income. If log income is normally distributed, the median of log income is the same as the mean of log income, that is, $\int \log(y(p))dp$. This is the logarithm of the limit of the Atkinson index when $\alpha = 1$. The log-differenced growth rate of median income is thus the same as the log-differenced growth rate of the Atkinson index.

6. Formally, let $\lambda$ be the fraction of the transfer that "leaks" when a dollar of income is transferred from a rich person (with income $y_R$) to a poor person (with income $y_P$). The relationship between $\alpha$ and $\lambda$ that holds social welfare constant is $1-\lambda=\left(\dfrac{y_R}{y_P}\right)^{\alpha}$. Pirttila and Uusitalo (2008) report results from a

survey of individuals in Finland who were asked directly about the tolerable amount of "leakage" and find evidence suggesting that $\alpha = 0.5$. However, other questions about wage inequality suggest much higher values of $\alpha$.

7. For a more systematic documentation of these stylized facts in different time periods and country samples, see Dollar, Kraay, and Kleineberg (2014).

8. This conclusion can be based on the evidence shown for the specific social welfare functions discussed in this chapter. But do the same conclusions hold for other social welfare functions not considered here? A useful tool to answer this question can be found in Shorrocks' (1983) concept of generalized Lorenz dominance. Shorrocks (1983) shows that for any increasing and concave social welfare function, social welfare unambiguously increases between two points in time if the growth rates of all the cumulative percentile shares of income are positive over the same period. Dollar, Kraay, and Kleineberg (2014) consider a large set of spells similar to those studied here and document that in over 80 percent of spells generalized Lorenz dominance holds; in other words, any increasing and concave social welfare function would be higher during these positive growth spells.

9. This decomposition was introduced in Datt and Ravallion (1992). A different implementation of the same idea is based on the Shapley (1953) method for game theory and was applied by Kakwani (1993) to decompose poverty variations into growth and redistribution effects. Subsequently, it was formulated under a more general scope by Shorrocks (2013) for any kind of decomposition, including that into population subgroups.

10. For a more detailed treatment of these two questions in the context of poverty measurement, see Ravallion (2011), on which the discussion in this section draws heavily.

## References

Alkire, S., and J. Foster. 2011. "Counting and Multidimensional Poverty Measurement." *Journal of Public Economics* 95: 476–87.

Atkinson, Anthony B. 1970. "On the Measurement of Inequality." *Journal of Economic Theory* 2.

Bangladesh Household Income and Expenditure Survey. 2010. http://catalog.ihsn .org/index.php/catalog/2257.

Becker, G. S., T. J. Philipson, and R. R. Soares. 2005. "The Quantity and Quality of Life and the Evolution of World Inequality." *American Economic Review* 95 (1): 277–91.

Birdsall, Nancy, and Christian Meyer. 2014. "The Median Is the Message: A Good-Enough Measure of Material Well-Being and Shared Development Progress." Center for Global Development Working Paper No. 351, Center for Global Development, Washington, DC.

Calvo, Cesar, and Stefan Dercon. 2013. "Vulnerability to Individual and Aggregate Poverty." *Social Choice and Welfare* 41 (4): 721–40.

Chen, Shaohua, and Martin Ravallion. 2013. "More Relatively-Poor People in a Less Absolutely-Poor World." *Review of Income and Wealth* 59 (1): 1–28.

Christiaensen, Luc J., and Kalanidhi Subbarao. 2005. "Towards an Understanding of Household Vulnerability in Rural Kenya." *Journal of African Economies* 14 (4): 520–58. doi: 10.1093/jae/eji008.

Dang, Hai-Anh H., and Peter F. Lanjouw. 2014. "Welfare Dynamics Measurement: Two Definitions of a Vulnerability Line and Their Applications." Unpublished manuscript, World Bank, Washington, DC.

Datt, Gaurav, and Martin Ravallion. 1992. "Growth and Redistribution Components of Changes in Poverty Measures." *Journal of Development Economics* 38 (2): 275–95.

Dollar, David, and Aart Kraay. 2002. "Growth Is Good for the Poor." *Journal of Economic Growth* 7: 195–225.

Dollar, David, Aart Kraay, and Tatjana Kleineberg. 2014. "Growth, Inequality and Social Welfare: Cross-Country Evidence." Policy Research Working Paper 6842, World Bank, Washington, DC.

Fleurbaey, M., and G. Gaulier. 2009. "International Comparisons of Living Standards by Equivalent Incomes (2009–04)." *Scandinavian Journal of Economics* 111 (3): 597–624.

Foster, James, Joel Greer, and Erik Thorbecke. 1984. "A Class of Decomposable Poverty Measures." *Econometrica* 52 (3): 761–66.

Greb, F., S. Klasen, S. H. Pasaribu, and M. Wiesenfarth. 2011. "Dollar a Day Re-Revisited." Courant Research Centre: Poverty, Equity and Growth Discussion Papers 91, University of Göttingen, Göttingen.

Jolliffe, Dean, Craig Gundersen, Laura Tiehen, and Joshua Winicki. 2005. "Food Stamp Benefits and Child Poverty." *American Journal of Agricultural Economics* 87 (3): 569–81.

Jones, C. I., and P. J. Klenow. 2011. "Beyond GDP? Welfare across Countries and Time." NBER Working Papers 16352, National Bureau of Economic Research, Cambridge, MA.

Kakwani, N. 1993. "On a Class of Poverty Measures." *Econometrica* 48 (2): 437–46.

Kraay, Aart. 2006. "When Is Growth Pro-Poor? Evidence from a Panel of Countries." *Journal of Development Economics* 80 (1): 198–227.

López-Calva, L. F., and E. Ortiz-Juarez. 2011. "A Vulnerability Approach to the Definition of the Middle Class." Policy Research Working Paper 5902, World Bank, Washington, DC.

Negre, Mario. 2010. "Concepts and Operationalization of Pro-Poor Growth." WIDER Working Paper 2010/47, United Nations University, Helsinki.

Okun, Arthur. 1975. *Equality and Efficiency: The Big Trade-off.* Washington, DC: Brookings Institution Press.

Piketty, Thomas. 2014. *Capital in the Twenty-First Century.* Harvard University Press.

Pirttila, Jukka, and Roope Uusitalo. 2008. "The 'Leaky Bucket' in the Real World: Measuring Inequality Aversion Using Survey Data." *Economica* 77 (305): 60–76.

Pritchett, Lant, Asep Suryahadi, and Sudarno Sumarto. 2000. "Quantifying Vulnerability to Poverty—A Proposed Measure, Applied to Indonesia." Policy Research Working Paper 2437, World Bank, Washington, DC. http://ideas .repec.org/p/wbk/wbrwps/2437.html.

Ravallion, Martin. 2011. "On Multidimensional Indices of Poverty." *Journal of Economic Inequality* 9 (2): 235–48.

Ravallion, Martin, and Shaohua Chen. 2011. "Weakly Relative Poverty." *Review of Economics and Statistics* 93 (4): 1251–61. doi: 10.1162/REST_a_00127.

Ravallion, Martin, Shaohua Chen, and Prem Sangraula. 2009. "Dollar a Day Revisited." *The World Bank Economic Review* 23 (2): 163–84.

Rippin, N. 2010. "Poverty Severity in a Multidimensional Framework: The Issue of Inequality Between Dimensions." Courant Research Centre: Poverty, Equity and Growth Discussion Paper 47, University of Göttingen, Göttingen, Germany.

———. 2012. "Distributional Justice and Efficiency: Integrating Inequality Within and Between Dimensions in Additive Poverty Indices." Courant Research Centre: Poverty, Equity and Growth Discussion Paper 128, University of Göttingen, Göttingen, Germany.

———. 2014. "Considerations of Efficiency and Distributive Justice in Multidimensional Poverty Measurement." PhD thesis, University of Göttingen. http://hdl.handle.net/11858/00-1735-0000-0022-5E2E-B.

Sen, Amartya. 1976. "Real National Income." *Review of Economic Studies* 43 (1): 19–39.

———. 1999. *Development as Freedom*. Oxford: Oxford University Press.

Shapley, L. 1953. "A Value for n-Persons Games." In *Contributions to the Theory of Games*, vol. 2, edited by H. W. Kuhn and A. W. Tucker. Princeton, NJ: Princeton University Press.

Shorrocks, Anthony. 1983. "Ranking Income Distributions." *Economica* 50: 3–17.

———. 2013. "Decomposition Procedures for Distributional Analysis: A Unified Framework Based on the Shapley Value." *Journal of Economic Inequality* 11 (1): 99–126,

Suryahadi, Asep, and Sudarno Sumarto. 2003. "Poverty and Vulnerability in Indonesia Before and After the Economic Crisis." *Asian Economic Journal* 17 (1): 45–64. doi: 10.1111/1351-3958.00161.

# CHAPTER FOUR

# Uncertainty, Downside Risk, and the Goals

There is considerable uncertainty about the future trajectories and distributional nature of growth in developing and emerging economies. This uncertainty, in turn, implies uncertainty about the future trajectories for global extreme poverty and shared prosperity. Some aspects of uncertainty about future growth can be modeled by looking at the variation and patterns observed in past growth. However, projections that extrapolate from patterns observed in past data are limited by fundamental uncertainty about the future and how it will differ from the past. For example, changes in technology, politics, conflict, climate, and financial conditions may lead to structural changes in economies in the future that differ from trends observed in the past. Such structural changes can also affect progress toward the World Bank goals—in positive and negative ways. However, knowing the precise magnitudes, probabilities, and timing of such changes is difficult, if not impossible. This chapter discusses uncertainty about growth rates and growth incidence and how it affects our understanding of the future trajectories of poverty and shared prosperity. Furthermore, the chapter focuses on a selection of sources of such uncertainty, particularly those posing downside risk to future growth and therefore compromising progress toward the goals.

The first part of the chapter illustrates how uncertainty about future growth rates, incidence, and sustainability can affect projections of global poverty and shared prosperity. The discussion of uncertainty about future growth rates includes simulations that explicitly incorporate uncertainty about future poverty projections, by allowing countries' projected growth rates and growth incidence to vary in accordance with past fluctuations in growth patterns, instead of being based on past averages, as is the case in chapter 1. These simulations demonstrate how projections of future global poverty seem quite uncertain when incorporating past variability in patterns and rates of growth. Furthermore, the simulations show that even under the most optimistic specifications of growth rates and growth incidence derived from past data, the 3 percent poverty target seems difficult to reach. Uncertainty about the long-term sustainability of economic growth and the associated implications for the World Bank goals are also discussed, but are not included in the set of simulations.

The second part of the chapter sets out a selection of key sources of uncertainty about future growth, poverty, and shared prosperity, with a particular focus on downside risks to the poverty and shared prosperity goals. Specifically, the discussion focuses on uncertainty about the magnitude, frequency, and impact of future economic and financial crises, political instability and armed conflict, climate change, and pandemics. These are sources of uncertainty for which the associated probabilities and impacts are not well understood but that can affect the evolution of shared prosperity and global poverty. They are difficult to incorporate in models or forecasts and, in turn, difficult to incorporate into scenarios for the goals. By no means are these the only sources of uncertainty and downside risks to the goals, but they illustrate the difficulty of projecting future growth, poverty, and shared prosperity.

The chapter emphasizes the extent to which uncertainties about the future affect the scenarios deployed in other parts of this report for assessing the twin goals. As with the rest of the report, the focus here is on the measurement and monitoring challenges posed by these uncertainties and not on the policy implications associated with addressing the sources or mitigating the uncertainties.

## How uncertainty affects assessment of the goals

Economic growth is the most important factor required for succeeding in reducing poverty and boosting shared prosperity toward 2030. In decomposing sources of pro-poor growth, Kraay (2006) finds that 70 percent of the variation in changes in poverty can be attributed to growth in average incomes. Similarly, and relevant for the shared prosperity goal, Dollar, Kleineberg, and Kraay (2013) find that that 77 percent of the cross-country variation in growth in incomes of the poorest 40 percent of populations can be attributed to growth in average incomes. Thus, understanding future growth patterns is essential to understanding the prospects for shared prosperity and global poverty. But substantial uncertainty about future growth performance—in terms of growth rates and growth incidence—leads to nontrivial uncertainty about projections for extreme poverty and shared prosperity.

As seen in chapter 1, getting to 3 percent extreme poverty by 2030 will likely require growth performance that is better than what has been observed over the past decade and much better than average growth in the developing world over the past 30 years. This challenge underscores how ambitious the target for global poverty is and the extent to which achieving the target relies on robust economic growth. From a measurement perspective, it also highlights how assessments of progress toward the poverty and shared prosperity goals are sensitive to assumptions and expectations for economic growth rates in developing countries over the next decades and how uncertainty about growth rates affects the goals.

### Forecasts of economic growth and thus poverty and shared prosperity

Forecasting economic growth is a difficult and imprecise exercise, even for the near future. Recently, this difficulty was illustrated by the inability to forecast the 2008 global financial crisis and its impact on global growth. In early 2008, when the financial crisis had already begun, the International Monetary Fund's five-year *World Economic Outlook* still forecasted that the global economy would grow at an average rate of 4.5 percent per year up to 2013. Actual growth turned out to be only 2.9 percent for the period (IMF 2014).

Over longer time periods, forecasting growth is even more difficult. A much-cited example of how difficult it can be to forecast long-term growth is Rosenstein-Rodan's attempt in the 1960s at predicting the economic performance of developing countries for the subsequent 15 years (Rosenstein-Rodan 1961). For the period from 1961 to 1976, Rosenstein-Rodan forecasted that the Republic of Korea would grow at 1.4 percent annually, while the actual growth rate was more than 6 percent per year, resulting in a more than doubling of average living standards over the period. In the same set of forecasts, Kenya was projected to grow at more than 2 percent annually, but it hardly grew at all over the subsequent two decades. In 1990, the World Bank forecasted Sub-Saharan Africa to grow at 3.8 percent for the decade leading up to 2000, but actual growth was only 2.6 percent (Fardoust and Dhareshwar 2013). Box 4.1 summarizes these and other examples that illustrate the difficulties and imprecision of long-term economic growth forecasting.

## Box 4.1 Uncertainty in forecasting economic growth

Forecasting economic growth is an extremely difficult and imprecise exercise, even for the near future. For example, in 2008 the IMF's five-year forecast for economic growth until 2013 was 4.5 percent per year. Actual growth, as reported in the 2014 *World Economic Outlook* was only 2.9 percent because of the overall growth slowdown associated with the 2008 global financial crisis. Compounded over six years, the slowdown meant that the world economy grew only 18.9 percent from 2007 to 2013, in comparison with the 30.3 percent forecasted in 2008 for the same period. Panel a in figure B4.1.1 illustrates the discrepancy between the forecasted and actual growth trajectories of the global economy, and panel b shows the discrepancy across country and regional groupings, showing how growth was lower than expected in all regions, with the gap particularly large for advanced economies.

It is even more difficult to forecast growth over decades, which is necessary to understand the viability of the goals of boosting shared prosperity and ending poverty by 2030. In the past, such World Bank projections systematically erred on the side of optimism: the realized growth rates of developing countries' aggregate output were lower than the projections in all the forecasts for the base-case scenario and in most of the forecasts even for the low-case scenario (Fardoust and Dhareshwar 2013). Therefore, long-run growth forecasting (more than five years) is sometimes compared with "throwing darts in the dark" and no longer part of the forecasts produced by international development institutions. Although international organizations do not produce long-term economic growth forecasts, some private sector entities do.

**Figure B4.1.1** The discrepancy between forecasted and actual growth since 2008

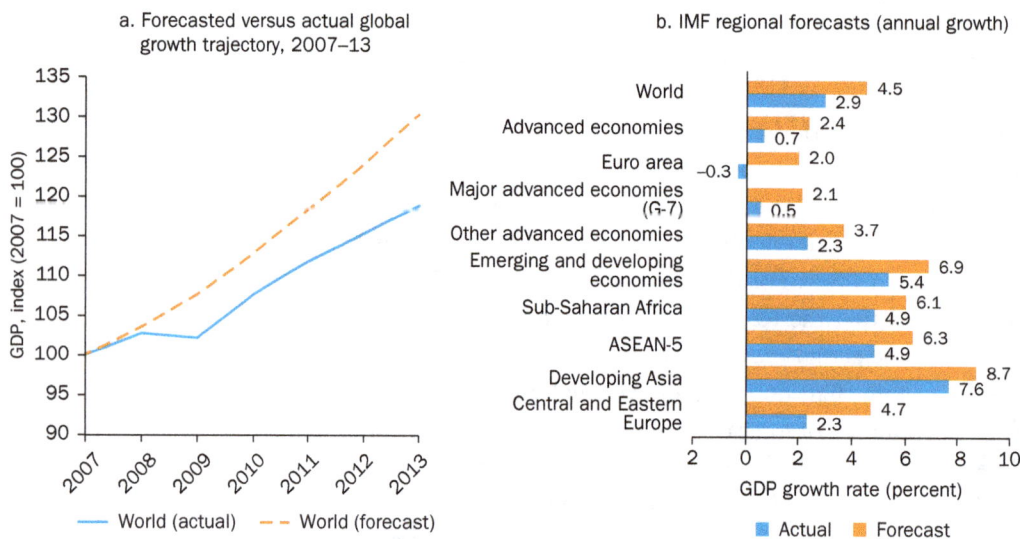

a. Forecasted versus actual global growth trajectory, 2007–13

b. IMF regional forecasts (annual growth)

*Sources:* Based on data from *World Economic Outlook* (IMF 2008, 2014).
*Note:* ASEAN-5 = Association of Southeast Asian Nations (Indonesia, Malaysia, the Philippines, Singapore, and Thailand); GDP = gross domestic product.

The inability to forecast economic growth with much confidence, even in the relative short term and in optimal data environments, has direct implications for the ability to develop long-term scenarios for poverty and shared prosperity, which this report projects until 2030. Given the strong relationship between growth and welfare of the poor, a substantial slow-down in economic growth—globally or regionally—could significantly compromise the global poverty goal. Given that it is estimated that more than two-thirds of the world's extreme poor lived in just eight countries in 2011, even a growth slowdown in a single country could have a significant impact on the global poverty headcount. A growth collapse in countries with high poverty in absolute numbers—such as Bangladesh, China, the Democratic Republic of Congo, India, or Nigeria—could contribute to a significant slowdown of progress toward the global poverty goal. But experience shows that knowing the probabilities and magnitudes of such events in the long term is close to impossible.

### Uncertainty in poverty projections

A pragmatic way to simulate future growth and the consequences for global poverty and shared prosperity is to draw on patterns observed in historical growth rates. For example, the set of projections of global poverty presented in chapter 1 essentially assumed that future growth would be identical to past average growth performance over some prespecified period and varied the reference period. As some past periods have seen faster growth than others, this approach creates different scenarios for the global poverty headcount in 2030. Similar to the projections in chapter 1, figure 4.1 shows three trajectories for global poverty based on projecting future per capita growth rates with observed growth in the 1980s, 1990s, and 2000s, respectively.[1] Per capita growth in developing countries was very low (and in many cases negative) in the 1980s, improved somewhat in the 1990s, and became even better in the 2000s. Correspondingly, projections based on growth rates from these three decades produce widely diverging projections for poverty. If future growth per capita is similar to the 2000s, the projection gives a headcount ratio of 4.8 percent, short of the 3 percent target, but nevertheless an impressive reduction in the number of poor people. If the next decades see growth rates similar to those of the 1990s or 1980s, however, the projections suggest much lower reduction in poverty, with a headcount ratio above 11 percent.

**Figure 4.1** Projecting global poverty headcount rates based on past growth rates, 2010–30

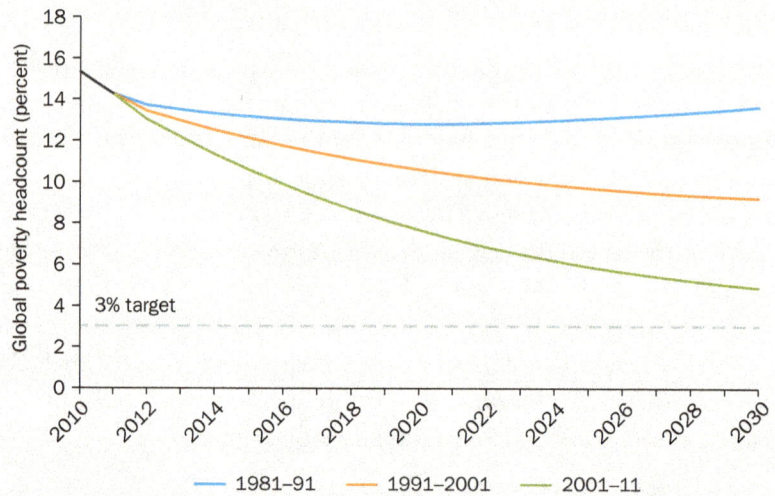

*Sources:* Based on data from the World Bank PovcalNet database and Penn World Table (version 8).
*Note:* Poverty projections assume distribution-neutral growth, based on historical growth patterns from different periods. Poverty headcount is estimated using a lognormal approximation of the income distribution. See box 4.2 for a full description of the methodology.

These very different trajectories illustrate that even when modeling future growth based on past observed growth rates, simply varying the period of past growth can generate large variations in projected poverty rates. Although patterns observed in the more recent past may be more reflective of patterns that can be expected in the near future (because of demographic and structural changes), the large variation in growth rates in the past illustrates large uncertainty about the future. Furthermore, as noted by Easterly and others (1993), correlations of growth rates across decades in the past have generally been low, highlighting that there is a lot of uncertainty that is not captured by looking at the past to project the future.

Growth also varies from year to year and across countries. Rather than basing projections for all countries on their past *average* growth rates, a more realistic approach is to treat and model future growth as uncertain in every country and produce probabilistic scenarios based on draws from past variation. Uncertainty about future growth can thus be modeled by taking random draws from the historical distribution of developing country growth rates. Such an approach explicitly incorporates uncertainty about future growth performance into scenarios of future growth by looking at past variation in growth rates. Box 4.2 describes in greater detail the methods used for these projections. Figure 4.2 shows the results from 10 simulations for the global headcount based on this approach and illustrates the widely varying poverty trajectories that are implied by past variation in growth.

## Box 4.2  Modeling uncertainty in poverty projections

The projections of poverty in this chapter rely on projecting growth rates based on past patterns and variation of growth. The derivation of poverty headcounts assumes that incomes are lognormally distributed in each country, with moments that match the observed survey mean and Gini coefficient. With the assumption of lognormality, country-level headcounts are estimated and aggregated to a global poverty headcount. Although the lognormal assumption is cruder than the more sophisticated distributional assumptions made in PovcalNet, this rough-and-ready approach does a reasonably good job of matching the PovcalNet estimates of the global headcount since the 1980s.

To simulate uncertainty about future growth, one can draw on observed variation of growth in the past. It is assumed that future growth is uncertain, but that uncertainty about future growth can be captured by taking draws from the historical distribution of developing country growth rates. Specifically, it is assumed that the historical data on growth are generated by the following simple empirical model:

$$g_{i,t} = \mu_i + \theta_i g_t + \varepsilon_{i,t}.$$

Real per capita consumption growth in country $i$ at time $t$, $g_{i,t}$, consists of a country fixed effect, $\mu_i$; the country's response to global shocks, $\theta_i g_t$; and an idiosyncratic component $\varepsilon_{i,t}$. Note that each country's growth may respond differently to a global

shock. It is simply assumed that global shocks are adequately proxied by the historical average world per capita consumption growth retrieved from the Penn World Table (version 8). More elaborate versions of a model like this could replace global growth with an unobserved common factor, whose distribution can be retrieved from the data with an unobserved components model.

The equation is estimated by ordinary least squares regressions for each of the 122 countries represented in the PovcalNet database, that is, estimates for $\mu_i$, $\theta_i$, and the country-specific variance of the error term, $\sigma_i^2$, are obtained for each country. With these estimates in hand, draws from the distribution of country growth rates are generated for each year between 2012 and 2030. Specifically, for each country, draws from a normal distribution are generated with mean $\hat{\mu}_i$ and variance $\hat{\sigma}_i^2$ corresponding to the country-specific component of the growth rate. In addition, identical draws are deployed for all countries from the distribution of historical global average growth rates, $g_t$; however, this is multiplied by a global shock by the country-specific response $\hat{\theta}_i$. Adding the country and global components gives annual growth rate projections that are cumulated forward to obtain a path for mean income for each country. Country-level and global poverty headcounts are then calculated with the same lognormal distributional assumptions about income distributions. Finally, this process is

*(continued)*

151

## Box 4.2   Continued

repeated 1,000 times, resulting in 1,000 trajectories of poverty for the global headcount.

In addition to uncertainty about growth rates, uncertainty about changes in inequality and thus growth incidence is added to the methodology described above. Similarly, draws are taken from the historical distribution of annual changes in the Gini coefficients with the spells from all developing countries that have available data in the PovcalNet database. Draws from this distribution are then generated for each country and for each year between 2012 and 2030, which are then cumulatively added to the country's Gini coefficient from 2012 onward. The projected growth rates and the projected Ginis are then used to calculate the global headcounts in the same way as before, and the procedure is repeated 1,000 times.

As an additional exercise, the effect that a possible proliferation of global or country-level crises could have on the global headcount is simulated. For this purpose, the simulation uses the global headcount corresponding to the average growth rate

projection and without distributional uncertainty as the benchmark scenario. To capture the effect of one additional global crisis, it is assumed that countries grow during one year at the lowest historical global growth rate instead of their annualized historical growth rate. Instead of choosing a particular year to replace the countries' average growth rate with this "global shock," the effect is spread out over the entire projection period. This smoothing of the shock over the projection period does not affect the global headcount projection in 2030 for which the exact timing of the crisis is irrelevant. To model additional country-specific shocks—as opposed to global shocks—the same exercise is performed, but instead of subtracting the lowest historical global growth rate, the lowest historical country-specific growth rate is subtracted. To estimate the effect of several additional crises, the negative growth shock is simply subtracted several times.

*Source:* Adapted from Chen and others (2013).

The range of trajectories for future poverty obtained from running 1,000 such simulations is shown in figure 4.3, drawing from growth rates observed from 2000 to 2010. This "fan chart" for the projected global headcount shows the median projection of the global headcount for each year, together with the 1st, 5th, 95th, and 99th percentiles, where these percentiles are calculated across the 1,000 replications (draws) for each country. The median poverty headcount across replications looks similar to some of the scenarios shown above and in chapter 1, with the poverty headcount declining smoothly over time to around 5.1 percent of the global population by 2030. However, there is substantial uncertainty around this trajectory, with the first percentile at around 3.8 percent of the global population and the 99th percentile at around 7.1 percent. This range results from relying on growth rates from the 2000s, which are optimistic for projecting into the future. Expanding the pool to include growth rates from previous decades would increase the headcount, as seen in figure 4.1,

**Figure 4.2** Drawing on past patterns and variation in growth to model uncertainty about future poverty rates, 2010–30

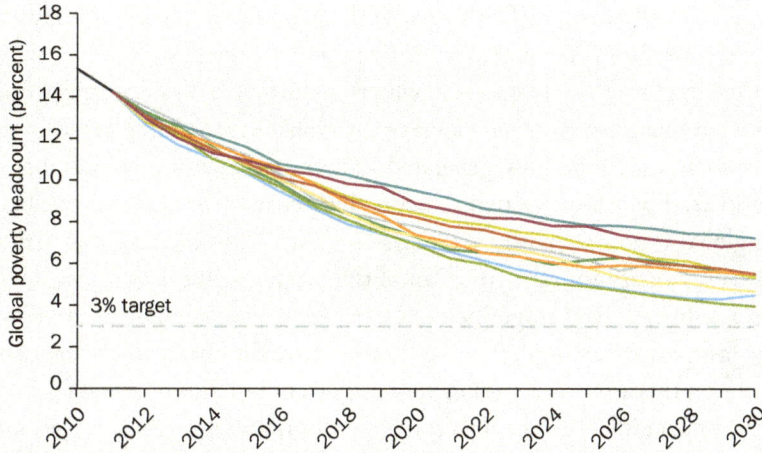

*Sources:* Based on data from the World Bank PovcalNet database and Penn World Table (version 8).
*Note:* The 10 lines shown in the graph represent a selection of poverty projections from 10 random draws of past growth rates. Projections assume distribution-neutral growth. See box 4.2 for a description of the methodology.

**Figure 4.3** Uncertainty about the trajectory of poverty based on growth, 2010–30

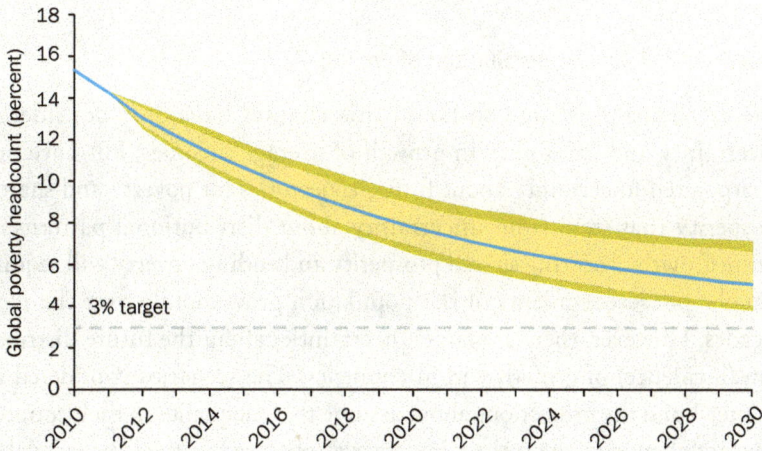

*Sources:* Based on data from the World Bank PovcalNet database and Penn World Table (version 8).
*Note:* The solid middle line is the median projection of the global headcount for each year and the shaded area shows the 1st/99th (light) and 5th/95th (darker) percentiles. These percentiles are calculated across the 1,000 replications (draws) for each country. Poverty projections assume distribution-neutral growth. See box 4.2 for a description of the methodology.

and also the range. These simulations show that when uncertainty about future growth rates is allowed to vary in line with the variation observed in the past, reaching the 3 percent global poverty goal appears uncertain and is still extremely difficult even with the most optimistic of draws of growth rates from the most optimistic periods of the past.

One might naturally question why this country-level uncertainty does not wash out at the aggregate level of the global headcount, given that the results combine randomly generated growth paths for a large number of countries. There are two main factors that account for uncertainty about the global trajectory with this method. First, the headcount measure of poverty is an asymmetric function of the mean—while very slow growth and resulting low-average incomes can result in very high headcounts, very fast growth and high incomes cannot drive the headcount below zero. However, this asymmetry is not very important in terms of the magnitude of the impact it has on the uncertainty about future growth rates. Second, and much more important, is the fact that there is a substantial global component to country growth rates in this model. Therefore, in the simulations, growth rates are correlated across countries in the same way that they are correlated across countries in the historical data. This correlation highlights how global shocks or slowdowns, and the associated uncertainty about the timing and magnitude of such shocks, contribute to uncertainty about shared prosperity and global poverty in the future.

### Uncertainty about the distribution of growth

The scenarios presented so far in this chapter have only considered uncertainty and variability in growth of average incomes, but have not incorporated uncertainty about future trajectories for poverty and shared prosperity that stem from uncertainty about distributional patterns of future growth. Boosting shared prosperity and ending poverty will require that the poorest segments of the population grow rapidly over the next decades. However, there are large uncertainties about the future distribution (incidence) of growth within countries. The scenarios considered in chapter 1 and the projections above assume that inequality in each country does not change in the future, but stays as observed in the latest available household survey. A similar approach is taken in the scenarios and simulations presented in Ravallion (2013). Only the location of the distribution shifts uniformly with the varying assumptions about growth in mean income, but not the growth incidence. Although this assumption may be

**Figure 4.4**  Uncertainty about inequality contributes to further uncertainty about future poverty, 2010–30

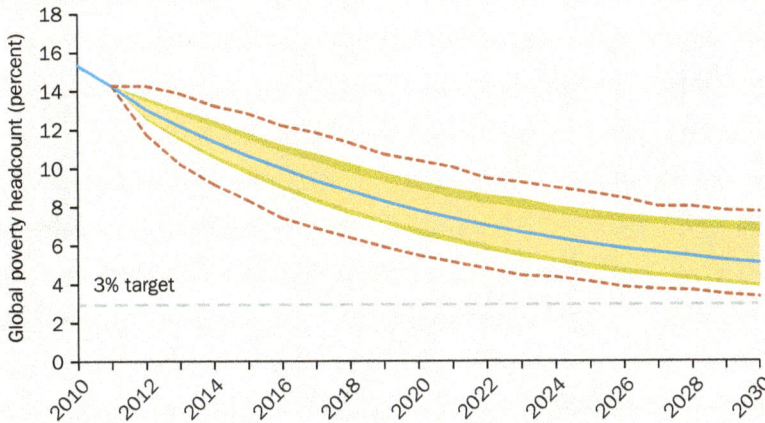

*Sources:* Based on data from the World Bank PovcalNet database and Penn World Table (version 8).
*Note:* The scenarios are the same as in figure 4.3, with the 1st and 99th percentiles from the simulations allowing inequality to vary superimposed (dashed red lines). See box 4.2 for a description of the methodology.

convenient for modeling the long-term evolution of poverty, it is clearly the case that income distributions and growth incidence do change over time.

As seen in chapter 2, the distribution of growth can vary significantly across time and countries. The simulations in chapter 2 show how different assumptions of future growth incidence can lead to quite different projections of future poverty rates. Rather than imposing a predetermined growth incidence on the projections, as is done in chapter 2, uncertainty about inequality can be incorporated into the projections by allowing future changes in inequality to vary in line with past observed variation in changes in inequality. Figure 4.4 incorporates variation in changes in inequality by allowing the Gini coefficient (a summary statistic for inequality in each country) to change based on patterns observed in the past. Uncertainty about inequality adds further uncertainty to the scenarios, increasing the "width" in the fan chart. But even in the most optimistic draw of changes in inequality (growth being distributed more to the poorest than the rich), the simulation falls short of the target, and the draws range from 3.3 percent in the most optimistic draw to 7.7 percent in the most pessimistic draw.

Although the incidence of growth can be influenced by policy, it is often also a result of external shocks that disproportionately affect the sectors

**Figure 4.5** The frequency of negative growth

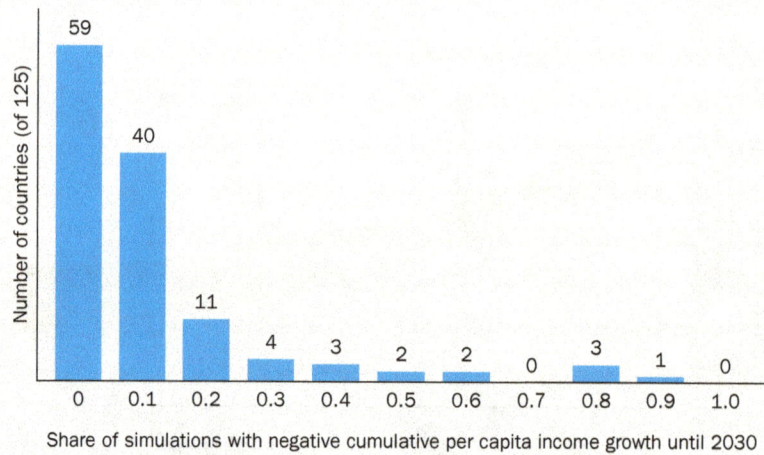

Sources: Based on data from the World Bank PovcalNet database and Penn World Table (version 8).
Note: See box 4.2 for a description of the methodology.

in which the poor work. For example, rising food prices can have a large effect on the poor who work in agriculture—either negative or positive, depending on whether the poor are net producers or consumers of agricultural products. On average, changes in the distribution of growth have been favorable to the poorest in many of the countries for which data are available in the recent decade, as seen in chapter 2 and documented by Narayan, Saavedra-Chanduvi, and Tiwari (2013). But there is no systematic evidence for such a trend in the longer time-series distribution data (Dollar, Kleineberg, and Kraay 2014).

The simulations of future growth used to provide projections of future global poverty rates can also be used to infer uncertainty about countries' shared prosperity growth. Because growth is assumed to be distribution neutral in these simulations, one can attribute the same growth to the bottom 40 percent of the population as what is being projected for the mean. From the simulations carried out, one can simply tabulate the frequency of each country experiencing zero or negative average growth between 2011 and 2030. Figure 4.5 shows the frequency of stagnation or deterioration in mean income for the period to 2030, implied by the scenarios discussed above, based on the relatively high growth rates observed in the 2000s. The bars show the percentage of simulated trajectories that project negative or stagnating growth. For example, of the 125 countries in the simulations presented here, 59 countries have a small risk of experiencing negative or zero growth, as only 0 to 10 percent of the 1,000 trajectories predict this outcome. However, for 40 countries, between 10 and 20 percent of the trajectories predict stagnating or decreasing per capita income. Finally, for a total of 8 countries, more than half of all estimated trajectories predict negative cumulative per capita income growth until 2030. Overall, these results highlight that sustaining positive shared prosperity growth is not a given, even if recent average trends have been positive in several regions and countries.

### Uncertainty about the long-term sustainability of development trajectories

In addition to high growth rates and a pro-poor growth incidence, the economic, environmental, and social sustainability of development trajectories will affect the ability to achieve and sustain progress toward the World Bank's two goals. In announcing its new goals, the World Bank stressed that the path toward them must be environmentally, socially, and economically sustainable over time (World Bank 2013a). In other words, achieving these goals through a blend of higher economic growth and inclusion should be sustainable and not achieved at the expense of later generations—either through excessive fiscal burdens, social strife, accelerated climate change, loss of biodiversity, or further environmental degradation. Poverty should end permanently and prosperity should be shared not only across populations, but also across generations. Thus, limiting the extent to which development trajectories over the next decades compromise future growth will be important.

Sustainable growth trajectories are needed to continue progress toward the goals in the medium and long run. For example, a development trajectory that relies on depleting natural resources, without consideration for how growth will be sustained beyond the resource boom, may result in reaching the goal in the short term but compromising growth thereafter. Similarly, fiscal stimulus programs or safety nets may be an effective way to boost growth among the poorest in the short run, but need to be implemented in a fiscally sustainable manner to ensure that shared prosperity is sustained across generations. The threats posed by climate change may be the most prominent source of uncertainty about future sustainability. Furthermore, it will also be important that development strategies are socially and politically sustainable. Political, social, and armed conflict is often associated with substantial growth slowdowns and increases in poverty. Persistent inequalities of opportunity can also contribute to social instability and unsustainable social contracts and compromise social cohesion.

However, as with average growth and growth incidence, forecasting at what degree development trajectories are sustainable and which are not is difficult. Future political events, technological evolution, and other factors that will determine the sustainability of development strategies are highly uncertain. A measure that can be useful in gauging the sustainability of growth trajectories, albeit imprecisely so, is the concept of adjusted net savings. Also known as genuine savings, it is a sustainability indicator that measures savings rates in an economy after taking into account investments in human capital, depletion of natural resources, and costs caused by pollution (Hamilton and Clemens 1999; Hamilton and Atkinson 2006). Similarly, the concept of "green growth" can be a useful framework for ensuring that countries achieve the rapid growth they need for poverty reduction and shared prosperity in the short term without causing costly and irreversible environmental damage, compromising future progress (Hallegatte and others 2012; World Bank 2012a).

## Sources of uncertainty about progress toward the goals

So far, this chapter has discussed, illustrated, and simplistically modeled how uncertainty affects the global poverty and shared prosperity goals, without discussing the origin of uncertainty in much detail. The remainder of the chapter reviews some of the sources of uncertainty that will affect the measurability and achievability of the goals. The discussion focuses on selected factors that may cause major economic shocks or change the nature of growth in the coming decades, including economic and financial crises, climate change, political and armed conflict, and pandemics. The chapter focuses on these selected factors in particular because they are shocks that may pose downside risk to the goals and may not be sufficiently taken into account when modeling future growth based on past patterns and variation in growth.

### Crises and recessions—economic, financial, and food price shocks

Economic crises are an important source of growth volatility. Uncertainty about the depth and frequency of future crises contributes to uncertainty around long-term average growth rates, poverty, and shared prosperity. Crises encompass a broad variety of events, including financial crises triggered by capital flight, bank runs, asset bubbles, currency crises, and sovereign default. Financial crises affect the real economy, as both consumer demand and private and public investment can depend on capital markets, as well as general economic confidence and aggregate demand. Much research has focused on how financial crises develop and how they might be prevented, but the literature has reached little consensus on how to prevent them (World Bank 2013b). Such crises will likely continue to occur in the years leading to 2030, which makes it important not to ignore them when assessing progress toward the goals and to continue efforts to anticipate them with better data and early warning systems.

Volatility, slowdowns, and poverty increases resulting from the sort of crises that have been observed in the past are, to a large extent, factored into the modeled trajectories with uncertainty presented in the previous section, as the model draws from past periods that also experienced crises. However, it is impossible to know exactly the frequency and magnitudes of these events. To understand better the downside risk to the goals posed by more crises, the poverty projection model can incorporate additional shocks equivalent to the country-specific worst growth rate, from one to five times over the period. The simulations smooth the impact of the shock, so that the effect is just in the aggregate, that is, the objective is to illustrate the impact at the end point (2030) and not the dynamic over time. The result of this exercise is presented in figure 4.6, which shows that adding five such shock years for each country adds nearly 4 percentage points to the simulated global poverty rate in 2030. These scenarios are for illustrative purposes and without any probability attached to them; it should be noted that for each and every country to experience several additional worst-case crisis years from 2011 to 2030 may be an unrealistically pessimistic scenario. A simulation adding global worst-case growth shocks shows similar, albeit more modest, impacts on poverty (up to 2 percent for five such shocks). Overall, a relatively small impact results from adding additional crisis-years to the simulation. This result is in contrast to the large impacts on the poverty headcount that result from assuming longer periods with lower average growth (as seen in past decades), as illustrated in figure 4.1. Importantly, the scenarios shown in figure 4.6 only consider effects on average incomes and do not allow for distributional heterogeneous effects of crises and downturns.

**Figure 4.6** Scenarios for global poverty under more frequent crises, 2010–30

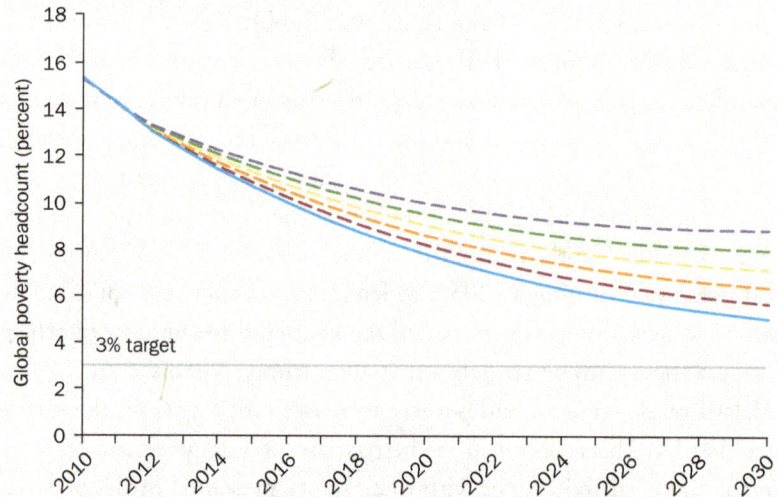

Sources: Based on data from the World Bank PovcalNet database and Penn World Table (version 8).
Note: Poverty projections assume distribution-neutral growth and baseline scenario growth rates the same as 2000–10. The dashed lines show scenarios for adding the negative growth impact of one to five additional worst-growth experiences for each country. See box 4.2 for a description of the methodology.

In addition to the frequency and magnitude of future crises, there is also uncertainty about the degree of contagion—spreading across countries and regions—caused by future crises. As the world becomes increasingly interlinked through trade and investment, the extent to which individual countries' growth is affected by other countries' growth rates is likely to be more important. For example, recent research by Drummond and Liu (2013) shows how the growing economic links between Africa and China, which have been positive overall for economic growth in Sub-Saharan Africa, also carry risks and added uncertainty for future growth. Based on panel data analysis, the authors estimate that a 1 percentage point decline in China's domestic investment is associated with an average 0.6 percentage point decline in Sub-Saharan African countries' export growth, with larger effects for resource-rich countries, especially oil exporters. This finding illustrates how economic integration can contribute to increased volatility and uncertainty about future growth in average incomes and poverty.

In contrast to the somewhat limited effect additional crises have on the aggregate simulations of poverty for the long run, evidence from large economic crises and periods of recession illustrate the potential negative impacts on poverty in the short term. The poverty headcount often

**Table 4.1    Increases in poverty before and during selected recessions**

| Country | Spell Start | Spell End | GDP per capita change (annual %) | Poverty headcount ratio ($1.25 PPP) Start | End | Change |
|---|---|---|---|---|---|---|
| Argentina | 1994 | 1995 | −4.1 | 1.9 | 3.9 | 2.0 |
| Argentina | 2000 | 2002 | −8.5 | 5.1 | 12.6 | 7.5 |
| Armenia | 2008 | 2010 | −6.1 | 1.3 | 2.5 | 1.2 |
| Belize | 1994 | 1995 | −1.6 | 8.9 | 14.0 | 5.1 |
| Brazil | 1982 | 1983 | −5.6 | 13.7 | 16.7 | 3.0 |
| Brazil | 1989 | 1990 | −5.9 | 13.7 | 17.2 | 3.5 |
| Colombia | 1996 | 1999 | −1.8 | 13.0 | 16.2 | 3.2 |
| Côte d'Ivoire | 1987 | 1988 | −2.3 | 8.7 | 13.8 | 5.1 |
| Ecuador | 1998 | 1999 | −6.6 | 14.5 | 23.9 | 9.5 |
| El Salvador | 2008 | 2009 | −3.6 | 5.4 | 9.0 | 3.5 |
| Honduras | 1993 | 1994 | −3.8 | 23.5 | 35.9 | 12.4 |
| Indonesia | 1996 | 1999 | −4.3 | 43.4 | 47.7 | 4.3 |
| Kyrgyz Republic | 2004 | 2005 | −1.3 | 14.2 | 22.9 | 8.7 |
| Mexico | 1994 | 1996 | −2.0 | 3.6 | 7.9 | 4.3 |
| Nigeria | 1992 | 1996 | −0.3 | 61.9 | 68.5 | 6.6 |
| Paraguay | 2001 | 2002 | −2.0 | 11.1 | 15.8 | 4.7 |
| Paraguay | 2008 | 2009 | −5.7 | 5.6 | 7.6 | 2.0 |
| Peru | 2000 | 2001 | −1.2 | 12.4 | 14.5 | 2.1 |
| Russian Federation | 1993 | 1996 | −6.7 | 1.5 | 2.8 | 1.3 |
| Venezuela, RB | 1987 | 1989 | −4.2 | 3.1 | 6.3 | 3.2 |
| Venezuela, RB | 2001 | 2002 | −10.5 | 9.6 | 15.9 | 6.3 |

*Sources:* Based on data from the World Bank PovcalNet database and the World Development Indicators database.

*Note:* A selection of growth spells of less than five years with negative per capita gross domestic product (GDP) growth over the period. PPP = purchasing power parity.

increases during crisis events because of loss of employment and overall reduction in aggregate demand. Table 4.1 shows changes in poverty rates before and during selected periods of negative economic growth for a selection of countries. The poverty headcount rose during crisis episodes in Latin America during the 1980s and 1990s and in Southeast Asia during the late 1990s. The table is limited to a selection of estimates where internationally comparable data are available. An overview of the impact of crises as measured by national poverty lines in the 1980s and 1990s is available in World Bank (2000). The 2008 global financial crisis affected developing nations less than the large regional downturns in past decades and what was foreseen by the World Bank and others at the outset of the crisis.

### Distributional effects of crises

The simulations of increased frequency of crises assume distribution-neutral impacts. Although the poor are often affected by crises, there is no systematic evidence that, on average, their welfare falls proportionately more in crises relative to richer segments of the population. Analysis of distributional change during past crises suggests that relative within-country inequality declines as often as it increases during recessions and crises, with no change on average (Ravallion 2008). Thus, the most appropriate assumption for estimating the effect of future economic crises on aggregate poverty headcounts is that the burden of crises will be uniformly proportional across the income distribution, as was assumed in the above simulations. However, in individual countries, crises may not be distribution neutral; certainly inequality falls in some countries and increases in others, but there is no systematic effect on average.

In some cases, the poor can be sheltered from crises by factors similar to those contributing to their poverty in the first place, such as geographic remoteness, poor connectivity with markets, and subsistence practices. Research by Ravallion and Lokshin (2007) on the Indonesian crisis of 1998 found sharp but geographically diverse increases in poverty, caused by uneven impacts and exposure. Proportionate impacts on extreme poverty were more likely in initially better-off and less unequal districts. A study by Friedman and Levinsohn (2002), also on the Indonesia crisis, found that although most households were affected, the urban poor suffered most, largely because poor rural households were able to produce food, which alleviated the worst impacts of the high inflation seen during the crisis. In stark contrast, the rural poor were more heavily affected in Thailand around the same time, partly because of their stronger link to the urban economy compared with the rural poor in Indonesia (Ravallion 2008).

Going forward, there is particular uncertainty regarding how global food prices will develop and affect the poor. Higher food prices could affect the poor negatively, but could also help them escape poverty more quickly, depending, to a large extent, on whether the poor are net producers or consumers of food. In countries like Cambodia, Tanzania, and Vietnam, many net sellers of food among the rural poor would benefit from higher prices (Mendoza 2009). Although net sellers of food comprise a much smaller fraction of the total poor in other countries, evidence from Bangladesh suggests that the benefits of higher crop prices over the past decade extend beyond net producers and that rural wages have also seen a positive effect (Jacoby and Dasgupta 2014). Similarly, in India, Jacoby (2013) found that once wage gains were taken into account, rural households across the income spectrum benefited from higher crop prices. In two recent studies of food prices and poverty globally, Headey (2013, 2014) finds evidence that, on average, higher food prices reduce poverty and inequality in the medium term. He finds evidence that the 2007–08 increase in global food prices has, in fact, accelerated global poverty reduction, contrary to assessments prior to the increase, which warned that price hikes would raise overall poverty in low-income countries considerably. The uncertainty about the future growth patterns in agriculture, and its potential impact on poverty and shared prosperity, is discussed further in the section on climate change below.

### Long-term impacts of economic crises

Crises can be caused by unsustainable economic policies, but can also compromise the fiscal sustainability of policies and programs that assist the poorest. High government debt resulting from crises may limit the government's ability to cushion future crises. Among developing countries, fiscal situations have significantly deteriorated since the 2008 financial crisis. A recent assessment suggests that 37 percent of developing countries saw their fiscal deficits rise by 3 percent of gross domestic product (GDP) or more between 2007 and 2013 (World Bank 2014). Although some of the fiscal resources certainly have been used on policies to cushion the impact of the crisis, such deterioration of the fiscal space available to governments for building up buffers to respond to future crises limits the possibility to assist those in need through safety nets or other government programs. This situation illustrates how crises can have lasting impacts on the vulnerability of economies beyond the crisis itself and the potential consequences for poverty and the economic welfare of the poorest households and, thereby, the viability of reaching the World Bank's goals.

Households, individuals, and families also take on debt and experience other long-term impacts of crises, with welfare losses often lasting a lot longer than the crisis period itself. As noted by Ravallion (2008), the food poor can be particularly vulnerable to long-term impacts of crises, as labor productivity may be significantly reduced at low levels of nutrition. That is, a negative shock could push a poor household past a tipping point to a level of consumption from which it is difficult to escape. Research on past crises has found lasting impacts of shocks well beyond the economic downturns with which they were associated. A study by Ravallion and Lokshin (2007) of the 1997–98 East Asian crisis finds that up to half of Indonesia's poverty in 2002 (long after broader economic recovery had taken place) was attributable to the 1998 crisis. Many of the actions poor families have to take to help protect their current living conditions also contribute to the lasting consequences of crises. For example, household debt often rises, key productive assets are sold, and children are temporarily or permanently withdrawn from school to save on fees or contribute labor activities, thus deteriorating human capital. Such drastic responses can be difficult to revert.

### Fragility: Political instability, conflict, and the goals

Periods of conflict and political instability can pose challenges to ending extreme poverty and boosting shared prosperity. Moreover, the unpredictable nature of political and conflict events renders it difficult to incorporate them into projections. Most armed conflicts are associated with lower growth and increases in poverty. A recent example of the sudden and unpredictable impact of conflict is the case of Syria. Syria's GDP was forecasted to grow 5 percent annually over the past three years; instead, the country's GDP has collapsed, with some estimates suggesting that more than two thirds of GDP has been lost since the onset of civil war, with undoubtedly large negative impacts also on poverty and shared prosperity (IMF 2011; UNDP 2014). Even in situations without direct armed conflict, periods of political instability and social unrest are associated with slower growth, especially in the short run, and consequently slower poverty reduction and shared prosperity.

Slowdowns and variations in economic growth associated with political instability and conflict are implicitly included in the projections presented earlier in this chapter, in that they were drawn from periods and countries that contained instability and conflict. However, future patterns of conflict and political instability may look different from those of the past. Data on conflict frequency and intensity show that political instability and conflict have declined markedly over past decades. For example, 2010 was the year

**Figure 4.7** The incidence of armed conflict in the world has declined since the early 1990s

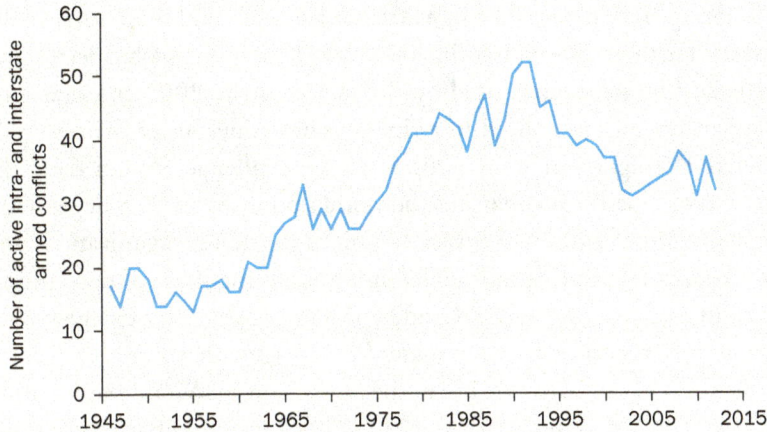

*Source:* Based on data from the Uppsala Conflict Data Program (Themnér and Wallensteen 2013).

with the lowest number of active conflicts since 1975 and much fewer than in the 1990s. (Figure 4.7 summarizes the trends in armed conflict.) Overall, the 2000s were the least conflict-affected decade since the 1970s (Themnér and Wallensteen 2013). This fact may have contributed to higher growth in the 2000s, particularly in Africa, and thus contributed to faster poverty reduction (thereby also contributing to relatively more optimistic trajectories for global poverty projections based on annualized growth rates from the 2000s). However, the incidence of future conflict and instability is largely unpredictable and may change in the years ahead. The recent increases in conflict in the Middle East and North Africa region is of particular concern, potentially causing reversals in poverty reduction and deteriorating progress toward shared prosperity. The threat of conflict is further complicated by its link to climate change as a potential contributor to increased conflict. Several studies show that as weather patterns become more volatile and as countries become warmer, the threat of conflict could likely increase (Hsiang, Burke, and Miguel 2013).

Poverty is high in most fragile and conflict-affected states (FCS) and extreme poverty will likely be further concentrated in these countries toward 2030. However, poverty data are very sparse for most FCS, which makes creating poverty estimates difficult and projections uncertain. An example is the Democratic Republic of Congo, a fragile state that is home to more than 50 million poor people, as of the last household survey, which was conducted in 2005. To date, the country has only one such consumption survey that can be used reliably for international poverty monitoring, and there is therefore little evidence of trends in poverty in the country. Furthermore, monitoring poverty in FCS from a global perspective has been further complicated by the fact that the 2005 International Comparison Program, used to estimate purchasing power parities, only covered 21 fragile states. In addition to the challenge of poor data, the question of exactly how many of the world's poor live in FCS depends on the definition of FCS, which varies significantly across organizations and researchers.[2] Depending on the definition used, the share of poor people living in FCS varies greatly.[3] Crude estimates, given the extremely poor data on poverty and growth in many FCS, suggest that about 17 percent of the world's poor currently live in the 36 FCS on the World Bank's list of FCS for 2014.[4] In contrast, when the OECD's longer list of 51 fragile states is used (also used by Chandy, Ledlie, and Penciakova [2013]), 44 percent of the world's poor currently live in countries classified as fragile.

Regardless of the definition of FCS, poverty is a persistent feature of many countries that fall under either definition. FCS tend to lag in economic growth and poverty reduction and do not easily escape their status as fragile states. In Africa, where nearly half the countries are defined as being fragile, growth performance and poverty reduction in FCS have been worse in fragile states (figure 4.8). In the most recent decade, in which many developing countries experienced high per capita growth, average annual real GDP per capita growth for FCS was only 1.7 percent (World Bank 2013c). Available estimates show that the poverty headcount has fallen more slowly over the past three decades in countries currently classified as FCS. The classification of FCS tends to be slow in changing. Andrimihaja, Cinyabuguma, and Devarajan (2011) note that the probability that an African fragile state in 2001 remained classified as fragile in 2009 is as high as 0.95. Globally, the 35 countries defined by the World Bank as fragile in 1979 were still classified as fragile in 2009—a pattern leading some researchers to suggest that there is a fragility trap (Andrimihaja, Cinyabuguma, and Devarajan 2011; Collier 2008).

There is great uncertainty about future patterns of fragility. The simulations deployed earlier in this chapter, to obtain projections of future global poverty, show that the share of the world's poor that live in countries that today are classified as FCS will at least double by 2030. This result is because of the weaker growth and higher initial poverty in many of these

**Figure 4.8**  Economic growth and poverty reduction are slower in Africa's fragile states, 1981–2010

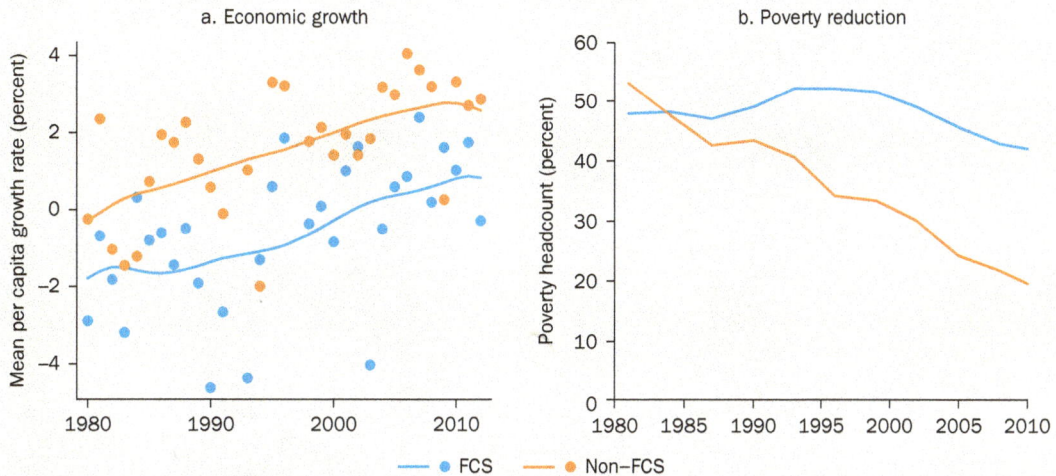

Sources: Based on data from the World Bank PovcalNet database and the World Bank World Development Indicators database.
Note: In panel a, average per capita growth rates are for non-oil producing Sub-Saharan African countries; dots represent annual growth rates and lines represent the mean trend in growth rates. Fragile and conflict-affected states (FCS) classification is that of World Bank for FY2014 and held constant over time.

countries. The absolute number of poor in fragile states would increase under these scenarios. Figure 4.9 shows the implied share of the global poor living in FCS (the figure uses the two definitions discussed above). The projection is for the relatively optimistic scenario of growth rates similar to those of the 2000s for all countries.

The observed patterns of slower economic growth and slower poverty reduction in fragile states are also reflected in the literature on the relationship between political instability or unrest and economic growth. Political instability has been associated with lower economic growth in several empirical reviews. In an early study, Alesina and others (1996) find that during periods of high "propensity of government collapse" in countries, GDP growth was significantly lower. Rodrik (1999) finds that weak institutional capacity and societal division were key determinants of economic growth collapses in the past. A more recent study by Aisen and Veiga (2013), looking at data from 169 countries between 1960 and 2004, finds that political instability is particularly harmful through its effects on declining total factor productivity growth and by discouraging the physical and human capital accumulation needed for growth. Similarly, Jong-A-Pin (2009) finds a significant, negative relationship between

**Figure 4.9** The share of the global poor living in fragile and conflict-affected states could double by 2030

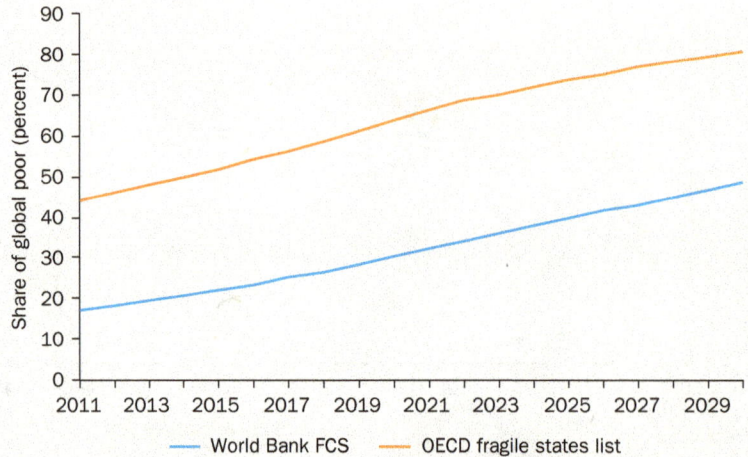

*Sources:* Based on data from the World Bank PovcalNet database and World Development Indicators database.
*Note:* Fragile and conflict-affected states (FCS) classifications are for FY2014 and held constant over time. OECD = Organisation for Economic Co-operation and Development.

regime stability and growth. Burger, Ianchovichina, and Rijkers (2013) demonstrate how political instability reduces foreign direct investment in tradable nonresource manufacturing and services, with negative implications for potential growth.

Governance transitions may also negatively affect growth in the short run, but often lead to stronger growth in the long run. Transitions, such as those recently seen in the Middle East and North Africa region, often affect economic growth patterns and may also have distributional impacts, with implications for the World Bank goals. A growing body of research finds that such transitions are associated, on average, with slow economic growth (some suggest for up to a decade), but that in the longer run growth is higher after the transition process (Acemoglu and others 2014; Rodrik and Wacziarg 2005; Freund and Jaud 2013; Khandelwal and Roitman 2013). Figure 4.10 shows an average trajectory of GDP for 10 years before and after transitions, based on data for 69 governance transitions between 1975 and 2000, which are studied by Papaioannou and Siourounis (2008). The figure shows a sharp decline and slowdown in growth around transition events but, on average, strong recovery. This pattern suggests that instability associated with political transitions may lead to a slowdown

**Figure 4.10** Governance transitions are associated with temporary economic downturns and stronger long-term growth

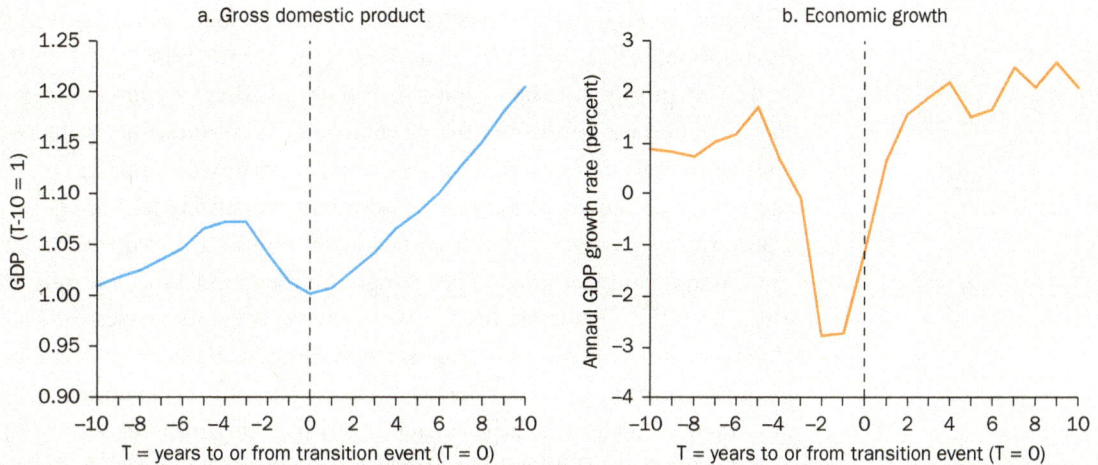

Source: Based on 69 partial and full democratization events as coded by Papaioannou and Siourounis (2008) merged with GDP data from the World Development Indicators. Growth rates are simple means.

of growth and poverty reduction, at least intermittently, as seen in many countries in the past. In the longer run, such periods are, on average, followed by sustained faster growth. Nevertheless, increased periods of political unrest could stall poverty reduction and delay progress toward the goals by 2030.

## Impacts of climate change and extreme weather

The two past assessments from the Intergovernmental Panel on Climate Change (IPCC) confirm that climate change is happening and having increasing impacts on societies (IPCC 2007, 2013). By 2030, climate scenarios suggest that the world will be, on average, approximately 1 degree Celsius warmer than it was in the late twentieth century with larger impacts in some areas, regardless of emissions of greenhouse gases in the next few decades. In the years up to 2030, in addition to higher average temperatures, climate change will likely contribute to increased intensity and frequency of extreme weather such as drought, flooding, and storms (IPCC 2014). Such changes can affect poverty reduction and economic growth; however, exactly how and by how much is subject to great uncertainty. In the longer term, beyond 2030, climate changes are expected to be much larger and to have considerable potential impact on economies. The following brief review first focuses on evidence of potential effects on average growth from climate change, before assessing potential distributional effects and effects on long-term sustainability.

The magnitude of the economic impacts of future climate change is highly uncertain and limits the possibility of understanding impacts of climate change on poverty and shared prosperity through impacts on average economic growth. Integrated assessment models (IAMs) are general equilibrium frameworks that have been commonly used to quantify various economic impacts of climate change and then model the net aggregate effect on GDP. The latest IPCC assessment report summarizes the likely effects of climate change on growth based on projections from such models. The report suggests that the overall aggregate global economic impacts of climate change are relatively small until warming of 3 degrees Celsius (IPCC 2014). A global mean average temperature rise of 2.5 degrees Celsius from preindustrial levels, which is not expected until well after 2050, is estimated by IAMs to lead to global economic losses between 0.2 and 2.0 percent of global GDP (Tol 2013; IPCC 2013). However, IPCC in its latest review concludes that losses are more likely to be greater, rather than smaller, than this range. The IPCC assessment also emphasizes that aggregate economic impacts disguise significant heterogeneity in impacts across regions, countries, and sectors. Relative to their income, the economic impacts of climate change are expected to be higher for poorer people and countries, thus contributing to global inequality (Eboli, Parrado, and Roson 2010; Tol 2013). Nevertheless, overall, these estimates of impacts on average incomes for 2030 are rather small compared with the aggregate growth expected over the next decades and would not have a great impact on poverty impacts if incorporated in the poverty projections provided for 2030 in this chapter.

The relatively modest impacts on economic output produced by the mainstream scenarios of the IAMs have recently been called into question. A growing literature argues that these models do not sufficiently account for the effects of climate change on economic output (Pindyck 2013; Stern 2013). In reviewing the IAM literature, Pindyck (2013) argues that many of the assumptions are largely arbitrary and can produce a wide range of results, and that there are neither theoretical nor empirical foundations to base the calibrations of the models on. Moreover, this literature argues that economic "damage functions" in the case of climate change should be understood in terms of depletion of stocks (capital), not only as reduction in flows. Models incorporating these aspects would show a more drastic impact on growth in the long run. Furthermore, there is increasing concern that growth models do not account for potential "tipping-point" risks for climate change with very rapid effects—such as the release of methane from the melting tundra in the arctic or large-scale crop failures. IAMs used to forecast growth prospects do not take into account such potentially dramatic effects of climate change. Therefore, estimates of the economic impact of climate change from these models remain largely uncertain.

Despite the limitations of the models, some analysts have used growth projections from IAMs to assess the impact of climate change on global poverty. One of the early applications was carried out by Anderson (2006), which looks at the impacts of climate change on $2-a-day poverty in 2100 based on GDP projections of the PAGE 2002 IAM model. Under a quite rapid climate change scenario under which mean temperature rises by 3.9 degrees Celsius by 2100, the predicted loss in per capita GDP from climate change is expected to be around 2.5 percent in India and Southeast Asia and 1.9 percent in Africa and the Middle East. When translated into poverty implications, the impacts are relatively small—between 24 million and 34 million additional people living on less than $2 a day at 2005 purchasing power parity. Assuming a worst-case scenario of the model at the 95th percentile of predicted impacts (where GDP per capita is lower in 2100 by between 9 percent and 13 percent than in the baseline scenario), the poverty impacts are larger, with an estimate of between 98 million and 149 million additional poor people, again as measured by the $2-a-day line in 2100. Skoufias and others (2011) update the long-term impacts of climate change on poverty with an alternative IAM, the Regional Integrated Model of Climate and the Economy (RICE). The authors look at impacts on $2-a-day poverty by 2055 (a higher poverty line and more than twice the time horizon compared with the World Bank's goals). The estimate they obtain using the RICE model is relatively small, with around 10 million additional people in poverty and the poverty headcount rate at 14.1 instead of 14.0 percent of the population, as measured at $2 a day. Given the relatively small impacts estimated with these models, it is clear that the use of scenarios from IAMs to assess poverty impacts for 2030 at the $1.25 poverty line would result in very small impacts on the global poverty headcount.

In contrast to the IAMs, a separate body of literature explores the links between weather changes and economic outcomes using data over a long time period, finding much more pronounced implications from warming on growth even in the short term, particularly for poor countries. This literature exploits variation in weather (rainfall, temperature, and storms) to identify effects on numerous economic outcomes, such as agricultural output, energy demand, labor productivity, mortality, manufacturing, trade, conflict, and migration.[5] A central study in this literature, by Dell, Jones, and Olken (2012), looks specifically at the link between temperature and overall economic growth by exploring a panel data set of more than 50 years of climate and growth data. The study finds that higher temperatures are likely to reduce economic output substantially in poor countries. Panel estimates that use data on year-to-year fluctuations suggest that for poor countries, per capita income growth falls by 1 percentage point for each 1 degree Celsius of warming.[6] In the medium term, a 1 degree Celsius increase in temperature reduces growth in poor countries by 1.9 percentage points. Furthermore, the findings suggest that higher temperatures affect growth through several channels, including by reducing agricultural output, industrial output, and even political stability. Of particular relevance for poverty reduction, the study finds that the impacts of temperature change are particularly marked in Sub-Saharan Africa. The estimates are much larger than what has been observed in the IAM literature. Although these results have large confidence intervals and are sensitive to specifications and country groupings, if the results are extrapolated into the future, they would lead to much larger impacts on growth and poverty than those found by the studies outlined above that rely on IAMs.

Despite the striking short-term evidence on the impact of weather changes on growth, such changes over relatively brief periods will not necessarily translate into long-run changes. As recognized by the researchers in this literature, the effect of a 1 degree Celsius higher temperature in a given country and year, as estimated by looking at past data, may not translate into comparable future changes for several reasons.[7] First, economies may adapt to long-term climate changes better than they adapt to shorter and more sudden annual or decade-long changes, such as droughts or floods. Adaptation can happen locally, for example, by changing farming practices, but also through innovation of adaptive technologies. Evidence from climate change in the United States in agriculture suggests that the effects persist for decades and that adaptation is only partial (Burke and Emerick 2013). Second, several potential effects of future climate change, including potential effects on sea levels, biodiversity, depletion of ground water, and storm and precipitation frequency and intensity, are not well captured in analysis of past data. Uncertainty around adaptation capabilities is great and makes assessing the impacts of climate change on poverty and shared prosperity difficult.

### Climate change and distributional impacts

The scenarios for climate change impacts discussed so far rely on effects through aggregate growth to assess impacts on poverty but ignore the potential distributional effects of climate change. Even if impacts on average growth may be modest in the medium term, the growth elasticity of poverty reduction may decline if sectors and natural resources that the poor rely more heavily on are severely affected by climate change. An increasing number of studies suggest that climate change will disproportionately affect the poorest because of their dependence on natural resources and ecosystem-based services or because the poorest have less capacity (financial, institutional, and technical) to adapt to climate change. A recent study by Angelsen and others (2014) measures environmental incomes, showing that environmental income shares are higher for low-income households than the rest. This is because the poor are more reliant on subsistence activities and products harvested from natural areas such as forests and lakes.

Increased frequency and intensity of weather shocks associated with climate change may also have lasting effects, especially on the poorest. Carter and others (2006), studying droughts in Ethiopia and Honduras, find that the poorest households struggle the most with shocks from natural disasters, adopting coping strategies that are costly and have lasting impact. Similarly, also studying rainfall shocks in Ethiopia, Dercon (2004) finds that droughts not only strongly affect consumption of the poorest in the short term, but also have impacts for as long as a decade. Loayza and others (2012) emphasize the heterogeneous impacts of natural disasters across sectors and, potentially, the income distribution, and emphasize the need to look at sectoral effects. Hallegatte and Dumas (2008) demonstrate theoretically how long-term income losses due to natural disasters are low if reconstructive capacity is high, while the impact can be large and negative when reconstructive capacity is low. This literature highlights how impacts on average growth can mask large differences across sectors and populations.

Another prominent concern for continued poverty reduction is the extent to which the poorest will be affected by the negative effects of climate change on agricultural yields and associated price shocks. Most of the poor worldwide live in rural areas, making impacts on agriculture particularly pertinent to assess. A substantial literature suggests significant negative impacts on agricultural productivity from climate change with potentially severe consequences for food security, particularly in South Asia and Sub-Saharan Africa—the regions with the largest share of the world's poor (Lobell and others 2008; Schlenker and Lobell 2010; Fischer, Shah, and Van Velthuizen 2002). The importance of agriculture in poverty reduction has further been corroborated by cross-country regressions that show that a 1 percent increase in agricultural per capita GDP, on average, reduces the extreme poverty gap squared by at least five times more than a 1 percent increase in GDP per capita outside agriculture, despite the smaller size of the agricultural sector (Christiaensen, Demery, and Kühl 2011). The potentially large impacts of climate change on the agricultural sector and the disproportional reliance of the poor on this sector could therefore alter the growth elasticity of poverty reduction, in comparison with what is observed in a world with less climate change.

Jacoby, Rabassa, and Skoufias (2011) propose a framework for estimating the distributional impacts of climate change in rural areas, with applications from India. The study estimates the impacts of climate change in 2040 on agricultural productivity and wages, taking into account adaptation (with district-level data). Their findings suggest that the impacts of climate change would lead to a substantial fall in agricultural productivity (17 percent overall) and a more modest consumption decline (of 6 percent on average) for most households in India in 2040, in comparison with a baseline scenario of no climate change. Furthermore, they show that climate change will have heterogeneous impacts across geographical areas and across the income distribution. Figure 4.11 shows the distributional effects found by Jacoby, Rabassa, and Skoufias relative to a baseline scenario of no climate change, showing a negative impact for all households across the income distribution. Although the effects from wages and land value (associated with a decline in agricultural production) are progressive, once cereal prices are taken into account, climate change impacts are regressive, falling more heavily on the poor than the rich. Integrating these findings into growth projections, the authors find an impact on $2-a-day poverty ranging from 0.6 to 4.8 percentage points in India in 2040, depending on the growth scenario—a quite large effect in comparison with other studies. The effects will be heterogeneous across space and time, given the different

**Figure 4.11** Climate change incidence curves for rural India, 2040

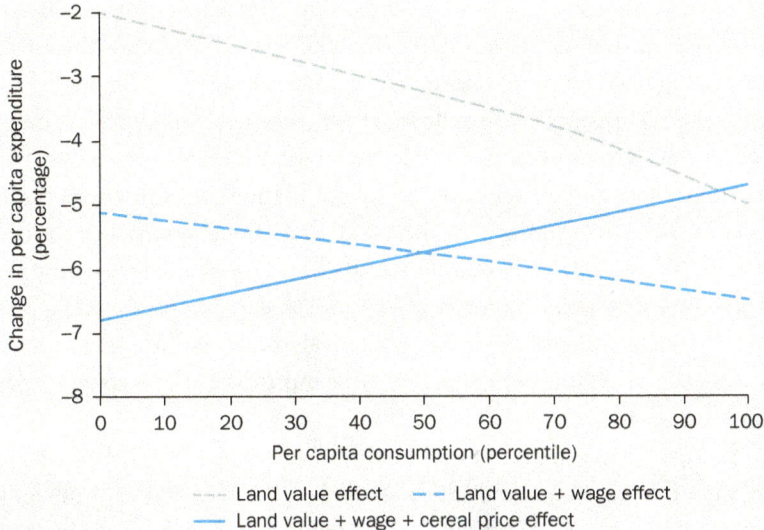

*Source:* Jacoby, Rabassa, and Skoufias (2011).
*Note:* Incidence curves assume a 17 percent decline in agricultural productivity from a projected 1.25°C temperature increase for the country as a whole by 2040, as laid out in Jacoby, Rabassa, and Skoufias (2011).

impacts of price shocks on agriculture incomes, as discussed in the section on crises and recessions above.

In addition to the impacts of climate change itself, there may also be distributional impacts of the adaptive strategies taken by individual countries and the world as a whole. Dercon (2012) posits that so-called "green growth" strategies, which are sensitive to environmental and climate change impacts of growth, may have unintended consequences for the poor that may even outweigh the benefits for the poor from higher average growth. The study highlights particularly how environmental regulation and pricing can have considerable harmful consequences for poor consumers. Understanding the impacts of adaptive strategies and how to get "green growth" right, globally and nationally, will be important to understand the full impact of climate change on poverty and shared prosperity.

## Uncertainty about climate change and long-term sustainability

Overall, despite the uncertainties, climate change will likely have a limited aggregate impact on extreme poverty and shared prosperity by 2030.

However, climate change could significantly affect the long-term sustainability of development progress beyond 2030, particularly in the latter part of the century when more catastrophic climate change would take place under current emissions scenarios. The effects of climate change are predicted to become more significant by mid-century. As climate change continues to happen in future decades and centuries, aggregate damages to economies could be considerable and have a larger effect on welfare, particularly for the poorest share of the population and those sensitive to shocks in the agricultural sector (Stern 2007). Although extreme poverty as the world knows it today would hopefully be eliminated by the latter part of the century, when more severe effects are expected to take place, a large share of people will still be living in relatively poor conditions. Sustained boosting of shared prosperity will likely be more difficult to sustain under such conditions.

It is clear that climate change could have a negative impact on average growth and the well-being of the poorest, but the magnitude of the long-term effects is uncertain. Although differing in terms of the magnitudes of the estimates, an emerging body of research provides evidence that climate change could slow the pace of global poverty reduction and shared prosperity growth, but that the overall, aggregate expected impact on the global poverty headcount will be relatively modest by 2030. Given the potentially more disastrous effects of climate change in the latter half of this century, one perspective is that the world now has a "window of opportunity" to eradicate poverty by 2030, and that increasing climate change impacts on growth and livelihoods after 2030 will make it more difficult and costly to do so later, particularly as the growth elasticity of poverty reduction may be reduced as a result of disproportional impacts on sectors and in regions on which the poorest depend and reside. Even if extreme poverty is successfully eradicated by 2030, climate change will likely continue to pose a real threat to many people living in near extreme poverty and compromise sustained progress toward shared prosperity.

### Global disease risk and pandemics

Global pandemics, such as influenza, plagues, smallpox, and AIDS, can have profound impacts on the economies, health, and well-being of societies and may be a threat to progress toward the poverty and shared prosperity goals. In an increasingly interconnected world, a pathogen transmitted to humans from poultry or livestock in a developing country can spread rapidly to other parts of the world within days (Jonas 2013; World Bank 2013b). Although the exact definition of a pandemic is contested, it generally refers to an epidemic of a new infectious disease occurring on a scale that crosses international boundaries, affecting a large number of people. Future pandemics are deemed likely to stem from zoonotic diseases (diseases caused by pathogens that can infect animals and humans), resulting in disease outbreaks among humans and animals (Jonas 2013; World Bank 2012b). Even when they do not turn into pandemics, infectious disease outbreaks can destroy the assets of the poor, for example through the collapse of markets for livestock and animal products. Furthermore, health, nutrition, and food security deteriorate when livestock and people are diseased. The poorest, often living close to livestock or wild animals, are the most vulnerable to such effects. Although the precise probability and magnitude of future disease outbreaks and pandemics remain very uncertain, they have the potential to hamper progress toward the poverty and shared prosperity goals. For example, the recent ebola outbreak in West Africa will likely reduce both growth and poverty reduction in the region.

The economic impact of a future pandemic will depend on its nature, scope, and scale, but could potentially be large. During a pandemic, shocks are likely in the transport, trade, financial, and tourism sectors. Global travel could collapse and affect economic growth in all regions. Only a quite limited literature has attempted to estimate the potential impacts, perhaps because of the lack of reliable data from past pandemics. A review of the available evidence by Burns, van der Mensbrugghe, and Timmer (2008) suggests that a dangerous form of influenza, similar to the 1918–19 flu, could kill more than 70 million people. A study by Murray and others (2007) finds that 96 percent of deaths from such a Spanish-flu-like pandemic would occur in the developing world, emphasizing the relative challenge posed to poor countries by such events, with direct consequences for the poverty goal. Based on the available evidence, Burns, van der Mensbrugghe, and Timmer (2008) estimate that the potential losses from such a severe influenza pandemic would be $3 trillion, or 4.8 percent of global GDP. They estimate that a moderate flu pandemic would have an impact of about half this amount; and weaker pandemics, such as the 2009 H1N1 flu pandemic, may have economic impacts of less than 0.5 percent of global GDP.

Some lessons for the impacts of large-scale disease can be drawn from the literature related to the HIV/AIDS pandemic, which has already had a large negative effect on economic development and poverty, particularly in

Africa. Early research on the economic impacts suggests that the pandemic reduced average national economic growth rates in the early 2000s by 2 to 4 percent a year across Africa (Dixon, McDonald, and Roberts 2002); however, the actual impact is thought to have been lower. Simulations by Bell, Devarajan, and Gersbach (2006) suggest that the South African economy could have shrunk to half its size at the time in about four generations in the absence of intervention. Beegle, De Weerdt, and Dercon (2008) find that such mortality shocks, especially among females, had a large impact on the consumption growth of households in Tanzania, illustrating the potential long-lasting impact of future pandemics. Although the effects of such disease can cause immense suffering and have huge social and economic costs on societies in aggregate, it is worth noting that high mortality can have perverse effects on key economic indicators, such as poverty headcount ratios and per capita growth. For example, Young (2005) suggests that the AIDS epidemic, on net, will improve future per capita consumption in South Africa, through the effect of high mortality on physical capital per worker. A similar effect was observed in European countries after the Black Death.

## Uncertainty and the ability to assess progress toward the goals

It is clear that future patterns of growth and, consequently, trajectories for poverty reduction and shared prosperity are highly uncertain. It is unrealistic to expect stable growth rates for all countries into the future. The first part of this chapter has shown that modeling future uncertainty about growth based on variation of past growth reinforces the conclusion from chapter 1 that the 3 percent target is very ambitious and highlights two further points. First, the considerable uncertainty about future growth performance implies considerable uncertainty about future trajectories for the global poverty headcount and shared prosperity. Second, even if under the fairly optimistic assumption that the growth pattern of the past decade, which has been quite favorable for developing countries, continues until 2030, once uncertainty is incorporated, even the most optimistic outcomes of these models, in terms of the 1 percent best possible draws from these models, imply a global headcount that still falls short of the target of 3 percent. And the most pessimistic draws suggest a rate far off the goal.

By reviewing selected sources of uncertainty that can pose substantial downside risk to the goals—economic and financial crises, political instability and conflict, climate change, and pandemics—it is clear that there are many factors that cannot be credibly incorporated into projections with defined probabilities and magnitudes, adding uncertainty about future poverty reduction and shared prosperity. Moreover, impacts from some of these uncertainties—especially climate change—will contribute to growth trajectories and variation that are different from those of the past. Although the impact of climate change on growth will likely be limited in the aggregate by 2030, there are highly diverging scenarios for both the distributional impacts and the long-term impacts on extreme poverty, which implies great uncertainty about the long-term sustainability of the poverty and shared prosperity goals. Future conflict and political stability may particularly challenge eradication of poverty in Africa, where many countries continue to be classified as "fragile" and have highly uncertain growth prospects, depending on whether they manage to escape the often vicious circle of instability and violence, which is detrimental to growth and poverty reduction. Progress toward the poverty goal in this region will crucially depend on continuing the trend of declining political instability and conflict.

Much of the discussion and analysis in this chapter has focused largely on uncertainties with negative impacts—such as climate change, conflict, and disease—which may act as obstacles to reaching the World Bank's goals. A fundamental source of uncertainty about future economic growth and poverty reduction that has not been extensively addressed in this chapter, but that also underpins many of the uncertainties in the chapter, is technological innovation. The development of new technologies may increase productivity and boost economic growth or mitigate some of the threats discussed. For example, a breakthrough in agricultural technology could improve the incomes of the poor. And renewable energy research or geo-engineering could have significant implications for mitigating the impacts or the rate of climate change. Innovations may also help improve policy and program design, making policies and programs more effective at reaching the poor and helping to improve future growth incidence in ways not seen in the past.

Overall, uncertainties in the projection of future poverty and shared prosperity can be reduced as more data, knowledge, and information become available. In particular, this chapter has highlighted the limitations of our knowledge of the distributional nature and long-term sustainability of various growth trajectories. More research and better data could help reduce the degree of uncertainty about future patterns of growth and poverty. In particular, having higher coverage and frequency of household survey data would allow improved research focusing on the direct effects of shocks on poverty and shared prosperity, as measured by changes in household consumption. Because of the lack of household survey data, much of the research that projects future impacts on poverty and shared prosperity relies on estimating changes in average GDP growth to infer changes in consumption. Furthermore, knowledge of the probabilities and magnitudes of complex issues can increase countries' and the international community's ability to assess what is required to reach the World Bank goals. Better data and ability to forecast and develop scenarios will not only help in better monitoring and assessing progress toward the goals, but also enable action to ensure that fewer people live in extreme poverty and that growth boosts the incomes of the poorest share of the population.

## Notes

1. These projections rely on a projection method that differs from those presented in chapter 1; thus, the results do not correspond one-to-one. Box 4.2 explains the projection method.
2. For a detailed review, see Sumner (2010).
3. Changes in the classification of FCS will likely continue in the years ahead. For example, Mali and Syria were only recently added to several FCS definitions.
4. The World Bank's list of "Fragile Situations" has either (a) a harmonized average Country Policy and Institutional Assessment (CPIA) country rating of 3.2 or less or (b) the presence of a United Nations or regional peace-keeping or peace-building mission during the past three years. The list includes only International Development Association–eligible countries and nonmembers or inactive territories or countries without CPIA data. The list excludes International Bank for Reconstruction and Development–only countries for which the CPIA scores are not currently disclosed. The list and more information can be found at http://siteresources.worldbank.org/EXTLICUS/Resources/511777-1269623894864/HarmonizedlistoffragilestatesFY14.pdf.
5. See Dell, Jones, and Olken (2014) for a complete overview of this literature.
6. Dell, Jones, and Olken (2012) define a "poor country" as having below-median purchasing power parity–adjusted per capita GDP in the first year the country enters the data set. This is not consistent with the World Bank's classification.
7. For a detailed discussion, see Dell, Jones, and Olken (2014).

# References

Acemoglu, Daron, Suresh Naidu, Pascual Restrepo, and James A. Robinson. 2014. "Democracy Does Cause Growth." NBER Working Paper w20004, National Bureau of Economic Research, Cambridge, MA.

Aisen, Ari, and Francisco José Veiga. 2013. "How Does Political Instability Affect Economic Growth?" *European Journal of Political Economy* 29: 151–67.

Alesina, Alberto, Sule Özler, Nouriel Roubini, and Phillip Swagel. 1996. "Political Instability and Economic Growth." *Journal of Economic Growth* 1 (2): 189–211.

Anderson, Edward. 2006. "Potential Impacts of Climate Change on $2-a-day Poverty and Child Mortality in Sub-Saharan Africa and South Asia." Unpublished manuscript, Overseas Development Institute, London.

Andrimihaja, Noro Aina, Matthias Cinyabuguma, and Shantayanan Devarajan. 2011. "Avoiding the Fragility Trap in Africa." Policy Research Working Paper 5884, World Bank, Washington, DC.

Angelsen, Arild, Sven Wunder, Ronnie Babigumira, Brian Belcher, Jan Börner, and Carsten Smith-Hall. 2014. "Environmental Incomes and Rural Livelihoods: A Global-Comparative Assessment." *World Development*. In press.

Beegle, Kathleen, Joachim De Weerdt, and Stefan Dercon. 2008. "Adult Mortality and Consumption Growth in the Age of HIV/AIDS." *Economic Development and Cultural Change* 56 (2): 299–326.

Bell, Clive, Shantayanan Devarajan, and Hans Gersbach. 2006. "The Long-run Economic Costs of AIDS: A Model with an Application to South Africa." *The World Bank Economic Review* 20 (1): 55–89.

Burger, Martijn, Elena Ianchovichina, and Bob Rijkers. 2013. "Risky Business: Political Instability and Greenfield Foreign Direct Investment in the Arab World." Policy Research Working Paper 6716, World Bank, Washington, DC.

Burke, Marshall, and Kyle Emerick. 2013. "Adaptation to Climate Change: Evidence from US Agriculture." University of California, Berkeley.

Burns, Andrew, Dominique van der Mensbrugghe, and Hans Timmer. 2008. *Evaluating the Economic Consequences of Avian Influenza*. Washington, DC: World Bank.

Carter, Michael R., Peter D. Little, Tewodaj Mogues, and Workneh Negatu. 2006. "The Long-Term Impacts of Short-Term Shocks: Poverty Traps and Environmental Disasters in Ethiopia and Honduras." *Basis Brief* 28. International Food Policy Research Institute, Washington, DC.

Chandy, Laurence, Natasha Ledlie, and Veronika Penciakova. 2013. "The Final Countdown: Prospects for Ending Extreme Poverty by 2030." Brookings Institution, Washington, DC.

Chen, Shaohua, Aart Kraay, Tatjana Kleineberg, and Peter Lanjouw. 2013. "The World Bank's Poverty Target of 3% in 2030: Assessing the Realism of This Goal and Exploring Some Country-Level Implications." Unpublished manuscript, World Bank, Washington, DC.

Christiaensen, Luc, Lionel Demery, and Jesper Kühl. 2011. "The (Evolving) Role of Agriculture in Poverty Reduction—An Empirical Perspective." *Journal of Development Economics* 96 (2): 239–54.

Collier, Paul. 2008. *The Bottom Billion. Why the Poorest Countries Are Failing and What Can Be Done About It.* New York: Oxford University Press.

Dell, Melissa, Benjamin F. Jones, and Benjamin A. Olken. 2012. "Temperature Shocks and Economic Growth: Evidence from the Last Half Century." *American Economic Journal: Macroeconomics* 4 (3): 66–95.

———. 2014. "What Do We Learn from the Weather? The New Climate-Economy Literature." *Journal of Economic Literature.*

Dercon, Stefan. 2004. "Growth and Shocks: Evidence from Rural Ethiopia." *Journal of Development Economics* 74 (2): 309–29.

———. 2012. "Is Green Growth Good for the Poor?" Policy Research Working Paper 6231, World Bank, Washington, DC.

Dixon, Simon, Scott McDonald, and Jennifer Roberts. 2002. "The Impact of HIV and AIDS on Africa's Economic Development." *BMJ: British Medical Journal* 324 (7331): 232.

Dollar, David, Tatjana Kleineberg, and Aart Kraay. 2013. "Growth Is Still Good for the Poor." Policy Research Working Paper 6568, World Bank, Washington, DC.

———. 2014. "Growth, Inequality, and Social Welfare: Cross-Country Evidence." Policy Research Working Paper 6842, World Bank, Washington, DC.

Drummond, Paulo, and Estelle X. Liu. 2013. "Africa's Rising Exposure to China: How Large Are Spillovers Through Trade?" IMF Working Paper 13-250, International Monetary Fund, Washington, DC.

Easterly, William, Michael Kremer, Lant Pritchett, and Lawrence H. Summers. 1993. "Good Policy or Good Luck?" *Journal of Monetary Economics* 32 (3): 459–83.

Eboli, Fabio, Ramiro Parrado, and Roberto Roson. 2010. "Climate-change Feedback on Economic Growth: Explorations with a Dynamic General Equilibrium Model." *Environment and Development Economics* 15 (5): 515–33.

Fardoust, Shahrokh, and Ashok Dhareshwar. 2013. "Some Thoughts on Making Long-term Forecasts for the World Economy." Policy Research Working Paper 6705, World Bank, Washington, DC.

Fischer, Günther, Mahendra Shah, and Harrij Van Velthuizen. 2002. "Climate Change and Agricultural Vulnerability." Special report prepared by the International Institute for Applied Systems Analysis.

Freund, Caroline, and Mélise Jaud. 2013. "Regime Change, Democracy and Growth." CEPR Discussion Paper 9282, Centre for Economic Policy Research, London.

Friedman, Jed, and James Levinsohn. 2002. "The Distributional Impact of Indonesia's Financial Crisis on Household Welfare." *The World Bank Economic Review* 16 (3): 397–424.

Hallegatte, Stephane, and Patrice Dumas. 2008. "Can Natural Disasters Have Positive Consequences? Investigating the Role of Embodied Technical Change." *Ecological Economics* 68 (3): 777–86.

Hallegatte, Stephane, Geoffrey Heal, Marianne Fay, and David Treguer. 2012. *From Growth to Green Growth—A Framework.* NBER Working Paper 17841, National Bureau of Economic Research, Cambridge, MA.

Hamilton, Kirk, and Michael Clemens. 1999. "Genuine Savings Rates in Developing Countries." *The World Bank Economic Review* 13(2): 333–56.

Hamilton, Kirk, and Giles Atkinson. 2006. *Wealth, Welfare and Sustainability: Advances in Measuring Sustainable Development.* Northampton, MA: Edward Elgar.

Headey, Derek D. 2013. "The Impact of the Global Food Crisis on Self-Assessed Food Security." *The World Bank Economic Review* 27 (1): 1–27.

———. 2014. "Food Prices and Poverty Reduction in the Long Run." IFPRI Discussion Paper No. 1331, International Food Policy Research Institute, Washington, DC.

Hsiang, Solomon M., Marshall Burke, and Edward Miguel. 2013. "Quantifying the Influence of Climate on Human Conflict." *Science* 341 (6151): doi:10.1126/science 1235367.

IMF (International Monetary Fund). 2008. *World Economic Outlook 2008.* Washington, DC: International Monetary Fund.

———. 2011. *World Economic Outlook 2011.* Washington, DC: International Monetary Fund.

———. 2014. *World Economic Outlook 2014.* Washington, DC: International Monetary Fund.

IPCC (Intergovernmental Panel on Climate Change). 2007. "Climate Change 2007: The Physical Science Basis." In *Contribution of Working Group I to the Fourth Assessment Report of the Intergovernmental Panel on Climate Change.* Cambridge, U.K.: Cambridge University Press.

———. 2013. "Climate Change 2013: The Physical Science Basis." In *The Working Group I Contribution to the IPCC Fifth Assessment Report.* Cambridge, U.K.: Cambridge University Press.

———. 2014. "Climate Change 2014: Impacts, Adaptation, and Vulnerability." In *Contribution of Working Group II to the Fifth Assessment Report of the Intergovernmental Panel on Climate Change.* Cambridge, U.K.: Cambridge University Press.

Jacoby, Hanan G. 2013. "Food Prices, Wages, and Welfare in Rural India." Policy Research Working Paper 6412, World Bank, Washington, DC.

Jacoby, Hanan, and Basab Dasgupta. 2014. "Household Exposure to Food Price Shocks in Rural Bangladesh." *Bangladesh Development Studies* 37 (1, 2).

Jacoby, Hanan G., Mariano Rabassa, and Emmanuel Skoufias. 2011. "Distributional Implications of Climate Change in India." Policy Research Working Paper 5623, World Bank, Washington, DC.

Jonas, Olga. 2013. "Pandemic Risk." Background paper for *World Development Report 2014*, World Bank, Washington, DC.

Jong-A-Pin, Richard. 2009. "On the Measurement of Political Instability and Its Impact on Economic Growth." *European Journal of Political Economy* 25 (1): 15–29.

Khandelwal, Padamja, and Agustin Roitman. 2013. "The Economics of Political Transitions: Implications for the Arab Spring." IMF Working Paper No. 13-69, International Monetary Fund, Washington, DC.

Kraay, Aart. 2006. "When Is Growth Pro-Poor? Evidence from a Panel of Countries." *Journal of Development Economics* 80 (1): 198–227.

Loayza, Norman V., Eduardo Olaberria, Jamele Rigolini, and Luc Christiaensen. 2012. "Natural Disasters and Growth: Going beyond the Averages." *World Development* 40 (7): 1317–36.

Lobell, David, Marshall Burke, Claudia Tebaldi, Michael D. Mastrandrea, Walter P. Falcon, and Rosamond L. Naylor. 2008. "Prioritizing Climate Change Adaptation Needs for Food Security in 2030." *Science* 319 (5863): 607–10.

Mendoza, R. U. 2009. "Aggregate Shocks, Poor Households and Children: Transmission Channels and Policy Responses." *Global Social Policy* 9 (1 suppl.): 55–78.

Murray, Christopher J., Alan D. Lopez, Brian Chin, Dennis Feehan, and Kenneth H. Hill. 2007. "Estimation of Potential Global Pandemic Influenza Mortality on the Basis of Vital Registry Data from the 1918–20 Pandemic: A Quantitative Analysis." *The Lancet* 368 (9554): 2211–18.

Narayan, Ambar, Jaime Saavedra-Chanduvi, and Sailesh Tiwari. 2013. "Shared Prosperity: Links to Growth, Inequality and Inequality of Opportunity." Policy Research Working Paper 6649, World Bank, Washington, DC.

Papaioannou, Elias, and Gregorios Siourounis. 2008. "Democratisation and Growth." *Economic Journal* 36: 365–87.

Pindyck, Robert S. 2013. "Climate Change Policy: What Do the Models Tell Us?" NBER Working Paper w19244, National Bureau of Economic Research, Cambridge, MA.

Ravallion, Martin. 2008. "Bailing Out the World's Poorest." Policy Research Working Paper 4763, World Bank, Washington, DC.

———. 2013. "How Long Will It Take to Lift One Billion People Out of Poverty?" *The World Bank Research Observer* 28 (2): 139–58.

Ravallion, Martin, and Michael Lokshin. 2007. "Lasting Impacts of Indonesia's Financial Crisis." *Economic Development and Cultural Change* 56 (1): 27–56.

Rodrik, Dani. 1999. "Where Did All the Growth Go? External Shocks, Social Conflict, and Growth Collapses." *Journal of Economic Growth* 4 (4): 385–412.

Rodrik, Dani, and Romain Wacziarg. 2005. "Do Democratic Transitions Produce Bad Economic Outcomes?" *American Economic Review* 95 (2): 50–55.

Rosenstein-Rodan, Paul Narziss. 1961. "International Aid for Underdeveloped Countries." *The Review of Economics and Statistics* 43 (2): 107–38.

Schlenker, Wolfram, and David B. Lobell. 2010. "Robust Negative Impacts of Climate Change on African Agriculture." *Environmental Research Letters* 5 (1): 014010.

Skoufias, Emmanuel, Mariano Rabassa, Sergio Olivieri, and Milan Brahmbhatt. 2011. "The Poverty Impacts of Climate Change: A Review of the Evidence." Policy Research Working Paper 5622, World Bank, Washington, DC.

Stern, Nicholas, ed. 2007. *The Economics of Climate Change: The Stern Review.* Cambridge, UK: Cambridge University Press.

———. 2013. "The Structure of Economic Modeling of the Potential Impacts of Climate Change: Grafting Gross Underestimation of Risk onto Already Narrow Science Models." *Journal of Economic Literature* 51 (3): 838–59.

Sumner, Andrew. 2010. "Global Poverty and the New Bottom Billion: What If Three-Quarters of the World's Poor Live in Middle-Income Countries?" IDS Working Papers 2010 (349), Institute of Development Studies, Sussex, U.K.

Themnér, Lotta, and Peter Wallensteen. 2013. "Armed Conflict, 1946–2012." *Journal of Peace Research* 50 (4): 519–21.

Tol, Richard. 2013. "Targets for Global Climate Policy: An Overview." *Journal of Economic Dynamics and Control* 37 (5): 911–28.

UNDP (United Nations Development Programme). 2014. *Syria: Squandering Humanity—Socioeconomic Monitoring Report on Syria*. Syrian Centre for Policy Research, Damascus.

World Bank. 2000. *World Development Report 2000/2001: Attacking Poverty*. Washington, DC: World Bank.

———. 2012a. *Inclusive Green Growth: The Pathway to Sustainable Development*. Washington, DC: World Bank.

———. 2012b. *People, Pathogens, and Our Planet: The Economics of One Health*. Washington, DC: World Bank.

———. 2013a. *World Bank Group Strategy, October 2013*. Washington, DC: World Bank.

———. 2013b. *World Development Report 2014: Risk and Opportunity, Managing Risk for Development*. Washington, DC: World Bank.

———. 2013c. *Global Monitoring Report 2013: Rural-Urban Dynamics and the Millennium Development Goals*. Washington, DC: World Bank.

———. 2014. *Global Economic Prospects: Shifting Priorities, Building the Future*. Volume 9. Washington, DC: World Bank.

Young, Alwyn. 2005. "The Gift of the Dying: The Tragedy of AIDS and the Welfare of Future African Generations." *The Quarterly Journal of Economics* 120 (2): 423–66.

# CHAPTER FIVE

# National Profiles of Poverty and Shared Prosperity, Data, and Methods

Implicit in the decision of the World Bank to establish the twin goals of reducing the global poverty rate to less than 3 percent and boosting shared prosperity is the view that setting goals helps focus efforts and resources. It is certainly the case that the global measures help to assess progress and influence the World Bank and other international agencies in terms of where funds are targeted. It must also be recognized that the most important actions taken to reduce poverty are not the result of global decisions, but rather policies, programs, and projects undertaken by individual countries. Poverty is reduced and shared prosperity is increased largely by national, not global, policies. Empirically informed policies to improve the well-being of the less well-off require several inputs, but a key to this process is a high-quality measure of household consumption that is comparable over time and space.

## Comparable household survey data for effective policy

Has poverty decreased? Has shared prosperity been boosted? Answering these fundamental questions requires having a *comparable* measure of well-being at multiple points in time. Over the past two decades, the availability of household consumption and expenditure data has increased dramatically. The 1990 global poverty count was based on analysis for only 22 countries and no country had more than one survey available (Ravallion, Datt, and van de Walle 1991). Today, consumption or expenditure information come from more than 1,000 surveys.

This significant improvement in the availability of consumption data experienced over the past two decades, however, has been accompanied by widening heterogeneity or differences in the instruments (for example, questionnaires) and methods used by countries to measure household consumption and expenditures. Although international guidelines for more harmonized instruments have been put forth by relevant organizations over the years, this has not resulted in greater harmonization. For example, Carletto, Zezza, and Banerjee (2013) argue that the lack of consensus on how to measure food security has led to a variety of data collection initiatives and resulted in a lack of comparable measures of food security across countries and within countries over time. The authors suggest that better use of present data collection efforts could improve the harmony of the measures. Fiedler, Carletto, and Dupriez (2013) offer some proposals for improving the comparability of this core measure of well-being.

Heterogeneity across countries in the measure of consumption is not necessarily an indication of poor quality. For example, a standardized questionnaire written for a middle-income country would have many nonsensical questions for a country with a high prevalence of extreme poverty. As another example, household surveys typically ask whether households have consumed food from a long list of items. A failure to customize the list to foods that are specific to the country will result in a low-quality measure of total food consumption—one that is neither reflective of the consumption level in the country nor useful for comparisons across countries. In these types of cases, heterogeneity in the questionnaire would potentially indicate that the instrument had been designed in a way that is sensitive to local conditions. When tailoring the questionnaire to local conditions produces data that are more useful to the country, then this sort of difference in the questionnaire design is desirable. It can help to produce policies that are more effective in reducing poverty.

In contrast, changes in the data collection process over time in a given country are sometimes not the result of changes in the underlying local conditions, but may be simply a result of the vagaries of the data generation process. For example, a change in the funding source for the data collection may result in a change in the instrument to reflect the funder's interests; similarly, simply a change of the personnel of the survey team can result in questionnaire changes. Changes to questionnaires are typically made based on the notion that they will improve the informational content of the data, but often little weight is placed on the cost imposed of creating data that are no longer comparable with previous data records. Simple questions like whether poverty has declined can become quite difficult to answer if, for example, the questionnaire has changed over time. The following section provides several examples of the types of differences that are observed in consumption and expenditure household surveys, across countries and in countries over time. The aim is to show how relatively innocuous changes can have very large effects on the measures of consumption, shared prosperity, and poverty.

## Questionnaire design and comparability of consumption and poverty

Research in data collection methods has well established that factors such as the recall period and the number of food items listed have a large effect on the resulting measure of estimated food consumption. One prominent example of differences in recall periods having large effects on measured poverty is described by Deaton and Kozel (2005). The India National Sample Survey Organization (NSSO),[1] which had historically used a uniform 30-day recall period, changed recall periods during the 1990s, which resulted in significantly divergent estimates of poverty.

After the change in recall periods, food expenditures increased by about a third, and total expenditure increased by about 17 percent. This increase in total expenditure reduced the estimated number of poor by close to 200 million (United Nations Statistics Division 2005). Another dimension of the change in the instrument was that the tails of the distribution for a 12-month recall period of infrequently consumed items were thicker (relative to the 30-day recall). This latter outcome has potentially significant implications for measures of shared prosperity, as will be demonstrated later in this chapter. The change in the questionnaires was not implemented as an experiment, and it was therefore difficult to disentangle the extent to which the change in measured poverty was real and how much was caused by the change in recall periods.

In contrast, Beegle and others (2012) carried out a careful experiment in Tanzania to examine how changing several aspects of the questionnaire affects measured consumption and thereby estimates of poverty. The authors selected eight random samples of 500 households each from the same population (and verified that indeed the samples were similar across many important attributes). They tested a variety of relatively common ways of collecting information about consumption, contrasting diary with recall, shorter recall with longer recall periods, and varying levels of disaggregation of the listed commodity items. For their experiment, they treated the person-level daily diary covering 14 days as the benchmark for comparison, in part because the diary collected information from each member of the household and in part because it was supplemented with frequent visits by enumerators who would help the respondents fill in the diary on each visit.

The extent to which the questionnaire designs deviated from the benchmark is striking. The benchmark personal diary provided the highest mean consumption level. The researchers are careful to acknowledge that asking each individual to identify his or her consumption level could result in double-counting or, more generally, overestimation. But for the purpose of understanding how variation in questionnaire design affects reported values, it is sufficient to observe variation in mean consumption across the instruments.

Figure 5.1 indicates the percent difference in the mean consumption level from each of the questionnaires relative to the benchmark personal diary. The long list, 7-day recall questionnaire resulted in a mean consumption level that was just 4 percent less than the benchmark personal diary. Simply changing the recall period from 7 days to 14 days though produced a mean consumption level that was 16 percent less than the benchmark.[2] If the benchmark is considered as the correct measure, then expanding the recall period by a week has the effect of lowering the measured mean of consumption by about 12 percent. Similarly, keeping the recall period the same but changing the number of prompts used to ask about consumption patterns also had large effects on the estimated mean consumption. While the long list with 7-day recall was 4 percent less, the questionnaire with 7-day recall combined with a highly collapsed list of items produced a mean consumption estimate that was 28 percent less than the benchmark.

The key implication of these findings is that seemingly innocuous changes to the questionnaire can easily result in measures of consumption that cannot be simply compared with each other over time. The lack of comparability has direct implications for poverty measurement. Beegle and others adjust the 2008 data back to the $1.25 poverty line (in 2005 purchasing power parity terms), which results in a poverty rate of 47.5 percent for the benchmark questionnaire. All the other questionnaires produced higher poverty estimates that ranged from 55 percent to 68 percent. Although the power of the tests to distinguish between the poverty estimates was relatively weak (with a confidence interval for the difference of approximately ±8 percentage points, based on the pooled standard error of about 4.2), four of the questionnaires resulted in statistically significantly higher poverty estimates. As one example, their results show that changing only the recall period from one week to two weeks (leaving everything

**Figure 5.1  Comparison of consumption measures resulting from different survey modules**

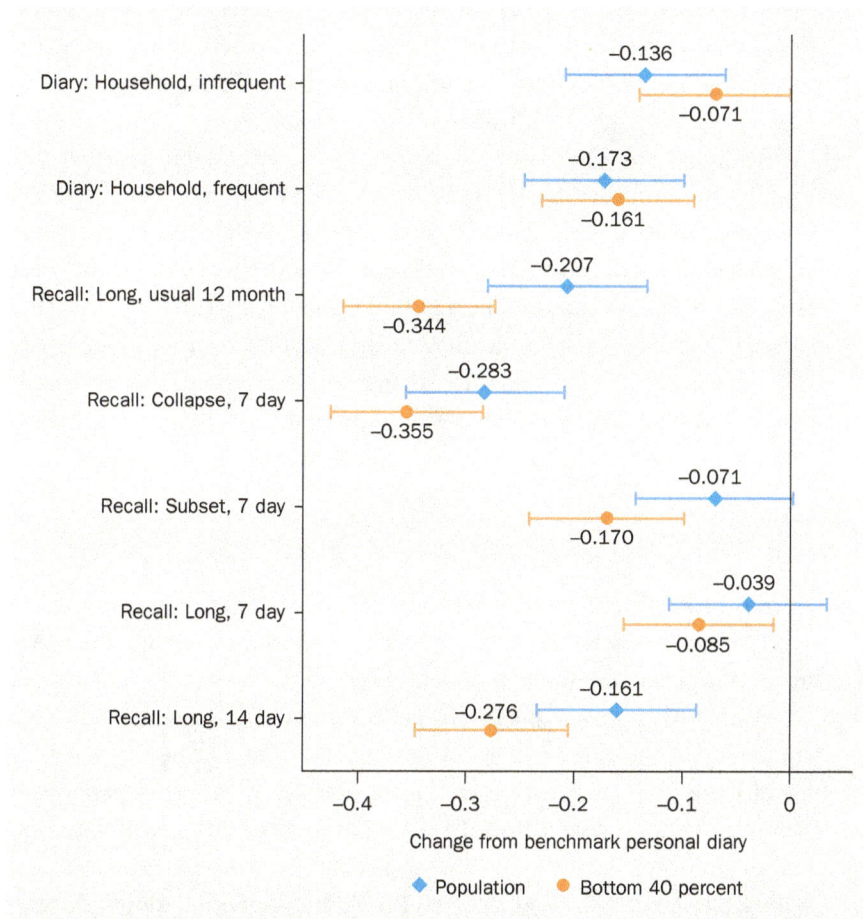

*Source:* Adapted from Beegle and others (2012).
*Note:* Chart plots results of a regression of log total per capita consumption expenditure on dummies indicating module assignment, omitting personal diary as a benchmark. Bars show 95 percent confidence interval. Enumeration area fixed effects are included. Due to the log specification, the estimated coefficients can be interpreted as percent deviations in mean value from personal diary.

else the same) has the effect of increasing poverty from 55 percent to 63 percent. The conclusion is that it is difficult to state whether poverty has changed over time if the underlying questionnaires have changed how they ask about consumption.

These findings are not unique to the population examined by Beegle and others (2012). Jolliffe (2001) presents findings from another between-groups experiment where two subsamples from the population of El Salvador were administered different questionnaires. Again, the balance of the design was

191

verified and there were no statistically significant differences between the two samples in terms of basic demographic characteristics, regional location, or measured income. One sample was administered a questionnaire that had a long, detailed list of consumption items (75 food items and 25 nonfood items) and the other sample was administered a short, collapsed list (18 food items and 6 nonfood items) questionnaire. For example, the long list questionnaire asked how much of each of three types of cheese was consumed while the collapsed list questionnaire asked how much cheese altogether was consumed. The recall period was the same, as well as other aspects of the instrument. The key finding from the experiment is that although the samples were the same in all relevant dimensions, because of the differences in the questionnaire design, the short questionnaire sample had a measured poverty rate that was 46 percent greater (because of lower measured consumption) than the long questionnaire sample.

### Questionnaire design and comparability of shared prosperity

An important implication of the studies is that changes in household survey questionnaires over time will result in spurious estimates of change in consumption and absolute poverty levels. This finding is true whether the change is from how the survey is administered (for example, diary or enumerated), the extensiveness of the survey (a short but comprehensive list of items compared with a long list of items), or the recall period (for example, 7-day compared with 14-day). For more discussion on this point and the importance of data quality in general, see Bamberger, Rugh, and Mabry (2006); Biemer and Lyberg (2003); and United Nations Statistics Division (2005).

Although there is a literature on questionnaire design and poverty, much less is known about how differences in instrument design have implications for the comparability of the variance of expenditure. Shared prosperity is inherently about changes in the distribution of well-being. To shed light on some of the same issues summarized in the literature about poverty, this report also presents new evidence based on the data used in Beegle and others (2012) on how questionnaire design affects shared prosperity.

Figure 5.1 reveals that all the measures of shared prosperity (that is, the mean consumption level of the bottom 40 percent) from the various questionnaires are lower than the benchmark instrument (that is, the intensive daily diary done for each individual). For example, the mean value of the bottom 40 percent from all the nondiary questionnaires ranges from 9 percent to 36 percent less than the benchmark. Shortening the list of consumption items that are asked about in the interview results in a decline in the mean value of the bottom 40 percent. Similarly, moving from a 7-day recall to a 14-day recall period results in a decline in the mean. To understand the importance of this experimental result, consider a country that initially had a 14-day recall period in the questionnaire and changed to a 7-day recall period. The experiment data from Tanzania indicates that this change would in and of itself result in a large and statistically significant increase in shared prosperity. Similarly, the evidence from Tanzania suggests that moving from a short, collapsed list of food items to a long list of food items would result in a statistically significant increase in shared prosperity.

The key finding from the analysis of shared prosperity is the same as with measuring consumption and poverty—seemingly harmless changes in how questions are asked produce significant changes in the measure of shared prosperity, rendering it incomparable across the surveys. The data also provide some indication that the shared prosperity measure appears to be somewhat more sensitive to changes in questionnaire design (relative to the overall mean). For the majority of the questionnaires, the difference in the mean of the bottom 40 percent and the benchmark instrument value is greater than the difference between the overall mean and the benchmark value. This finding is essentially a statement that the estimated mean and the variance of the distribution are affected by changes in the questionnaire. (Although the shared prosperity measure appears to be sensitive to changes in questionnaire design, box 5.1 presents evidence that it is robust to measurement error of the top earners.)

The findings in Beegle and others (2012) and the analysis in this report based on their data suggest that, on average, a 7-day recall with a long list of food items performs well compared with more expensive and onerous methods, such as the administration of food consumption diaries at the household and individual level, with the latter often considered the gold standard. Given that 7-day recall is widely used and is probably the most suitable method for scaling up collection of food consumption data, the findings are encouraging. However, testing the external validity of the findings beyond the cases cited here would be important to do before trying to impose more standardization of this recall period. Thus, to improve data comparability and quality, there is a continued need for survey experimentation on how to collect better consumption data, as discussed by Deaton and Grosh (2000).

## Box 5.1   Shared prosperity is robust to measurement error in top earners

An overlooked attribute of the shared prosperity measure is that it is largely unaffected by measurement problems associated with anyone who is not in the bottom 40 percent of the distribution. Unit nonresponse tends to be a much more significant problem in rich countries (see Meyer, Mok, and Sullivan [2009] for a discussion of nonresponse in the United States) and has historically been low in low-income countries. But as countries get richer, item and unit nonresponse become more pervasive as measurement problems. The standard presumption, which is supported by some evidence from richer countries and consistent with observed gaps between survey data and national accounts data, is that refusal rates are increasing with income.

An implication of this relationship is that measures of inequality that are derived from household survey data may fail to reflect the full magnitude of changes in inequality if the top earners are not represented in the samples. Because the shared prosperity measure essentially places no weight on anyone above the 40th percentile, nonresponse of top earners has a relatively small effect on the measure. When the rich completely drop out of the survey, the "bottom" 40 percent will somewhat overstate the location of the 40th percentile, but the effect on the mean of the bottom 40 percent is much smaller than the change in the mean of the distribution and the measure of inequality (both of which place the highest weights on the richest; see the discussion in chapter 3). However, if top earners participate in the survey, but underreport consumption or income, then the measure of shared prosperity is completely robust to this sort of measurement problem.

Nepal potentially provides some anecdotal evidence of this phenomenon. Table B5.1.1 shows trends in the Gini, shared prosperity index, and mean and median values of real per capita expenditure from 1995 to 2011. Data from the Nepal Living

**Table B5.1.1   Inequality and shared prosperity in Nepal, 1995–2011**

| Indicator | 1995-96 | 2003-04 | 2010-11 |
|---|---|---|---|
| Gini | 34 | 44 | 33 |
| | (0.009) | (0.015) | (0.007) |
| Shared prosperity | 3,067 | 4,319 | 6,798 |
| | (40.4) | (46.7) | (58.4) |
| Mean, real per capita expenditure | 6,171 | 10,645 | 13,301 |
| Median | 4,874 | 7,067 | 10,757 |

*Sources:* Nepal Living Standards Survey I, II, III and World Bank (2006).

*Note:* Estimates are population-weighted estimates expressed in constant 1995 Nepalese rupees. Standard errors (in parentheses) account for weights and clustering; those for the Gini coefficient are based on Jolliffe and Krushelnytskyy (1999).

Standards Survey (NLSS) show that the Gini coefficient increased from 34 to 44 between 1995 and 2003, but then fell to 33 by 2010–11. The up and down swings are of such a large magnitude that they are nearly noncredible. Extensive efforts to recreate the consumption variable in a completely comparable way increased the Gini by two points in 2010–11, but the pattern remains very challenging to explain. Indeed, World Bank (2006) used a decision rule to exclude some large observations in 2003–04 and reduced the Gini by 3 points (although this decision rule was not used in earlier or later years).

If policy focused only on the Gini coefficient, the inference from the estimates would be that the period between 1995–96 and 2003–04 was a time of incredibly unequal growth. Because of its focus, the shared prosperity index reveals that over this time period, average consumption of the bottom 40 percent increased in real terms by more than 40 percent. Similarly, the median individual's consumption increased by 45 percent.

*(continued)*

## Box 5.1 Continued

These statistics indicate significant growth for the bottom part of the distribution. In the latter part of the decade, between 2003 and 2010, shared prosperity and the median continued to grow by more than 50 percent, while the Gini dropped significantly and the mean increased by only 25 percent. A candidate explanation for this pattern is that there were significant measurement error problems for top earners in 2003–04, which led to severe changes in the Gini. The shared prosperity index presented a much more stable pattern, with lower growth of shared prosperity between 1993 and 2003, followed by higher growth in the latter half of the decade.

### Timing of fieldwork and comparability of consumption, poverty, and shared prosperity

In addition to changes in the questionnaire, changes in the implementation of the survey can also have significant effects on measured poverty and shared prosperity. It is well understood that changes in the quality of the training, supervision, enumeration, and data entry can all affect data quality and compromise comparability over time. Perhaps somewhat less discussed, but well recognized, is that simply changing the timing of the fieldwork can also affect the comparability of the measures over time.

Khandker and Mahmud (2012) report that more than 80 percent of the world's poor reside in rural areas and most of the poor depend on agricultural activities for their livelihood.[3] Agricultural activities are seasonal by nature and, in many countries, the seasons occur at fairly similar times for many households. When livelihoods are closely linked with agriculture, well-being will also follow the seasonal pattern of agriculture, with relatively better-off periods around harvest time and lean seasons, typically postplanting when stocks have dwindled. For example, in Bangladesh the cycle was historically so pronounced in certain areas that there is a specific term in Bangla for the phenomena—*Monga*—which essentially identifies the lean months as a period of death and destruction.

An implication of the seasonality of well-being is that if fieldwork for data collection occurs one year during the lean season and then, in the following year, during the postharvest period, it will appear as if poverty has reduced significantly over time. In some ways, it is accurate to suggest that poverty has decreased in this case, but the decrease described here reflects the seasonal cycle of poverty and not necessarily improvement over the years.

An example based on data from Afghanistan provides a relatively extreme example of how the timing of fieldwork can influence the estimate of poverty. The 2007/08 National Reconstruction and Vulnerability Assessment survey for Afghanistan collected data from more than 20,500 households covering all 34 provinces, and the fieldwork for the survey took an entire year. An important attribute of the sample design is that it was implicitly stratified by quarters of the year so that each quarter could be viewed as a nationally representative sample.[4] D'Souza and Jolliffe (2012, 2013) show that the quarterly subsamples are similar in terms of time-invariant attributes.[5]

During this time period, several factors combined that accentuated the seasonal fluctuations in well-being (for example, the food price crisis struck that year and Afghanistan's lean period was worse than normal because of the drought the preceding year). The data therefore provide an example where the seasonal effect is high, but still quite informative for understanding the extent of potential variation in poverty and shared prosperity within a year. The temporal stratification allows the interpretation of each quarter subsample as being representative of the population. Table 5.1 shows that the estimated poverty rate more than doubled within the year, while the measure of shared prosperity ranged from a low of Af 847 to a high of Af 1,122. An implication is that if, for example, in one year data were only collected during a lean quarter and then in the following year fieldwork occurred during a better quarter, it would be very difficult to know whether the improvements observed in poverty and shared prosperity were because of improvements over the year or simply reflected the changed time period

**Table 5.1**  Poverty and shared prosperity by quarter

| Indicator | Quarter 1 (fall) | Quarter 2 (winter) | Quarter 3 (spring) | Quarter 4 (summer) |
|---|---|---|---|---|
| Real per capita consumption (Afghani) | 2,023 | 1,717 | 1,519 | 1,477 |
| Poverty (headcount, %) | 21 | 31 | 43 | 46 |
| Shared prosperity (mean of bottom 40%, Afghani) | 1,122 | 972 | 878 | 847 |

*Source:* Afghanistan National Risk and Vulnerability Assessment 2007/08.
*Note:* Estimates are population-weighted means for the full sample. Real values reflect adjustments for spatial and temporal price differences, covering 13 months of fieldwork.

of data collection. The data from Afghanistan suggest that simply changing the quarter of data collection could lead to an increase in shared prosperity of more than 20 percent. The prototypical Living Standards Measurement Study (LSMS) survey is designed to be in the field for 12 months (Grosh and Muñoz 1996). While the primary motivation for time in the field is to reduce nonsampling error through smaller, more manageable teams, an important attribute of this design is that the resulting annual estimates will average out seasonal variation.

## Cost-of-living differences and comparability of consumption, poverty, and shared prosperity

The discussion up to this point has been about maintaining the comparability of key indicators over time for the purpose of measuring whether shared prosperity is increasing and poverty is declining over time in a country. An additional important element to consider is subnational comparability in a country. If the cost of living is twice as high in the capital city as in rural areas, the measure of consumption that underlies the poverty and shared prosperity indicators needs to account for this difference. A failure to account for differences in prices or the cost of living in a country would result in misidentification of the poor. Knowing the regions where the poor reside and, in particular, whether extreme poverty is more prevalent in urban or rural areas, hinges on having good measures of differences in costs in the country. Without this sort of information, national policy will fail to both correctly identify the poor and properly tailor poverty reduction policies for those most in need. As progress in reducing poverty continues and poverty rates diminish within countries, improved targeting of poverty policies is likely to become ever more important.

The United States provides a useful illustration of the connection between poverty estimation, spatial differences in the cost of living, and poverty policy. Poverty policy in the United States has a long history of targeting more resources to rural areas, in part because of the perception that poverty is significantly higher there. The most recent poverty estimates from 2012 indicate that poverty in areas outside metropolitan statistical areas is more than 3 percentage points higher (or more than 20 percent higher) than poverty in metropolitan areas (DeNavas-Walt, Proctor, and Smith 2013). Correspondingly, poverty estimates figure prominently in determining the distribution of large sums of cash and in-kind benefits from state and federal government programs, with federal block grants for community development being linked to county-level poverty estimates and benefit assistance, such as supplemental nutritional assistance programs (commonly referred to as the food stamp program) being linked to nominal income. Data from the 2003 Current Population Survey indicate that per capita benefits were 39 percent higher in U.S. nonmetropolitan (nonmetro) areas than in metropolitan (metro) areas. If poverty is indeed higher in nonmetro areas, then this is an example of effective geographic targeting.

However, these poverty rates do not account for differences in the cost of living across the United States. The poverty thresholds in major urban centers are the same as for rural, lower-cost areas of the country. To examine the extent to which differences in the cost of living might affect poverty comparisons, Jolliffe (2006) uses data from a U.S. government housing program that subsidizes housing costs for qualified poor participants. The value of the subsidy is adjusted to account for differences in local area rental costs and is priced to cover the gross rent (utilities included) at the 40th percentile for "standard" quality housing. The effect of adjusting for the differences in the cost of housing (treating all other prices as if they are the same level in nonmetro areas as in metro areas) has a qualitatively and statistically significant effect of reranking the relative poverty rates over the 10-year span examined. Figure 5.2 illustrates these findings for the period 1991 to 2002. In the last year in the figure, nominal poverty rates in nonmetro areas were 22 percent higher than in metro areas. Once adjusted for differences in the cost of standardized shelter, nonmetro poverty was 15 percent lower than metro poverty rates.

In most countries, it tends to be the case that urban areas, in general, and capital cities, in particular, are more expensive to live in than other parts of the country. As seen in the U.S. example above, failing to account for this difference will incorrectly portray the levels of poverty in rural and urban areas of the country. An example from Jolliffe, Datt, and Sharma (2004) shows a similar situation in the case of the Arab Republic of Egypt. The authors estimate region-specific poverty lines and find that use of these lines as a correction for spatial differences in the cost of living significantly increases the estimated poverty rate of metropolitan cities in Egypt (that is, Cairo, Alexandria, and Giza). The poverty rate of those cities was less than 10 percent in 1997. Accounting for price differences more than doubled the rate to 26 percent, indicating that poverty in metropolitan areas was approximately the same rate as in the rest of the country. This adjustment for price differences also resulted in the complete elimination of the difference between Upper and Lower Egypt. Conventional wisdom

**Figure 5.2** Percentage difference between metro and nonmetro poverty in the United States, 1991–2002

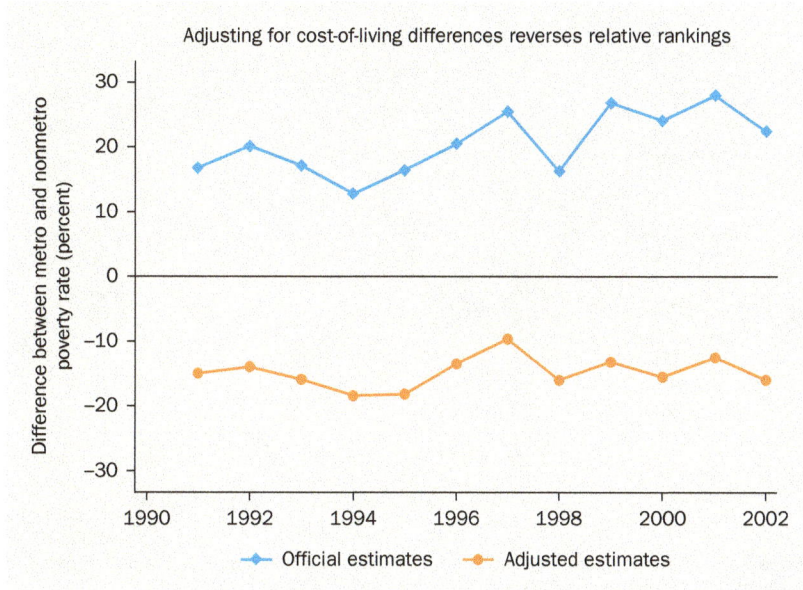

Source: Adapted from Jolliffe (2006).

held that poverty was significantly higher in Upper Egypt, but the survey data indicated that the cost of living was substantially less in Upper Egypt relative to Lower Egypt, and once this was accounted for, the difference in poverty rates essentially vanishes.

Bangladesh provides another example of the importance of adjusting for differences in the cost of living. The government of Bangladesh estimates rural and urban poverty lines for divisions of Bangladesh, and these are interpreted as reflecting variations in the cost of maintaining a comparable bundle of basic food and nonfood needs. Figure 5.3 shows that costs vary substantially across rural and urban areas, are lower in the western divisions (areas that had previously been designated as less integrated), and are much higher in Dhaka and Chittagong (the two largest cities).

Poverty estimates for the earlier part of the 2000 decade, which accounted for price differences, highlighted the need for creating economic opportunities for narrowing the development gap between the east and the west of Bangladesh (Narayan and Zaman 2008). While the east was rapidly improving and benefiting from its geographical proximity to growth poles, the western region of Bangladesh had been lagging behind. This finding

199

**Figure 5.3**   Spatial variation in cost of basic needs, Bangladesh, 2010

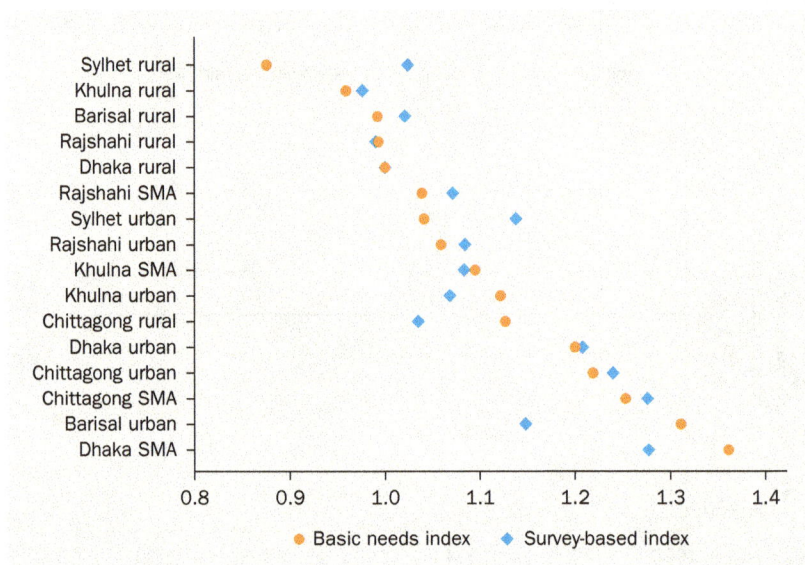

*Source:* Adapted from Gimenez and Jolliffe (2014), based on 2010 Bangladesh Household Income and Expenditure Survey. Used with permission; further permission required for reuse.
*Note:* SMA = statistical metropolitan area.

buttressed many decisions to invest in bridges and roads projects. By the end of the decade, the 2010 poverty estimates describe a changed Bangladesh. Not only did the western divisions (Barisal, Khulna, and Rajshahi) experience larger reductions in poverty, they also managed to reach levels of poverty that are closer to those of their eastern counterparts (Chittagong, Dhaka, and Sylhet). But, if one failed to correct for spatial differences in prices, the geographic profile of poverty would have appeared as if the east-west divide still existed. In short, accounting for spatial differences in the cost of living within countries is critical to get the geographic profile of poverty correct.

## Large data gaps and new technologies and methods

Although the stock of household surveys has increased tremendously over the past three decades, the annual flow of surveys is still relatively low. Figure 5.4 graphs the annual counts of household surveys in the PovcalNet database, and box 5.2 provides a stocktaking of household surveys. Although 129 countries are currently represented by more than 1,000 surveys, in a typical year, there are only about 20 to 40 new surveys available.

**Figure 5.4** Number of surveys in PovcalNet and reference years, 1978–2012

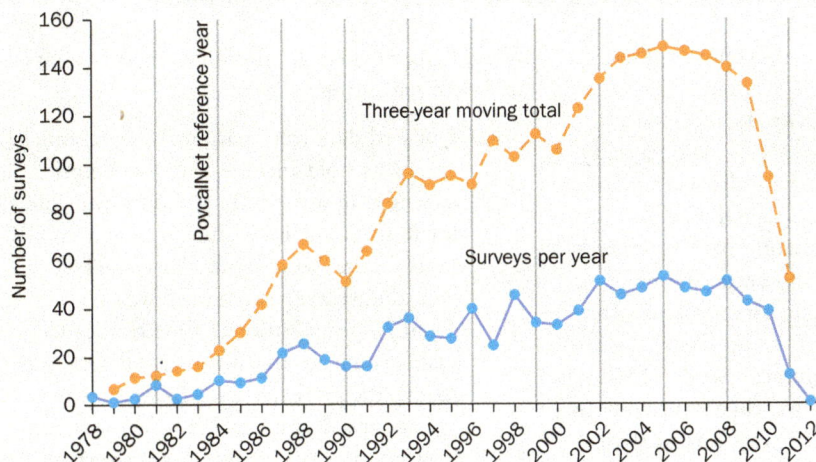

*Source:* Based on data from the World Bank PovcalNet database (accessed August 2014).
*Note:* It is common for there to be a delay of some months between when a survey is collected, when it is published, and when it becomes available in PovcalNet. The decline between 2010 and 2011 illustrated in the figure therefore reflects the fact that many surveys collected in 2011 are not yet available in PovcalNet, rather than a substantial decline in the number of surveys collected in 2011.

With the World Bank's focus on the twin goals, there has also been a call for much more frequent reporting on poverty and shared prosperity statistics. Many have suggested this means that there is a need for annual household survey data, but in the short- to medium-term future, it is not feasible to imagine this occurring in a manner that supports institutional development of the national statistical organizations largely responsible for the collection of these data. A proposed path forward is to increase efforts in data collection while also exploiting new technologies to improve data collection and methodological advances in imputation techniques that can significantly help to improve the quality and frequency of poverty and shared prosperity analysis.

## Technology to improve data collection: CAPI, GPS, and cell phones

Household surveys have traditionally been implemented with pencil-and-paper interviewing (PAPI). Advances in mobile technology and computer-assisted personal interviewing (CAPI) software platforms have made CAPI a viable alternative that is increasingly utilized for household survey data collection in the developing world. Caeyers, Chalmers, and De Weerdt (2011) note that errors commonly present in PAPI are often systematically

## Box 5.2 Household income and consumption surveys at the World Bank

At the core of any national assessment of poverty lies a household income or consumption expenditure survey. Over the past two decades, the availability of such data has increased exponentially. With their early efforts, Ahluwalia, Carter, and Chenery (1979) and Ahluwalia and others (1980) laid the foundation for the World Bank to systematically compile and harmonize measures of living standards through household surveys. Their work was an important impetus to the World Bank's Living Standards Measurement Study (LSMS) project, which has evolved over time from a purely research-focused undertaking to a core analytical tool that supports the World Bank's operational work.

The World Bank in 1990 for the first time applied a concerted effort to estimate a global poverty headcount based on survey data available for only 22 countries (Ravallion, Datt, and van de Walle 1991). The most recent version of the World Bank's PovcalNet database today holds over 1,000 surveys from 129 countries, covering almost 85 percent of the developing world's population.

However, because household income and expenditure surveys are resource and time intensive, in a typical year, only about 20 to 40 new surveys become available. Surveys often take about a year to collect data and are relatively costly, often involving multiple visits to thousands or tens of thousands of households, depending on the sample size.

Given the push for more frequent monitoring of poverty and shared prosperity as a result of the World Bank's twin goals, the following two points are worth reiterating:

(a) Updated data from nationally representative household income and consumption expenditure surveys are still only available for most countries in intervals of several years. In the World Bank's PovcalNet database, the average gap between two surveys is about 2.7 years. However, this average hides vast regional heterogeneity: in Sub-Saharan Africa, the gap between surveys is on average about 5.2 years; in Latin America and the Caribbean, the average gap between two surveys in a given country is about 1.6 years.

(b) Even if surveys are conducted more often, there is still a considerable lag between when the data are collected and when they become available for policy makers and the wider public to analyze.

Map B5.2.1, of the most recent household survey available in the World Bank's Africa region, illustrates these two challenges. On average, the most recent survey is from 2009. In the design of national poverty reduction programs, this lag time can be long enough to have an adverse impact on the effectiveness of targeting and resource allocation. The oldest survey, for Eritrea, is from more than 20 years ago. In Kenya the most recent household survey data were collected as part of the 2005/06 Kenya Integrated Household Budget Survey.

*(continued)*

correlated with household characteristics, which they suggest can be mitigated with the use of CAPI. In a PAPI-CAPI experiment, they show that in the case of estimated consumption, CAPI significantly reduces the variance of consumption and increases the mean, thereby reducing the measures of poverty and inequality. Fafchamps and others (2012) offer some cautionary

## Box 5.2   Continued

**Map B5.2.1**   **Most recent household consumption survey available in Africa**

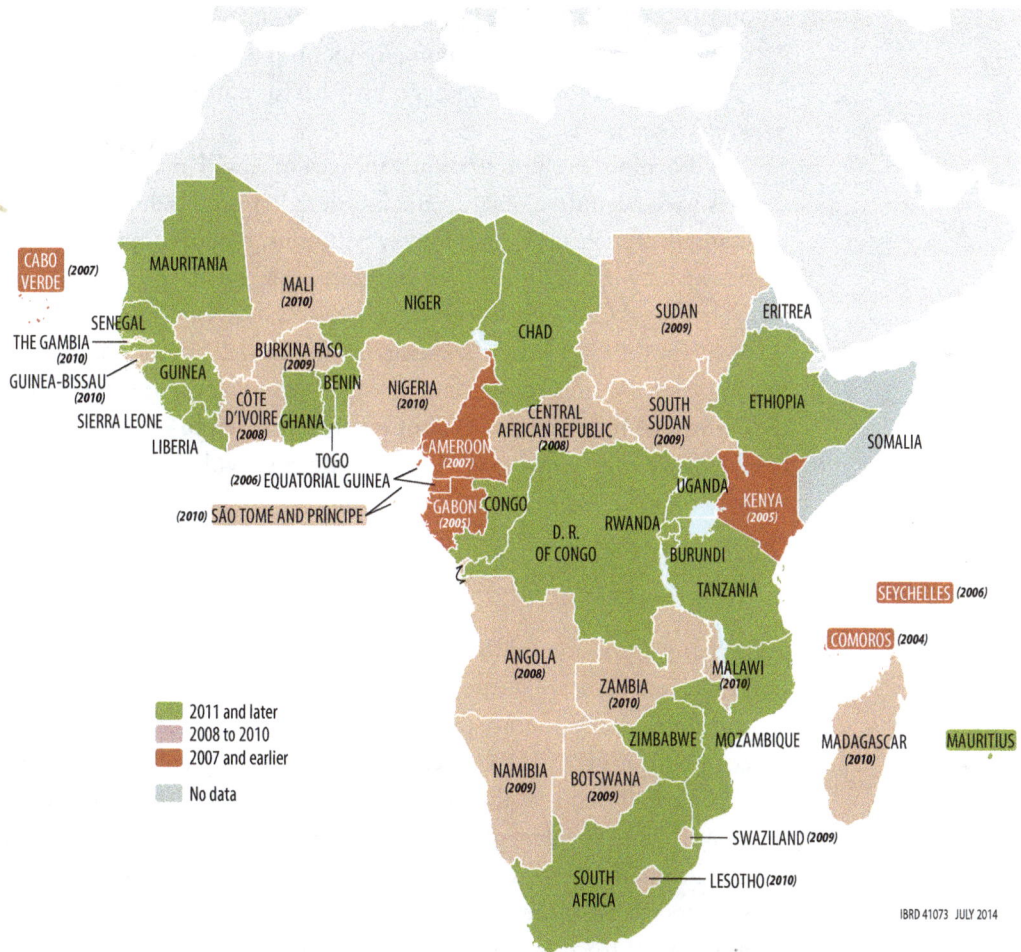

CABO VERDE *(2007)*
MAURITANIA
MALI *(2010)*
NIGER
SUDAN *(2009)*
ERITREA
SENEGAL
THE GAMBIA *(2010)*
BURKINA FASO *(2009)*
CHAD
GUINEA-BISSAU *(2010)*
GUINEA
BENIN
NIGERIA *(2010)*
ETHIOPIA
CÔTE D'IVOIRE *(2008)*
GHANA
CENTRAL AFRICAN REPUBLIC *(2008)*
SOUTH SUDAN *(2009)*
SIERRA LEONE
LIBERIA
SOMALIA
TOGO *(2006)*
EQUATORIAL GUINEA
CAMEROON *(2007)*
*(2010)* SÃO TOMÉ AND PRÍNCIPE
GABON *(2005)*
CONGO
UGANDA
KENYA *(2005)*
D. R. OF CONGO
RWANDA
BURUNDI
TANZANIA
SEYCHELLES *(2006)*
COMOROS *(2004)*
ANGOLA *(2008)*
ZAMBIA *(2010)*
MALAWI *(2010)*
ZIMBABWE
MOZAMBIQUE
MADAGASCAR *(2010)*
MAURITIUS
NAMIBIA *(2009)*
BOTSWANA *(2009)*
SWAZILAND *(2009)*
LESOTHO *(2010)*
SOUTH AFRICA

- 2011 and later
- 2008 to 2010
- 2007 and earlier
- No data

IBRD 41073  JULY 2014

*Source:* World Bank Africa Region, Statistics Practice Team.

evidence that some of the quality gains anticipated from CAPI might not be accrued in certain circumstances.

The attractiveness of CAPI is rooted primarily in the reduction of the time lag between data collection and data analysis and in the presumed improvements in data quality by carrying out automatic checks and quality control at the point of the interview. A well-designed CAPI platform can (a) minimize coding errors and conduct complex intrasurvey and intersurvey module consistency checks; (b) accommodate with ease the dynamic structure of household survey questionnaires, in which information is collected at varying levels of (at times interconnected) observations depending on the topic; and (c) be positioned to integrate key ancillary data collection (such as Global Positioning System [GPS] capture and photo, video, and sound recording and other sensor-based information) into household survey operations.

To exploit the potential advantages of CAPI many software packages have been developed in the last decade for household surveys.[6] One example of such software is Survey Solutions, presently being developed as freeware by the World Bank's research department. Survey Solutions is a tablet-based CAPI software platform that is designed for the management of survey personnel and their assignments, as well as the collection, validation, and transmission of data. Despite higher up-front costs for preparation of the instrument, CAPI offers the potential to increase significantly the quality and timeliness of data and can provide lower interview times without affecting response.

### Geocoding to improve measures of location, distance, and size

When the poor do not benefit from economic growth, it may sometimes be because they are located in remote areas, disconnected from markets and public infrastructure that would allow them to share in the benefits of economic growth. In many cases, some of the key constraints to improving the well-being of the poor are linked to issues such as distance from facilities and the geographic characteristics of the location of residence. Traditionally, distances and measures of land size have been based on self-reports by the respondent, and data on the location of the residence was limited to coarse geographic descriptions. The introduction of cheap and reliable GPS instruments has significantly changed these measures by providing the ability to pinpoint a location with high precision and thereby also allow for the linking of geocoded complementary data.

Carletto, Savastano, and Zezza (2013) use GPS-measured plot size to shed new light on the long-standing issue of whether there is an inverse relationship between plot size and land productivity. Their findings indicate not only that the presumed inverse relationship exists, but that, in fact, GPS measurement suggests the relationship had historically been underestimated. Gibson and McKenzie (2007, 217) find four channels through which GPS can improve data collection by "i) clarifying policy externalities and spillovers; ii) improving the understanding of access to services; iii) improving the collection of household survey data; and iv) providing data for econometric modeling of the causal impact of policies." They further note that geocoded data allow analysis to control for spatial correlation that can significantly improve econometric analysis and the informational content of the data.

Although geocoding introduces some new concerns about maintaining the confidentiality of the respondents, protocols exist on how to handle these. For example, the Living Standards Measurement Study–Integrated Surveys on Agriculture (LSMS-ISA)[7] regularly collect the geocoded location of the enumerated households but release only the location of the enumeration area with a small amount of random noise introduced to the coordinates. This noise largely does not diminish the ability to link the data to complementary data sources (for example, land quality or rainfall data), yet does prevent the identification of specific households. The overall benefits of GPS instruments are large. They offer significantly higher precision in terms of location, distances, and sizes and allow for greater integration of different data libraries.

### Cell phone opportunities in data collection

Another important technological advance that is increasingly contributing to data collection and surveys in particular is the use of cell phones. Although phone interviews cannot reliably substitute for lengthy surveys like the LSMS, cell phones can serve as a potential tool for quality control and follow-up questioning of in-person interviews. Research by Croke and others (2012) shows that in Africa, rapid collection of high-frequency, wide-range data can be done in a cost-effective manner, with increased flexibility on question formulation, while minimizing respondent fatigue, attrition, and nonresponses.

The World Bank has explored some key initiatives with cell phone data collection tools such as Listening to Africa, which does not rely exclusively on phone interviews but uses a face-to-face baseline survey first and then follow-up phone interviews. The advantage to combining the two approaches is that it is feasible to collect a rich set of information during the face-to-face interview and then follow up with a few key questions at later points in time to learn about the dynamics of well-being in a few limited dimensions. Another such World Bank initiative is Listening to LAC for Latin America and the Caribbean.

### Imputation methods to help fill the gaps

In addition to advances in survey methodology and data collection methods, new imputation methods have helped in the generation of high-quality poverty profiles. Imputation refers to the process of replacing missing values with "plausible" values, based on a variety of estimation models and methods. Imputation can be used in at least three related ways. First, by imputing missing values within single data sets, analysts can avoid biased estimates or the loss of statistical power caused by samples getting smaller by dropping observations. Second, to improve the frequency of longitudinal data, for example, to generate more recent or more frequent poverty estimates than existing survey data would allow, survey-to-survey (or cross-survey) imputation can be used to fill in data gaps. Third, imputation techniques can help in combining various data sources, for example, from household surveys and censuses, to generate small area estimates that allow the measurement of poverty at high levels of geographic disaggregation. Overall, imputation methods can be seen as flexible tools rather than prescriptions for specific contexts. The imputation method underlying many of the World Bank's poverty maps, for example, can also be used to impute values in non–spatially defined dimensions or nonincome dimensions between survey years.[8]

### The quality of survey data: Imputation to deal with missing values

Missing item values are highly prevalent in all public use data sets, particularly in the context of low- and middle-income countries. Surveys of household consumption expenditure or other inputs to poverty analysis almost always contain a substantial number of missing values for at least some variables. A variety of imputation methods have thus been developed to address the problem of missing data, including simple strategies such as casewise deletion.[9] More complex imputation approaches are used to fill in values that are missing for various reasons of nonresponse, including item and unit nonresponse as well as measurement errors.

The appropriateness and efficiency of various ways to handle missing data depend fundamentally on the pattern of missing data and the specific application. Broadly speaking, simply deleting missing or apparently corrupted observations in a data set may lead to biased point estimates and incorrect standard errors caused by shrinking sample sizes.

A flexible technique that offers a solution is multiple imputation, which was developed by Rubin (1987, 1996). In multiple imputation approaches, missing values are replaced with a (relatively small) number of simulated alternatives.[10] Multiple imputation assumes that the missing data are "missing at random," which, following Rubin's (1976) definition, means that whether or not data are missing may depend on observable factors but not on unobservable factors. An example of data that are missing at random would be a situation in which respondents in a household survey are less likely to report their consumption if they are employed in a particular sector.[11]

Operationally, the multiple imputation approach takes the perspective that the data collector and the data analyst of public use data sets are two distinct entities and that once the missing data have been imputed by the data collector, the new data set should allow the data analyst to make valid inferences with traditional estimation methods for complete data sets. Such an approach, if done correctly, has appeal for public use data such as the surveys that serve as inputs to the World Bank's poverty and inequality estimates. The approach would allow for standardized treatment of some missing values, which could potentially improve comparability and replicability.

In Rubin's framework, the data collector uses an imputation model to generate multiple complete data sets. Various approaches can be used for this imputation, including Markov Chain Monte Carlo methods as in Schafer (1997). Each missing value from the original data set is replaced with a set of plausible values. Once all imputations have been generated, each of the complete data sets is analyzed with standard statistical models and methods. The combined results then allow reliable estimates and confidence intervals that reflect the uncertainty associated with the missing data.

A recent empirical application of multiple imputation techniques for missing data is the use of GPS data in the measurement of farm plot sizes. The inverse relationship between the land area cultivated by farmers and the productivity per unit of land used has long been discussed in the empirical literature, starting with the work of Sen (1962).[12] With the arrival of GPS data over the past two decades, a new set of studies has attempted to reassess the relationship, for example, Carletto, Savastano, and Zezza (2013), discussed above. However, GPS-based measures of plot size can suffer from significant item nonresponse. This might be the case because it is not practical for respondents to accompany enumerators to agricultural plots located far from the original interview location, or it could be the case that the plot was too large to walk around with the GPS instrument.

Kilic and others (2013) explore this issue in detail with public survey data from Uganda and Tanzania, where land plot sizes are collected through self-reporting and through GPS-based measurement. Similar to other studies, the authors find a large number of missing values, accounting for 35 and 18 percent of the plot samples in Uganda and Tanzania, respectively. They also find that in both countries, plots with missing GPS data differ systematically from plots with GPS data. Plots with missing GPS data are on average farther from the household location and tend to lack desirable features in terms of soil quality and slope. The authors conjecture that the data are largely "missing at random," since missingness is correlated with observable characteristics. They find that use of the complete, multiply imputed data set, as opposed to an incomplete data set of GPS plot size data, further strengthens the evidence for the existence of an inverse farm scale–land productivity relationship.

Vermaak (2012) provides a useful example of using multiple imputation for the estimation of poverty and inequality in the context of missing and interval-reported earnings data (that is, earnings that are reported to fall within a range rather than a specific value). In the context of labor force survey data from South Africa, she finds that the multiple imputation approach, as opposed to the naïve approach of assigning midpoints to interval values, does not significantly alter the estimate of poverty (primarily because reporting of intervals occurs for individuals with earnings above the poverty line).

### From improved quality to increased frequency: Survey-to-survey imputation techniques

Multiple imputation was originally designed to be a technique for filling in missing values in public use data sets. It is now commonly used to overcome problems of insufficient data availability in many other contexts. In the context of poverty analysis, higher frequency can be achieved through imputation between two surveys of the same type over time and, possibly more commonly, by combining data from different surveys, for example, an expenditure survey that is fielded once every few years and a labor force survey that is fielded once every quarter.

An early application of survey-to-survey imputation between two surveys of the same type is the work by Deaton and Dreze (2002) and Kijima and Lanjouw (2003) on poverty estimation in India.[13] They estimate the potential impact of a change in the survey methodology of the Indian National Sample Survey (NSS) related to a change in recall periods for reporting consumption expenditures.[14] Without taking into account these methodological changes, consumption expenditure estimates for 1999/2000 were argued to be fundamentally higher than those for 1993/94, resulting in underestimated poverty levels for 1999/2000 and an overestimated rate of poverty reduction during the 1990s period of economic liberalization in India. To project consumption expenditure as if the recall period had been unchanged, Deaton and Dreze (2002) and Kijima and Lanjouw (2003) estimate a model of household consumption expenditure with survey data from the 1993/94 round of the NSS, restricting the explanatory variables to those that are strictly comparable between the 1993/94 and 1999/2000 rounds of the NSS. Deaton and Dreze use a nonparametric method to estimate corrected poverty levels (and incorporate spatial and temporal price adjustments); Kijima and Lanjouw use the fully or semiparametric methodology of Elbers, Lanjouw, and Lanjouw (2002, 2003; henceforth ELL). Both approaches find similar results, showing that poverty during the 1990s declined much less rapidly than the official figures suggested.

The similar findings of the two approaches suggest that various imputation models for poverty estimation based on the same type of survey between two years, when constructed carefully, can provide comparable results. Figure 5.5 plots the results from a simple empirical exercise by Yoshida (2014) that uses data from two consecutive rounds of the Sri Lanka Household Income and Expenditure Survey (HIES). Poverty headcounts are estimated for rural and urban areas in 2009/10, based on a consumption expenditure model created with data from the earlier round in 2006/07. Changes in the questionnaire were minimal between the two rounds. The consumption model is estimated in two ways, using the ELL methodology and following the multiple-imputation approach by Rubin (1987). As a benchmark, actual poverty in 2009/10 as measured directly by the survey is provided in the figure. Abstracting from a longer discussion of the methodological differences between approaches, these empirical results suggest that in this relatively basic application, the two imputation methods provide comparable results.

Focusing in more detail on the imputation approach developed by ELL, Christiaensen and others (2012) provide a validation assessment of poverty-tracking methods based on imputation over time between the

**Figure 5.5**    Comparison of imputation models for Sri Lanka's poverty rate

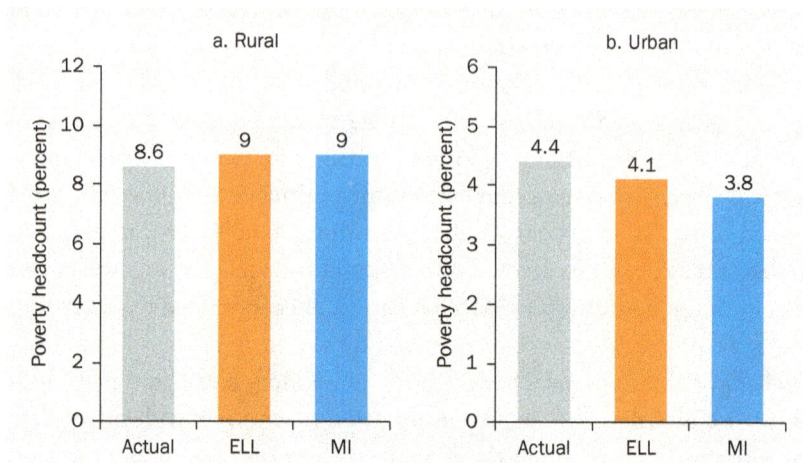

*Source:* Adapted from Yoshida (2014), based on Sri Lanka Household Income and Expenditure Survey 2006/07 and 2009/10.
*Note:* Poverty rates for 2009/10 are estimated based on models created with 2006/07 data. ELL refers to estimates based on a model following Elbers, Lanjouw, and Lanjouw (2003). MI refers to estimates based on the multiple-imputation approach following Rubin (1987).

same or comparable surveys. Christiaensen and others rely on two highly comparable cross-sections from the Vietnam Living Standards Survey and four years of panel data from two rural Chinese provinces. They chose economic environments with significant structural changes and marked reductions in poverty to assess the predictive power of various specifications of imputation-based models under demanding conditions. As described above, the simple intuition behind the ELL methodology for survey-to-survey imputation in this context is to first estimate a model of household consumption based on various household characteristics in year $t$, and then predict household consumption in year $t+1$ with the available information at that time, combined with the parameter estimates from year $t$. Through the use of explanatory variables that are comparable across surveys, the approach ensures an identical definition of consumption across surveys, but assumes that the relationship between consumption and its correlates remains stable over time (Christiaensen and others 2012, 272).

To illustrate how the choice of correlates can affect poverty predictions, Christiaensen and others (2012) estimate nine increasingly complex models of consumption: (a) food expenditures excluding rice; (b) all food expenditures; (c) nonfood expenditures using a 30-day recall period;

(d) nonfood expenditures using a one-year recall period; (e) total nonfood expenditures irrespective of recall period; (f) geographic and demographic household indicators; (g) geographic, demographic, and education-related variables; (h) geographic and demographic variables and education, housing, and consumer durables; and (i) geographic indicators, housing, and consumer durables. For the case of Vietnam, the various specifications of the ELL approach perform well in tracking poverty over time.[15] Figure 5.6 plots the poverty headcount based on both cross-sections of the data. As a benchmark, the solid blue line shows the actual levels of poverty with 95 percent confidence intervals. The orange hollow diamonds plot the predicted poverty point estimates, based on different specifications. It is notable that in four of the nine cases, the point estimates are not statistically different from the observed poverty headcount. Christiaensen and others conclude that there is no clear basis for preferring consumption-based over nonconsumption-based models, but note that excluding rice consumption from the food component improves the predictive power of the models.

Another approach to obtain higher-frequency data is through combining data from different surveys. Douidich and others (2013) apply the same methodology developed by ELL in the case of Morocco to combine data from detailed consumption expenditure surveys, which are fielded every few years, with higher-frequency data obtained from a quarterly labor force survey (LFS). They rely on two cross-sections of Morocco's National Survey on Consumption and Expenditure from 2000/01 and the National Living Standards Survey from 2006/07 to consider two models: they estimate consumption in the 2000/01 data to impute "forward" and they estimate consumption in the 2006/07 data to impute "backward." Both consumption models produce nearly identical poverty trends, irrespective of whether

**Figure 5.6** Various imputation-based poverty estimates and actual poverty headcount between two cross-sections of household surveys in Vietnam, 1992/93 and 1997/98

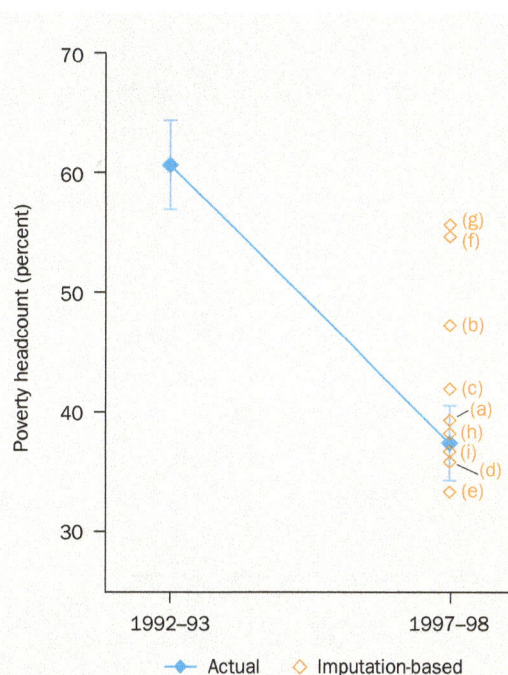

*Source:* Adapted from Christiaensen and others (2012), based on Vietnam Living Standards Surveys (VLSS).
*Note:* Four out of nine models fall into the 95 percent confidence interval around the estimated poverty rate using actual data. Letters indicate variables included in the model: (a) food: nonrice; (b) food: nonrice and rice; (c) nonfood: 30-day recall; (d) nonfood: annual recall; (e) nonfood: 30-day and annual recall; (f) nonconsumption assets: geographic and demographic; (g) nonconsumption assets: geographic, demographic, education/profession; (h) nonconsumption assets: geographic, demographic, education/profession, housing quality, consumer durables; (i) nonconsumption assets: geographic, housing quality, consumer durables.

**Figure 5.7** Backward and forward imputation using combined data from two household surveys from Sri Lanka, 2006 and 2009

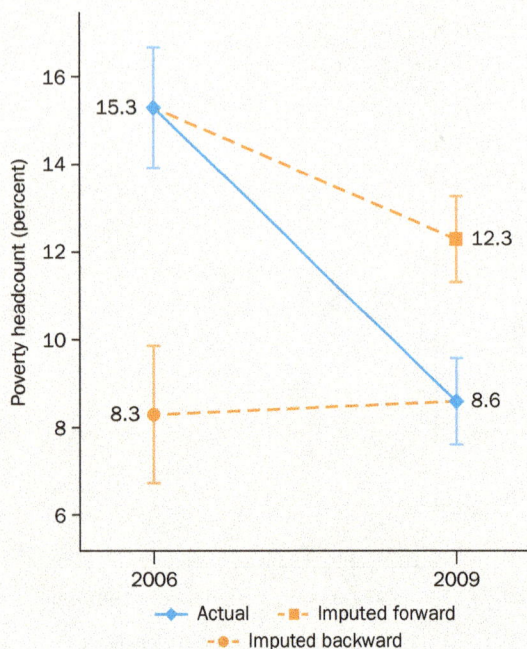

*Source:* Adapted from Newhouse and others (2014), based on Sri Lanka Household Income and Expenditure Survey (HIES) and Labor Force Survey (LFS).
*Note:* Forward imputation refers to a consumption model estimated in the HIES 2006 data, imputed into the 2009 LFS data; backward imputation refers to a consumption model estimated in the 2009 HIES data, imputed into the 2006 LFS data. Range shows 95 percent confidence intervals. Imputation does not include additional wage data as shown in Newhouse and others (2014).

projecting forward or backward. Imputation-based poverty headcounts from both models closely match measured poverty headcounts based on actual survey data. Douidich and others then apply both consumption models to LFS data for the period 2001 to 2010 and find almost overlapping quarterly poverty trends.

Do these promising results hold in other contexts? Newhouse and others (2014) replicate the approach of Douidich and others (2013) for the case of Sri Lanka. Newhouse and others combine the 2006/07 and 2009/10 rounds of the HIES with quarterly LFS data. They similarly estimate two consumption models, one with the 2006 HIES data to impute forward into the 2009 LFS data and another one with the 2009 HIES data to impute backward into the 2006 LFS data. Projected poverty rates are then compared with estimated poverty based on actual survey data from HIES. Figure 5.7 plots the results, which show significant discrepancies between projected and actual poverty headcounts. The authors attribute the discrepancies in the case of Sri Lanka to incompatibilities of survey questionnaires between the HIES and the LFS for urban areas and to a lack of common variables between the surveys, which adequately explain changes in poverty for rural areas. Overall, the study illustrates that survey-to-survey imputation approaches to generate higher-frequency data based on two survey sources do not necessarily work well in all contexts. Moving forward, careful validation of various models will remain a priority.

In addition to providing higher-frequency point estimates of poverty based on several surveys, imputation approaches can be used in the construction of synthetic panel data. In this application, imputation methods are used to combine several rounds of cross-section data. Panel data are the foundation for household-level analysis of income mobility, poverty dynamics, and vulnerability to poverty. However, relatively few panel data sets with national coverage are available for developing countries. One approach to address the problem of data availability has sometimes been by following age cohorts across multiple survey cross-sections (Deaton and Paxson 1994).

To allow for analysis at levels more disaggregated than age cohorts, Dang and Lanjouw (2013) and Dang and others (2014) build on the methodology developed by ELL. The intuition behind their approach follows the approach of the applications described above. A model of household consumption expenditure is estimated in the earlier round of cross-section data using a specification that includes only time-invariant covariates. The parameter estimates from this model are applied to the same set of covariates in the later cross-section to estimate consumption in the earlier period (for households surveyed in the later period). Poverty dynamics can then be observed by use of actual consumption from the later period compared with estimated consumption in the earlier period. For the cases of Indonesia and Vietnam, where actual panel data allow validation, this approach produces reasonable upper- and lower-bound estimates of mobility.

Synthetic panel data estimated with this approach can be combined with the analytical framework proposed by Dang and Lanjouw (2014) to identify population groups that are either in poverty, vulnerable to falling into poverty, or not vulnerable anymore and thus part of what could be described as the secure "middle class." In its upcoming flagship report on income inequality in South Asia, the World Bank uses this approach to analyze poverty dynamics in the region. Figure 5.8 illustrates the results for India between 2004 and 2009. After estimating a monthly vulnerability line of 988 rupees per capita, three groups of households are identified in the synthetic panel data: the poor below the poverty line, the vulnerable above the poverty line and below the vulnerability line, and the middle class above the vulnerability line. The results show welfare improvements for the poor category and the middle class, while the vulnerable group remains almost the same, accounting for a little less than 50 percent of the population in both periods. More broadly, this application illustrates the viability of using the synthetic panel approach of Dang and others (2014) for large-scale analyses of poverty dynamics.

## From improved frequency to improved resolution: Combining surveys for small area estimates

A specific application of imputation techniques with particularly strong appeal for policy makers is the generation of small area estimates. As explored in chapter 1, poverty reduction is an uneven process and poverty

**Figure 5.8** India consumption transition dynamics based on synthetic panel data estimated using the ELL approach, 2004–09

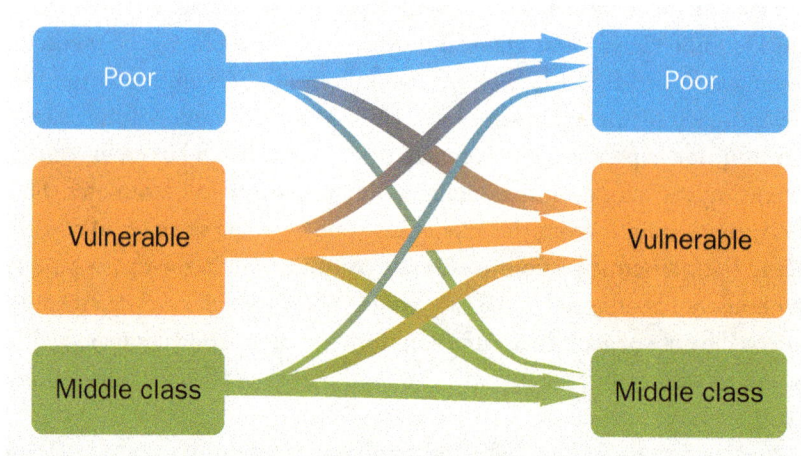

*Source:* Based on data from Dang and Lanjouw (2014).
*Note:* The vertical size of the boxes represents the total population share of the respective group; the width of the arrow represents the percentage of population that is transitioning. All numbers are weighted using population weights, vulnerability index defined as $P(Y2 < Z2|Z1 < Y1 < V1)$, and set at 20 percent (that is, a vulnerability line of 998 Rs per month at 2004 prices).

may be more concentrated in some areas of a country than in others—in absolute numbers as well as in poverty rates. In the design and assessment of resource allocation mechanisms for poverty reduction programs, governments may thus wish to understand better the spatial patterns of poverty, and when possible, how they are changing over time. This is not only important for effectively targeting antipoverty spending and identifying the households with the greatest needs, but also more broadly for coordinating and allocating resources across government actors and between various administrative levels. By integrating spatial analysis into welfare programs and aid systems, governments and donors can also overcome politically sensitive questions in locational decisions regarding program and project implementation and funding allocation (see box 5.3 for examples of two policy applications).[16] Although the intuitive appeal and policy relevance of small area estimates of poverty are clear, the provision of such data is less straightforward. This is because typical national household income and expenditure surveys that form the basis for poverty estimates usually are not designed in a way that allows reliable estimates at such a disaggregated level.

One method to overcome such data limitations and address policy demands is to use poverty maps in which household survey data are

## Box 5.3 Poverty maps and public policy: The case of Mexico

Over the past decade, Mexico has seen large reductions in poverty, in part as a result of robust economic growth and well-targeted social policies such as the Progresa-Oportunidades conditional cash transfer program. Yet, while headline poverty rates continued to fall, the mid-2000s also brought increasing awareness that poverty reduction had not been equally shared. In particular, poverty in the urban sector seemed to remain persistent. In addition, in 1997 the Mexican government undertook major reforms to the federal system that entailed a substantial increase in fiscal resources available to state and municipal governments. These factors contributed to an increased need for spatially disaggregated poverty estimates.

The first poverty map, estimated using the imputation approach developed by Elbers, Lanjouw, and Lanjouw (2002, 2003), was published in 2005 under the lead of the Mexican Ministry of Social Development and the United Nations Development Programme (UNDP) in Mexico. Poverty mapping has since been a central part of social policy planning and implementation.

First, in the fiscal system, the spatially disaggregated data generated as part of the poverty mapping process have provided a new foundation to assess and discuss budget allocations. Many poor municipalities experienced unprecedented budget inflows.

Second, the data serve as an input into various social programs, for continued improvements in targeting of existing programs such as Habitat, a program designed to improve living standards in poor urban households, as well as in the design of new programs.

Another immediate effect of constructing the first Mexican poverty map in 2005 was that UNDP Mexico reestimated the Human Development Index (HDI) at the municipal level, which in turn led the Mexican government to announce a special development program that would focus on the 50 municipalities with the highest poverty rates and lowest HDIs.

*Source:* Adapted from López-Calva, Rodriguez-Chamussy, and Szekely (2007).

combined with population census data to impute income or consumption at levels of precision that are comparable to those of commonly used survey-based welfare estimates—but for small areas such as single towns or communities (Ghosh and Rao 1994; Hentschel and others 2000; Elbers, Lanjouw, and Lanjouw 2002, 2003). By combining both sources, small area estimation techniques build on the respective strengths of each source. Censuses allow for the highest possible level of geographic disaggregation (such as cities, villages, or communities), but they typically only contain a limited numbers of questions and are conducted infrequently. Household surveys are conducted more frequently and provide detailed information on a broad range of socioeconomic characteristics, but since they often comprise only several thousand households, they typically do not have the statistical power to provide estimates at high levels of disaggregation. Most household surveys only allow estimates at the level of the first subnational administrative unit, such as the state or province.

In small area estimations, both sources are linked by predicting in a regression framework the variable of interest (for example, household consumption expenditure to calculate poverty headcounts) on the basis of explanatory variables that are common to the census and the household survey (for example, household size, age, and education). In a first step, household survey data are used to estimate such regressions at the lowest level of disaggregation for which the survey is representative. In a second step, the estimated coefficients from the survey data are applied to census data from approximately the same period, based on the variables that are common to both sources, to impute the variable of interest. In this process, obsolete, inaccurate, or incomplete census data can potentially introduce an error directly by providing a faulty baseline for the highest level of disaggregation as well as indirectly by providing low-quality expansion factors (or sampling weights) for the household surveys, as noted in the next chapter.

Because small area estimation techniques depend on a set of explanatory variables that are common to both data sources, the power of such estimates can be improved by including a wider range of socioeconomic variables in the census questionnaire. To resolve the tension between the requirement of universal coverage in a census and the availability of more detailed data (and thus higher costs), censuses often utilize a "short form" and "long form" questionnaire (United Nations Statistics Division 2008). The short form questionnaire contains only limited information and is used to enumerate the whole population, while the long form contains more detailed questions but is only administered to a smaller percentage of households (for example, one in six for the 2000 long form in the United States). See box 5.4 for an example from the 2000 U.S. Census.

As of 2014, more than 60 poverty maps have been constructed for about 45 countries.[17] What, then, can we learn from small area estimates of poverty? Ravallion (1993) and Elbers and others (2007) assess whether higher degrees of spatial disaggregation by poverty maps can help to improve government poverty reduction programs. They consider the distribution of a hypothetical budget to a country's population, assuming that the only information available for targeting is the geographic location of households and the level of poverty at each location. Elbers and others (2007) use poverty maps constructed for Cambodia, Ecuador, and Madagascar to

## Box 5.4  U.S. Census 2000: Short and long form details

To resolve the tension between the requirement of universal coverage in a census and the availability of more detailed data and thus higher costs, censuses often use a "short form" and "long form" questionnaire. More detailed census forms not only tend to be more costly, they also tend to have adverse effects on response rates. In a traditional census with short and long forms, the short form usually only contains a few questions and is intended to maintain universal coverage. The long form is used to collect more detailed information from a smaller sample of households, for example, on areas such as housing or fertility. Both forms are administered during the same time frame.

In the United States, the 2000 Census administered short and long forms. The short form contained just six questions related to the population and one question on housing. On average, the form takes about 10 minutes to complete. This form was given to about five of every six households. The long form asks the same questions plus 27 more, on a total of 34 subjects, taking on average 38 minutes to complete. The long form was given to about one of every six households. The table below provides a list of all the questions.

With the 2010 Census, the U.S. Census Bureau stopped administering the long form. Instead, it now collects more detailed socioeconomic information through the American Community Survey (ACS), which is conducted on a more frequent basis. Through a rolling sample, the ACS is designed to produce small area estimates.

*Short form*
*Population:*  Name, sex, age
Relationship, Hispanic origin, race

*Housing:*  Tenure

*Long form, additional questions*
*Population:*  Marital status
Place of birth, citizenship status, year of entry
School enrollment and attainment
Ancestry, migration
Languages spoken
Veteran status
Disabilities
Grandparents as caregivers
Labor force status (current)
Place of work and journey to work
Work status last year
Industry, occupation, and class of worker
Income (previous year)

*Housing:*  Units in structure
Number of rooms
Number of bedrooms
Plumbing and kitchen facilities
Year structure built
Year moved into unit
House heating fuel
Telephone
Vehicles available
Farm residence
Value of home
Monthly rent (including congregate housing)
Shelter costs (monthly costs)

*Source:* U.S. Census Bureau (1999) and data available online at http://www.census.gov.

simulate two transfer schemes. In both schemes, transfers are made based on knowledge about poverty levels in progressively smaller subpopulations. The simulated transfers are then benchmarked against a uniform transfer across the whole population. The authors find that in all three countries, more disaggregated data on poverty leads to increasingly clear benefits from geographic targeting.

There are many policy-relevant uses of poverty maps, but in terms of geographic targeting (one of the most common uses of poverty maps), the utility of poverty maps hinges on two issues. First and most fundamental, the accuracy and explanatory power of the consumption model underlying the poverty estimates will determine whether the constructed map can convincingly distinguish between localities in terms of poverty. Second, even if poverty estimates at the highest possible geographic level of detail are precise, the constructed map will only be helpful if living standards within this level are relatively uniformly distributed. Targeting will be less effective in cases where the poorest communities also exhibit high inequality of living standards.

## Notes

1. The NSSO was started in the 1920s, representing the first major system of household surveys based on probability sampling in the world.
2. In more detail, the 7-day recall would ask whether (and how much) a particular item was consumed in the past 7 days, and then this value would be annualized. The 14-day recall asks exactly the same question, but simply inquires whether (and how much) was consumed in the past 14 days, and then this value is annualized.
3. Livingston, Schonberger, and Delaney (2011) estimate this statistic at 75 percent of the world's poor living in rural areas and deriving significant portions of their livelihood from activities related to agriculture.
4. For more discussion on the Afghanistan National Risk and Vulnerability Assessment sample and sample design, see D'Souza and Jolliffe (2014). For a discussion of implicit stratification, see Kish (1995).
5. D'Souza and Jolliffe (2012, 2013) exploit the temporal stratification to examine how conflict and price variation affect food security.
6. A comparative software assessment was conducted by the World Bank's research department for CAPI software packages. The full report is publicly available on http://www.worldbank.org/lsms-isa. This exercise and field experience with the existing software packages subsequently led to the development of Survey Solutions to fill the gaps observed in the market, particularly on survey management capability. For more information, see http://www.worldbank.org/capi.

7. For more details on LSMS-ISA, see http://www.worldbank.org/lsms-isa.

8. It would go beyond the scope of this report to provide a more detailed methodological discussion of the various imputation approaches. Elbers, Lanjouw, and Lanjouw (2002, 2003) provide a technical summary of the imputation approach commonly used for small area estimates. Ridder and Moffitt (2007) provide a comprehensive technical overview of data combination methods.

9. Case deletion may lead to biased inferences if data are not "missing completely at random."

10. See Schafer (1999) for a nontechnical introduction.

11. The definition of data that are "missing not at random" (MNAR), following Rubin (1976), is when the probability of a missing value depends on unobservable factors. An example would be if respondents in household surveys are less likely to report their consumption when they have higher consumption. In empirical reality, the "missing at random" (MAR) assumption is often impossible to determine, while the treatment of MNAR missing data is nontrivial. Giusti and Little (2011) provide a discussion and present two sensitivity analyses to deal with data that are potentially not MAR.

12. Barrett, Bellemare, and Hou (2010) provide an introduction to the literature and various reasons for the potential relationship.

13. Also see Tarozzi (2007) for a more recent application in the same context.

14. See Deaton and Kozel (2005) for an overview of "the great Indian poverty debate."

15. The findings from Christiaensen and others (2012) for China are qualitatively similar to the findings for Vietnam; the findings for China are not reported here for brevity.

16. Bedi, Coudouel, and Simler (2007a) and other contributions in Bedi, Coudouel, and Simler (2007b) provide further details and various country case studies on policy applications of poverty maps.

17. According to data compiled by the World Bank's Poverty Global Practice.

# References

Ahluwalia, Montek S., Nicholas G. Carter, and Hollis B. Chenery. 1979. "Growth and Poverty in Developing Countries." *Journal of Development Economics* 6 (3): 299–341. doi:10.1016/0304-3878(79)90020-8.

Ahluwalia, Montek S., John H. Duloy, Graham Pyatt, and T. N. Srinivasan. 1980. "Who Benefits from Economic Development? Comment." *American Economic Review* 70 (1): 242–45.

Bamberger, Michael, Jim Rugh, and Linda Mabry. 2006. *Real World Evaluation: Working under Budget, Time, Data, and Political Constraints.* Thousand Oaks: Sage Publications.

Barrett, Christopher B., Marc F. Bellemare, and Janet Y. Hou. 2010. "Reconsidering Conventional Explanations of the Inverse Productivity–Size Relationship." *World Development* 38 (1): 88–97. doi:10.1016/j.worlddev.2009.06.002.

Bedi, Tara, Aline Coudouel, and Kenneth Simler. 2007a. "Maps for Policy Making: Beyond the Obvious Target Applications." In *More Than a Pretty Picture: Using Poverty Maps to Design Better Policies and Interventions*, edited by Tara Bedi, Aline Coudouel, and Kenneth Simler, 3–22. Washington, DC: World Bank. http://ideas.repec.org/b/wbk/wbpubs/6800.html.

———, eds. 2007b. *More Than a Pretty Picture: Using Poverty Maps to Design Better Policies and Interventions*. Washington, DC: World Bank. http://ideas.repec.org/b/wbk/wbpubs/6800.html.

Beegle, Kathleen, Joachim De Weerdt, Jed Friedman, and John Gibson. 2012. "Methods of Household Consumption Measurement through Surveys: Experimental Results from Tanzania." *Journal of Development Economics* 98 (1): 3–18.

Biemer, Paul P., and Lars Lyberg. 2003. *Introduction to Survey Quality*. Wiley Series in Survey Methodology. Hoboken, NJ: Wiley. http://search.ebscohost.com/login.aspx?direct=true&scope=site&db=nlebk&db=nlabk&AN=85511.

Caeyers, Bet, Neil Chalmers, and Joachim De Weerdt. 2011. "Improving Consumption Measurement and Other Survey Data through CAPI: Evidence from a Randomized Experiment." *Journal of Development Economics* 98 (1): 19–33. doi:10.1016/j.jdeveco.2011.12.001.

Carletto, Calogero, Sara Savastano, and Alberto Zezza. 2013. "Fact or Artifact: The Impact of Measurement Errors on the Farm Size–Productivity Relationship." *Journal of Development Economics* 103 (July): 254–61. doi:10.1016/j.jdeveco.2013.03.004.

Carletto, Calogero, Alberto Zezza, and Raka Banerjee. 2013. "Towards Better Measurement of Household Food Security: Harmonizing Indicators and the Role of Household Surveys." *Global Food Security* 2 (1): 30–40. doi:10.1016/j.gfs.2012.11.006.

Christiaensen, Luc, Peter Lanjouw, Jill Luoto, and David Stifel. 2012. "Small Area Estimation-Based Prediction Methods to Track Poverty: Validation and Applications." *The Journal of Economic Inequality* 10 (2): 267–97. doi:10.1007/s10888-011-9209-9.

Croke, Kevin, Andrew Dabalen, Gabriel Demombynes, Marcelo Giugale, and Johannes Hoogeveen. 2012. "Collecting High Frequency Panel Data in Africa Using Mobile Phone Interviews." Policy Research Working Paper 6097, World Bank, Washington, DC.

Dang, Hai-Anh, and Peter Lanjouw. 2013. "Measuring Poverty Dynamics with Synthetic Panels Based on Cross-Sections." Policy Research Working Paper 6504, World Bank, Washington, DC. http://ideas.repec.org/p/wbk/wbrwps/6504.html.

———. 2014. "Welfare Dynamics Measurement: Two Definitions of a Vulnerability Line and Their Empirical Application." Policy Research Working Paper 6944, World Bank, Washington, DC. http://ideas.repec.org/p/wbk/wbrwps/6944.html.

Dang, Hai-Anh, Peter Lanjouw, Jill Luoto, and David McKenzie. 2014. "Using Repeated Cross-Sections to Explore Movements into and out of Poverty."

*Journal of Development Economics* 107 (March): 112–28. doi:10.1016/j. jdeveco.2013.10.008.

Deaton, Angus, and Jean Dreze. 2002. "Poverty and Inequality in India." *Economic and Political Weekly* 37 (36): 3729–48.

Deaton, Angus, and Margaret Grosh. 2000. "Consumption." In *Designing Household Survey Questionnaires for Developing Countries: Lessons from 15 Years of the Living Standards Measurement Study*, edited by Margaret Grosh and Paul Glewwe. Washington, DC: World Bank.

Deaton, Angus, and Valerie Kozel. 2005. "Data and Dogma: The Great Indian Poverty Debate." *The World Bank Research Observer* 20 (2): 177–99. doi:10.1093/wbro/lki009.

Deaton, Angus, and Christina Paxson. 1994. "Intertemporal Choice and Inequality." *Journal of Political Economy* 102 (3): 437–67.

DeNavas-Walt, Carmen, Bernadette D. Proctor, and Jessica C. Smith. 2013. *Income, Poverty, and Health Insurance Coverage in the United States: 2012.* U.S. Census Bureau, Current Population Reports P60-245. Washington, DC: U.S. Government Printing Office.

Douidich, Mohamed, Abdeljaouad Ezzrari, Roy Van der Weide, and Paolo Verme. 2013. "Estimating Quarterly Poverty Rates Using Labor Force Surveys: A Primer." Policy Research Working Paper 6466, World Bank, Washington, DC.

D'Souza, Anna, and Dean Jolliffe. 2012. "Rising Food Prices and Coping Strategies: Household-Level Evidence from Afghanistan." *Journal of Development Studies* 48 (2): 282–99.

———. 2013. "Conflict, Food Price Shocks, and Food Insecurity: The Experience of Afghan Households." *Food Policy* 42 (October): 32–47. doi:10.1016/j. foodpol.2013.06.007.

———. 2014. "Food Insecurity in Vulnerable Populations: Coping with Food Price Shocks in Afghanistan." *American Journal of Agricultural Economics* 96 (3): 790–812. doi:10.1093/ajae/aat089.

Elbers, Chris, Tomoki Fujii, Peter Lanjouw, Berk Özler, and Wesley Yin. 2007. "Poverty Alleviation through Geographic Targeting: How Much Does Disaggregation Help?" *Journal of Development Economics* 83 (1): 198–213. doi:10.1016/j.jdeveco.2006.02.001.

Elbers, Chris, Jean O. Lanjouw, and Peter F. Lanjouw. 2002. "Micro-Level Estimation of Welfare." Policy Research Working Paper 2911, World Bank, Washington, DC. http://elibrary.worldbank.org/doi/book/10.1596/1813-9450-2911.

———. 2003. "Micro-Level Estimation of Poverty and Inequality." *Econometrica* 71 (1): 355–64. doi:10.1111/1468-0262.00399.

Fafchamps, Marcel, David McKenzie, Simon Quinn, and Christopher Woodruff. 2012. "Using PDA Consistency Checks to Increase the Precision of Profits and Sales Measurement in Panels." *Journal of Development Economics* 98 (1): 51–57. doi:10.1016/j.jdeveco.2010.06.004.

Fiedler, John, Calogero Carletto, and Olivier Dupriez. 2013. "Still Waiting for Godot? Improving Household Consumption and Expenditures Surveys

(HCES) to Enable More Evidence-Based Nutrition Policies." *Food and Nutrition Bulletin* 33 (3, supplement): 242–51.

Ghosh, M., and J. N. K. Rao. 1994. "Small Area Estimation: An Appraisal." *Statistical Science* 9 (1): 55–76. doi:10.1214/ss/1177010647.

Gibson, J., and D. McKenzie. 2007. "Using Global Positioning Systems in Household Surveys for Better Economics and Better Policy." *The World Bank Research Observer* 22 (2): 217–41. doi:10.1093/wbro/lkm009.

Gimenez, Lea R., and Dean Jolliffe. 2014. "Inflation for the Poor: A Comparison of CPI and Household Survey Data." *Bangladesh Development Studies* 37 (1/2): 57–81.

Giusti, Caterina, and Roderick J. A. Little. 2011. "An Analysis of Nonignorable Nonresponse to Income in a Survey with a Rotating Panel Design." *Journal of Official Statistics* 27 (2): 211–29.

Grosh, Margaret E., and Juan Muñoz. 1996. "A Manual for Planning and Implementing the Living Standards Measurement Study Survey." LSMS Working Paper No. 126, World Bank, Washington, DC.

Hentschel, Jesko, Jean Olson Lanjouw, Peter Lanjouw, and Javier Poggi. 2000. "Combining Census and Survey Data to Trace the Spatial Dimensions of Poverty: A Case Study of Ecuador." *The World Bank Economic Review* 14 (1): 147–65. doi:10.1093/wber/14.1.147.

Jolliffe, Dean. 2001. "Measuring Absolute and Relative Poverty: The Sensitivity of Estimated Household Consumption to Survey Design." *Journal of Economic and Social Measurement* 27 (1–2): 1–23.

———. 2006. "Poverty, Prices, and Place: How Sensitive Is the Spatial Distribution of Poverty to Cost of Living Adjustments?" *Economic Inquiry* 44 (2): 296–310. doi:10.1093/ei/cbj016.

Jolliffe, Dean, Gaurav Datt, and Manohar Sharma. 2004. "Robust Poverty and Inequality Measurement in Egypt: Correcting for Spatial-Price Variation and Sample Design Effects." *Review of Development Economics* 8 (4): 557–72. doi:10.1111/j.1467-9361.2004.00252.x.

Jolliffe, Dean, and Bohdan Krushelnytskyy. 1999. "Bootstrap Standard Errors for Indices of Inequality: INEQERR." *Stata Technical Bulletin* 51 (1): 28–32.

Khandker, Shahidur R., and Wahiduddin Mahmud. 2012. "Seasonal Hunger and Public Policies: Evidence from Northwest Bangladesh." Directions in Development: Poverty 70268, World Bank, Washington, DC.

Kijima, Yoko, and Peter Lanjouw. 2003. "Poverty in India during the 1990s— A Regional Perspective." Policy Research Working Paper 3141, World Bank, Washington, DC.

Kilic, Talip, Alberto Zezza, Calogero Carletto, and Sara Savastano. 2013. "Missing(ness) in Action: Selectivity Bias in GPS-Based Land Area Measurements." Policy Research Working Paper 6490, World Bank, Washington, DC.

Kish, Leslie. 1995. *Survey Sampling.* New York: Wiley.

Livingston, G., S. Schonberger, and S. Delaney. 2011. "Sub-Saharan Africa: The State of Smallholders in Agriculture." International Fund for Agricultural Development, Rome.

López-Calva, Luis F., L. Rodriguez-Chamussy, and Miguel Szekely. 2007. "Poverty Maps and Public Policy: Lessons from Mexico." In *More Than a Pretty*

*Picture: Using Poverty Maps to Design Better Policies and Interventions*, edited by Tara Bedi, Aline Coudouel, and Kenneth Simler, 3–22. Washington, DC: World Bank. http://ideas.repec.org/b/wbk/wbpubs/6800.html.

Meyer, Bruce D., Wallace K. C. Mok, and James X. Sullivan. 2009. "The Under-Reporting of Transfers in Household Surveys: Its Nature and Consequences." NBER Working Paper 15181, National Bureau of Economic Research, Cambridge, MA. http://www.nber.org/papers/w15181.

Narayan, Ambar, and Hassan Zaman. 2008. *Bangladesh Poverty Assessment: Creating Opportunities and Bridging the East-West Divide.* 26. Bangladesh Development Series. Washington, DC: World Bank.

Newhouse, D., S. Shivakumaran, S. Takamatsu, and Nobuo Yoshida. 2014. "How Survey-to-Survey Imputation Can Fail." Policy Research Working Paper 6961, World Bank, Washington, DC.

Ravallion, Martin. 1993. "Poverty Alleviation through Regional Targeting: A Case Study for Indonesia." In *The Economics of Rural Organization: Theory, Practice, and Policy*, edited by Karla Hoff, Avishay Braverman, and Joseph E. Stiglitz, 453. New York: Oxford University Press.

Ravallion, Martin, Gaurav Datt, and Dominique van de Walle. 1991. "Quantifying Absolute Poverty in the Developing World." *Review of Income and Wealth* 37 (4): 345–61. doi:10.1111/j.1475-4991.1991.tb00378.x.

Ridder, Geert, and Robert Moffitt. 2007. "The Econometrics of Data Combination." In *Handbook of Econometrics*, edited by James J. Heckman and Edward E. Leamer, Volume 6, Part B, 5469–5547. Handbooks in Economics. Amsterdam: North-Holland. http://www.sciencedirect.com/science/article/pii/S1573441207060758.

Rubin, Donald B. 1976. "Inference and Missing Data." *Biometrika* 63 (3): 581–92. doi:10.1093/biomet/63.3.581.

———. 1987. *Multiple Imputation for Nonresponse in Surveys*. New York: John Wiley & Sons.

———. 1996. "Multiple Imputation after 18+ Years." *Journal of the American Statistical Association* 91 (434): 473–89. doi:10.1080/01621459.1996.10476908.

Schafer, Joseph L. 1997. *Analysis of Incomplete Multivariate Data*. London; New York: Chapman and Hall/CRC.

———. 1999. "Multiple Imputation: A Primer." *Statistical Methods in Medical Research* 8 (1): 3–15. doi:10.1177/096228029900800102.

Sen, Amartya. 1962. "An Aspect of Indian Agriculture." *Economic and Political Weekly* 14: 243–46.

Tarozzi, Alessandro. 2007. "Calculating Comparable Statistics From Incomparable Surveys, With an Application to Poverty in India." *Journal of Business and Economic Statistics* 25 (3): 314–36. doi:10.1198/073500106000000233.

United Nations Statistics Division. 2005. *Handbook on Poverty Statistics: Concepts, Methods and Policy Use*. New York: United Nations. http://unstats.un.org/unsd/methods/poverty/pdf/un_book%20final%2030%20dec%2005.pdf.

———. 2008. *Principles and Recommendations for Population and Housing Censuses*. Revision 2. Statistical Papers 67. New York: United Nations.

United States Census Bureau. 1999. *The Long and Short of It: Why Does the Census Ask So Many Questions?* Washington, DC: U.S. Census Bureau. http://www.census.gov/dmd/www/pdf/d3239a.pdf.

Vermaak, Claire. 2012. "Tracking Poverty with Coarse Data: Evidence from South Africa." *Journal of Economic Inequality* 10: 239–65.

World Bank. 2006."Nepal Resilience Amidst Conflict: An Assessment of Poverty in Nepal, 1995–96 and 2003–04." Poverty Assessment No. 34834-NP. World Bank, Washington, DC. http://www-wds.worldbank.org/external/default/WDSContentServer/WDSP/IB/2006/07/13/000090341_20060713084841/Rendered/PDF/348340NP.pdf.

Yoshida, Nobuo. 2014. "Comparison of MI and ELL: Empirical results." Paper presented at the Poverty and Inequality Measurement and Analysis Practice Group special session on multiple imputation, Washington, DC, June 18.

# CHAPTER SIX

# Global Profiles of Poverty and Shared Prosperity, Data, and Measurement Issues

Frequent and reliable data are crucial for consistently measuring changes in poverty and shared prosperity over time and, thereby, for helping to build momentum to achieve the World Bank's new goals. This chapter focuses on the complementary data that are needed to estimate the global profile of poverty and shared prosperity. As noted in earlier chapters, the poverty goal is global and requires adding up the count of poor people in all countries. In contrast, the shared prosperity goal is specific to each country and is not aggregated up to a global measure. This fundamental difference in the two measures results in different supplemental data needs for each. Both need household survey data for relatively frequent and comparable measures of consumption or income and its distribution across households. Both use sampling weights typically derived from census data, and both need supplemental data on inflation. Estimating the total number of poor in the world though requires some additional complementary data, which is not needed for measuring shared prosperity, in particular, national accounts growth data, and data on purchasing power parity (PPP). The purpose of this chapter is to describe the role played by each of these additional data sources and illustrate the importance of ensuring quality data inputs to produce reliable and regular shared prosperity and global poverty estimates.

Population data are a critical input for producing an estimated poverty rate (that is, the percentage who are poor), an estimated count of the poor, and the shared prosperity measure. Without credible census data (or some population frame), it is difficult to make any inferences about the population of a country as a whole from a sample-based household survey.

For cross-country comparisons, additional data are needed to adjust for differences in the cost of living across countries. Making a statement about poverty in a particular country is a long way from being able to compare the poor in a consistent way across countries, because countries define minimum needs differently. Someone who is deemed not poor in one country may well be consuming at a level that would be considered poor in another country. The global count of the extreme poor aims to identify a poverty line that has the same value across all countries. To do this, additional data are needed that measure differences in the cost of living across countries. The key data for this are the PPP data collected by the International Comparison Program (ICP).

When household surveys are not conducted on an annual basis, additional data are needed to produce a consistent time series for poverty data. As noted in chapters 1, 2, and 5, household survey data do not exist for every country for every year. The most recent global poverty count is for 2011, but for most countries there was no household survey done in 2011. In some countries, household survey data may exist for 2011, but for others the data source may either be several years old or, in some cases, more recent than 2011. Rather than only estimate the poverty count based on the very small set of countries that have household survey data from 2011, PovcalNet extracts as much information as possible from existing surveys by interpolation and extrapolation methods that essentially project the measure of consumption to a fixed point in time.[1] Two key data sources for this "lining up" process are national income accounts data for estimates of real growth over time and consumer price index (CPI) data for estimates of the change in price levels over time.

The purpose of this chapter is to explain how each of these complementary data sources is used to line up household survey data so that the total count of the poor refers to the same point in time. The discussion will illustrate the importance of each of these data sources, with the primary objective of emphasizing the need for well-developed national statistical systems that are capable of collecting high-quality, timely, and well-documented inputs for improved policy making. The discussion on accounting for differences in prices across countries is particularly extensive, primarily because these data have significant implications for the global poverty estimates.

## Why census data are needed to count the poor

Population data are needed to produce poverty counts and poverty rates. The total number of poor people in a country is estimated as the product of the poverty rate and the total population. A key input to estimate the count of poor people, therefore, is to have a total count of the population for all countries. Population data are also needed to estimate the *rate* of poverty from household surveys. Poverty estimation is based on sample data, with samples that are drawn from a population with some known probability. It is the knowledge of the probability of selection into the sample that enables inferences back to the population. No matter how large the sample or how well the survey data are collected, without a population and housing sampling frame, surveys cannot make inferences about the population as a whole or, thereby, produce unbiased estimates of the percentage of the population who are poor. Census data are the primary source of sampling frames and benchmark statistics for household surveys (United Nations Statistics Division 1984, 2008).

## Coverage of census data

Population censuses are usually conducted in 10-year frequencies. In the current 2010 round (from 2005 to 2014), the United Nations World Population and Housing Census program has scheduled at least one census in 227 of 235 program countries or areas (map 6.1). Of the 227 countries that have scheduled censuses, 205 have already conducted the census. In the 8 countries that have not scheduled a census, data availability ranges from the year 1997 in Iraq to 1943 in Lebanon (table 6.1).

The most comprehensive effort to provide time-series data on total populations by age and sex, combining census and other population data, is the World Population Prospects (WPP) database maintained by the United Nations Population Division (United Nations 2009, 2011, 2013). The database is reviewed and updated every two years. At the World Bank, the WPP population estimates serve as inputs to the World Development Indicators (WDI) database and as the baseline for official regional and global poverty estimates.

## Quality of census data

Census data are necessary to produce sampling weights (adjustment factors that account for the varying probability of an individual being included in the survey) to ensure the survey is nationally representative. If the census data are of low quality, the census will produce poor quality survey weights and therefore poor quality population statistics. Similarly, an obsolete population census in a country that is growing or demographically changing will produce an outdated sampling frame. Any sample from an outdated

**Map 6.1    Census data coverage for the 2010 round**

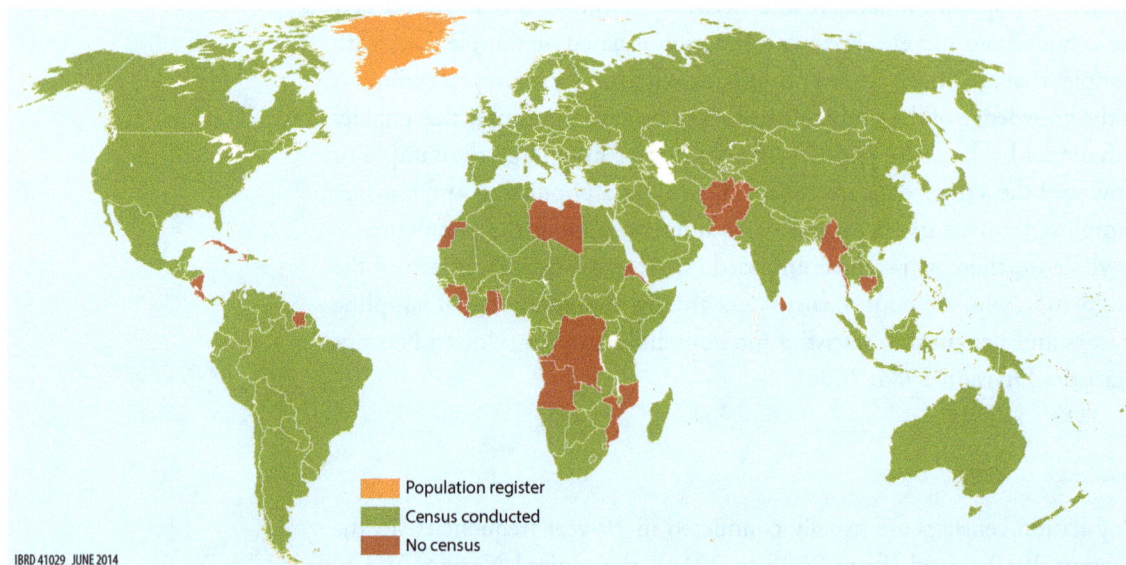

Population register
Census conducted
No census

IBRD 41029  JUNE 2014

*Source:* United Nations Department of Economic and Social Affairs, Statistics Division, World Population and Housing Census program.

frame can only make inferences to the population as it was comprised at the time of the census and will therefore likely fail to represent important groups or areas of the population. For example, if there are large population realignments by area, say through rural-to-urban migration, and if poverty prevalence differs significantly by area, an outdated frame will provide incorrect population expansion factors (or weights) and will produce biased poverty counts. Overall, obsolete, incomplete, or inaccurate census data can give rise to substantial nonsampling error (coverage or frame error).[2]

The quality of household surveys hinges on keeping a current sample frame (United Nations Statistics Division 2005, 2008). Maintaining a current sampling frame can be challenging, particularly in environments where there are significant demographic or residential changes. But in organized statistical environments, where administrative data systems are strong, there are several steps that national statistical organizations can take to keep a fresh frame. The first-best solution to deal with an obsolete, incomplete, or inaccurate frame is a countrywide, complete update of the old frame, accomplished by undertaking a new census. In many cases, this might be too time-consuming and costly, so a compromise is to update the frame only in areas of a country where the largest demographic shifts

**Table 6.1    Countries with outdated censuses**

| Country | Year of last census | Years since last census |
|---|---|---|
| Jordan (planned for 2015) | 2004 | 10 |
| Syrian Arab Republic | 2004 | 10 |
| Yemen (planned for 2014) | 2004 | 10 |
| Central African Republic | 2003 | 11 |
| Comoros | 2003 | 11 |
| Haiti | 2003 | 11 |
| Uganda (postponed to 2016) | 2001 | 13 |
| Ukraine | 2001 | 13 |
| Pakistan | 1998 | 16 |
| Iraq | 1997 | 17 |
| Madagascar | 1993 | 21 |
| Somalia | 1986 | 28 |
| Congo, Dem. Rep. (planned for 2015) | 1984 | 30 |
| Eritrea | 1984 | 30 |
| Afghanistan (2011 ongoing Socio-Demographic and Economic Survey by province) | 1979 | 35 |
| Lebanon | 1943 | 71 |

*Source:* United Nations Department of Economic and Social Affairs, Population Division, based on analysis in July 2014 of the implementation of the World Population and Housing Census program since 1948.

have occurred. In most higher-income countries, census data are regularly updated with data on deaths and births from vital statistics derived from civil and vital registrations, or sample estimates of fertility and mortality rates from health surveys (but uncertainty often remains for local population estimates based on postcensal trends in internal and international migrations, especially if these new trends are different from the previous intercensal period). In some cases, construction data for new housing structures can be used to correct for internal migration patterns—potentially reflecting growth in urban or peri-urban areas—and administrative data can be used to control for duplicates or out-of-scope units.

In low- and middle-income countries, where census data are often not available, outdated, or not reliable, demographic models and complementary data such as surveys, population registrars, or administrative records, combined with indirect estimation techniques (Moultrie and others 2013), are often the only option to provide consistent population counts by country and region (United Nations 2014). Indirect estimation approaches are typically based on independently estimating sources of demographic change, integrating separate estimates for fertility, mortality, and migration, if available, into a cohort-component projection framework. Investing in well-functioning census systems is an important way to reduce reliance on modeling and estimation approaches (box 6.1).

One way to assess the quality of census data and population projections is to compare population projections with actual population estimates in the census year. For example, the most recent census for Bangladesh was carried out in 2011. Prior to the census, the Bangladesh Bureau of Statistics projected the population of Bangladesh to be approximately 150 million in 2011. In contrast, the United Nations WPP 2008 revision projected the population to be approximately 164 million. Although the discrepancy is large, it is not unsurprising. Population projections are most accurate in the year following a census and deteriorate as the projections move further in time away from the census year. In the case of Bangladesh, the final results from the 2011 census indicated that the total population was about 152 million—quite close to the government's estimate, but about 7 percent less than the United Nations estimate. The numbers converged in subsequent revisions of the United Nations WPP: in the 2010 revision, the United Nations revised the total population count for 2010 down to approximately 149 million, a reduction of about 9.5 percent. In the 2012 revision, the 2010 total population was revised upward slightly, to about 151 million.

With each new release of the United Nations biennial *World Population Prospects*, the World Bank updates the WDI database to reflect the updated numbers. The WDI then serves as an input to population totals in the PovcalNet database. As a result, with each update of PovcalNet, the total number of poor will change even when the poverty rate does not change (figure 6.1). Given that the poverty rate using the $1.25 international poverty line for Bangladesh was 43 percent in 2010, the estimated count of poor people in 2010 changed significantly based on the various population estimates from approximately 71 million (as estimated in 2011, based on the 2008 WPP estimate) to 64 million (as estimated in 2012, based on the 2010 WPP estimate), and finally 65 million (as estimated in 2014, based

## Box 6.1   Nonsampling error in population estimates

One way that nonsampling error enters into population estimates is through modeling of input data. Figure B6.1.1 illustrates how the United Nations Population Division (UNPD) draws from numerous data sources to produce an estimate of the total fertility rate (TFR) for Niger. This rate feeds into the population projections and can, in some cases, also be used as a check on the credibility of current population counts. The figure contains several short lines, which represent TFR estimates based on a wide variety of data sources. All the estimates differ, which helps to illustrate how challenging estimating the fundamental population statistic can be. The lower orange line (labeled

2) in the figure shows the official TFR estimates based on census data from 1988 and 2001. When UNPD estimated the TFR based on all existing data, the analysis indicated a significantly higher TFR, as shown by the blue line (labeled 1). The lesson learned from this comparison is that even though there is no sampling error associated with census data, population estimates may nonetheless be measured with nonsampling error. Investing in maintaining high-quality, well-functioning census systems is an important element in reducing the reliance on significant levels of modeling and estimation approaches in estimating population levels.

**Figure B6.1.1**   Niger total fertility estimates, multiple data sources and methodologies, 1970–2012

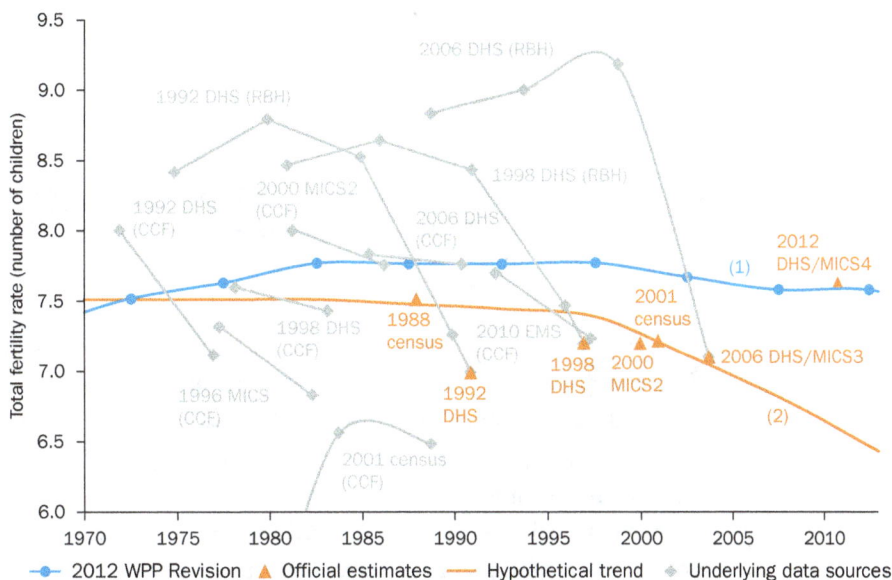

*Source:* Based on data from United Nations (2014).
*Note:* The blue line (1) represents the total fertility rate estimates between 1970 and 2012 from the 2012 revision of the UN World Population Prospects (WPP). The orange line (2) represents the uncorrected estimates of total fertility in Niger, based on the 1988 and 2001 censuses as well as the values for several Demographic and Health Surveys (DHS) that were available at the time. CCF = completed cohort fertility; EMS = Enquête sur la Survie et la Mortalite des Enfants; MICS = multiple indicator cluster survey; RBH = retrospective birth histories.

**Figure 6.1**  Changing population projections and effects on poverty estimates, Bangladesh, 2005–15

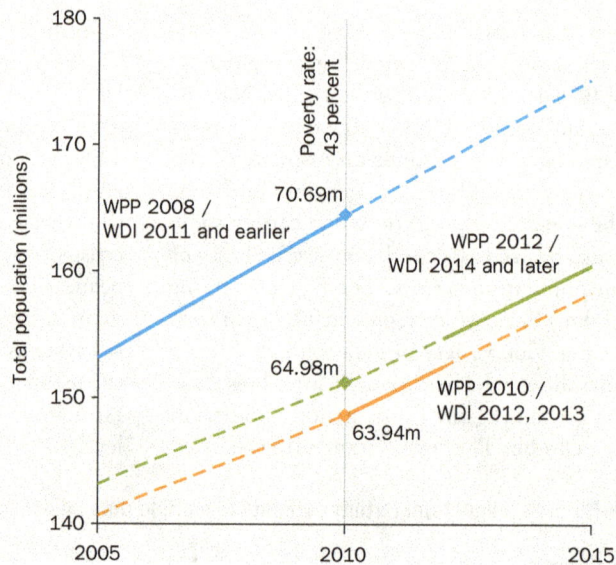

*Sources:* Based on data from United Nations (2009, 2011, 2013) and the World Bank PovcalNet database.
*Note:* The figure shows poverty estimates over time using population data from two alternative data sources: the World Bank's World Development Indicators (WDI) database and the United Nations' World Population Prospects (WPP) database. m = million.

on the 2012 WPP estimate). Between 2011 and 2014, the change in the estimated total population would reduce the global count of the poor by more than 5 million people, even if the estimated poverty rate were to stay unchanged.

In an extensive review of the state of population counts, the United States' National Research Council (2000) assessed the overall quality of population projections across the globe. Across several sets of United Nations and World Bank forecasts, the absolute value of the errors in projected country populations averaged 4.8 percent in five-year projections and 17 percent in 30-year projections. Given that many censuses occur once every 10 years, a reasonable benchmark to think about errors in poverty counts induced by errors in population projections is the five-year value. Considering that the most recent count of the global poor estimates that about one billion people live in extreme poverty, an error rate of 5 percent in population projections would translate into approximately 50 million people being misclassified. The misclassifications are more important in terms of thinking about the geographic profile of poverty than the overall count of the poor. (Because some of these misclassifications will be under-counts and some will be overcounts, the total count will be less affected by the projection error.) The National Research Council review shows that the example of Bangladesh discussed above is not exceptional, illustrating the importance of credible population counts for estimating global poverty.

## Purchasing power parity data: A unifying standard for measuring the poor

To count the number of people in the world who live in extreme poverty it is necessary to have a poverty line that is comparable across countries. PPP index numbers from the ICP are needed to adjust for differences in the cost of living across countries. The PPP numbers allow conversion from an estimated international poverty line into local currencies and then assessment of the number of people consuming at levels below this threshold in each country. There is an extensive literature documenting the sensitivity of poverty estimates to shifts in the poverty line.[3] By extension, poverty estimates are similarly sensitive to changes in the PPP data. This section describes how the global poverty line is selected and how it is made comparable across countries. The section provides a brief history of the interaction between the PPP data and estimates of global poverty and discusses the decision to postpone adoption of the 2011 PPP data for the 2011 global poverty estimates.

### PPPs and global poverty in 1979

The World Bank has a long tradition of producing global poverty counts. Ahluwalia, Carter, and Chenery (1979) provided some of the first modern counts of global poverty. Their work used as a global yardstick of basic minimum needs the consumption level associated with the 46th percentile of consumption in India, based on data from 1975. With this global poverty threshold established, the next task was to convert the line, denominated in Indian rupees, into the local currencies of all other countries included in the global count. It is well documented that currency exchange rates fail to provide a conversion that maintains equivalent costs of living across countries.[4] To convert the value of the Indian line, Ahluwalia, Carter, and Chenery thus used an index based on price data for a comparable bundle of goods across many countries. The price index used came from the ICP, which was started in 1968 as a collaborative effort of the United Nations Statistics Division and the University of Pennsylvania.

The first round of ICP data was collected in 1970 and covered 10 countries. Subsequent rounds of the ICP have occurred on an occasional basis. Between 1970 and 2013, there have been eight rounds of ICP data collection, with the coverage of countries increasing from 10 to 199 countries in the most recent 2011 round of data collection.[5]

Combining census population estimates, imputation to fill data gaps, and a variant of the ICP price index from 1975, Ahluwalia, Carter, and Chenery produced global poverty estimates for 36 countries based on data from 25 countries.[6] The key finding of their work was that the poor largely had not shared in the growth of the previous decade. Producing a global count of the poor was an input to this finding but also helped illustrate the complex choices necessary to estimate global poverty.

Ahluwalia, Carter, and Chenery's (1979) use of the 1975 ICP data provides one example of the complex choices needed to estimate global poverty. The 1975 ICP price data covered only 16 countries, but Ahluwalia, Carter, and Chenery needed to make comparisons across all 36 countries. To do this, they relied on an imputation approach described in Kravis, Heston, and Summers (1978), which ultimately produced a PPP conversion factor (Kravis-PPP) based on, but different from, the ICP data. Kravis, Heston, and Summers constructed a multi-equation model to predict price levels across 100 countries. They carefully cautioned that the estimates were sensitive to modeling assumptions and were weak in power. As an example of the sensitivity of their model to choices, they noted that the price level for Indonesia varied by 32 percent across two models considered.

As another example of the complexity of adjusting for differences in price levels, Ahluwalia, Carter, and Chenery (1979) compared the profile of poverty across countries based on the Kravis-PPP index and market exchange rates (table 6.2). Although they clearly argued against the use of market exchange rates to make cross-country comparisons, the poverty estimates based on exchange rates nonetheless offer some useful insights. Since the poverty line used was defined in terms of the 46th percentile of the Indian income distribution, nothing happens to the count of the poor in India (table 6.2) if one uses the ICP-based price index or exchange rates (arguably a desirable feature, since if most or all of the poor were in India, using India as a base would help mitigate the sensitivity of global poverty estimates to changes in the PPP index). However, the exchange rate–based count of the poor does change (and is lower than the ICP-based poverty rates) for all countries other than India. This difference indicates

**Table 6.2** Poverty estimates from 1979 based on market and PPP-adjusted exchange rates

| Region or country | 1975 ICP-based index | 1975 exchange rate |
|---|---|---|
| All less developed countries | 38 | 35 |
| India | 46 | 46 |
| Low income | 51 | 49 |
| Middle income | 31 | 24 |
| High income | 13 | 8 |

*Source:* Based on data from Ahluwalia, Carter, and Chenery (1979).

*Note:* ICP = International Comparison Program; LDCs = less developed countries; PPP = purchasing power parity.

that official exchange rates overstated the value of total consumption (or understated the cost of purchasing a basic needs bundle of goods) in the less developed countries (LDCs), relative to India.[7] This explains the slightly lower poverty rate based on exchange rates relative to the estimate based on the ICP price index for the set of LDCs. However, the difference between the exchange rate and the ICP-based price index within the set of LDCs is relatively small.[8] When examining richer countries, the exchange rate fares much worse relative to the ICP price index and produces significantly lower poverty estimates. If exchange rates are viewed as an alternate measure of price differences across countries, then, as relative price differences between rich and poor countries increase, the poverty rate decreases in better-off countries relative to poorer countries.

This pattern hints at a difficult issue for global comparisons as the ICP is revised over time. Updates or changes to the spatial price index used to denominate the poverty line in standardized PPP units can result in large shifts in the overall level of poverty, as well as significant reranking of countries in terms of the size of their population of poor. This is a lesson that returns with each release of the ICP PPP data.

## PPPs and the "dollar-a-day" international poverty line

Following the 1975 ICP estimates, which were used in the global poverty counts, the ICP released updates in 1980 and 1985. The 1980 data were not used for global poverty counts, but the World Bank's 1990 *World Development Report* (World Bank 1990) on poverty did base a global count of poverty on the 1985 PPP data, which covered twice as many countries as before. However, although country coverage for the PPP data had increased, country coverage of household surveys had not. A background paper for the World Bank's 1990 poverty estimates (Ravallion, Datt, and van de Walle 1991) used data from 22 countries and extrapolated poverty estimates for 64 countries. Although the extrapolation approach directly estimated poverty, conversion factors were still needed to convert national accounts data on per capita consumption to U.S. dollars using the PPP factors estimated by Summers and Heston (1988) based on the 1985 ICP data.

A choice was also made in Ravallion, Datt, and van de Walle (1991) on how to estimate the international global poverty line. The approach they followed has subsequently become standard practice in the World Bank's global poverty calculations. To address concerns about the sensitivity of choosing a global poverty line based on one country, Ravallion, Datt, and van de Walle proposed an approach based on pooling 33 national poverty lines, essentially those from all the countries they could gather. National poverty lines vary from country to country, in part reflecting differences in subjective assessments of minimum needs; differences in the extent of public service provision of some basic needs; and many other factors, such as climate, tastes, and behavioral norms. The approach aimed to find a typical poverty line influenced by the choices, on average, of many poor countries and not solely determined by one country.

Ravallion, Datt, and van de Walle (1991) noted how in many countries poverty lines tended to increase in value with increases in income—suggesting that even "absolute" poverty lines have embedded in them a relative component that accounts for broader needs to participate in society, in addition to some minimum cost of basic needs. For the poorest of countries, however, there was no correlation between poverty lines and income levels, suggesting that for this set of countries poverty lines must be reflective of the absolute cost of basic needs. The researchers' analysis of 33 poverty lines suggested that the typical poverty line reflecting only basic needs (essentially for the poorest of countries) ranged from about $23 per month to $30.42 per month. Although they presented findings from both, they preferred the $30.42 per month measure, which closely matched the value of poverty lines from eight of the poorer countries in their sample.[9] The value of this line was about $1.01 per day, and was thereafter referred to as the "dollar-a-day" line.[10] The resulting global count of the poor was 1.1 billion persons.[11]

With new consumption data and expanding country coverage, global poverty estimates have been regularly updated since then, with some important modifications over time. Chen and Ravallion (2001) provided updates to the global poverty estimates with the newer 1993 PPP data. They also reestimated the global poverty line—following essentially the same methodology of identifying the average poverty line across a small set of low-income countries—and found its value to be $1.08 a day in 1993 prices. One way to interpret this change is to view poverty lines as reflecting the expenditure necessary to reach some minimum level of well-being. Changes in this value over time thus reflect the increasing cost of obtaining this minimum level of well-being (assuming that for the poorest of countries, minimum needs stayed unchanged). Moreover, while the value of this line is expressed in U.S. dollars, increases in the value of the line are not linked to changing price levels in the United States. Indeed, if the dollar-a-day ($1.01 in 1985 PPP terms) had been adjusted by the U.S. consumer price index, the 1993 poverty line would have been substantially higher, at $1.35. This divergence indicates that the value of the global poverty line would have purchased much less in the United States over time, but continued to reflect changing price levels (at least as defined by the cost of purchasing basic needs) in the poorest of countries.

Following Chen and Ravallion's (2001) analysis, the $1.08 line became the new global poverty line, although it was still referred to as the dollar-a-day line. The 1993 PPP index, combined with an increasing stock of household survey data, had some other effects on the global poverty estimates.[12] For example, the overall prevalence of poverty was about a percentage point lower than if one had continued to use the past PPP data (and the previous dollar-a-day line). More substantively, the 1993 PPP data implied a shift in relative prices across regions. While poverty rates in South and East Asia were largely unaffected by the new PPP data, the regional poverty estimate for Sub-Saharan Africa increased by about 10 percentage points, while that for Latin America dropped by about 8 percentage points (both relative to what they would have been if the 1985 PPP index had been used).

Given the large changes in poverty estimates that can follow revisions to PPP data, prior to adopting the 1993 PPP index for global poverty estimation, Chen and Ravallion (2001) argued that the decision to change the PPP index used for poverty estimation should only be made after careful examination of new PPP data. One reason for this is that global poverty estimates are particularly sensitive to potential errors in the PPP indexes. As one key example, Ravallion, Datt, and van de Walle (1991) identified errors in the PPP for China and showed that these have large implications for poverty estimation.

## 2005 PPP and "the world is poorer than we thought"

For many years following 1993, the ICP did not release any revisions to the PPP data, but the 2005 release of the PPP data had significant implications for global poverty estimates. After a lengthy review and some important adjustments to the PPP data for China, India, and Indonesia—based primarily on concerns that price data in these countries were not representative of prices in rural areas—Chen and Ravallion (2010) incorporated the 2005 PPP price data into the global poverty count. The most substantial change occurred when Chen and Ravallion once again reestimated the global poverty line. Based on a larger pool of countries for which poverty lines existed, they now estimated the global poverty line as the simple average of the 15 poorest countries in the world. This revision increased the global poverty line to $1.25 for 2005. This revision was an important factor behind a large increase in the count of poor people. The 1993 count of the poor, based on the $1.08 poverty line and 1993 PPP numbers, estimated that 1.3 billion people were poor. Back-casting the 2005 PPP index to 1993, based on the new $1.25 poverty line, resulted in an estimated count of 1.8 billion people who were poor. Adopting the new index and revising the poverty line essentially resulted in increasing the estimated number of people who were poor in 1993 by 500 million. Table 6.3 illustrates the sensitivity of the number of people

**Table 6.3** Estimates of the percentage of the poor in 1993 based on three PPP indexes

| Indicator or region | ICP PPP index | | |
|---|---|---|---|
| | 1985 | 1993 | 2005 |
| Poverty line (US$) | 1.01 | 1.08 | 1.25 |
| East Asia and the Pacific | 26.0 | 25.2 | 50.8 |
| Europe and Central Asia | 3.5 | 3.5 | 4.3 |
| Latin America and the Caribbean | 23.5 | 15.3 | 10.1 |
| Middle East and North Africa | 4.1 | 1.9 | 4.1 |
| South Asia | 43.1 | 42.4 | 46.9 |
| Sub-Saharan Africa | 39.1 | 49.7 | 56.9 |
| Poverty prevalence | 29.4 | 28.2 | 39.2 |
| *Poverty population (millions)* | *1,350* | *1,304* | *1,799* |

*Source:* Based on data from Deaton (2010).

who are estimated to be poor and the regional profile of poverty to changes in the PPP index. In the case of the PPP rounds from 1993 and 2005, Chen and Ravallion (2001) and Ravallion, Chen, and Sangraula (2009) provide the evidence used to justify adopting these revisions to the PPP indexes.

The 2005 revision produced a healthy debate on how to identify an international poverty line and the resulting measure of global poverty. As one example, Deaton (2010) argued that the methodology used to estimate the global poverty line should be weighted by the size of the poor population across all countries, and not be a simple average of selected poverty lines. In the same spirit of trying to identify the "typical" poverty line, Deaton argued that countries with very large counts of poor should contribute more heavily to the estimation of the international poverty line. He focused on the fact that India, a country with one of the largest populations of poor people, had prior to the 1993 ICP round been included among the set of selected poor countries, but had "graduated" out of the set of the 15 poorest countries by 1993. India's national poverty line had been particularly low, and the country's migration out of the poverty line sample had the effect of increasing the international poverty line. This had the perverse consequence that as India's income grew, India was dropped from the set of countries determining the international poverty line— causing the line to increase and thereby to increase the number of Indians who were deemed poor by the global poverty count.

The recent release of the 2011 ICP PPP data once again highlights the potential role for price data to alter the overall profile of global poverty. Whereas the 2005 PPP data indicated a significant increase in price levels (resulting in a large increase in poverty), the 2011 PPP data suggest a large drop in price levels and poverty counts. Chandy and Kharas (2014) suggest that global poverty (based on the $1.25 poverty line) is more than halved (more than 600 million people deemed not poor) when the estimation uses the 2011 PPP data rather than the 2005 PPP data. One inference Chandy and Kharas extract from this, which aligns with the view of this report, is that "the size of the changes are a reminder that while our knowledge about the number of people living in extreme poverty and their location is improving, it remains far from complete."

History has shown that with each release of the PPP data, there has been a careful review and critique of the data. In some cases, the PPP data have not been used; in other cases, they have been modified either to fill gaps or account for potential problems in measuring poverty. For example, past ICP rounds have not adequately reflected the fact that prices tend to be lower in rural areas than in urban areas, which have required adjustments when estimating poverty in several countries. The ICP PPP conversion factors are based on national averages; however, the extent to which these prices are representative of rural and urban areas is not well documented.

Chen and Ravallion (2010) uncovered an urban bias in several countries in the past round of the ICP, which required careful adjustments. Chen and Ravallion (2008) found that the 2005 ICP survey in China was confined to only 11 cities, and therefore the researchers chose to treat the ICP 2005 PPP as an urban PPP index for China and use the ratio of urban-to-rural national poverty lines to estimate the rural poverty line in local currency units.[13] Correcting for the urban bias in the ICP data reduced the poverty estimate for China in 2005 by nearly half, from 26.4 percent to 15.6 percent, which had a large impact on the global count. Similarly, Ravallion (2008) found that for India, rural areas were underrepresented in the 2005 round of the ICP. Ravallion made corresponding adjustments to make sure that lower rural prices were properly accounted for in the poverty estimates. Understanding the extent to which there is urban bias in the 2011 ICP is one area of research, among many, that needs to be pursued before producing robust poverty numbers based on the 2011 PPPs.

Deaton and Aten (2014) believe that the 2011 PPP data are superior to the 2005 PPP data, in part because the new data reverse an error in the 2005 PPP estimates. The 2005 PPP data are essentially the product of two price indexes—one index established PPP *within* regions and the other established a price index *across* regions. The cross-region index is based on data from a set of 18 so-called ring countries, in which a distinct commodity list was used to price out goods that were not unique to any particular region. Deaton and Aten argue that the cross-region ring index is the key source of error in the 2005 PPP data, resulting in an overestimation of the price levels in Africa, Asia, and Western Asia by 20 to 30 percent.

The findings by Ravallion (2014) suggest almost the opposite interpretation, indicating that there are potentially significant concerns about the 2011 PPP data. He argues that the downward drift in prices observed for much of Asia (but not China) is in contrast to what would be expected given the observed rate of economic growth. A part of his interpretation of the data rests on the dynamic Penn Effect (Ravallion 2013), which suggests that the ratio of the PPP index to the market exchange rate rises with economic growth. Ravallion offers a hypothesis that over time the bundle of goods used for the PPP index has become more heavily weighted toward internationally traded goods (for which prices exist) and this has led to a downward shift in price levels relative to market exchange rates (conditioning on growth rates).

### Need for careful review of PPP revisions

The release of new PPPs always brings potential change to the understanding of global poverty. This change comes about through raising or lowering the overall count of the global poor, as well as through reranking countries in terms of their population of poor. Adapting the 2011 PPP data without any revisions or adjustments would result in a significant decline in the overall level of poverty. At this point in time, there are still several questions raised in the initial analysis of these data that require answers prior to determining the appropriate application of the 2011 PPP data for the poverty estimates. Getting the global poverty count correct is essential for assessing progress in the goal to eradicate extreme poverty. Similarly, to ensure that this goal is reached efficiently, it is critical to identify correctly the countries in which poverty rates are the highest, as this knowledge helps to focus efforts and resources appropriately in those countries most in need.

Because eliminating poverty is a key objective of the World Bank's mission, it is critical to be able to understand fully and readily explain any decision to change these estimates. New rounds of PPP data can provide improved understanding of the cost of living across countries, as well as expand the number of countries for which PPP data are available. However, careful review has occurred with each release of the PPP data. In some years, it was decided not to revise the poverty estimates; in other years, the new PPP data were incorporated. For example, well after the release of the 2005 PPP numbers and after extensive review of the underlying data, the World Bank incorporated the 2005 PPP data into the global poverty counts. There are many questions about the preliminary analysis of the 2011 PPP data that cannot yet be answered, and prudence suggests that it is wise to learn from the past and ensure that the PPP data are well understood before revising the global poverty estimates. The view of this report echoes that of the ICP that ". . . additional research will be necessary before international poverty rates can be estimated using the ICP PPPs" (International Comparison Program 2014, 24).

## Measures of inflation and growth to align data to the same year

When household survey data are not available on an annual basis, two additional data sources are needed. The ICP PPP index provides an instrument to adjust for differences in prices across countries at a fixed point in time, but does not provide a measure of the change in price levels over time. If household survey data existed for all countries in every year, the PPP data and population projections combined with household survey data would be sufficient to estimate global poverty. This is far from the case though: as illustrated in chapter 5, in any given year, there have almost never been more than 50 countries with household survey data. To line up temporally the existing surveys, it is necessary to have data on inflation and estimates of real growth rates. To measure changes in shared prosperity, it is important to keep the underlying measure of well-being in real terms. To measure poverty counts at the same point in time, it is necessary to inflate poverty lines to the same year. To handle both of these problems, data on inflation are needed for all countries.

### Why inflation data are needed to measure poverty and shared prosperity

When household surveys are not available on an annual basis, household consumption expenditure or income at current prices in each year needs to be deflated to one common base year. Equivalently, for poverty estimates, a given absolute poverty line could be held constant in real terms and adjusted by inflation to match the survey year. Most commonly, various types of consumer price indexes are used for such price adjustments. CPIs reflect changes in average prices in an economy by measuring the prices of a representative basket of goods and services.

The inflation adjustment in the World Bank's PovcalNet database, which also serves as the basis for calculating shared prosperity, largely follows standard practices (Chen and Ravallion 2010). PovcalNet uses country-specific, annual CPI data to deflate all survey data on household consumption expenditure or income to constant local prices of the ICP base year (currently 2005). After all surveys are converted to constant 2005 prices, the ICP PPP index is used to adjust for price differences across countries. This is equivalent to converting the international poverty line at constant 2005 PPP into constant local currencies in 2005 for all countries and then converting the line to the local prices prevailing at the time of the relevant household survey. Although the poverty line is expressed in terms of U.S. dollars, it is useful to note that the value of this line has not been fixed over time in terms of purchasing power in the United States; in principle, the value has been fixed in real terms to the cost of basic needs in the 15 poorest countries of the world (box 6.2).

### Box 6.2 U.S. inflation and the international poverty line

A comparison of the difference between the changes in the global poverty line over time with the rate of inflation in the United States, rather than the rate of individual countries' inflation, highlights how price-level changes across countries vary significantly.

The global poverty line was initially equal to $1.01 in 1985 dollars. For the years between 1985 and 1993, the value of this poverty line was inflated for each country by the country's rate of inflation. With the first estimates based on the 1993 PPP index, the poverty line was reestimated: the new value was $1.08 in 1993 dollars. As a point of comparison, the consumer price index in the United States during this period increased by 34 percent.

If the $1.01 poverty line had been adjusted to reflect changes in the U.S. price level, the 1993 poverty line would have been $1.35.

With the 2005 PPP index, Chen and Ravallion (2010) again reestimated the poverty line and now put the value at $1.25. As a point of reference, if the line had been adjusted over the entire time period by the U.S. rate of inflation, the line would be set at $1.82 in 2005 dollars. In other words, the constant U.S. dollar value of $1.01 from 1985 is $1.82 in 2005 dollars. The divergence between the U.S. inflation rate and the increase in the estimated value of the global poverty line thus reflects that prices have been increasing faster in rich countries relative to poor countries.

### Common problems with CPI data for poverty measurement

Comparisons of poverty and shared prosperity over time can be highly sensitive to measures of inflation. Although most countries have well-established statistical systems in place for collecting relatively high-frequency price data, the quality of CPI data varies significantly across countries and, similar to other complementary data, suffers from many potential sources of error. For a detailed discussion of common problems with CPI data, see International Labour Office (2004). Furthermore, the estimation of poverty has particular requirements that differ at times from those for national CPI data collection. First, CPI data are sometimes collected only in urban areas of countries and thereby fail to reflect price changes in rural areas, where oftentimes the majority of the poor live (Deaton 1997).

Second, changes in relative prices over time can create problems in deflating poverty lines (or, similarly, consumption). Suryahadi, Sumarto, and Pritchett (2003) use the case of Indonesia to illustrate how large changes in relative prices can make it difficult to maintain comparability in measures of well-being over time.[14] If all prices in an economy change uniformly over time, deflation of current expenditures or income can be achieved with appropriate price indexes. In Indonesia during the Asian financial crisis of 1997, however, the prices of food rose by 160 percent between 1996 and 1999, while the prices of nonfood items rose by 81 percent in the same period.[15] How should analysts estimate the inflation faced by individual households, given the vastly different relative prices? Suryahadi, Sumarto, and Pritchett consider various approaches that put different weights on food price inflation to calculate the change in poverty rates from a given level in 1996 to their postcrisis level in 1999. Depending on the method used, the increases in the estimated poverty rate range between 53 percent and 124 percent.

A third example, linked to the weights used by CPI data, is that the bundle of goods that are priced are almost always designed to reflect average consumption patterns and therefore typically do not reflect the consumption patterns of the poor (nor necessarily the types of markets where the poor are more likely to shop). The average person most likely consumes many products that the poor never purchase and, similarly, staple goods, which represent a large portion of the poor person's budget, typically form a relatively smaller share of the average bundle of goods. If the prices of staple goods rise much faster than the prices of other goods, as was experienced during the global food price crisis in 2009, inflation as experienced by a poor person is much higher than as experienced by the average person. Although this is a clear case where CPI data will underestimate inflation as experienced by the poor within countries, the evidence available to date suggests it is not a major concern for cross-country comparisons of poverty. Deaton and Dupriez (2011) and the Asian Development Bank (2008) find that the relative change in weights is fairly similar across countries and does not seem ultimately to affect poverty levels.

Fourth, price deflators may provide a poor proxy for the change in real living standards in transition economies or in environments of large shocks. If (poor or nonpoor) consumers shift away from goods that are rapidly increasing in prices and if this shift is not captured by the official CPI, the rise in the cost of living may be overstated. Gibson, Stillman, and Le (2008) use Engel curves for the food budget share of Russian households during the transition period of the economy to show that the official Russian CPI has significantly overstated the rise in prices and thus understated real income and household consumption growth.

In some cases, subnational inflation data are needed. For the large majority of surveys, PovcalNet relies on national-level CPI data to adjust for changing price levels. However, there are a few important exceptions. In the cases of China and India, subnational CPIs are used for the rural and urban sectors.[16] For Indian surveys, PovcalNet follows the methodology of the Indian National Sample Survey (NSS). In rural areas, the official CPI for agricultural laborers is used to deflate household consumption; in urban areas, the official CPI for urban nonmanual employees is used. Box 6.3 provides a detailed discussion of this issue and an example of how the choice of the price index itself can affect the poverty count.

### Alternatives when CPI data are not available

The cases discussed above illustrate that CPI data that have national coverage (including urban and rural areas), as well as the potential to provide measures of prices faced by the poor (and not just the average consumer), greatly improve the quality of measures of change in shared prosperity and poverty. Careful institutionalization of good practices in compiling CPI data is the first-best outcome. However, because CPI data are of questionable quality in many countries (at least in terms of their use for poverty estimation), there are several examples of countries that use household survey data to capture inflation. In some cases, the survey data provide direct measures of some prices (although rarely of nonfood items) and scope exists for producing a comparable bundle as consumed by the poor over time.

To address the case where survey data cannot be used directly to produce a price index and where the quality of CPI price data is also suspect, Olsen Lanjouw and Lanjouw (2001) propose a price index based on cost of basic needs (CBN) poverty lines. They show that reestimation of the poverty lines based on the CBN method can produce comparable poverty lines in real terms when the following set of assumptions hold: (a) the consumption measures are monotonically increasing in total expenditures (akin to Engel's Law), (b) relative prices that determine consumption patterns are stable across time and the groups being compared, and (c) there is no (or limited) measurement error in the expenditure data. Olsen Lanjouw and Lanjouw demonstrate that the CBN method allows measurement of poverty and price changes over time without having to rely on the existence of a price index.

Bangladesh is an example of a country that has essentially followed the Olsen Lanjouw–Lanjouw approach. In recent years, concern has been expressed by policy makers and the policy research community that the CPI has consistently underestimated the rising cost of living as experienced by the poor in Bangladesh. A special government of Bangladesh committee determined that this divergence was sufficiently large to use reestimated poverty lines, rather than the CPI, to produce comparable poverty

## Box 6.3 Impact of spatial and temporal price differences on national poverty estimates: The controversial case of India

The case of India serves as a good example of how the choice of a specific price deflator can affect poverty estimates. The choice of the appropriate deflator in India has been subject to intense debate (Deaton and Kozel 2005). As Deaton and Tarozzi (2005) remark, in a country where states are bigger than most nations and where rural-urban differences remain stark, the measurement of overall inflation is not the only role that price indexes play in the measurement of poverty. In India, price indexes are also used to establish the differences in price levels between states and, within states, between rural and urban areas. Individual rural and urban poverty lines at the state level define the official poverty headcount. As a result, any problems with price indexes will be reflected in any official estimates of poverty (and poverty reduction).

Until the mid-1990s, India's Planning Commission used two poverty lines for rural and urban areas, held constant in real terms by the implicit price deflator of consumption from the national income accounts. However, this deflator not only likely did not reflect the changes in prices for households near the poverty line, but also did not account for differences in inflation between rural and urban areas. In 1993, the Planning Commission's expert group on poverty measurement thus recommended that special rural and urban price indexes should be calculated and used to adjust national- and state-level rural and urban poverty lines (Government of India 1993).

Deaton (2003, 2005, 2008) and his coauthors have long criticized the use of these indexes—specifically the poverty estimates based on adapted versions of the consumer price index for agricultural laborers (CPI-AL) and the consumer price

index for industrial workers (CPI-IW), because the weights of these price indexes were updated infrequently. Deaton and Kozel (2005) described that, until 1995, the CPI-AL used weights based on expenditure patterns from a 1960/61 survey. To make the index more relevant for people near the poverty line, the CPI-AL was reweighted with food shares of households near the poverty line in 1973/74.

Deaton argued that because food prices have *fallen* since 1999/2000 relative to nonfood prices, the use of outdated weights that overstate the fraction of household spending on food means that the poor are assigned a price index that rises less rapidly than the overall cost of living. Nominal poverty lines would thus be understated and the official poverty headcount would be too low. Deaton estimated that, as a result, the official poverty headcount in 2004/05 should not have been 28.3 percent but 31.0 percent of the population.

As an alternative, Deaton recommended that nominal poverty lines should be calculated with alternative price indexes based directly on the National Sample Survey (NSS) data. Such an approach was adopted by the latest expert group on poverty measurement of the Planning Commission ("Tendulkar Committee"), which proposed to update India's various poverty lines with implicit prices derived from quantity and value data collected in the NSS (Government of India 2009). Using these lines instead, the all-India rural poverty headcount ratio in 2004/05 was estimated at 41.8 percent, in comparison with the 28.3 percent previously reported. Accordingly, the official Indian poverty estimates based on the 2009/10 and 2011/12 household surveys used revised poverty lines based on implicit price indexes.

**Figure 6.2** **Poverty over time in Bangladesh: Comparison of inflation indexes, 2000–10**

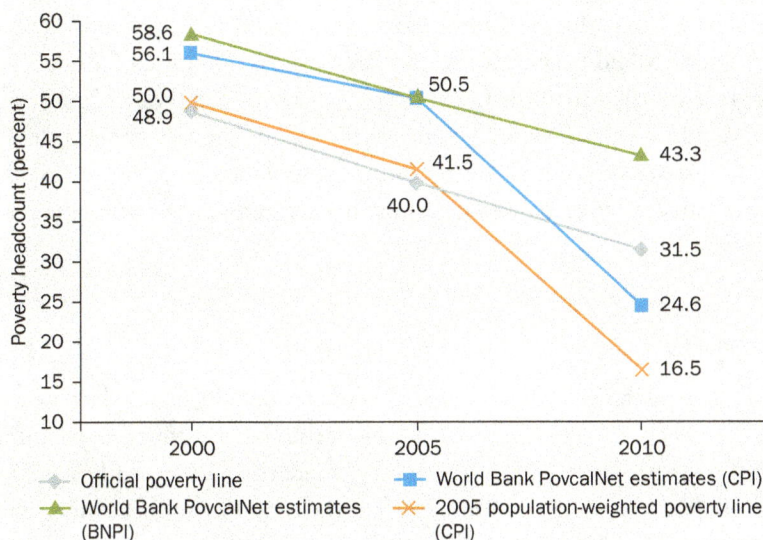

*Source:* Based on data from Gimenez and Jolliffe (2014).
*Note:* The figure shows poverty rates over time calculated with two alternative inflation indexes: the basic needs price index (BNPI) and the consumer price index (CPI).

comparisons over time. The implications of this decision had a substantial effect on the estimated poverty rate. If one considers the $1.25 poverty line (in 2005 dollars), poverty based on inflating the poverty line by the CPI is estimated to be 43 percent in Bangladesh. Treating the change in poverty lines as the relevant measure for inflating the $1.25 line results in a poverty estimate of 25 percent: a reduction in poverty of more than 40 percent from the CPI-based poverty rate. Figure 6.2 illustrates the differences in the $1.25 line and the government of Bangladesh's national poverty line, using different price indexes. That there is such a large divergence in the estimates raises serious concerns about the quality or perceived quality of CPI data for the purposes of measuring poverty in Bangladesh. For the purposes of the global poverty count, the World Bank ultimately decided that the decision by the government of Bangladesh was sufficiently substantiated that it was incorporated into the global estimates.

Bangladesh and India (discussed in box 6.3) provide examples of the sensitivity of the global poverty counts to the quality of inflation data. If

Deaton is correct, the use of the two CPI data sources in India resulted in an underestimation of poverty by 3 percentage points, which, in a country with one of the largest populations of poor people, is indeed a large underestimation. Similarly, the example for Bangladesh illustrates that the count of the poor would be almost twice as large if PovcalNet used CPI data for Bangladesh rather than the index based on reestimated poverty lines.

Overall, this discussion illustrates that, to compare poverty and shared prosperity across countries when annual survey data are not available, high-quality inflation data that accurately capture prices faced by the poor are needed.

### Why growth rates are needed to measure poverty

Data on growth rates are also needed when household survey data are not available in every year. To see this, consider the case of estimating the number of poor people in 2011 in a country where the most recently available household survey data was from 2009. If the economy of this country had grown between 2009 and 2011, the household survey data alone would not be able to reflect this. Given that growth is the primary source of poverty reduction (Kraay 2006), failing to reflect the observed growth will in most cases result in overestimating poverty.

In countries where household survey data are not available on an annual basis, growth rates from national income accounts data can be used to project consumption or income forward (or backward, as needed) to line up data into reference years, so that poverty can be estimated at the same point in time across all countries.[17] National accounts data represent the activities of economic actors (for example, individuals, firms, and government) at the most aggregated level, usually on an annual basis, and provide the well-known gross domestic product (GDP) aggregate. Unlike household surveys, national income accounts are highly standardized and are widely available at relatively high frequency.

Of the 126 countries currently represented in the PovcalNet database, 18 have only one survey available. In those cases, the survey mean is adjusted backward or forward to the reference year using the real growth rate in private consumption or income per capita from the national accounts, under the assumption of constant relative inequality—that is, leaving the Lorenz curve unchanged. If a reference year falls between two household surveys, the means of both surveys are adjusted forward and backward toward the reference year with the same national accounts data. The poverty headcount for the reference year is then calculated as a weighted average of the two surveys, based on how close the surveys fall relative to the reference year (box 6.4).

## Discrepancies in household survey data and national income accounts data

When household survey data and national income accounts provide significantly different estimates of consumption and growth, the estimation of poverty levels, poverty projections, and the elasticity of poverty to growth all become very challenging. This challenge poses many questions. Given

---

**Box 6.4    Lining up country surveys for aggregate poverty estimates**

The World Bank's official regional and global poverty estimates are generated by "lining up" the underlying survey data into reference years. Under the assumption of constant relative inequality, survey means are adjusted with the real growth rate in private consumption or income per capita from the national accounts, as shown in figures B6.4.1 and B6.4.2.

*Example 1. Syrian Arab Republic: Adjusting survey data to calculate headcounts in two years*
For Syria, the World Bank PovcalNet database contains only a single household survey, conducted in 2004. In this case, the survey mean from the year 2004 ($\mu_{2004}$) is adjusted forward and backward to

both reference years 2002 and 2005, using the real growth rate in private consumption per capita for each year ($g$). An adjusted mean of consumption per capita for each reference year is thus calculated based on the 2004 survey ($\mu_{2002\,(2004)}$ and $\mu_{2005\,(2004)}$, where $\mu b_{(t)}$ is the estimated mean for reference year $b$ using the survey for year $t$). With these means, one can then calculate the poverty headcounts in 2002 and 2005.

*Example 2. Mali: Reference year falls between two surveys*
Estimating poverty in Mali for 2005 provides another useful example. Mali had a household survey before 2005, in 2001, and one afterward, in

**Figure B6.4.1    Illustration of open-ended lineup of survey into reference years**

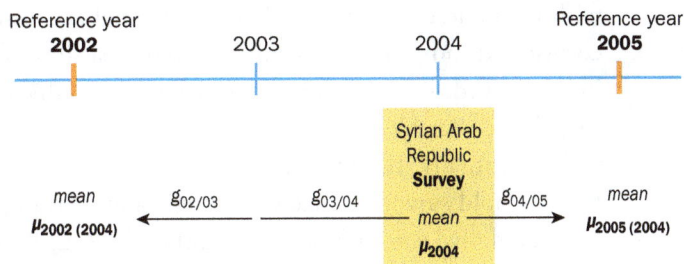

*(continued)*

## Box 6.4 Continued

2006. To calculate the poverty headcount in reference year 2005, the survey means from both surveys ($\mu_{2001}$ and $\mu_{2006}$) are adjusted toward the reference year, again using the real growth rate in private consumption per capita ($g$) for each year. The calculation results in two means and two headcounts for the same reference year, based on the two surveys ($\mu_{2005\,(2001)}$ and $\mu_{2005\,(2006)}$, and $h_{2005(2001)}$ and $h_{(2005)(2006)}$, respectively). The poverty headcount in 2005 is then calculated as the weighted average of the two, weighted according to the number of years between the survey and the reference year.

**Figure B6.4.2** Illustration of lineup into reference years between two surveys

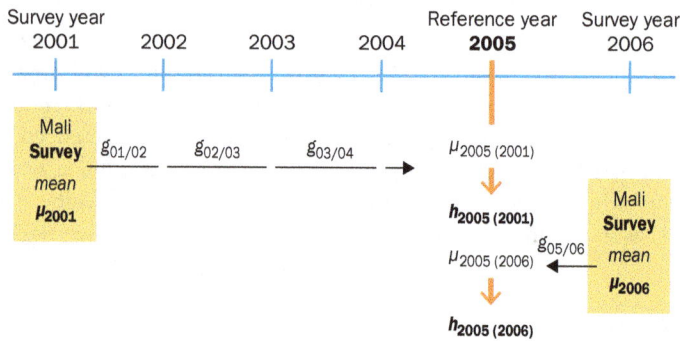

*Source:* Adapted from Chen and Ravallion (2004).

that the estimates of global poverty and global inequality typically rely—in one way or another—on a combination of national accounts statistics and survey data, how comparable are the two sources, in levels and over time, within and across countries? Which national accounts aggregate would correspond most closely to survey-based measures of consumption and income? And, if surveys and national accounts diverge, which measure would be preferable?

Conceptually, the two most obvious national accounts counterparts to household survey estimates of income and consumption are GDP and household final consumption expenditure (HFCE).[18] GDP can be defined as the value of all goods and services for various final uses. It is equal to final consumption expenditure, plus gross capital formation, plus net exports

(Commission of the European Communities and others 1993). The first component, final consumption expenditure, can be broken down into final consumption of households (HFCE), nonprofit institutions serving households, and general government consumption. HFCE includes almost all goods consumed by households, whether durable or nondurable. Both GDP and HFCE aggregates might imply different biases, and the existing literature discusses various arguments for and against the use of each aggregate. Anand and Segal (2008) provide a useful summary of this literature. For the purposes of lining up survey data to reference years, a reasonable assessment is that in countries where total consumption is used to measure poverty, HFCE is conceptually more closely linked, whereas GDP is more useful for lining up survey data in countries where income is used to measure poverty.

In spite of the conceptual connections, it turns out that empirically HFCE is closer in overall levels to household consumption and income as measured by household survey data. Using the most recent year for all consumption surveys available in the World Bank's PovcalNet database, the simple average ratio of survey consumption to GDP is 0.46 (or 0.38 in a population-weighted average). By contrast, the simple average ratio of survey consumption to HFCE is considerably higher, at 0.64 (or 0.58 in a population-weighted average). The ratios are comparable for countries that have household income data in PovcalNet, with a simple average of 0.44 for household income to GDP and 0.64 for household income to HFCE. To complicate things further, Deaton (2005) plotted these ratios (survey-based measures of consumption and income over national accounts aggregates) by overall GDP per capita and found that the ratio declines with increases in GDP. Updates to this analysis present the same finding—the divergence between survey data and national accounts becomes systematically larger with increases in GDP.

Differences in levels are not necessarily problematic for the purposes of lining up survey data, if the growth rates are the same. Ravallion (2003) analyzed 142 spells of growth between successive household surveys in the 1980s and 1990s and found that about half the growth rate in national accounts consumption is reflected in the survey-based growth rate. Ravallion's calculation is revisited below with more recent data. In line with the calculations of shared prosperity in previous chapters, 67 country spells are matched as closely as possible to the period 2005 to 2010 (figure 6.3). Regressing the average annual growth in household survey mean on the average annual growth of national accounts consumption (HFCE) reveals

**Figure 6.3** Growth rates of survey consumption versus growth rates of national accounts consumption

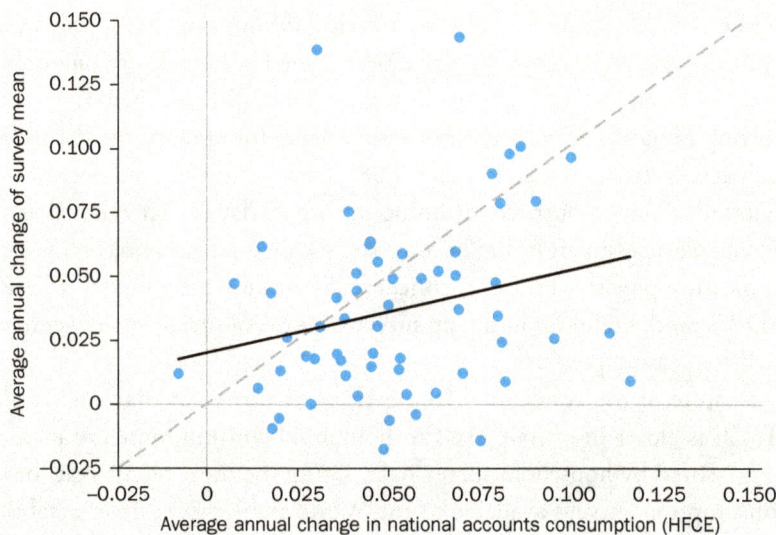

*Sources:* Based on data from the World Bank PovcalNet database and adapted from Ravallion (2003).
*Note:* Solid line shows a linear fit. Growth rates are calculated as annualized average growth rates in mean household consumption expenditure per capita from household surveys and household final consumption expenditure (HFCE) per capita from national accounts over the period 2005 to 2010. Given the data available from PovcalNet for each country (as of July 2014), surveys are matched as closely as possible to this period within a bandwidth of +/- 2 years, that is, the earlier survey must be between 2003 and 2007 and the later survey must be between 2008 and 2012. In cases where several spells of growth can be constructed in this range, spells are selected in order of the following priorities: (a) closest match, (b) latest spell and (c) longest period. This generates 67 spells with an average length of 4.8 years.

that about a third of the growth rate in national accounts consumption is reflected in the survey-based rate. Deaton (2005) took a different approach by calculating population-weighted growth rates of survey means in a (changing) set of developing countries over a 10-year period. Irrespective of whether growth is calculated as the average over the decade or as a logarithm regressed on time, Deaton found that the growth rate of survey consumption was about half the growth rate of national accounts—in all three cases, the growth in mean consumption as measured by household survey data is much lower than the growth rate estimated from national accounts data.

These findings indicate that the use of national accounts data to line up survey years is a troublesome element of global poverty estimation. The literature has so far failed to provide a compelling explanation for the divergence between household survey and national accounts data, leaving

**Figure 6.4**  Projection error in poverty estimates that use HFCE to scale up consumption, 2004–10

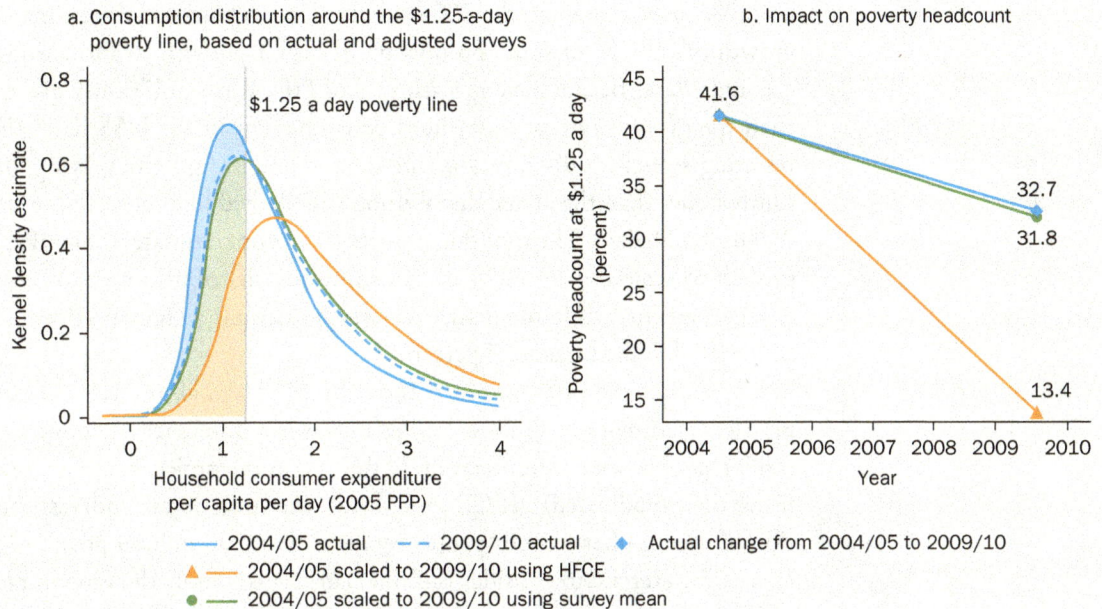

a. Consumption distribution around the $1.25-a-day poverty line, based on actual and adjusted surveys

b. Impact on poverty headcount

- 2004/05 actual
- – – 2009/10 actual
- ◆ Actual change from 2004/05 to 2009/10
- ▲ — 2004/05 scaled to 2009/10 using HFCE
- ● — 2004/05 scaled to 2009/10 using survey mean

*Sources:* Based on data from India National Sample Survey (61st and 66th rounds), World Bank PovcalNet database, and World Bank World Development Indicators database.
*Note:* The methodology to estimate poverty illustrated here follows Ravallion 2008. HCFE = household final consumer expenditure; PPP = purchasing power parity.

analysts in a difficult position. When survey data are a few years old and all evidence suggests the economy is growing, ignoring national accounts growth estimates will almost certainly result in failing to account for progress in poverty reduction. Alternatively, the use of national accounts growth estimates on average (over all countries) will in expectation overstate progress in poverty reduction.

Figure 6.4 uses data from India to illustrate an example of how the divergence of growth as estimated by national accounts and survey means can affect poverty estimates. Panel a in this figure presents several distributions of total household consumption, and panel b shows the poverty rates corresponding to each of the distributions. Following the methodology to estimate poverty in India proposed by Ravallion (2008) and used in the World Bank's official poverty calculations, the estimated poverty headcount for India in 2004/05 was 41.6 percent (reflected in panel a as the area to the left of the $1.25 a day vertical line and under the solid blue line depicting the consumption distribution in 2004/05).

253

Consider the hypothetical situation if PovcalNet did not have the 2009/10 India NSS data. In this case, PovcalNet would estimate poverty in 2009/10 by scaling up the 2004/05 distribution based on the estimated growth of HFCE (or some proportion of HFCE growth) from national accounts data. Because the growth rate of HFCE is significantly greater than the growth rate of household consumption in the NSS data, the resulting scaled-up distribution (the orange line in figure 6.4) is significantly richer than the actual distribution (the dashed line) observed in the 2009/10 NSS data. The resulting poverty headcount estimate using HFCE growth to scale up the 2004/05 consumption distribution to 2009/10 is 13.4 percent, while the actual poverty headcount as measured by the 2009/10 NSS data was 32.7 percent.

Given that the population in India in 2010 was about 1.15 billion people, the difference in these two estimates is a difference of about 222 million people. One interpretation of this is that the projection error from using the (unadjusted) HFCE growth rate amounts to an underestimation of the number of poor people by more than 200 million people. An alternative exercise to consider is if one had access to only the growth rate of NSS consumption and used this to scale up the 2004/05 distribution (the green line in figure 6.4). The estimated poverty rate would be 31.8 percent (an underestimate of less than 1 percentage point). The implication of this is that the divergence between estimated growth based on national accounts and on household survey data can result in very large differences in estimated poverty rates.

The purpose of this example is to highlight two points. The first point is simply to illustrate the importance of improving our understanding of the sources of divergence between survey data and national accounts data, to better understand global poverty. The second point is that extrapolating growth in household survey consumption measures based on national accounts growth rates (see example 1 in box 6.4) is a modeling approach that is heavily relied on and has the potential to introduce large errors in the poverty estimates. To illustrate the extent to which this extrapolation is used, consider the poverty estimates for 2010. In the summer of 2014, 79 percent of the country-level poverty estimates were based on projecting an earlier survey forward in time based on national accounts growth estimates. With the update of PovcalNet in the fall of 2014, this figure drops to 27 percent. Prior to the update, most countries' poverty rates were based on projecting survey data forward based on national accounts growth data. Indeed, when considering the most recent poverty estimates from PovcalNet at any given point in time, it will be the case that the vast majority of the estimates will be based on growth projections (as compared with interpolations between two household surveys). Out of concern for gross errors such as the India example described above, PovcalNet does not provide poverty projections for years where the poverty counts for large countries, such as India, would be based on national accounts growth extrapolations. Although this choice results in less frequent release of the poverty estimates (for example, continuing this rule would prevent the release of annual poverty estimates), it does help to significantly reduce the overall error rate.

The discussion in this chapter about the complementary data sources for global poverty estimation has sought to explain how each source affects poverty estimates and also to illustrate the overall sensitivity of the poverty counts to changes or errors in the complementary data. Bangladesh, a country with a relatively large portion of the global count of the extreme poor, has been used to illustrate how changes in population projections and inflation estimates change the classification of millions of individuals from either poor or not poor. Similarly, the example of the use of national accounts growth rates to project poverty in India illustrates the magnitude of the potential error and serves as an example for why PovcalNet does not provide annual lineups (but essentially waits until key household survey data become available). Ultimately, complementary data are essential for producing the global poverty count, and the aim of this chapter has been to describe the many ways in which the quality of complementary data affects global poverty estimates. The importance of complementary data is often overlooked, but always to the detriment of the ability to understand accurately the overall level of global poverty and its geographic profile.

## Notes

1. PovcalNet is an interactive tool that allows users to replicate World Bank poverty estimates. Throughout this chapter, PovcalNet refers to the data and estimates produced from the interactive tool. For details, see: http://iresearch .worldbank.org/PovcalNet.
2. See Biemer and Lyberg (2003) for a broad overview of data quality in surveys.
3. Ravallion and Bidani (1994) illustrate how shifts in the poverty line affect poverty estimates in Indonesia across various definitions of well-being. Ruggles (1990) provides an example of the sensitivity of the United States poverty rate to various indexing methods for the poverty line (see table 3.4 therein). Blackburn (1998) uses data on 11 countries from the Luxembourg Income Study to show how poverty estimates vary significantly as the poverty

line is set at different proportions of the line. Jolliffe, Datt, and Sharma (2004) illustrate how changing the poverty line for different price assumptions significantly alters the profile of poverty in Egypt.

4.  For a discussion of this, see Taylor and Taylor (2004). Frenkel (1981) argues that the empirical literature on this point is clear, but that this can also be concluded by simply observing how real exchange rates (market currency exchange rates multiplied by the ratio of national price indexes) fluctuate and deviate substantially from one. See also Kravis, Heston, and Summers (1978), who show that real exchange rates deviate from one to a greater extent for low-income countries than for high-income countries.

5.  For more discussion of the history of the ICP, see http://go.worldbank.org /WLPETUYSO0.

6.  Ahluwalia, Carter, and Chenery (1979) list 36 countries, but footnote 1 states that data for 11 of the 36 countries was imputed from cross-country comparisons for the purpose of ensuring sufficient population and geographic coverage. Including the imputed data, their sample covers 80 percent of the population of countries in the developing world, excluding China.

7.  Or, as Deaton (2005, 2) states, "[m]aking comparisons in PPP units corrects, or at least diminishes, the gross understatement of living standards in poor countries relative to rich."

8.  This in part reflects the fact that India was a low-income country in 1975, but it also reflects the fact that relative exchange rates within the less developed category of countries were similar to the relative ratios of the ICP-based price index.

9.  The national poverty lines for six countries (Bangladesh, Indonesia, Kenya, Nepal, Morocco, and Tanzania) were within one dollar of the $30.42 per month line. Pakistan and the Philippines were also close to this value. For the purposes of comparison, India's poverty line was $23 per month in 1985 PPP terms. If the Indian line had been used, the resulting global poverty line would have been about 76 cents per day, rather than the "dollar-a-day" line that was selected.

10. It is worth noting that the identified methodology was not intended to establish a dollar a day as the global poverty line, but rather to estimate a globally accepted measure of minimum needs as (essentially) an average of poverty lines from some of the world's poorer countries.

11. Coverage of the estimate was based on data from 22 countries, with extrapolation models used for an additional 64 countries.

12. The global poverty estimates were based on significantly more household surveys than had previously been available—more than 120 surveys from 67 low- and middle-income countries were used to estimate poverty. There was another change in methodology with these estimates as well: poverty estimates for countries without data were now based on regional averages rather than the modeling approach that had been previously used.

13. Deaton and Heston (2010), both of whom served on the ICP technical advisory board, note that this problem was recognized. The Asian Development Bank, which was the relevant regional authority, reweighted the collected prices with the aim of making them reflective of all of China. However, the

correction did not take into account differences between urban and rural prices (it just essentially reweighted the data from the 11 cities), thus Deaton and Heston assume that the price data collected were too high overall.

14. Indonesia provides a rich case study of the many practical difficulties in estimating poverty. See Frankenberg, Thomas, and Beegle (1999); Pradhan and others (2000); and Suryahadi and Sumarto (2003) for a comprehensive treatment of the poverty impact of the 1997 financial crisis. Haughton and Khandker (2009, chapter 11) provide a summary of the deflation problem for the case of Indonesia.

15. This differential can largely be attributed to the substantial real devaluation of the Indonesian rupiah during the crisis, which made food imports relatively more expensive.

16. For Indonesia, PovcalNet provides separate Lorenz curves for rural and urban areas but uses only one economywide CPI.

17. In addition to using national accounts data to shift household survey data forward or backward in time, these data have also sometimes been used to adjust household survey data at a specific point in time. The fundamental assumption underlying this adjustment is that the mean value of consumption as measured by household survey data is wrong, but the distribution of consumption from the same survey is correct. Under this approach, revised distributions are constructed by rescaling all levels of consumption or income in a survey by the ratio of the national accounts aggregate (such as GDP per capita) to the survey mean. This approach has a long tradition in the estimation of global inequality, where national distributions are first rescaled using national accounts and then aggregated to derive regional or global estimates. Examples include the work by Ahluwalia, Carter, and Chenery (1979); Berry, Bourguignon, and Morrisson (1983); Bhalla (2002); Bourguignon and Morrisson (2002); and Sala-i-Martin (2006).

18. Deaton (2005) and Anand and Segal (2008) present detailed conceptual discussions that provide the basis for this paragraph.

# References

Ahluwalia, Montek S., Nicholas G. Carter, and Hollis B. Chenery. 1979. "Growth and Poverty in Developing Countries." *Journal of Development Economics* 6 (3): 299–341. doi:10.1016/0304-3878(79)90020-8.

Anand, Sudhir, and Paul Segal. 2008. "What Do We Know about Global Income Inequality?" *Journal of Economic Literature* 46 (1): 57–94. doi:10.1257/jel.46.1.57.

Asian Development Bank. 2008. *Research Study on Poverty-Specific Purchasing Power Parities for Selected Countries in Asia and the Pacific.* Manila, Philippines: Asian Development Bank.

Berry, Albert, Francois Bourguignon, and Christian Morrisson. 1983. "The Level of World Inequality: How Much Can One Say?" *Review of Income and Wealth* 29 (3): 217–41. doi:10.1111/j.1475-4991.1983.tb00643.x.

Bhalla, Surjit S. 2002. *Imagine There's No Country: Poverty, Inequality, and Growth in the Era of Globalization.* Washington, DC: Institute for International Economics.

Biemer, Paul P., and Lars Lyberg. 2003. *Introduction to Survey Quality.* Wiley Series in Survey Methodology. Hoboken, NJ: Wiley.

Blackburn, McKinley L. 1998. "The Sensitivity of International Poverty Comparisons." *Review of Income and Wealth* 44 (4): 449–72. doi:10.1111/j.1475-4991.1998.tb00293.x.

Bourguignon, François, and Christian Morrisson. 2002. "Inequality among World Citizens: 1820–1992." *American Economic Review* 92 (4): 727–44. doi:10.1257/00028280260344443.

Chandy, Lawrence, and Homi Kharas. 2014. "What Do New Price Data Mean for the Goal of Ending Extreme Poverty?" Brookings Institution, Washington, DC. http://www.brookings.edu/blogs/up-front/posts/2014/05/05-data-extreme-poverty-chandy-kharas.

Chen, Shaohua, and Martin Ravallion. 2001. "How Did the World's Poorest Fare in the 1990s?" *Review of Income and Wealth* 47 (3): 283–300.

———. 2004. "How Have the World's Poorest Fared since the Early 1980s?" *The World Bank Research Observer* 19 (2): 141–69. doi:10.1093/wbro/lkh020.

———. 2008. "China Is Poorer Than We Thought, but No Less Successful in the Fight against Poverty." Policy Research Working Paper 4621, World Bank, Washington, DC.

———. 2010. "The Developing World Is Poorer Than We Thought, But No Less Successful in the Fight Against Poverty." *The Quarterly Journal of Economics* 125 (4): 1577–1625. doi:10.1162/qjec.2010.125.4.1577.

Commission of the European Communities, International Monetary Fund, Organisation for Economic Co-operation and Development, United Nations, and World Bank. 1993. *System of National Accounts 1993.* System of National Accounts, Brussels/Luxembourg, New York, Paris, Washington DC.

Deaton, Angus. 1997. *The Analysis of Household Surveys: A Microeconometric Approach to Development Policy.* Baltimore, MD: Johns Hopkins University Press

———. 2003. "Prices and Poverty in India, 1987–2000." *Economic and Political Weekly* 38 (4): 362–68.

———. 2005. "Measuring Poverty in a Growing World (or Measuring Growth in a Poor World)." *Review of Economics and Statistics* 87 (1): 1–19. doi:10.1162/0034653053327612.

———. 2008. "Price Trends in India and Their Implications for Measuring Poverty." *Economic and Political Weekly* 43 (6): 43–49.

———. 2010. "Price Indexes, Inequality, and the Measurement of World Poverty." *American Economic Review* 100 (1): 5–34. doi:10.1257/aer.100.1.5.

Deaton, Angus, and Bettina Aten. 2014. "Trying to Understand the PPPs in ICP 2011: Why Are the Results so Different?" Princeton University, Princeton, NJ. http://www.princeton.edu/~deaton/downloads/Deaton_Aten_Trying_to_understand_ICP_2011_V3_1.pdf.

Deaton, Angus, and Olivier Dupriez. 2011. "Purchasing Power Parity Exchange Rates for the Global Poor." *American Economic Journal: Applied Economics* 3 (2): 137–66. doi:10.1257/app.3.2.137.

Deaton, Angus, and Alan Heston. 2010. "Understanding PPPs and PPP-Based National Accounts." *American Economic Journal: Macroeconomics* 2 (4): 1–35. doi:10.1257/mac.2.4.1.

Deaton, Angus, and Valerie Kozel. 2005. "Data and Dogma: The Great Indian Poverty Debate." *The World Bank Research Observer* 20 (2): 177–99. doi:10.1093/wbro/lki009.

Deaton, Angus, and Alessandro Tarozzi. 2005. "Prices and Poverty in India." In *The Great Indian Poverty Debate*, edited by Angus Deaton and Valerie Kozel, 381–411. New Delhi: MacMillan.

Frankenberg, Elizabeth, Duncan Thomas, and Kathleen Beegle. 1999. "The Real Costs of Indonesia's Economic Crisis." Labor and Population Program Working Paper 99-04, RAND Corporation, Santa Monica, CA. http://www.rand.org/pubs/drafts/DRU2064.html.

Frenkel, Jacob A. 1981. "Collapse of Purchasing Power Parities during the 1970s." *European Economic Review* XVI (1): 145–65.

Gibson, John, Steven Stillman, and Trinh Le. 2008. "CPI Bias and Real Living Standards in Russia during the Transition." *Journal of Development Economics* 87 (1): 140–60. doi:10.1016/j.jdeveco.2007.06.005.

Gimenez, Lea R., and Dean Jolliffe. 2014. "Inflation for the Poor: A Comparison of CPI and Household Survey Data." *Bangladesh Development Studies* 37 (1/2): 57–81.

Government of India, Planning Commission. 1993. *Report of the Expert Group on Estimation of Proportion and Number of Poor*. New Delhi: Government of India.

———. 2009. *Report of the Expert Group to Review the Methodology for Estimation of Poverty*. New Delhi: Government of India.

Haughton, Jonathan Henry, and Shahidur R. Khandker. 2009. *Handbook on Poverty and Inequality*. Washington, DC: World Bank.

International Comparison Program. 2014. *Purchasing Power Parities and Real Expenditures of World Economies: Summary of Results and Findings of the 2011 International Comparison Program*. Washington, DC: World Bank.

International Labour Office. 2004. *Consumer Price Index Manual: Theory and Practice*. Geneva: International Labour Office.

Jolliffe, Dean, Gaurav Datt, and Manohar Sharma. 2004. "Robust Poverty and Inequality Measurement in Egypt: Correcting for Spatial-Price Variation and Sample Design Effects." *Review of Development Economics* 8 (4): 557–72. doi:10.1111/j.1467-9361.2004.00252.x.

Kraay, Aart. 2006. "When Is Growth Pro-Poor? Evidence from a Panel of Countries." *Journal of Development Economics* 80 (1): 198–227. doi:10.1016/j.jdeveco.2005.02.004.

Kravis, Irving B., Alan W. Heston, and Robert Summers. 1978. "Real GDP Per Capita for More Than One Hundred Countries." *Economic Journal* 88 (350): 215–42.

Moultrie, Tom, Rob Dorrington, Allan Hill, Kenneth Hill, Ian Timaeus, and Basia Zaba, eds. 2013. *Tools for Demographic Estimation*. Second impression. Paris: International Union for the Scientific Study of Population.

National Research Council (U.S.). 2000. *Beyond Six Billion: Forecasting the World's Population*, edited by John Bongaarts and Rodolfo A. Bulatao. Washington, DC: National Academy Press.

Olsen Lanjouw, Jean, and Peter Lanjouw. 2001. "How to Compare Apples And Oranges: Poverty Measurement Based on Different Definitions of Consumption." *Review of Income and Wealth* 47 (1): 25–42. doi:10.1111/1475-4991.00002.

Pradhan, Menno, Asep Suryahadi, Sudarno Sumarto, and Lant Pritchett. 2000. "Measurements of Poverty in Indonesia—1996, 1999, and Beyond." Policy Research Working Paper 2438, World Bank, Washington, DC.

Ravallion, Martin. 2003. "Measuring Aggregate Welfare in Developing Countries: How Well Do National Accounts and Surveys Agree?" *The Review of Economics and Statistics* 85 (3): 645–52.

———. 2008. "A Global Perspective on Poverty in India." *Economic and Political Weekly*, October, 31–37.

———. 2013. "Price Levels and Economic Growth: Making Sense of Revisions to Data on Real Incomes." *Review of Income and Wealth* 59 (4): 593–613. doi:10.1111/j.1475-4991.2012.00510.x.

———. 2014. "An Exploration of the International Comparison Program's New Global Economic Landscape." Georgetown University, Washington, DC.

Ravallion, Martin, and Benu Bidani. 1994. "How Robust Is a Poverty Profile?" *The World Bank Economic Review* 8 (1): 75–102. doi:10.1093/wber/8.1.75.

Ravallion, M., S. Chen, and P. Sangraula. 2009. "Dollar a Day Revisited." *The World Bank Economic Review* 23 (2): 163–84. doi:10.1093/wber/lhp007.

Ravallion, Martin, Gaurav Datt, and Dominique van de Walle. 1991. "Quantifying Absolute Poverty in the Developing World." *Review of Income and Wealth* 37 (4): 345–61. doi:10.1111/j.1475-4991.1991.tb00378.x.

Ruggles, Patricia. 1990. *Drawing the Line: Alternative Poverty Measures and Their Implications for Public Policy*. Washington, DC: Urban Institute Press.

Sala-i-Martin, Xavier. 2006. "The World Distribution of Income: Falling Poverty and . . . Convergence, Period." *The Quarterly Journal of Economics* 121 (2): 351–97. doi:10.1162/qjec.2006.121.2.351.

Summers, Robert, and Alan Heston. 1988. "A New Set of International Comparisons of Real Product and Price Levels Estimates for 130 Countries, 1950–1985." *Review of Income and Wealth* 34 (1): 1–25. doi:10.1111/j.1475-4991.1988.tb00558.x.

Suryahadi, Asep, and Sudarno Sumarto. 2003. "Poverty and Vulnerability in Indonesia Before and After the Economic Crisis." *Asian Economic Journal* 17 (1): 45–64. doi:10.1111/1351-3958.00161.

Suryahadi, Asep, Sudarno Sumarto, and Lant Pritchett. 2003. "Evolution of Poverty During the Crisis in Indonesia." *Asian Economic Journal* 17 (3): 221–41. doi:10.1111/j.1467-8381.2003.00184.x.

Taylor, Alan M, and Mark P. Taylor. 2004. "The Purchasing Power Parity Debate." *Journal of Economic Perspectives* 18 (4): 135–58. doi:10.1257/0895330042632744.

United Nations Statistics Division. 1984. *Handbook of Household Surveys*. Revised Edition. Studies in Methods 31. New York: United Nations.

———. 2005. *Household Sample Surveys in Developing and Transition Countries*. Studies in Methods 96. New York: United Nations.

————. 2008. *Designing Household Survey Samples: Practical Guidelines.* Studies in Methods 98. New York: United Nations.

United Nations, Department of Economic and Social Affairs, Population Division. 2009. "World Population Prospects: The 2008 Revision, Volume I: Comprehensive Tables." ST/ESA/SER.A/287. United Nations, New York.

————. 2011. "World Population Prospects: The 2010 Revision, Volume I: Comprehensive Tables." ST/ESA/SER.A/313. United Nations, New York.

————. 2013. "World Population Prospects: The 2012 Revision, Volume I: Comprehensive Tables." ST/ESA/SER.A/336. United Nations, New York.

————. 2014. "World Population Prospects: The 2012 Revision, Methodology of the United Nations Population Estimates and Projections." Working Paper ESA/P/WP.235. United Nations, New York.

World Bank. 1990. *World Development Report 1990: Poverty.* New York: Oxford University Press.

# About the Team

**Dean Jolliffe** is a senior economist in the Development Economics Research Group of the World Bank and a member of the Living Standards Measurement Study (LSMS) team. He has also worked in the South Asia region at the World Bank on poverty assessments for Afghanistan and Bangladesh. Previously, he was a research economist at the Economic Research Service of the United States Department of Agriculture, an adjunct professor at the Johns Hopkins University School of Advanced International Studies, an assistant professor at the Center for Economic Research and Graduate Education in Prague, and a postdoctoral fellow at the International Food Policy Research Institute. His research interests include poverty, food security, economics of education, health economics, and how data collection methods affect measurement. Dean holds appointments as a research fellow with the Institute for the Study of Labor in Bonn, and as a Research Affiliate with the National Poverty Center at the University of Michigan. He received his PhD in economics from Princeton University.

**Peter Lanjouw**, a Dutch national, is research manager of the Poverty Group in the Development Economics Research Group of the World Bank. His research has focused on rural development, notably the study of a village economy in rural India and the broader analysis of rural non-farm diversification, as well as a number of methodological questions in the measurement of poverty and inequality. He has taught at the Vrije University in Amsterdam, University of California at Berkeley, University of Namur, and Foundation for the Advanced Study of International Development in Tokyo, and he is an honorary fellow of the Amsterdam Institute of International Development, Amsterdam. He is an associate editor of the *World Bank Economic Review* and a past editorial board member of the *World Bank Economic Review* and the *Journal of African Economies*. He joined the World Bank in 1995 after earning a PhD in economics from the London School of Economics and Political Science.

---

**Shaohua Chen** is a lead statistician in the Development Economics Research Group of the World Bank. Her main research interests over the past 20 years have focused on poverty and inequality measurement. She has managed the global poverty monitoring and online computational tool PovcalNet at the World Bank since 1991. She is also responsible for the measurement and projection of global poverty for the World Bank's major reports such as the World Development Indicators and Global Monitoring Reports. Before joining the World Bank, Shaohua was a lecturer at the Huazhong University of Science and Technology. Her research findings have been published in major economic and statistical journals, including the *Quarterly Journal of Economics, Review of Economics and Statistics, Journal of Development Economics*, and *Journal of Public Economics*. She received her MSc in statistical computing from the American University.

**Aart Kraay**, an economist, is a senior adviser in the Development Economics Research Group at the World Bank. His research interests include international capital movements, growth and inequality, governance, and the Chinese economy. His research on these topics has been published in scholarly journals such as the *Quarterly Journal of Economics*, the *Review of Economics and Statistics*, the *Economic Journal*, the *Journal of Monetary Economics*, the *Journal of International Economics*, and the *Journal of the European Economic Association*. He is an associate editor of the *Journal of Development Economics*, and is an adjunct professor at the School of Advanced International Studies at Johns Hopkins University. He has also held visiting positions at the International Monetary Fund and the Sloan School of Management at MIT. He joined the World Bank in 1995 after earning a PhD in economics from Harvard University, and a BSc in economics from the University of Toronto.

**Christian Johannes Meyer** is a consultant with the Poverty and Inequality Team in the Development Economics Research Group. Before that, he was a research associate at the Center for Global Development, where he worked on poverty and inequality in Latin America and the

Caribbean, fiscal incidence analysis, as well as labor markets and industrial organization in Sub-Saharan Africa. He previously worked with the United Nations Conference on Trade and Development, the European Commission, and the German federal government. Christian holds a BA from WHU Vallendar and a MPP from the Hertie School of Governance, Berlin. He is currently a PhD candidate in economics at the European University Institute in Florence.

**Mario Negre** is a senior economist in the World Bank Development Economics Research Group seconded by the German Development Institute. He has worked at the European Parliament, first as an adviser to the chairman of the Development Committee and then for all external relations committees. Since 2012, he has been a senior researcher at the German Development Institute. His fields of specialization are pro-poor growth, inclusiveness, inequality and poverty measurement, as well as development cooperation policy, particularly European. Mario holds a BSc in physics from the University of Barcelona, an MA in development policies from the University of Bremen, and a PhD in development economics from the Jawharlal Nehru University, India.

**Espen Beer Prydz** is an economist in the World Bank's Development Economics Research Group. His research interests include issues of poverty, inequality, and survey methods. He has previously worked with the World Bank in Cambodia, South Sudan, and Indonesia, on poverty, social protection, and economic policy. Prior to joining the World Bank, Espen undertook research on poverty, labor markets, and gender with the OECD Development Centre and the Abdul Latif Jameel Poverty Action Lab (J-PAL). Espen is a Norwegian national who holds an MPA in international development from the Harvard Kennedy School and a BS from the London School of Economics.

**Renos Vakis** is a lead economist in the Poverty and Inequality Research team in the Development Economics Research Group and a member of the Living Standards Measurement Study (LSMS) team. His research focuses on poverty reduction, equity, and gender issues. He has written extensively on issues related to poverty dynamics and mobility, risk management, social protection, gender, market failures, and rural development, especially in Latin America and South Asia. He has also been involved in the design of impact evaluation of antipoverty interventions. At the

World Bank, he has previously held positions at the Poverty Reduction and Economic Management Unit of the Latin America and the Caribbean Region, as well as the Social Protection Network. He has also taught economics at Johns Hopkins University (SAIS). Renos holds a PhD from the University of California at Berkeley.

**Kyla Wethli** is a consultant with the Poverty and Inequality Team in the Development Economics Research Group. In 2013, she was a member of the core team for the World Development Report 2014 *Risk and Opportunity: Managing Risk for Development.* Prior to joining the World Bank, she was an assistant economist at Her Majesty's Treasury in the United Kingdom, focusing on macroeconomic policy and international economic developments, and an economic attaché at the British Embassy in Washington, DC. Kyla holds a BS in government and economics and an MS in economics from the London School of Economics and Political Science.

# Index

Boxes, figures, maps, notes, and tables are indicated by *b, f, m, n*, and *t*, respectively.

## H

## I

www.ingramcontent.com/pod-product-compliance
Lightning Source LLC
Chambersburg PA
CBHW080414270326
41929CB00018B/3025